Zimbabwe: The Past is the Future

Zimbabwe: The Past is the Future

Edited by

David Harold-Barry

Published by Weaver Press
Box A1922, Avondale, Harare. 2004
www.weaverpresszimbabwe.com

© This collection: Silveria House. Each chapter: the author.

Typeset by Fontline Electronic Publishing Pvt Ltd, Harare

Cover Design: Danes Design, Harare

Cover Photographs courtesy of National Archives of Zimbabwe and *The Standard*, Zimbabwe

The editor and the publisher would like to express their thanks to Diakonia, the Konrad Adenauer Foundation and Silveria House for their generous support of this publication.

Diakonia is a Swedish ecumenical and development organisation that was formed in 1964.

Silveria House is a leadership training and development education centre, begun by the Jesuits in 1964. Besides its major work in training courses, the centre also publishes material on development.

The Konrad Adenauer Foundation <www.kas.de> is a political foundation of the Federal Republic of Germany. By its international co-operation it works for the safeguard of human rights and for the promotion of the values of representative democracy, social market economy, social justice and sustainable development. The foundation's main areas of activities are: civic education, political and social research, promotion of political participation and collaboration with civil society organisations and the media. The Konrad Adenauer Foundation does not necessarily subscribe to the opinions of contributors.

All rights reserved. No part of the publication may be reproduced, stored in a retrieval system or transmitted in any form by any means – electronic, mechanical, photocopying, recording, or otherwise – without the express written permission of the publisher.

ISBN: 1 77922 025 1

Contents

Notes on contributors		vii
Forward – *Archbishop Pius Ncube*		xiii
Preface – *David Harold-Barry*		xv
1.	Current politics in Zimbabwe: confronting the crisis *Brian Raftopoulos*	1
2.	Robert Mugabe: revolutionary or rebel? *Dieter B. Scholz*	19
3.	What happened to our dream? *The Zimbabwe Liberator's Platform*	31
4.	The people's liberation struggle *Duduzile Tafara*	43
5.	The long way home: one man's story *Alexander Kanengoni*	47
6.	Environmental impacts of the fast-track land reform programme: a livelihoods perspective *Emmanuel Manzungu*	53
7.	Land reform and farm workers *Lloyd M. Sachikonye*	69
8.	The culture of party politics and the concept of the state *David Kaulemu*	77
9.	Continuity and change in the Zimbabwean religio-cultural landscape in the era of HIV/AIDS *Paul H. Gundani*	87
10.	The Zimbabwe economy 1980-2003: a ZCTU perspective *Godfrey Kanyenze*	107
11.	Travails of opposition politics in Zimbabwe since Independence *Eldred Masunungure*	147
12.	The onslaught against democracy and the rule of law in Zimbabwe in 2000 *Geoffrey Feltoe*	193
13.	Sticks and stones, skeletons and ghosts *A. P. Reeler*	225

14. Opportunities for political renewal in Zimbabwe
    Fay Chung 239

15. One country, 'two nations', no dialogue
    David Harold-Barry 249

Chronology 261

Notes on Contributors

Fay King Chung holds a D. Phil. in Education (University of Zimbabwe) and has wide experience in her field. She has taught in pre-independence township secondary schools as well as in adult literacy and adult education. She lectured at the University of Zambia and prepared primary and secondary school teachers during the liberation struggle. She was Director of Teacher Education, Curriculum Development for the Department of Education of the Zimbabwe African National Union (ZANU) Liberation Movement. Subsequently she was Chief of Educational Planning and later Chief of the Curriculum Development Unit in the Ministry of Education, Zimbabwe. She became Chairperson of the Zimbabwe Foundation for Education with Production (ZIMFEP), Member of Parliament and Minister first of Education and Culture and later for Employment Creation and Cooperatives. She then became Chief of UNICEF Education Section and Special Advisor on Education to the Organization of African Unity. She has written widely on education and values with particular reference to Zimbabwe.

Geoff Feltoe is an Associate Professor of Law at the University of Zimbabwe. He is currently a Trustee of the Legal Resources Foundation and the Amani Trust and was a member of the executive of the Catholic Justice and Peace Commission from 1975 until 1982. He has published a large number of legal textbooks and articles. He has written extensively on human rights issues.

Paul Henry Gundani is Associate Professor of Church History in the University of South Africa. Previously he taught Christian History and Thought in Africa in the Department of Religious Studies, Classics and Philosophy at the University of Zimbabwe and at the Faculty of Theology at Africa University in Mutare. He has also taught and written on the relationship between Christianity and culture in Africa, contributing over thirty academic articles to accredited journals and chapters to books published in Africa and internationally. He has written one book on this subject and co-edited two others.

David Harold-Barry taught history at St Ignatius College before moving to Silveira House Leadership and Development Training Centre in Chishawasha, as Director of Training and subsequently Director of the Centre. He is a Jesuit priest and spent some years in the training of young members of the Society of Jesus. Later he joined the leadership team of the Jesuits in Zimbabwe and has now returned to Silveira House as a writer in the Research Department.

David Kaulemu was the Chairperson of the Department of Religious Studies, Classics and Philosophy at the University of Zimbabwe where he lectured in Philosophy. He also lectures at Arrupe Jesuit College of Philosophy and Humanities and from there co-ordinates the African Forum for Catholic Social Teaching, a regional programme for Eastern and Southern Africa aimed at making more visible this social teaching in the African church and society. He has published, with Professor Hilary Homans, modules on the role of philosophy in health care. He is deeply concerned with analysing the morality of institutions of African modernity. He has written on the African township as a social formation as well as on the morality of the market, the state and civil society and the invention of traditions.

Alexander Kanengoni trained as a teacher and taught briefly before going to join the liberation struggle in 1974. After Zimbabwe's independence in 1980, he went to the University of Zimbabwe and majored in English literature. In 1983 he joined the Ministry of Education and Culture as project officer responsible for the education of ex-combatants and refugees. In 1988 he joined the Zimbabwe Broadcasting Service and worked there until 2002, when he became a farmer. Alexander's previously published work includes the novels: *Vicious Circle* (1983), *When the Rainbird Cries* (1988) *Echoing Silences* (1997) and a collection of short stories, *Effortless Tears* (1993).

Godfrey Kanyenze is the Director of the Labour and Development Research Institute of Zimbabwe (LEDRIZ). He presents papers on economic and labour issues in Zimbabwe at various conferences such as the Poverty Reduction Forum. He also works with civil society organisations like the Africa Forum for Debt and Development (AFRODAD) on issues to do with poverty reduction.

Emmanuel Manzungu holds a Ph.D. in irrigation management from Wageningen University of Environmental Sciences in the Netherlands. He has written extensively on irrigation and water resources management, the major highlights of which are four books on this theme. Currently he is a research associate with the Department of Soil science and Agricultural Engineering, University of Zimbabwe, where he is conducting research on various aspects of water management in southern Africa.

Eldred Masunungure is the Chairman of the Department of Political and Administrative Studies at the University of Zimbabwe where he also teaches various courses in public policy and political science at both postgraduate and undergraduate levels. He also co-ordinates and contributes to teaching the Governance and Policymaking course of the Masters in Policy Studies of SAPES Trust. His research interests are in public policy processes, governance and state-society relations.

Notes on contributors

Brian Raftopoulos is an Associate Professor at the Institute of Development Studies, UZ. He has written widely on Zimbabwean history and politics and serves as an overseas editor of the influential *Journal of Southern African Studies*. He is also a civic activist who served on the first executive of the National Constitutional Assembly, and is currently the Chairperson of the Crisis In Zimbabwe Coalition, the largest civic alliance in the country. Brian Raftopoulos is also a regular political commentator on the politics of Zimbabwe.

Anthony Peter Reeler did an M.Sc. in Clinical Psychology at the University of Leeds and is now Regional Human Rights Defender, with the Institute for Democracy in Southern Africa [Idasa]. He has wide experience in community mental health, treating victims of organised violence and torture, advocating human rights and in training, research, and reporting. He has both lectured and run a private practice in Clinical Psychology. He was a founder member and the Clinical Director of Amani Trust. He has been a consultant and member of a variety of committees and panels dealing with questions of human rights and mental health in the countries of Southern Africa and beyond and has published over a 100 papers and articles in academic journals and newspapers. He has also collaborated with C.H.Todd in a number of Nurse-Counsellor Manuals

Lloyd Sachikonye is a senior researcher based at the Institute of Development Studies, University of Zimbabwe. His main research interests revolve around labour studies, agrarian issues and governance. He was co-editor with Brian Raftopoulos of the book: *Striking Back: The Post-Colonial State and Labour in Zimbabwe*, (2001), editor of the Zimbabwe Human Development Report (2001) and author of the report on 'The Situation of Commercial Farm Workers after Land Reform' (2003).

Dieter Scholz is the Director of Silveira House Leadership and Development Training Centre in Chishawasha, Zimbabwe. He is a Jesuit priest with experience in both rural and urban ministry. He worked both before and after Independence at Marymount Mission, bordering Moçambique. Jailed and expelled from the country during the Smith era for his work with the Catholic Justice and Peace Commission, he spent a number of years setting up the worldwide Jesuit Refugee Service of which he was the first director.

Dududzile Tafara is the Chimurenga name of a war veteran who has worked in the field of rural development in Zimbabwe since independence.

The Zimbabwe Liberators' Platform is a registered non-partisan, non-government organisation formed by war veterans whose core business is to advocate for peace, democracy, good governance and development. Their first objective is to set up a forum for refocusing on the original aims and objectives of the liberation struggle. Its membership is countrywide and drawn from former liberation war fighters, detainees and war collaborators, workers, youth, peasants, students, trade unionists, members of churches and civic organisations.

Freedom for supporters of the government only, for members of one party only - no matter how numerous they might be - is no freedom at all. Freedom is always freedom for those who think differently.

Rosa Luxemburg

Justice is the first condition of humanity.

Wole Soyinka

In one way the Zimbabwe election sets an example to all democrats. It inspires even as it appals. It is a brilliant moment in the history of elections, in Africa or anywhere else. It registers the attraction and the power of democracy as they've seldom been seen before. Where in our own continent of ingrates, would people queue for 15 minutes, let alone 20 hours, to make their point? Where, simultaneously, has any other leader gone to such lengths as Robert Mugabe to confer democratic legitimacy on himself? While he serially violates the substance of democracy, he can't do without its semblance. Each side, voter and dictator, pays tribute to what democracy is meant to be. It could be called a kind of apotheosis.

Hugo Young
The Guardian, *March 12, 2002*

Foreword

We are in a time of great suffering in Zimbabwe, but one thing is clear: never before has there been such a wealth of documentation about the events of our history as there is today. However, documentation itself is like an unexploited seam of ore until it is mined and processed and refined. Therefore, I welcome this collection of essays, which does just that. Jesus told us: 'Do not be afraid of them. For everything that is now covered will be uncovered, and everything now hidden will be made clear' [Matt 10:26].

The writers you will meet here make things clear. I share with them the great desire that we all understand what has been happening in our country and learn from the sad events we are witnessing. The government wants docile acceptance of its policies and actions. But if truth dwells within us we cannot accept the trampling on human rights that have marked our recent past.

I believe we are called to preach the values of the Kingdom of God: love, holiness, humility, respect for others and their property, to promote peace and non-violence; we are called to feel for others, to be gentle, compassionate, understanding, sincere, truthful; we are called to be human and integrated.

This means that we put people before things, that we are God-centred, forgiving, self-controlled, prayerful, that we become healers and are ready to sacrifice ourselves for others and not to take advantage of them, that we suffer for the truth and judge ourselves before we judge others, that we are joyful, the salt of the earth and the light of the world. We are called to respect the poor, to be renewed with God's vision [John 3:5], to be motivated by the Holy Spirit, to be free and to free others [John 8:36] and to be full of hope.

Unless we can stretch our heads, our hands and our hearts to such desires we will be doomed to repeat the cycle of violence and the struggle we are now experiencing. I believe these essays are an excellent contribution to the process of awareness and conversion that our country needs today.

Pius A Ncube
Archbishop of Bulawayo

Preface

'We build the road and the road builds us.' This adage, much used in development parlance, can easily apply to the struggle for Zimbabwe. We thought there was a certain closure about the date 1980 – that the victory was won and all we had to do was 'enjoy the fruits'. Events around the turn of the new century have shown how naïve we were. We now realise that the 'fruits' do not tumble into our laps. We have to wrestle everyday with forces bent on appropriating these fruits to selfish ends. And in that continuing struggle for justice we ourselves are built into a new people.

In the present crisis people ask, 'how is it possible that we have reached where we are now?' No one can claim to have foreseen the extent of the catastrophe we now experience. The papers in this collection grew out of a desire at Silveira House, Chishawasha, to understand what has happened. They are not the findings of a symposium nor were they produced under pressure. They are the considered reflections from different angles on our history since independence. The editor has made no attempt to point the writers in any particular direction. As a result, although there is much common ground, there are also remarkable divergences of view about recent events and their origins. There is also much divergence of method. Some of us are academics, some practitioners in daily civic struggles and some of us are 'the ordinary people' who go about their daily business but have something to say.

I would particularly like to thank all the contributors for the time they have taken to write. They are actors in the ongoing drama and it has not been easy to create space for measured reflection. Dieter Scholz, the director of Silveira House, suggested the collection in the first place and Janice McLaughlin solicited many of the papers. I am particularly indebted to Irene Staunton and Murray McCartney of Weaver Press for their patience in seeing this collection through all its stages of delivery. They worked closely with Rosalie Wilson in the final stages of editing. Finally Diakonia of Sweden, in the person of Ulf Riccardsson, and the Konrad Adenauer Foundation of Germany, in the person of Anton Bösl, have provided the encouragement and the resources to enable us to spend much time on this task.

If this collection contributes to an understanding of where we have come from and helps us to design our future wisely, it will have done well.

David Harold-Barry SJ
Silveira House, Chishawasha
March 2004

Current politics in Zimbabwe: confronting the crisis

Brian Raftopoulos

All authoritarian regimes face limitations that impose constraints on the politics of repression. These limitations take various forms: the economic crisis that such regimes may not have caused, but certainly accelerate, the erosion of national legitimacy as a result of the perceived betrayal of a vision of renewal, the emergence of an alternative political movement, and the growing criticisms of the international community.

All these have been present in the recent history of Zimbabwe. The origins of our crisis pre-date independence. It is necessary to restate this in the light of the revulsion which has grown towards the present government. It is analytically impossible to discuss the problems of internal politics, economics and land reforms, without an understanding of the colonial inheritance.

Yet the knee-jerk reaction to this argument is to dismiss it because of its association with the endless diatribe of a ruling party in a seemingly inexorable slide towards defeat. The Zimbabwe African National Union – Patriotic Front (ZANU PF) can be likened to the Titanic, with its captain, in this case, positively in search of icebergs. But for all of us in search of alternatives, the pressing issues of our past await serious consideration and action.

My intention is to describe the post-colonial context of the present crisis in Zimbabwe. I shall analyse the ways in which a formerly strong nationalist party, with a broad social mandate, has seen its legitimacy eroded over the last two decades. For a state to maintain its right to rule, it must continuously engender the consent of its citizens, through an overall management of society with a minimum use of force.

In addition, it must provide space for dissenting voices to emerge, through processes and structures that are characterised by openness, accountability and the possibility of a peaceful transition to an alternative political regime. These are difficult conditions to guarantee, especially in the context of the economic crisis that prevails in Zimbabwe today, but they are terms that most Zimbabweans now demand as a prerequisite for a political contract with any future ruling party.

As a nation, we are at the most critical point of our history, struggling to chart a peaceful path beyond our present devastating political and economic conditions. It is appropriate that we should pause to reflect on the post-independence years and gather the 'resources of hope' that we desperately require for the decades of reconstruction ahead.

The first and second parts of this chapter provide an overview of the economic and political developments of the 1980s and 1990s. The third section reflects on the more recent developments in the country and examines possible future trends. The extreme conditions in the country demand that we plot a path out of the current crisis. Failure to do this would be to submit to one of the most dangerous effects of authoritarian rule, namely, the inability to see alternatives. Such an exercise demands we avoid looking for easy scapegoats and face honestly the many factors that have brought us to where we are. President Mugabe is a major contributing factor to the Zimbabwean crisis. But he is part of a broader set of obstacles and in the long term these – many of which are beyond our borders – will have to be confronted.

1980s – years of restoration and hope

At independence in 1980, the new government embarked on a vision of 'national reconciliation' that, in economic terms, sought to combine a continuity of existing production structures with policies to improve the conditions of the majority of the population neglected during the colonial years.

Confronted with the dilemma of a mass support base seeking immediate redress to long-existing inequalities, the new state sought to pursue a policy of high economic growth rates, increased incomes and social expenditures, and the promotion of rural development. The first Minister of Economic Planning and Development observed that 'our development strategy goes beyond the mere increase in the material wealth of society. Equity in the distribution of wealth and income is one of the cornerstones of our economic policy.'

The broad objectives of the policy document *Growth with Equity* [1981] were:

- The establishment of a socialist society.
- Rapid economic growth.
- Balanced development and equitable distribution of income and productive resources.
- Economic restructuring.
- The development of human resources
- Rural development.

- Worker participation.
- The development of economic infrastructure and social services.
- Fiscal and monetary reform.

Following this statement of policy, the government launched the Transitional National Development Plan to achieve these objectives. Consequently, much of the 1980s saw an impressive expansion in the social services, as the new government stretched its resources to achieve a rapid delivery of benefits to a highly expectant constituency. This emphasis in policy underlined the state's concerns with equity in the social sectors and the use of aid funds to develop this process.

A reform government consolidating its power

The government's policy on land in this period, and indeed until 1997, was based on a cautious, market-based approach to reform. One leading land expert described the process thus:

> *Land was purchased by the state for redistribution following willing-buyer, willing-seller procedures. This framework was agreed to at the Lancaster House Conference. The private sector led the identification and supply of land available for resettlement, while central government was a reactive buyer choosing land on offer. The government provided land to beneficiaries selected mainly by its district officials under the direct supervision of central government officials.[1]*

In addition to this legal process of land acquisition, the 1980s witnessed low-intensity land occupations, or 'squatting', carried out by various communities, sometimes unofficially supported by party officials. For the most part, the ruling party opposed such processes of self-provisioning, preferring to follow the legal, market-driven process. Prime Minister Robert Mugabe told 'squatters':

> *If we were to ask your forefathers whether they lived in the same area as their ancestors' graves, the answer would be in the negative. Now that we are buying farms to resettle people, who will stay there if you want to protect ancestors' graves? Of course we must protect our ancestors' graves but we must stay on arable land where we can be productive.[2]*

---

[1] Moyo, Sam (2000) 'The Interaction of Market and Compulsory Land Acquisition Processes with Social Action in Zimbabwe's Land Reform'. Paper presented at the SARIPS Annual Colloquium on Regional Integration: Past, Present and Future, Harare, September 2000.

[2] *The Herald*, 20 August 1985.

Using the willing-buyer, willing-seller process, some three million hectares of land were acquired by the end of the 1980s for resettlement. Recent research on what happened during this period indicates that many positive developments resulted, with settlers acquiring access to potable water supplies, dip-tanks, clinics, schools, improved toilets, housing loans, roads and marketing depots. And these areas witnessed a drop in cases of alcoholism, decreased domestic violence and reduced rates of suicide.[3] So, while the process was certainly slower than many land-starved rural dwellers might have wished, and it witnessed problems of implementation and funding, it produced some positive and sustainable results. In the current environment of a highly politicised, fast-track process, these achievements are often forgotten.

In the field of labour relations the state took several policy measures to protect workers, such as the Minimum Wages Act and the Employment Act, both passed in 1980. Independence witnessed a series of wildcat strikes where workers expressed their general desire for the immediate fruits of freedom, and the more particular desire of equity with white workers in the same job in the same industry. Through its legislative interventions the government sought to improve both income levels and employment security. In 1985, the government passed the Labour Relations Act, giving greater recognition to workers' rights to join trade unions while also retaining a measure of control in the hands of the Minister of Labour, similar to the role of the minister under the old colonial Industrial Conciliation Act. The persistence of such powers indicated the new state's nervousness about conceding power in these early years.

While such policies provided some protection for workers in the 1980s, the longer-term trends in income and employment levels were largely negative. While real wages increased in mining, industry and commerce from 1980-82, thereafter they either declined or remained static for much of the 1980s. In the lowest wage sectors of agriculture and domestic employment, wages increased for much of the 1980s. With regard to employment, growth levels averaged a low 1,72 per cent between 1980 and 1989.

In economic terms, the 1980s were a time of social welfare expenditure, slow land reform, cautious minimum-wage regulation and limited economic growth. The hope that growth would provide a trickle-down effect to the poorest in the country proved forlorn. For a new state, in need of establishing its legitimacy, such trends were disturbing and they indicated a need for a major policy change at the macro-economic level. Given the dramatic collapse of socialist regimes in 1989-90, and

---

[3] Kinsey, Bill (1999) 'Land Reform, Growth and Equity: Emerging Evidence from Zimbabwe's Resettlement Programme'. *Journal of Southern African Studies*, 25,2 173-96.

the growing orthodoxy of economic liberalism, there was pressure for the government to move towards a structural-adjustment programme, as had happened in other parts of Africa and the Third World.

In the political field, 1980 witnessed the victory of an uneasy alliance of the two major nationalist parties in the country. Their popular support, as a result of their roles in the liberation struggle, ensured them a strong legitimacy in the immediate post-colonial years. However, the ruling party also had to establish control over the state and over those sections of the population where its support base was weak.

During its first five years, the new government Africanised the state and created a national army out of former warring elements. This was a considerable achievement, taking place as it did against the background of a hostile apartheid state to the south. At the local government level, legislation in 1985 created politically appointed governors in the country's provinces – a move geared towards the consolidation of the ruling party's power in the rural areas. This process of extending the reach of the state marginalised traditional authorities in the country and was a sign of a confident new regime forging its vision of modernity for the young nation.

In carrying out this task, there was a strong element of 'command', reflecting the continuing influence of the often militarist politics of the liberation movements. Such politics emerged in the context of the struggles against a colonial regime embedded in repressive politics and offering few opportunities for democratic participation.

Moreover, this emphasis on the transfer of state power from the old to the new was effected with little concern for the civic rights of individuals – a common feature in post-colonial states. This style of state management soon became apparent in many spheres of Zimbabwean politics.

In the area of labour relations, the countrywide wildcat strikes of 1980-82, already referred to, led to strong government intervention, creating a labour movement subject to party control. The legacy from before independence, a weakened and divided labour movement, allowed the state to set up the Zimbabwe Congress of Trade Unions (ZCTU) in 1981, as an arm of the ruling party.

For much of the 1980s, workers were regularly reminded about their subordinate role to the party, and, when on strike, chastised for their ingratitude towards the liberation parties. Additionally, the war veterans were active in mobilising support for ZANU PF at the workplace in the early 1980s, pressurising employers to employ war veterans, and becoming involved in workers' committees.

During this period of fragile relations between employers and the state, businesses often adopted the strategy of employing 'politically-connected lobbyists to walk the corridors of power, to network with the new authority figures, and to represent the interests of their employers. Business leaders built on the work of these lobbyists to forge their own links with the new civil servants and politicians.'[4] This approach was apparent until the mid-1980s, when the new structures of industrial relations began to exert their force, and the ruling party settled into a slower economic-reconstruction programme.

The dominance of ZANU PF could also be seen in its influence over women's organisations, the student movement, and other civic groups. Non-governmental organisations adopted a low profile and complementary approach to the state, seeking to assist the social welfare policies of the government. The authority of the ruling party went largely unquestioned, as the majority of organisations in the country fell into line behind the development project of the state.

If there were criticisms, they were muted, and few sought to challenge the message of national unity that was invoked at every stage. The emphasis on nation building, across racial and ethnic boundaries, was one that few sought to dispute in the fragile early years of independence. At this stage the ruling party had an immense amount of ideological capital at its disposal, and had a fairly wide margin for political error, a luxury that would begin to dissipate by the end of the first decade of independence.

Yet the veneer of national unity was soon torn asunder in the crisis that developed in Matabeleland and the Midlands in the mid-1980s. The unity between the two major liberation movements, ZANU and the Zimbabwe African People's Union (ZAPU), forged in the late 1970s under the Patriotic Front, had been based largely on the tactical requirements of negotiations for a political settlement. The tensions that existed between the two movements remained and were heightened after the ZANU PF election victory in 1980. The immediate causes of the outbreak of violence between 'dissidents' and government forces was 'a distrust within, and then repression by, the newly-formed Zimbabwe National Army.'[5] The repressive response of the state to the crisis marked the post-colonial history of Zimbabwe in ways that have yet to be confronted.

Moreover, the immunity given to the perpetrators of this violence mirrored the action of the Smith regime, in particular during the Internal Settlement period 1978-80, and led to an intensified militarisation of violence and politics in Zimbabwe. An important start to this process would have been for the government to respond to the report produced by the Catholic Commission for Justice and Peace and the Legal Resources Foundation on the violence inflicted on the people of

---

[4] Dean, Howard (2001) 'The Labour Wars: Invasions of Firms and Businesses – Hostage Taking as the New Face of Labour Negotiations'. *Labour Relations Information Service*, April 2001.
[5] Alexander, Jocelyn, Jo Ann McGregor and Terence Ranger (2000) *Violence and Memory: One Hundred Years in the 'Dark Forests' of Matabeleland*. Oxford: James Currey.

Matabeleland, entitled *Breaking the Silence, Building True Peace: A Report on the Disturbances in Matabeleland and Midlands 1980-88*, which was published in 1997.

Growing authoritarianism and the emergence of dissenting voices

The broad impact of this crisis on Zimbabwean politics was to produce a culture of fear and intolerance. The Unity Agreement of 1987, which led to peace between ZANU PF and ZAPU, stopped the violence. But it also ushered in a significant increase in the powers of the executive, in the form of the Constitution of Zimbabwe Amendment Act Number 7. This effectively marginalised the legislature but, as an unintended consequence, placed increased emphasis on the role of the judiciary in restraining the executive.

Added to this were the uneven conditions provided by the state for electoral politics. These included the lack of an independent Electoral Supervisory Commission, the complete domination of the electronic media by the ruling party, the abuse of state funding and resources by the ruling party for electoral purposes, state-led violence against opposition forces and irregularities in the voters' rolls.

The disparity between the *de jure* rights and freedoms enshrined in the Zimbabwean constitution and the *de facto* political rules developed by the state, have provided opposition parties and civic groups opposing the ruling party with important openings for contesting ZANU PF domination.[6] The battles in the courts over the abuse of executive powers and the uneven playing field provided by present electoral laws became the focus for action by civil society groups, especially in the 1990s. Such issues were to feature as a central part of the campaign for constitutional reform after 1997.

By the late 1980s the authoritarianism of the government began to show itself in the move towards a one-party state and in the growing corruption of a ruling elite that displayed little regard for deepening structures of accountability. The Willowgate Scandal in 1988, and the executive pardoning of its perpetrators, was indicative of these trends. It showed the state using a process that could be described as 'class formation behind closed doors'.

In opposition to these developments, dissenting voices began to emerge in the form of student protests, a restructured trade union movement with a strong leadership, and an opposition party – the

---

[6] Nordlund, Per (1996) 'Organising the Political Agora: Domination and Democratisation in Zambia and Zimbabwe'. D. Phil. Thesis, Uppsala. See also the important book by John Makumbe and Daniel Compagnon (2000) *Behind the Smokescreen: The Politics of Zimbabwe's 1995 General Elections*. Harare: University of Zimbabwe Publications.

Zimbabwe Unity Movement (ZUM) led by Edgar Tekere – formed as a result of challenges within the leadership of the ruling party. Despite its short history, ZUM performed well in the 1990 general election, capturing 17 per cent of the total vote and 26 per cent of the urban vote. In the presidential campaign Tekere won 16 per cent of the votes cast.

The most significant development was the emergence of a revitalised labour movement which, from the mid-1980s, developed a more critical and autonomous position towards the state and began to expand its critique of the government from strictly economic concerns to broader issues of political accountability. Additionally, the trade unions began to nurture political alliances with other social groups, such as students, in a process of building a larger consensus around the need for state accountability.

Thus the first decade of independence ended with growing economic problems, an embryonic opposition movement, and serious fractures in the notion of national unity imposed by the ruling party.

The 1990s – economic liberalisation and political challenge

It was clear by the late 1980s that the government's impressive policies on the expansion of social expenditures were being implemented on the basis of a shrinking economic base. Employment levels were low, growing at only 2,5 per cent between 1985-90,[7] and the prospects for new investment were not encouraging. In a global economic context in which economic liberalisation was the established orthodoxy, and the international financial institutions were the determining agencies for financial assistance, the state adopted the Economic Structural Adjustment Programme in 1990.

There has been a mountain of academic work devoted to the effects of structural adjustment in Africa, and a great deal of debate on its effects in Zimbabwe. Much of the literature has established the negative effects of the programmes on the continent. The indicators for Zimbabwe tend to confirm this trend. Employment growth decreased from 2,5 per cent between 1985-90 to 1,5 per cent in the years 1996-99. Different figures on wage levels indicate sharp declines. The ZCTU point to a drop in real wages from an index of 122 in 1982 to 80,7 in 1999, while a leading annual-earnings survey indicates that the average income in 2000 was 19 per cent lower than in 1980.

---

[7] In addition, the much-hailed expansion in the education system required a similar expansion in the employment market to accommodate all the school-leavers, eager for work, whose families had invested in their education. See also Brian Raftopoulos, 'Education and the Political Crisis in Zimbabwe'. Paper presented at the Canon Collins Memorial Lecture, London, 28 May 2003.

Estimates of the levels of those considered poor increased from 62 per cent in 1995 to 75 per cent in 2000. Looking at the distribution of the gross domestic income (GDI), while the proportion going to wages decreased from 54 per cent in 1987 to 39 per cent in 1999, the share of profits increased from 47 per cent to 61 per cent during the same years.[8] When one adds to these indicators the deteriorating social services in the country, it is clear that the deregulation of the economy has shown few positive benefits for the majority of Zimbabweans. Moreover, such signals were apparent even before the ruling party embarked on the criminalisation of politics that we have witnessed since 2000.

Rising civic awareness in the mid-1990s

The escalating crisis in the economy during these years predictably provided the conditions for dramatic developments in the political sphere. Within the ruling party, the internal fissures became more apparent as a number of party cadres, frustrated by the lack of accountability of party structures, pursued their political fortunes as 'independents'. In the election process, the courts became a central arena for disputing irregular procedures, casting a growing shadow over the unfairness of the existing election laws.

The case of Margaret Dongo in Harare South in 1995 was a significant development in this struggle. An ex-combatant from the ruling party, she challenged ZANU PF in an urban constituency and, after a legal battle over irregular election procedures, won the seat as an independent. This victory was an important signal of the growing disenchantment with the ruling party, and the importance of using the judiciary to challenge the election conditions established by ZANU PF. Nevertheless, Dongo's success also underlined the limitations of various small opposition groups with a limited membership and provided little sense of a general political alternative to ZANU PF.

Labour relations in the 1990s

In the labour relations field, the decline of workers' incomes resulted in more strike actions, characterised by several features: the involvement of increasing numbers of workers and more sectors, more nationwide actions, more regular recourse to strike action as a tool in the collective-bargaining process, recurring actions over unresolved grievances, and

---

[8] Kanyenze, Godfrey (2001) 'The Labour Market Under Economic Reform: The Case of Zimbabwe'. Paper prepared for SAPRIN/Poverty Forum. See also Ch. 10 by Dr Kanyenze in this book for a full evaluation of ESAP.

the growing militancy of public sector workers.[9] The national public sector strike in 1996, in particular, strengthened the links between the ZCTU and the public sector workers, and shook the confidence of the state. The general strike of December 1997 and the mass stay-aways of 1998 established the potential effectiveness of labour as a social movement, signalling the escalating momentum for change in the country.

The skill of the labour movement in developing a broad social alliance against the government showed that effective changes had taken place in the leadership of the ZCTU. A central figure in these changes was Morgan Tsvangirai, a former clerk in the mining industry and a one-time political commissar of ZANU PF, who epitomised the new and challenging voice of labour.

Tsvangirai led a group of unionists in the deepening of shop-floor union structures, the training of union members and the strengthening of the policy content of ZCTU interventions. As the economic crisis in the country deepened, the ZCTU leadership articulated the linkage between this crisis and the problems of governance. Taking this linkage further, the ZCTU played a central role in the formation of the National Constitutional Assembly (NCA) in 1997, which had as its major objective the need for constitutional reform.

Thus, the ZCTU developed a strong alliance with a wide range of civic organisations around the issues of democratisation and human rights, a terrain on which the ruling party was weak. Moreover, this strategy connected local pressures for change with a global discourse around these concerns. The campaign around constitutional reform became a dominant feature of Zimbabwean politics in the late 1990s. The NCA developed a successful mass campaign, and triggered a process of discussion on reform within the ruling party itself, forcing the government to set up a constitutional commission in 1999.

The cumulative effect of this alliance between the ZCTU and other civic groups was the build-up of pressure for the creation of an opposition party. In addition to the campaign for constitutional reform, the ZCTU organised the National Working People's Convention in February, 1999, which was attended by some 1,000 delegates, to discuss the crisis in Zimbabwe and chart a way forward.

One of the recommendations that emerged from the convention was that the labour movement should facilitate the formation of a new political party. Thus, as a result of a broad-based discussion amongst civic organisations, the Movement for Democratic Change (MDC) was formed

---

[9] See Saunders, Richard (2001) 'Striking Ahead: Industrial Actions and Labour Development in Zimbabwe,' in B. Raftopoulos and L. Sachikonye (eds) *Striking Back: The Labour Movement and the Post-Colonial State in Zimbabwe 1980-2000*. Harare: Weaver Press, 133-173.

in September, 1999, threatening to provide the biggest political challenge to ZANU PF since 1980.

In the space of two decades the ZCTU had moved from a weak and divided movement, under the shadow of a dominant nationalist party, to be the facilitator of a broad opposition alliance that was challenging for state power. It was not surprising that the labour movement should play this role since, as in other developing countries, trade union movements are often the only civic groups with the national organisational capacity to undertake such political initiatives.

The war veterans' intervention

Parallel to these developments, the ruling party faced an even more convulsive challenge from within its own ranks. The war veterans, who had formed a lobbying association in 1992, challenged the authority of the party and the president in 1997, by demanding gratuities for their role in the liberation struggle. The veterans had always been a key factor in ZANU PF politics, having since 1980 played a significant role in marginalising ZIPRA forces in the new national army, and then providing a mobilising force for ZANU PF in the workplace in the early 1980s. Their vital role after the events of 2000 will be discussed in the next section. A recent analysis of the role of the war veterans in Zimbabwean politics describes their interventions as follows:

> Since independence, the political dynamics between war veterans and the ruling party have been remarkably consistent. Their relationship has been characterised by collaboration, conflict, and accommodation. Veterans and the party have used each other to pursue their different, though often overlapping, objectives. The party has used veterans to build its power and legitimacy. It has sanctioned and encouraged veterans' violence against its opponents and rewarded them for work well done. It has invoked its role in the liberation struggle to justify its use of veterans and its objectives. Veterans have used their allegedly superior contribution to the liberation struggle to justify their claims for preferential access to state resources – jobs, promotions, pensions, land. In trying to enforce their demands, they have often used violence and intimidation against competitors for resources, as well as party leaders and bureaucrats whom they believed were blocking their progress. For 20 years they have also sought allies within both the party (members of parliament, cabinet ministers, senior party officials) and state institutions (bureaucrats, the army, the police)...[10]

[10] Kriger, Norma (2001) 'Zimbabwe's War Veterans and the Ruling Party: Continuities in Political Dynamics'. *Politique Africaine*, 81, 80-100.

The challenge to the president in 1997, in the midst of the growing crisis of legitimacy of ZANU PF, presented a crucial moment for his survival. The decision of President Mugabe to give in to the demands for a Z$50,000 payment to each veteran saved the president's position, but created a host of other problems for Zimbabwe.

It precipitated a decisive crash in the Zimbabwean dollar, many of the effects of which are still with us today. The president's decision confirmed the centrality of 'commandist' politics in his thinking, effectively marginalising more democratic participation by a broader range of civic groups. The decision also made it clear that, as the party's support base eroded, the president would become increasingly reliant on coercive measures of mobilisation.

In addition to the demands of the war veterans, ZANU PF faced increasing pressures from other groups, such as the Indigenous Business Development Centre (IBDC) and the Affirmative Action Group (AAG), formed in the 1990s, that lobbied the government for more direct state intervention to assist black entrepreneurs. Confronted by all these demands and with the long-standing pressure for land reform – and with an economy that was contracting through liberalisation – the government faced a massive demand for action to reduce poverty. The move towards more direct state acquisition of land in 1997, and part of the rationale for sending troops to the Democratic Republic of the Congo (DRC) in 1998 in search of new sources of income, were directly related to the deepening crisis in the Zimbabwean economy.

As the 1990s drew to a close, the political scene was marked both by signs of a strong emergent opposition and the menacing presence of coercive party structures being used to consolidate the position of a weakening executive. The millennium opened on a promising, but also threatening, balance of political forces.

2000 and beyond

It is always difficult to isolate the origins of a crisis in society, but it is easier to identify watershed years. The year 2000 constituted an important junction of political events. The government presented its draft constitution, opposed by the NCA, to a referendum in the hope of marginalising the process that had been suggested by the NCA. In the event, the draft was rejected in the referendum and with it the government's hope of taming a process that had escaped its control.

At one level the government's defeat was a result of the way it ignored important views from its outreach programme, which were voiced by the NCA. In particular, this related to the excessive power of the executive. More generally, the rejection was a vote of disillusion with the government. The 'No' vote represented the first major defeat for the ruling party since independence, and the protest threatened to translate itself into an election defeat later in the year.

The response of the ruling party was almost immediate, and ruthless. The president and other party leaders blamed the defeat on the white minority and some western countries and promised retaliation in volatile political language. President Mugabe sought to cast his political response in terms of a general anti-imperialist discourse, that demonised internal opposition forces as unpatriotic 'enemies of the state', and therefore beyond the pale of the rule of law.

This discourse sought to justify the denigration of civic and political rights as minority concerns, in the name of a selective manipulation of redistributive issues around the land question. A combination of war veterans, unemployed party youths and other party members began a series of violent land occupations throughout the country. The effect of these was to connect with a popular grievance around land reform, but in ways that removed the land issue from the arena of broader public accountability, and consolidated ZANU PF's waning support through violence.

The occupations and the violence continued up to the June 2000 parliamentary elections and beyond, and served to destroy emergent opposition party structures in the rural areas, cordoning them off to opposition campaigning. The result was the worst election violence in Zimbabwe's history. Some 35 people were killed before and during the elections, and many human rights abuses were committed, mainly by ZANU PF. Opposition politicians and their supporters continue to face death, violence, harassment, and prosecution under the Public Order and Security Act (POSA) and the Access to Information and Protection of Privacy Act (AIPPA) that replaced the draconian Law and Order Maintenance Act, a key instrument of oppression during the colonial period.

Despite the levels of violence unleashed by the ruling party, the opposition MDC won 57 seats to ZANU PF's 62 seats. For a party that had been in existence for only nine months, this result was a substantial achievement. And further, because of the level of violence the legitimacy of the result was immediately questioned, both nationally and internationally, and the MDC went on to challenge the election results in 39 constituencies.

The MDC won four of those challenges, bringing it almost on a par with ZANU PF with regard to elected seats, though the ruling party can rely on the 30 parliamentary un-elected seats controlled by the president under the present constitution. The case for constitutional reform has never been so strong, while the legitimacy of the government in power is at its lowest point since independence.

This weak legitimacy is reflected in the way the government continued to act in the country. In 2001, the violence of the land occupations and the elections continued in the by-elections in Bikita West and Marondera West, as well as in the mayoral elections in Masvingo. Equally disturbing have been ZANU PF's attacks on its own state structures, state officials and laws.

There was a sustained campaign by the executive and the war veterans against the judiciary, leading to the 'early retirement' of the chief justice and the resignation of two High Court judges. Pursuant to this were the factory occupations led by the ZANU PF-sponsored Zimbabwe Federation of Trade Unions (ZFTU), supported by a 'labour committee' of senior party officials and war veterans, which contravened the Labour Relations Act and the established machinery of industrial relations in order to resolve outstanding labour disputes.

We have also seen the sacking and intimidation of teachers, health workers and local government employees by war veterans because of their alleged support for the MDC. Through these measures state structures and personnel have been attacked in order to re-establish the dominance of the ruling party. This strategy has caused consternation among certain leaders in ZANU PF, who fear the loss of control of the party to more anarchic elements. On 19 January 2001, the *Zimbabwe Independent* reported the national chairman of the ruling party, John Nkomo, warning of 'an element of insolence and indiscipline by some war veterans,' reminding the latter that 'the party comes first'. Such concerns were also expressed by Nkomo over the factory invasions.

In the area of the media, the new Broadcasting Services Act (No. 3 of 2001), fast-tracked through parliament in April 2001, is an attempt to control alternative opinions in the electronic media, particularly through the radio which is the dominant source of information for the rural population. The banning of the recent programme sponsored by the National Development Association (NDA), *Talk to the Nation*, emphasised the government's intolerance, even towards sympathetic organisations. The words of a Zimbabwe Broadcasting Corporation (ZBC) official justifying the withdrawal of the programme showed a total lack of awareness of the irony of authoritarian regimes:

> *It is not all about money. Live productions can be tricky and dangerous. The setting on the NDA productions was professionally done but maybe the production should not have been broadcast live. You do not know what someone will come and say and there is no way of controlling it.*[11]

---

[11] 'ZBC switches off NDA sponsored live TV programme,' *The Herald*, 6 June 2001.

The government has also introduced legislation to control foreign financing of political parties, and has moved to control non-governmental organisations (NGOs) by stopping their involvement in civic education. Both these positions are designed to proscribe the viability of opposition forces. Combined with these measures, the ruling party has established its own civic bodies to rival the influence of those organisations that have formed the basis for opposition politics in the country. In the students' movement, the ruling party has sponsored the Zimbabwe Progressive Students' Union (ZPSU) and the Zimbabwe Congress of Students' Unions (ZICOSU) to counter the influence of the Zimbabwe National Students' Union (ZINASU). The established ZCTU has been confronted by the ZFTU.

Similar developments have also occurred in the area of constitutional reform, where the NDA was set up to confront the NCA, and rival municipal residents' associations have been sponsored to offset the more critical structures. The common denominator of these organisations is their lack of a substantive membership base. Once again, these actions resemble the survival strategies attempted by the Smith regime in the dying days of settler colonialism.

Escalating repression of dissent

The central purpose of all these measures was to eliminate centres of dissent and create more conducive conditions for a ZANU PF victory in the presidential elections. For much of the independence years, the party was prepared to tolerate a minimum level of electoral competition as long as single-party dominance was not threatened. The existence of civic groups complemented its service delivery to the state. But when this situation no longer prevailed and the possibility of defeat became more apparent, the governing elite lost its facade of tolerance and unleashed its repressive party and state machinery. Yet this strategy of intimidation began to have diminishing returns and even backfired. The Masvingo mayoral election showed that the MDC could win even under violent conditions.

The intention of the factory invasions was to provide quick victories for workers and undermine the ZCTU with alternative structures and so weaken the urban base of the MDC, but the results proved disastrous for the government. While the ZCTU structures were certainly strained and divisions were engendered by the splinter unions set up by the ZFTU, the labour movement has survived the assault. Many workers used the invasions to settle long-standing issues without surrendering the autonomy of their union structures and so proving the importance of strong institutional structures among non-state organisations. Moreover, the invasion of certain international NGOs and South African companies drew strong criticisms from both the international community and, more significantly, the South African government. The loss of employment resulting from this strategy, combined with the stalling of the fast-track land reform programme, provided the more reform-minded members of the government with the opportunity to reassert the legal structures of the state, and temporarily place some restraints on the invasions.

The final futility of the factory invasions was that it succeeded in doing, in a few months, what the opposition had been trying to do since the land occupations began: it shifted the national discussion from the land question to the more general issue of the economy, on which the ruling party's position is extremely weak.

Conclusion

In conclusion, there are three major points to be stressed about the political crisis in Zimbabwe. The first concerns the pervasive violence of the Zimbabwean state. In the early 1980s the Mugabe regime used the war veterans to consolidate its control of the state, and then proceeded to demobilise this force when its position in power was more secure. Similarly, the state marginalised the influence of traditional authorities, as it extended its powers to local government level. After two decades of independence, and in the context of a massive loss of state legitimacy, we have witnessed certain reversals in that process. The embattled regime has once again turned to the war veterans to enforce its party dominance, by attacking those state structures and personnel considered 'disloyal' to the ruling party. The regime has also breached its own laws in order to maintain state power. This coercive strategy has attempted to destroy those civic organisations and processes that have been critical of the post-colonial state. It is as though an influential faction of the ruling party has used the unpopularity of the state to attack its own structures, as an opposition force, in order to reconsolidate ZANU PF dominance.

Second, it is clear that a severe break has developed between the discourse and politics of the liberation struggle and that of the civic struggles for democratisation in the post-colonial period. In part, this tension can be traced to the period of the emergence of mass nationalism in the 1950s and 1960s.[12] However, the differences have deepened over

---

[12] See Raftopoulos, Brian and Ian Phimister (eds) (1997) *Keep on Knocking: A History of the Labour Movement in Zimbabwe 1900-1997*. Harare: Baobab Books. Raftopoulos, Brian and Tsuneo Yoshikuni (eds) (1999) *Sites of Struggle: Essays in Zimbabwe's Urban History*. Harare: Weaver Press. Moyo, Sam, John Makumbe and Brian Raftopoulos (2000) *NGOs, the State and Politics in Zimbabwe*. Harare: Sapes Books; Raftopoulos, Brian 'Problematising Nationalism in Zimbabwe: A Historiographical Review'. *Zambezia*, 1999, 26,2.

the last decade. The dichotomy was neatly captured in a *Daily News* report at the time of the Bindura by-election, which described the two candidates in the following terms: 'Pfebve, 32, represents the new politics of democracy, while Manyika, 46, epitomises the old politics of the liberation struggle.'[13]

This tension has developed in the context of a declining liberation movement that has drawn a lethal distinction between a violently driven anti-imperialist project, centred around the land question, and the politics of human rights which it has characterised as an imposition of global imperialist politics. Any sense of national ownership of such rights issues is lost in this characterisation. This position is captured in the simplistic ruling party slogan, 'The land is the economy, the economy is the land', which has been translated into politics of exclusion, racial essentialism, and violence.

On the other hand, the civic opposition has espoused its project largely through the language of citizenship rights, articulated most clearly in the campaign for constitutional reform. Yet these politics of democratisation have not sufficiently negotiated their connections, as well as their differences, with the legacy of the liberation struggle.

The interventions of the Zimbabwe Liberators' Platform, a group of war veterans that have opposed the current strategy of ruling party violence, are an important attempt to make such connections. Zimbabweans are in a very good position to advance such a dialogue, which is an issue that is confronting all the countries of Southern Africa that have emerged from settler colonialism after an extended liberation struggle.

Third, and emerging from the previous point, is the manner in which the role of violence has been articulated in Zimbabwean politics. For the ruling party, violence in the post-colonial period is an extension of the liberation struggle – a necessary means to achieve a political agenda. The dehumanising and delegitimising effects of this strategy on Zimbabwe citizens have been considered essential for maintaining state power.

In response, the forces of opposition have used their critique of this violence as a pivotal part of their demand for alternative politics. Yet this critique has not acknowledged sufficiently the systemic violence to which post-colonial states, like Zimbabwe, continue to be subjected by the forces of global finance. And so they are not sufficiently prepared for the difficult confrontations and choices that any government in a marginalised state will have to make in a project of economic and political reconstruction.

---

[13] *The Daily News*, 24 July 2001.

Zimbabwe: The Past is the Future

At present, the future of Zimbabwe is balanced on a knife-edge, as an ageing and increasingly unpopular nationalist leader struggles to secure his position. The test of a political transition is upon us as a nation, and the failure to deal with this challenge could lead to heightened civil conflict. We must make every effort to avoid such a disastrous option.

Robert Mugabe: revolutionary or rebel?

Dieter B. Scholz

When President Julius Nyerere of Tanzania arrived in Harare for the Zimbabwe independence celebrations on 18 April 1980, he greeted Prime Minister Robert Mugabe with the words, 'You have inherited a jewel. Keep it that way.' At the donor conference two years later representatives from western countries hastened to offer aid to rebuild the country, which had been ravaged by nearly ten years of civil war, leaving an estimated 80,000 people dead. Dozens of non-governmental organisations were founded to respond to every imaginable need of individuals and communities, including the demobilised ex-combatants. Zimbabwe had become the darling of the international community.

What happened, in just twenty years, to make this same country, with its extraordinarily resourceful and courageous people, the pariah of the same international community? President Robert Mugabe puts the blame squarely on the whites. He accuses them of having rejected the hand of reconciliation extended at independence and of having systematically undermined his policies, especially on land reform. Other commentators argue that the economic structural adjustment programme imposed in the 1990s by the International Monetary Fund (IMF) and the World Bank, coupled with poor governance and rampant corruption, are to blame for our present deplorable state.

These factors have contributed to Zimbabwe's decline. But we have to look further for a fuller explanation. It is enlightening to compare the situation of Zimbabwe in 1980 with Germany after the Second World War. Jürgen Moltmann was a 22-year-old German prisoner of war in Britain towards the end of the war and he described how he was first inspired to study theology in captivity. He learnt the power of hope, reconciliation and forgiveness and he began lifelong friendships with young British and American students. When he was repatriated, 'the hour of the new beginning' (as it was called), had already passed. He discovered with dismay and sadness that the chance of a radical new start had been missed. In civil life, in politics, and especially among the Christian churches, reconstruction had taken the form of restoring the pre-war status quo. The churches, he wrote, had installed themselves comfortably in post-war Germany and gained more influence on education, the press, politics and economics than was good for them, for they were being used by powerful politicians and economic interests. The one force that could have challenged them, the Confessing Church of Dietrich Bonhoeffer[1] had been marginalised. Germany grew rich and powerful, but the hope he had cherished for a new beginning had vanished. For countless young people in Europe after the war, a journey of intellectual and social agnosticism culminated in the student uprisings of 1968 when the universities of Frankfurt and Paris were literally set on fire. Blind violence against authority – any established authority: policemen, politicians, bankers – became the ultimate expression of their anger at the missed chance of a new beginning after the war. Something similar has happened in Zimbabwe.

The people's war: experiences from Rushinga

When I returned to Zimbabwe in 1990, after an absence of twelve years, I had the same feelings as Jürgen Moltmann returning to post-war Germany. My first assignment was pastoral ministry at Mary Mount Mission in eastern Rushinga, where I had worked in the early sixties and again in the early seventies. By 1990, this huge rural parish hosted 50,000 Mozambican refugees – victims of the atrocious war between *Resistencia Naçional Moçambique* (Mozambique National Resistance – Renamo) and *Frente de Libertaçao de Moçambique* (Mozambique Liberation Front – Frelimo). The price this remote district near the Mozambique border paid for the liberation of Zimbabwe was staggering. Four out of every five young men I had taught in Forms III and IV twenty years earlier had not returned from the war and no one knew where they had fallen and been buried. A whole generation seemed to be missing.

Not a single head of cattle remained in the whole of eastern Rushinga ten years after independence. Ian Smith's soldiers had deliberately infected the animals with anthrax, as a measure of 'communal punishment' under the Law and Order (Maintenance) Act. Despite many promises, the government of independent Zimbabwe had still not given the people a single cow or ox by 1990. I saw elderly women laboriously tilling their fields with small home-made hoes. They started work long before sunrise to avoid the stifling heat, and by mid-morning were exhausted. They were among the frequent patients at our hospital seeking relief from excruciating back pain.

Each year, during the rains, we found the skeletons of ZANLA fighters – sometimes in the bush, often in the fields and, on one occasion,

---

[1] Bonhoeffer was murdered by the Nazis on 9 April 1945, just as the war was ended.

crouching in a cave – but it was not until the mid-nineties that a cemetery was set up near Rushinga to give them a decent burial. Party officials came and went. They promised to match every coffin that the mission would donate with one of their own. With funds from abroad we paid skilled wood workers among the Mozambican refugees to make the coffins. They were extremely well crafted, worthy to receive the remains of those who had fallen for Zimbabwe. But when the time of the solemn reburial came, only half the bodies could be laid to rest because the coffins promised by the party had not materialised.

For several years, the mission hospital treated a constant stream of patients from Chapinduka with gastro-enteric infections caused by water from their polluted dam. From that village alone I knew at least a dozen young men who had given their lives for the liberation of Zimbabwe. Government and ZANU PF party officials were invited to come and see the dam and its murky water. They did come and were hosted by the mission. They visited the dam and the hospital and promised that a borehole would soon be provided. It never was. We even went to the extent of taking a bottle of the greenish-brown water to Harare and placing it on the desk of the minister who had made the promise, but to no effect. In the end, the mission raised the money from abroad and, with the technical assistance of the District Development Fund, drilled and constructed the borehole.

The mission also facilitated an extensive programme of income-generating projects for young people. There were two village bakeries, four grinding mills, several tuck-shops and a large number of agricultural and livestock projects. Acting on a circular from the Ministry of Health, that all public places had to have properly built Blair toilets, an overzealous district environmental health officer ordered the closure of one project after another which did not have the required facilities. Similar action was taken against schools, stores and grinding mills. Representations were met with further threats. In the end, a government minister had to be brought in to stop such uncivil acts and explain to the district officials the meaning of the words 'civil' and 'servant'. However, the damage had already been done. We reminded the authorities that the only other time this had happened in Rushinga was when, at the height of the liberation war, Ian Smith's security forces closed down all schools, stores and grinding mills to punish the people for harbouring and collaborating with the 'terrorists'. The people had not forgotten that connection too. 'We are living in Mozambique here,' they told a delegation of party officials.

Drought

Between 1990 and 1995, Rushinga was hit by two severe droughts. On the last Sunday of March 1995, at the end of Mass, Magion Chimbende, the youth leader at Chimandau, stepped forward and showed me a basket of grass seeds, which he said several families in his community were now reduced to eating. The seeds were pounded to make a fine powder that was then mixed with water and cooked. Magion had planted ten acres of maize and six acres of millet that year. He did not reap a single cob of maize or bucket of millet. The sun burnt the maize and the more drought-resistant millet was destroyed by an invasion of army worm.

I felt a great admiration for Magion, for whenever I passed his field he would be working there by himself in the scorching midday sun. He had borrowed two oxen from Chitange and a plough from another village, which he had carried on his back over a distance of twelve kilometres. One day he came to Mass, obviously in pain. When I asked him what was wrong, he rolled back the collar of his shirt and showed me several deep cuts across his shoulders and upper back from carrying the plough. From the beginning of January, he would spend the nights on a small platform he had built across two huge branches of a century-old baobab tree to protect his crops and chase away wild pigs and baboons. For three months Magion did not have a single night of uninterrupted sleep.

Magion told me that for their relish with the porridge made from grass seeds, the people were eating armoured crickets, known as *mamunye*, or *taguta padare*. What neither he nor I knew at the time was that these little creatures have to be properly cleaned and cooked or they will cause a serious illness of the bladder often mistaken for bilharzia. After having completed the second Mass that day in a village on the Mozambique border, I returned to the mission, took all the available cash and returned to Chimandau, so that Magion and some other members of the relief committee the people had formed that Sunday could go and buy maize at Rushinga the following day.

While Magion and his team went to buy maize, I went to see the district administrator in Rushinga on the Monday morning. I took with me a small plastic bag with grass seeds, which I put on his desk, and a glass jar with two armoured crickets marinated in methylated spirit. We had a fruitful discussion. Then I went to see the Member of Parliament for Rushinga, a prominent businessman in Mount Darwin, who was equally understanding. From there I continued to Harare where a friend assisted by inviting a team of journalists. They came to Mary Mount a few days later, spoke with the people, sampled some of the food, took photographs and wrote a story in the local *Sunday Gazette*. The following week a team of Zimbabwe Broadcasting Corporation television reporters turned up to verify if things were really that bad. They had assumed that the story in the *Sunday Gazette* was exaggerated. We suggested they go and have lunch with the people at Chimandau and Nyabawa. They agreed. About three weeks later, a government grain-lending scheme got underway.

Robert Mugabe: revolutionary or rebel?

Such was the real tragedy around Mary Mount. People were eating grass and crickets at Chimandau, while there were mountains of maize at the Grain Marketing Board, just 80 kilometres away. When a calamity occurred in Rushinga, the party and the government always seemed the last to know – and sometimes the least to care. We began wondering; where is the people's revolution?

The Christian church

And was the local church more successful in making a new beginning? In our parish, I was told the story of an elderly woman who, defying the landmines of the Rhodesian soldiers as well as the guns and sticks of ZANLA fighters, had walked on foot, every other month, from Chitange village to Mount Darwin (182 kilometres away) to attend Mass and receive the Eucharist. I followed up with discreet enquiries in other communities and discovered that when the expatriate missionary was forced to leave and the indigenous religious sisters were taken to Mozambique, the faithful were quite able 'to drink from their own well,' to borrow a phrase from the Latin American liberation theologian Gustavo Gutierrez. They had developed a new way – their own way – of living their Christian faith centred around the Word of God when they prayed together in small groups of families, without priests, brothers and sisters. But when the war was over, the priests, brothers and sisters returned, and the mission station once again became the centre, taking over the pastoral leadership of the parish. As in post-war Germany, I felt a moment of grace seemed to have been missed.

Chimurenga: rebellion or revolution?

Max Gluckman, the eminent social anthropologist, said in his 1953 Frazer Lecture at the University of Glasgow, 'in African political life, men were rebels and never revolutionaries'.[2] The statement summed up his research over many years among the peoples of south-eastern Africa – at a different time from the struggle for Zimbabwe and in an altogether different social setting. Nevertheless, the statement captures a striking insight into the dynamics and psychology of social change. A rebellion is the overthrow of a government, whereas a revolution is the overthrow of a social order in favour of a new system of social structures and values. A rebellion replaces one set of individuals with another, while a revolution brings about a fundamental change in the social, political and economic conditions of society.[3] Rebels want to take the place of the rulers they displace, while revolutionaries want to build a new social order.

---

[2] Gluckman, Max (1963) *Order and Rebellion in Tribal Africa.* London: Cohen and West, 127.
[3] *Concise Oxford Dictionary,* 1990.

23

Zimbabwe: The Past is the Future

Our War of Liberation was a rebellion, in that Robert Mugabe's ZANU PF replaced Ian Smith's Rhodesian Front without creating a new social order or changing the fundamental values that had shaped colonial society. Within the colonial shell of post-independent Zimbabwe – and often in conflict with the demands of modern government – the social structures, relationships, needs and allegiances of African society have reasserted themselves and contributed, substantially, to the crisis Zimbabwe now faces. Richard Dowden, Africa editor of *The Economist*, has explored this factor in the wider context of the continent, arguing that neither racial prejudice nor bad governance, alone or jointly, can explain the prevailing disorder of so many African countries, and that the key to understanding lies in the reality of African societies.

> *Each African country is different, but common to all is an attitude to politics, which begins and ends with power and wealth. Doesn't it in every nation? But in Africa there is nothing else. Its states, and their institutions, were imposed by foreign powers, instead of evolving from the history of the people. The 6 000 to 10 000 political entities, which existed in Africa in the middle of the [nineteenth] century, were destroyed or emasculated by imperial rule and replaced by lines drawn on the map. Yet the ethnic, religious or business networks of pre-colonial Africa have survived and developed under the surface of nation states. On the surface, the institutions ... inherited from France, Britain and Portugal, remained largely in place. One is constantly struck by how British or French the style of justice and administration still is. Yet those institutions have been hollowed out. An independent judiciary or an impartial police force or civil service may exist in form but, in many cases, the substance has changed. Operating through non-official networks, the ruler gets his way by bypassing the official structures, or turns them into his own fiefdom by ensuring that anyone in a position of power in those institutions is either a relative or in some way beholden to him. There is no loyalty to the state itself, let alone to the development of the people. In many African countries the president does not distinguish between the national treasury and his own private bank account, or between the police force and his private militia. Political opponents complain but, the evidence is that when they win, they try to do the same thing. ... Such leaders and their attitudes to power emerge from African societies and from the complex relationships between those societies and Africa's artificial nation-states and the rest of the world. It has nothing to do with the racial stereotype of 'the African'.*[4]

---

[4] Dowden, Richard (1999) 'What's wrong with Africa?' *The Tablet*, 16 January. p.73.

The difference is the same

In Zimbabwe, despite the rhetoric of a glorious socialist revolution brought about by the armed struggle, the colonial structures and Rhodesian way of life persist. Arguably, at independence, black Zimbabweans had better access to education, health services and social welfare. But these improvements were quantitative rather than qualitative, peripheral rather than central. They did not lead to the emergence of a new society built on the vision of justice for all – as developed, for example, in the series *From Rhodesia to Zimbabwe*, published jointly, during the war years, by Silveira House and the Catholic Commission for Justice and Peace. And these post-independence achievements were relegated to second place as soon as choices had to be made between education, health and social services, on the one hand, and the defence budget or the dictates of economic structural adjustment, on the other.

While race was no longer the criterion for access to power and wealth, the tiny white elite was replaced by a tiny white and black elite. The blacks in this elite of *nouveaux riches* were preponderantly those few men, and even fewer women, who had either directed the war from the top floor of ZANLA headquarters in central Maputo or been away acquiring degrees in Britain or the United States. (The first person to apply after independence to the Zimbabwe Project in London for a scholarship for his children at an exclusive boarding school, was not a refugee or war veteran but a newly appointed cabinet minister who had spent the war years working as an international civil servant for the United Nations in Geneva. And his application was not a request but a demand.)

Initially, the likeness between Rhodesia and Zimbabwe was somewhat obscured by the Soviet-style *nomenklatura* of the ruling party's leadership structures. Designations such as Central Committee and Politburo baffled white Zimbabweans and made those who had come into contact with real communism cringe. Robert Mugabe boldly proclaimed himself a Marxist-Leninist and yet was delighted to be invited to speak at a Catholic Youth Congress, where he waxed eloquent to a crowd of 6,000 young people about the sanctity of the sacrament of marriage. A bishop could not have been more orthodox. Nor was the friendship with eastern European countries as warm and close as it appeared to outsiders. At a meeting during the war, Mugabe told me of his frustration with his East German donors who, in response to his appeal for food and strong footwear, had sent him soup powder ... infested with worms, and flimsy tennis shoes.

After independence, tribal trust lands were renamed communal lands, and African purchase areas became small-scale commercial farms, but the structure, distribution patterns and unjust economics of the

Rhodesian segregationist Land Apportionment Act remained largely intact.

Another clear indication that Zimbabwe was born from a rebellion rather than a revolution was the ruling party happily governing the country under the semi-colonial Lancaster House Constitution for twenty years without making more than a handful of amendments. They only hastily drafted their own constitutional proposals – which actually gave the president greater powers – when an alliance of civil society groups formed the National Constitutional Assembly to propose a new constitution more in line with the people's aspirations. Both the First Chimurenga and the Second Chimurenga were about land, but land only became a burning issue when the government lost the referendum on a new constitution and hastily put the land issue centre stage as the only thing left to offer people in return for their votes.

Even more striking, the Zimbabwe government retained Rhodesia's infamous Law and Order (Maintenance) Act, complete with the vast body of supporting security legislation built around it during years of mounting pressure from African nationalism. Sir Robert Tredgold, a third-generation Rhodesian, Minister of Defence, Federal Chief Justice and Acting Governor-General, had this to say about the Act in 1969:

> *The culmination [of the spate of repressive legislation] came in 1960, when the government published its Law and Order Maintenance Bill. An eminent lawyer described the proposal as vicious and a leading newspaper as hysterical and neither epithet was unjustified. It almost appeared as though someone had sat down with the Declaration of Human Rights and deliberately scrubbed out each in turn. ... The cumulative effect of the security laws was to turn Rhodesia into a police state. The word has an emotional content and many white Rhodesians became very angry if it was used of their country. Yet, as I understand it, a police state is a state in which the police and the executive are given or assume complete control over all political activity. In this sense it is manifestly true of the Rhodesia of today. ... This was not the end of such legislation. In the succeeding years its severity has been increased. The mandatory death sentence has been laid down for certain offences. Some new political offences have been created. One shocking feature is that a distinction has been made for the purposes of punishment between offences committed for political purposes and ordinary offences, and the former must now be treated more severely, regardless of the circumstances. ... That the legislation brought much injustice I have no doubt at all. Men and women, and some who were little more than boys or girls, were severely punished for acts that in most countries would be regarded as little*

more than outbursts of political exuberance. Compulsory punishments were imposed out of all proportion to the offences.[5]

It was that Act, more than any other piece of legislation, which had contributed to the isolation of Rhodesia and, ultimately, its downfall. Under that law, hundreds of young women and men trying to make their way across the border to Mozambique were arrested, tried, condemned and executed; journalists were persecuted, prosecuted and expelled from the country;[6] newspapers were closed; entire districts like Rushinga, had their cattle (as previously mentioned) and crops destroyed, homesteads burnt down and whole families arrested, as 'communal punishment'. During the liberation war, this law, in conjunction with the Indemnity and Compensation Act,[7] gave Ian Smith's security police the licence 'lawfully' to abduct, torture and murder political opponents.

Despite appeals from many quarters, the Zimbabwe government kept this law on the statute books after independence and applies it today in the same manner, with the same rigour and for similar ends, as its Rhodesian predecessor. In doing so, the ZANU PF government has placed itself in the ideological vicinity of the former apartheid era of the National Party government of South Africa, which originally designed these draconian laws. Recently this Act has been superseded by the Public Order and Security Act. Social and political commentators observed that it is even more repressive than the original.

The Rhodesian state and way of life subsisted not only in the laws and administrative structures of Zimbabwe, but also, of course, in the racial prejudices of some whites. Robert Mugabe is right when he complains that the hand of friendship and reconciliation he extended to white Rhodesians on the eve of independence was rejected. He is also right when he accuses white farmers of having undermined his earlier attempts at land reform. Stunning examples of unrepentant white racism are the utterances in recent years of Ian Smith on the conduct of his security forces during the independence war. Delivering a speech at the Oxford Union, Smith spoke of the people he used to govern in less than endearing terms, at some points calling them 'rapists and murderers'.

---

[5] Tredgold, Sir Robert (1969) *The Rhodesia that was my life*. London: George Allen & Unwin, 229-33.

[6] For example, Father Michael Traber SMB, editor of *Moto*, was expelled in 1972 after publishing a cartoon, with the caption: "The proposed new Constitution will ensure that government will be retained in responsible hands ..." a fist, dripping with blood, squeezing a crowd of black people.

[7] For a comment on the Indemnity and Compensation Act, see Robert Tredgold (1976) 'The Indemnity and Compensation Act: A Profoundly Shocking Law,' in *Civil War in Rhodesia*, a report by the Catholic Commission for Justice and Peace (Salisbury) and CIIR (London), 95.

'The more we killed, the happier we were. We were fighting terrorists ... We had no atrocities... We never killed civilians.'

The fact that Smith's troops did kill tens of thousands of civilians between 1972 and 1980 is meticulously documented from corroborated eye witness accounts in reports by the Catholic Commission for Justice and Peace.[8] It is significant that when the authors of these reports were prosecuted by the Rhodesian Front judiciary, they were charged under the Official Secrets Act and the Law and Order (Maintenance) (Emergency Powers Regulations) Act. Their offence was not misrepresenting the facts but 'causing alarm and despondency'. In their defence – and, more important, in defence of the ordinary people who had brought their complaints to the commission – the authors chose not to oppose the state's claims that they had revealed 'military secrets' and 'caused alarm and despondency' among white Rhodesians, who, up to the day of independence (and beyond), were made to believe that this war was about defeating external communist terrorists.[9] They were victims of Ian Smith's warped leadership. One of his former elite soldiers, Bruce Moore-King, described the situation in this way:

> *It was greed that sent us to war. This is part of what I have seen. It is not my truth, my accusation. The elders showed me this truth, showed it through their careless petty actions, and their poisonous lessons to the children. I point no finger; accuse no man for the war, for the past. I was part of it, contributed as much as any to its horror. The elders' guilt is their own, and it will hound them until they face it honestly. Only then will they be able to bury the past. But for the bitter, destructive, petty, murderous actions, deeds and words of my tribe since peace was brought to this land, for these I accuse many. The high priest I accuse particularly. His betrayal has been absolute and constant. Yet his recent actions have helped me to see another part of the truth, and for that I thank him. Like the elders, the high priest has publicly declared the truth about himself.*[10]

---

[8] See *Man in the Middle – Torture, Resettlement and Eviction* (1975); *Civil War in Rhodesia* (1976) reports compiled by the Catholic Commission for Justice and Peace in Rhodesia (Salisbury) and CIIR (London).
[9] *The Herald*, (Harare) 2 November 2000, quoting *The Guardian* (London).
[10] Moore-King, Bruce (1988) *White Man, Black War*. Harare: Baobab Books, 113. Emmerson Mnangangwa, then Minister of Justice, Legal and Parliamentary Affairs, said about this book: 'A different and remarkable book. Its publication marks a significant step in our own growth and maturity: it demonstrates that we have progressed, through reconciliation and self-criticism, to a point where we can say these things to each other in a spirit of openness and frankness.' From the review printed on the dust cover.

So what did happen to the Jewel?

The jewel Mugabe inherited at independence was a country divided into two nations.[11] At first sight the legacy he will be passing on to the next generation is a country even more deeply divided. Yet, on closer examination, the ten-year War of Liberation and the subsequent two decades have in fact brought the 'two nations' closer together. This is the real revolution that has been taking place over the past 30 years, one that continues now among ordinary Zimbabweans, black and white. There are many signs of this. The struggle for liberation was not in vain. For many whites, a freedom greater and deeper than political independence has been achieved. Attitudes and behaviour patterns have changed. And there is hope that Zimbabwe, during the next generation, will be one nation, made up of gifted people, where race or tribe will be irrelevant.

The lingering tragedy is that neither those whites who cling to the past nor the black nationalists of the governing party seem able to understand this. Both appear locked in the political and mental stereotypes of Rhodesia. The closer the end of the liberation war came, the louder Ian Smith trumpeted, 'The Africans will never rule this country. Not in a thousand years. Never, ever.' Today, Robert Mugabe affirms, 'Let the MDC side with Europeans and the British, but we will conquer them together. I am firmly asserting to you that there will never come a day when the MDC will rule this country. Never, ever.'

But things have changed. And the people have changed. The younger generation of black Zimbabweans who come to learn here at Silveira House[12] simply do not understand what the ZANU PF leadership are talking about. They want to learn a trade, pass their tests, find work, start a family and get on with life. The majority of real war veterans strongly dissociate themselves from the farm invasions, murders and other forms of violence perpetrated by others in their name. We know this, because some of our trainers and instructors are real ex-combatants. Most whites are profoundly embarrassed when Ian Smith opens his mouth and tries to resuscitate the racist myths of his Rhodesian Front: 'I still don't believe majority rule was the correct solution.' Most black Zimbabweans are too sophisticated and mature to take offence: they simply laugh and put it down to the old man's age. Many white farmers developed good working relationships with their black colleagues in the communal lands and would readily assist them with tillage, fertiliser

---

[11] Gray, Richard (1960) *The Two Nations*. London: Oxford University Press; Mason, Philip (1958) *The Birth of a Dilemma*, Oxford University Press, London; Mason, Philip, 1960, *Year of Decision*, Oxford University Press, London.

[12] Silveira House was established in 1964 by Father John Dove to provide leadership and development training to urban and rural communities and organisations. Its objectives have not always pleased successive governments.

and seeds. While some whites opposed land reform there were many eager to help facilitate a thorough land resettlement process in Zimbabwe. We know this because a Jesuit at Silveira House was deeply involved in mediation between the government, the farmers and the people who invaded and occupied commercial farmland.[13]

True, the current troubles are real and serious. And they are dangerous. But they are artificially fabricated and imposed from the top. The racist rhetoric of 'striking fear into the heart of every white' has singularly failed to ignite black feelings. If such utterances were based on 'the will of the people', Zimbabwe would be on fire. But Zimbabwe is not at war with itself. It will never be, again. Those who fought in the war for independence, and survived – with scars both physical and emotional – will not allow this to happen. And they will tell their children not to allow war to happen ever again in their country. To allow one of Ian Smith's former Grey Scouts say it in his own words:

> *My homeland stretches before me, a quilt of thriving forests and fields. Never have I seen such peace in my homeland. The truth I have found since my return is not that we were wrong, not that war is murderous and degrading, not that our leaders lied and misled and used us. Those are mere facts. The truth is that our fellow countrymen have shown us the meaning of the words we once spoke so easily. The truth is that they have shown us how a civilised people conduct themselves. We have much to learn about civilised, honest behaviour. To those who cling to and revel in the past, I offer a simple test: Take your son by the hand and show him his homeland as it is today. Show him those things that have come about which were worth killing to prevent. ... But if you can see no such things, then call yourself Zimbabwean, with all that the word means, and set about rebuilding our war-ravaged homeland. Understand, explain to your son, that these are the only two choices available to you; there can be no compromise, no procrastination. Choose to be Zimbabwean or choose to be the enemy. We of the scarred generation, who have begun to question, to think, and to see, will allow you no other choice. The people of this land will allow you no other. You have exhausted your privileges as elders and parents. Make your choice, then live or die by it.*[14]

---

[13] Fidelis Mukonori, SJ, spent hours in this mediation process in 2000 and 2001, which is credited with preventing further murders of commercial farmers.
[14] Moore-King, Bruce, op.cit. ft. 10. 132.

What happened to our dream?

The Zimbabwe Liberators' Platform[1]

In 1980, the new government of independent Zimbabwe took over a resilient country, which had survived fifteen years of international sanctions. A major donor conference at the time demonstrated intense international interest and led to offers of significant development assistance. Initially the economy grew rapidly as a result of the lifting of sanctions coupled with donor assistance. The policy of national reconciliation after the bitter war caught the imagination of both the country and the world. Peace, stability and social integration seemed attainable.

Yet within ten years of independence the economy showed signs of decline and the slide has accelerated up to the present.[2] The volume of manufacturing output, for example, went down after an initial surge in the first year of the Economic Structural Adjustment Programme (ESAP).[3] How did this happen? How did the same leadership that inherited a promising Zimbabwe in 1980 manage to change the country from prosperity and hope to what eventually became economic collapse, desperation and isolation in a space of twenty years?

We believe that the answer to this question lies in the history of the liberation struggle itself and our purpose in this chapter is to explain our present difficulties in the light of the role played by the freedom fighters – their aspirations, hardships and frustrations – as they travelled the arduous road from colonial oppression to independence and then on to a brutal dictatorship.

One aim, different aspirations

Zimbabwe's national liberation struggle was driven by grievances engendered by decades of colonial subjugation. The struggle had the ultimate goal of freedom. Successive colonial administrations used

---
[1] The Zimbabwe Liberators Platform was formed in 2000 (see page 39).
[2] National Accounts 1985-2000. Harare: Central Statistical Office, March 2002.
[3] CSO Quarterly Digest of Statistics. Cited in Bond, Patrick, and Masimba Manyanya (2002) *Zimbabwe's Plunge*. Durban: University of Natal Press; Harare: Weaver Press.

political power to suppress the black majority through legislation backed by force. Blacks could not form political parties to articulate their grievances and economically they were limited to designated areas. Access to education and jobs and social centres – hotels, restaurants, etc, – was restricted. The Land Apportionment Act of 1931 expropriated fertile land from blacks and confined them to sandy, often arid, soils. The Land Tenure Act of 1969 tried to enshrine this division permanently. All of these grievances united black people to fight for their rights and freedoms.

Their first response was to form 'nationalist' parties – groups of people bonded together with the aim of winning political freedom. These parties were at the forefront of the struggle for independence here as in the rest of Africa. Nationalist leaders who were jailed for demanding freedom became the youth's role models. But as the struggle developed, it became clear that young people, who formed the bulk of the freedom fighters, had more far-reaching aspirations. Yes, they shared the experience of deprivation and the denial of dignity. Yes, they too were inspired by the success of the nationalist struggles in Africa, Cuba and China, but gradually there emerged a difference in their aspirations once the armed struggle began.

Their political education wove the diverse individual and national grievances into a system that expressed itself politically, economically, socially and culturally. They realised there was need to wrest power from the colonial regime not just to gain freedom but also to address the structures in the country. It gradually became clear that the old nationalist parties simply wanted to take power, change the name, flag and anthem and put black people into positions where whites had been before. These old parties did not want radical change in a way that would open up opportunities for the masses of the people. This difference in perspective did not reveal itself immediately. We need to review the story of the struggle to see how it arose. The independence movement that originated in the 1940s simply focused on resistance to colonial rule. The early nationalist leaders: Joshua Nkomo, James Chikerema and George Nyandoro, began the Southern Rhodesia African National Congress (later the Zimbabwe African People's Union – ZAPU) in 1957 with this intention. Ndabaningi Sithole, Leopold Takawira and others broke away in 1963 to form the Zimbabwe African National Union (ZANU) but they had the same basic aims as the parent party. Realising that nationalist struggles were not yielding results ZAPU and ZANU resolved separately to change their strategy from politics to arms. This momentous decision opened the way for more comprehensive aspirations. The aim now was not simply a transfer of power from white to black but a whole restructuring of society.

Once the decision to take up arms was made, ZANU and ZAPU began recruiting people for military training in Cuba, China, the Soviet Union

What happened to our dream?

or Ghana. There was some pressure to do this owing to the prospect of the Organisation of African Unity (OAU) withdrawing its financial support if there were no fighters in military camps. Initially, volunteers to join the liberation armies were hard to come by and this explains why a number of unemployed Zimbabweans in Zambia were enticed to join the struggle under the false impression that they would get jobs and scholarships. Among such people was the late Ernest Kadungure, a former Minister of Defence in Mugabe's cabinet. The abduction, however, of 291 students and workers from St Albert's Mission in Mount Darwin in July 1973 was more the result of over-zealousness on the part of Commander Thomas Nhari than the policy of ZANLA. At that time ZANLA was freely getting recruits from the operational zones and could do without the forcible abduction of school children – many too young to become soldiers. Nhari was reprimanded by the High Command for his adventurist and irresponsible attitude.[4]

The real military struggle began after the Unilateral Declaration of Independence by the Rhodesians in 1965. Guerrilla bands crossed into the country from Zambia and launched sabotage operations using such weapons as petrol bombs. There were no significant military successes during this period and a strategic re-appraisal of the war effort followed towards the end of the 1960s leading to the adoption of a 'people's war' based on the mobilisation and organisation of the masses. The notion of a quick military victory was abandoned and the need to wage a protracted war was adopted. In the early 1970s large numbers of young people joined the guerrilla army.

Internal difficulties

In 1971, James Chikerema from ZAPU and Nathan Shamuyarira from ZANU moved to combine the two guerrilla groups – ZAPU and ZANU – into the Front for the Liberation of Zimbabwe (FROLIZI) which sought and received recognition from the OAU with support from Libya. But it was resisted by the leadership of ZANU and ZAPU as an attempt to destroy the two parent parties. Their response was to form their own Joint Military Command (JMC) under Herbert Chitepo, the national chairman of ZANU. This move effectively undermined FROLIZI.

In 1974, some the Zimbabwe African Liberation Army (ZANLA - the armed wing of ZANU) fighters – a group led by the same Thomas Nhari mentioned above – rebelled against the JMC and kidnapped some of its leaders, but the rebellion was suppressed. Nhari himself, Dakarai Badza,

---

[4] This version of the kidnapping is also recorded in *On the Frontline – Catholic Missions in Zimbabwe's Liberation War*, Janice McLaughlin (1996). Harare: Baobab Books, 72-108.

Fidian Kashiri, Cephasis Tichatonga, Siza Molife, Sam Chandawa and Timothy Chiridza were rounded up and executed.[5] ZAPU experienced similar problems at the beginning of the 1970s.

Detente and the intensification of the war

The mid-1970s saw an intensification of the war. The Rhodesian regime suffered increased numbers of casualties and was forced to seek military support from South Africa and Australia. It also sought British and US assistance to contain the situation. The South Africans had been involved in Rhodesia's war from as early as 1967 following a joint military campaign by the Zimbabwe People's Revolutionary Army (ZIPRA – the armed wing of ZAPU) and Umkhonto weSizwe (The Spear of the Nation – the military wing of the African National Congress of South Africa) in the Victoria Falls area that year.

A plan was drawn up in 1974 by Zambia and South Africa to end the fighting following the decolonisation of Mozambique and Angola – events that exposed the flanks of both Rhodesia and South Africa militarily. Moreover, Zambia was feeling the strain of the protracted struggle, which cost her £112m in the eighteen months from January 1973 alone.[6] The collapse of Portuguese rule threatened South Africa's use of the port of Lourenço Marques, the flow of labour from Moçambique to its mines and access to the electricity generated at Cabora Bassa. The President of Zambia, Kenneth Kaunda, and the Prime Minister of South Africa, John Vorster, worked for a negotiated settlement. The freedom fighters were extremely suspicious of these moves, but they were effectively leaderless with Ndabaningi Sithole under suspicion and Joshua Nkomo, the leader of ZAPU, being unacceptable to ZANU and ZANLA. The fighters suspected that the former's commitment to the struggle was waning. His readiness to embrace the détente initiative spearheaded by Vorster and Kaunda was viewed as a betrayal by the ZANLA fighters. They saw it as a ploy to derail the struggle. At one point Sithole told a group of fighters, 'I am a teacher and can always go back to the classroom but what about you?'[7] Nkomo was not acceptable to ZANU and its fighters because of the split in the early 1960s which had shown his weak and indecisive leadership through his inclination to accept the unfair 1961 Constitutional proposals. Ethnicity was not an issue at the time of the split in 1963.

---

[5] Bhebe, Ngwabi, (1999) *The ZAPU and ZANU Guerrilla Warfare and the Evangelical Lutheran Church in Zimbabwe*. Gweru: Mambo Press, 57.
[6] Sir Robert Jackson, co-ordinator of UN assistance to Zambia, quoted in Martin, David and Phyllis Johnson (1981) *The Struggle for Zimbabwe*. London: Faber and Faber, 346.
[7] Personal recollection, Wilfred Mhanda.

Meanwhile the Rhodesians worked to cause division and confusion in the liberation movements with the intention of reducing, and eventually stopping, military activity inside the country and thus providing a breathing space. Nationalist leaders were released from detention in Rhodesia to take part in the talks brokered by Zambia and South Africa, to end the fighting. An attempt was made by Abel Muzorewa of the African National Council (ANC), Joshua Nkomo of ZAPU, Ndabaningi Sithole of ZANU, and James Chikerema of FROLIZI, to respond to the call of the 'frontline leaders', especially Nyerere and Kaunda, to unite as one organisation. They did so by placing themselves under the umbrella of a 'United' African National Council (UANC). (The original ANC was an *ad hoc* party formed under Muzorewa in 1971 by ZAPU and ZANU members within Rhodesia to oppose the recommendations of the Pearce Commission for a settlement based on a revised constitution. The proposals theoretically, at least, would have given Africans increased representation in parliament.) ZANU and ZAPU were officially banned in Tanzania and Zambia as they were in Rhodesia.

Further confusion occurred in March 1975 when the Zambian authorities arrested and detained the ZANU leadership in exile, following the death by a car bomb of the party chairman, Herbert Chitepo, in Lusaka. Subsequently all ZANLA fighters in Zambia were disarmed and detained at Mboroma Camp for nine months. The fighters in Mozambique were similarly disarmed but not detained. This virtually brought the war in Rhodesia to a halt.

The formation of ZIPA and the Patriotic Front

In the same year (1975), after a strike among the detained ZANLA forces, the Zambian government brought Chikerema, Nkomo, Sithole and Muzorewa together to form the Zimbabwe Liberation Council (ZLC). Sithole supported the ZLC but ZAPU did not because of Chikerema's involvement. Division between Sithole as ZANU leader and the ZANLA forces deepened when Sithole appointed a new high command without consultation and ignored the incumbent military leadership. Furthermore, Sithole acquiesced in the unprovoked shooting of unarmed ZANLA commanders at Mboroma by the Zambian army. The division came to a head when ZANLA commanders gathered at Mgagao in Tanzania, and issued the Mgagao Manifesto denouncing Sithole and calling for the resumption of the liberation war. In support of this, the OAU and the Tanzanian government told ZANLA to co-operate with ZIPRA. Mozambique also supported unity between ZANLA and ZIPRA and wanted a commitment to prosecuting the war. Under pressure from their backers, ZIPRA and ZANLA formed the Zimbabwe Peoples Army (ZIPA) in 1975. The next step was to integrate the fighting forces inside Mozambique as well as those in training camps in Morogoro and Mgagao. The war resumed in January 1976 without the involvement of the political leadership.

However, conflicts between ZANLA and ZIPRA soon began in the training camps in Tanzania resulting in some deaths, and consequently the fighters proposed that there should be political leadership over the fighting forces. Samora Machel resisted the inclusion of Robert Mugabe because he was said to be against unity. Nevertheless, ZANLA chose him as their leader. ZAPU was represented by Jason Moyo, John Nkomo, George Silundika and others, but by the middle of the year the ZIPRA component of ZIPA withdrew from the integration effort and returned to Zambia.

While the nationalist armies were moving apart the political leaders, Joshua Nkomo and Robert Mugabe, were coming together. They formed the Patriotic Front in October 1976 and went to Geneva for talks with the British and the Americans.

Power and ideological struggle[8]

The divisions and constantly shifting alliances on the military front and within the political leadership continued with the 'Vashandi' incident – the arrest, by the ZANU leaders, of 50 commanders: the ZIPA military committee members, commanders from the battlefront, and camp commanders. Of the 50, twenty-five were kept in Beira and the rest at Cabo Delgado. The reasons given for the detentions revealed the underlying differences between the nationalist leaders and the fighters on the ground, divisions that ran right throughout the whole liberation struggle.

- It was alleged that the commanders wanted to stamp their authority on the fighting forces that were making an impact on the battlefield.
- The young commanders in the field were ideologically very clear. They wanted a democratic revolution that would lead to the social and economic restructuring of the country.
- They were insisting on political unity between ZANU and ZAPU – something Mugabe vehemently opposed.

The fighters suspected that the commitment of the nationalist leaders to the liberation struggle was not wholehearted. They showed no inclination to work for the transformation of society or to serve the interests of the majority, namely the peasants and the workers. In January 1978 there was another incident in which a group of ZANU political leaders and a

---

[8] A detailed account of the ideological struggle within ZANLA and the Vashandi incident can be found in McLaughlin, J (1996) op.cit. ft. 4. 52-68.

few commanders were arrested for allegedly planning to take over the leadership of the liberation movement. All the detainees were released at independence in April 1980. But a few days afterwards some former ZIPA commanders were again detained. Among them were Dzinashe Machingura, James Nyikadzinashe, Parker Chipoyera and David Todlana. Later that year, eighteen of the former prisoners were re-arrested and detained for ten days by the police who seized all their documentation on the liberation struggle, apparently on Mugabe's instructions. Nkomo as Minister of Home Affairs ordered their release.

The role of war veterans during and after the struggle

During the liberation war, the freedom fighters claimed to have a clear vision of a new Zimbabwe: independent, free, democratic and economically prosperous. Society was to be transformed in pursuit of social justice in the interests of the people. They had to sell this vision and so be 'political soldiers'. This spirit of service guided them during the war, hence the song 'Nzira dzamasoja dzokuzvibata nadzo' (the way in which soldiers should conduct themselves), that is, their guiding principle was to be respect for people and self-discipline. Freedom fighters served as role models to the youths and the rest of society through their heroic acts and readiness to sacrifice their lives for the liberation of their country. It is, however, also true that some fighters were guilty of terrible deeds against the people, which tarnished their name and reputation. The majority of these incidents took place during the later years of the war.

After the struggle, the freedom fighters were relegated to a secondary role. They were not given an opportunity to articulate their vision, mission, values and objectives. The revolution was hijacked partly during the struggle, partly during the Lancaster House negotiations, and partly during the post-independence era.

Why did this happen? There was a convergence of interests between the nationalists and the Western powers. The freedom fighters had been largely influenced by eastern European (Marxist) and Chinese (Maoist) ideology, while the nationalists were a product of the West where they were educated and moulded. Yet the nationalists, in terms of ideology, were stuck in the 1940s and '50s – while the West had moved on in terms of human rights and accountable governance. There was also an uneven development in political consciousness between nationalists and freedom fighters. The fighters were exposed to a new outlook after going through the political and military mill. They learnt that their task was to fight for and serve the people The nationalists never had this experience. They did not fight and they simply saw themselves as leaders. The fears and concerns that had given rise to the Vashandi phenomenon became a reality. All the nationalists were ever interested in was to step into the shoes of the former white oppressors and become the new masters.

Post-independence history

After independence, the fighters – first known as ex-combatants and much later as 'war veterans' – can trace their project through four stages.

(i) Demobilisation

When the war of liberation and the Lancaster House talks brought independence to Zimbabwe, soldiers from the Rhodesian regime and the liberation movements (ZAPU and ZANU) were integrated into one national army. The size of this army was too big for the country, so many of the former liberation forces as well as the Rhodesian military were demobilised, as agreed at Lancaster House. To make demobilisation attractive, the Zimbabwe government offered the former fighters job opportunities in government departments and parastatals, and training opportunities. The demobilised were paid a sum that was not enough to enable them to start a new life. No counselling accompanied demobilisation or the cash payment, and as a result, some of the war veterans were soon destitute. It is true that some were assisted as was pointed out by Judith Todd in 2000,[9] 'Of the 41,000 demobilised, 5,000 went to school, 1,000 undertook vocational training, 5 000 formed co-operatives of one kind or another and a further 40,000 found employment.' But in the final analysis, the demobilisation exercise did not achieve its intended goal because of lack of commitment, poor planning and corruption.

What was needed was a sound policy for the rehabilitation of the former fighters into society. Some of the current problems involving war veterans can be traced back to these early failures. Unscrupulous politicians took advantage of war veterans and abused them for their own selfish ends. For example, in the 1990s, when the war veterans were poor and desperate, they were easy prey to manipulation by the ruling party, as we shall see.

(ii) The formation of the War Veterans' Association

In the early 1980s, war veterans from ZANLA and ZIPRA made efforts to form an organisation that would unite them, look after their interests, and ensure that the gains, objectives and values of the liberation struggle were defended and consolidated. The government and the ZANU PF leadership deliberately frustrated these efforts. The only logical explanation for the leadership's behaviour is:

---

[9] *The Daily News*, 15 September 2000.

What happened to our dream?

a) their fear that a strong war veterans' organisation would pose a threat to their own positions of power and control over decision-making; and
b) their awareness that such an organisation would question the leadership's agenda.

However, in 1990, the Zimbabwe National Liberation War Veterans Association (ZNLWVA) was launched with Mugabe and Emmerson Mnangagwa in attendance. War veterans began to make demands for recognition, rehabilitation, financial and educational assistance. When Chenjerai Hunzvi, who was not a war veteran, took over the leadership of the association in 1997, he increased pressure on the government for gratuities. Hunzvi had been an office worker at ZAPU HQ in Lusaka during the struggle and moved to Harare at the time of independence in 1980. He continued to work as an Administrative Assistant at Nkomo's residence under Mrs Ndlovu, the Administrative Officer. In 1982 he went to Poland for medical studies, returning to Zimbabwe in 1988.

In 1997 the government eventually gave in and paid out Z$2.5bn to the war veterans. The controversy surrounding the gratuities has refused to go away. War veterans are still haunted by it to this day, as if it was not justified. (Incidentally, former Rhodesian soldiers are still receiving their pensions, partly in foreign currency.) Then war veterans' association leaders became ambitious. Seeing an opportunity to enter the government, they delivered the organisation to ZANU PF, which welcomed it with open hands. It is important to note that Hunzvi's gravitation to ZANU PF was to seek immunity for his embezzlement of the war veterans' funds. Thanks to his support for ZANU PF, he placed himself beyond the arm of the law and was never prosecuted for the crimes he committed. Hunzvi campaigned for ZANU PF in parliamentary elections and was rewarded with a parliamentary seat. He failed, however, to secure a ministerial portfolio but he remained ambitious. He was subsequently heavily involved in the land invasions that began in 2000, often inciting the invaders to violence. The ZNLWVA also campaigned for Mugabe's re-election as President in 2002. Today, the association is perceived by the Zimbabwe public as a violent organisation, whose members support a ruling party responsible for ruining the country.

(iii) The formation of the Zimbabwe Liberators' Platform

The events of 2000 – violent land invasions, political coercion and the breakdown of the rule of law – were in part perpetrated in the name of war veterans. Yet those events negated and betrayed the aims, objectives and values of the liberation struggle. The associated violence and anarchy tarnished the image of genuine war veterans. Those developments prompted the formation in 2000 of the Zimbabwe Liberators' Platform (ZLP), whose purpose was to salvage the honour of the war veterans as well as help the nation refocus on the original aims and objectives of the struggle: freedom, democracy, respect for human rights, equality, peace and social justice.

(iv) War veterans and land invasions

When ZANU PF lost the constitutional referendum in February 2000, it realised that its popularity had plunged. Faced with parliamentary elections within a few months, the ruling party formulated an election campaign strategy with land as its only trump card. Land helped shift the focus away from the liability of a troubled economy. As the whites appeared to be supporting the opposition Movement for Democratic Change (MDC), they became the targets. So the strategy was to grab their land by force.

The ZANU PF leadership used the state apparatus to invade white-owned commercial farms, and later invited war veterans to participate in the exercise. With war veterans at the forefront, it would be easy to sell the idea to the Zimbabwean public: war veterans were demonstrating against the unequal distribution of land. Surely the government would be criticised if it failed to redistribute land to the landless Zimbabweans. After all, the liberation war was fought over land violently seized by white colonialists who had paid no compensation.

The government ignored the chaotic nature of the land invasions even when they became violent and bloody. Mugabe openly told the nation that the invasions were political, and justified, rendering the police powerless. The war veterans associated with the invasions did so in the name of the ZNLWVA, which now had close links with ZANU PF. However the association as such never passed a resolution supporting the land reform exercise The violence, murder, rape, intimidation and torture that characterised the invasions came to be associated with the war veterans and the public perceived them as violent rapists and murderers.

However, the reality is that less than 50 genuine war veterans actively spearheaded the land invasions and some criminal elements helped to create that perception. The majority of the invaders were not war veterans, though later a sizeable number did join the initial invaders and acquired some land. The farm invasions of 2000 were largely state sponsored with a few incidents of spontaneous actions, though most of these were reversed by the authorities. Ian Smith's farm in Shurugwi, for instance, was invaded for a time until it was realised it was in a catchment area. The invaders were used by the ZANU PF leadership to carry out their dirty work. True to form, the ZANU PF leaders later evicted war veterans from the farms they had occupied for up to two years, in order to make way for the ZANU PF elite, some of whom now own several farms. The consequences of the land invasions are hunger, food shortages, loss of exports, acute poverty, unemployment, environmental degradation, and a loss of production.

Present aspirations versus reality

Did the liberation struggle achieve its intended objectives? Is the nation still guided by those values that made many Zimbabweans sacrifice their resources, time and lives? If not, what went wrong?

Zimbabwe today faces its deepest political, economic, social and humanitarian crisis ever. The ZANU PF government has enacted repressive legislation denying Zimbabweans their basic rights and freedoms. Elections have been rigged to perpetuate ZANU PF rule. The rule of law is not respected and there is selective application of justice. Corruption in the judiciary is now widespread. The economy has virtually collapsed. The country generates very little foreign currency, as the agricultural base has collapsed, resulting in the shortage of fuel, with all the dire economic consequences associated with that. Foreign currency shortages have also affected imports of water treatment chemicals, electricity, drugs, agricultural and industrial inputs and equipment. Unemployment has reached a record high of 70 per cent. Hyperinflation is over 500 per cent. Bank notes are in short supply. The chaotic and violent land invasions have created acute shortages of agricultural products such as maize and maize meal, wheat and bread, sugar, fertiliser and seed. There is a humanitarian crisis caused by misguided political and economic policies, rampant institutionalised corruption and mismanagement.

People are starving because of food shortages and skewed distribution of food assistance where party supporters are prioritised. The AIDS pandemic is taking a heavy toll on the nation deprived of adequate food. Political repression has created internal refugees and land invasions have displaced farm workers who have no land, home or income.

Socially, the education system and health delivery system have collapsed. The shortage of foreign currency has adversely affected the health of the population. Essential drugs and medical equipment are in short supply. Students at boarding schools and tertiary institutions are malnourished due to food shortages. The public transport system virtually collapsed until fuel was allowed to find a market level which makes travel to and from work the largest item for a wage earner.

Conclusion

In Zimbabwe today, virtually everything that can go wrong has gone wrong. There is political chaos and anarchy. Economic meltdown is nearly complete. Desperation and frustration are polluting the atmosphere and political intransigence persists. The 'Jewel of Africa' is in the intensive care unit. Political leaders who delivered independence and short-lived economic prosperity have become rogues.

As far as the war veterans are concerned, their aspirations have turned into a nightmare; the ideal is totally divorced from a very painful reality. With the exception of independence and the national flag, nothing else forms part of their original aspirations. No economic opportunities, no political freedoms or rights, no food, no cash, no values, and no culture. Zimbabweans in general feel hollow; genuine war veterans in particular feel worse because their sacrifices were in vain.

4

The people's liberation struggle

Duduzile Tafara

As I reflect now on the struggle for Zimbabwe, I wonder if I was even conscious of what was happening at the time. How many of us could talk articulately about the struggle then? What exactly happened in those camps? And, when we were home, was there a place for us? Most of these questions remain unanswered inside of me, and I am very reluctant to write about them now. This is because of the pain for me, as a former fighter, when I recall the many friends who died in the camps or during the early years of independence, and the many former fighters who are now languishing in poverty in the present economic hardships.

What did the former fighters think was the point of the struggle? Even today not many of us are able to speak about it. Our education during the struggle was narrow. We saw the enemy as the white people. They had stolen our land and our task was to win it back. We did not need to go beyond that. This motivation was enough to drive people in large numbers to join the liberation struggle. It was simple: wealth was in the hands of the few, while the many suffered poverty.

Efforts were made to try to create awareness among the people in the camps about the purpose of the liberation struggle, but because those who conducted the classes had limited education themselves, the instruction was restricted to turning people into killing machines of the white people. Everything bad that had happened back home was because of white people. As soon as they were removed, everything would be good back home. Maybe the leaders knew more, but this was the 'education' of the ordinary combatant.

But it became for me like the story of the hunter and his dog. The hunter knows what he is looking for, but it is the dog that does the actual chasing of the animal until it is caught. The story of the former fighters is one of a struggle for survival that started the day they joined the War of Liberation. We were told that all the wealth of the whites would be used for the benefit of poor blacks. We were going to have a democratic Zimbabwe where everyone was going to exercise his or her right through the ballot box. We were all going to be equal. But what these equal rights were was never explained.

The leapfrogging of steps and processes that the gun was going to bring in both politics and economics turned into a fantasy. 'Tichasangana kuMeikles', we would say, referring to one of the most well-known hotels in town, 'we will meet in Meikles in a free Zimbabwe.' It is still not clear to me, or to many of my companions, what the economic impact of the freedom struggle is. We are now realising that economic independence requires long-term planning, which takes into account issues of training, access to capital, resources and sustainability. This was never clear to us. All we knew was that the specific aim of the liberation struggle was to establish black majority rule.

In the power dynamics of that time, there were astronomically high levels of fear instilled into people through members of the intelligence units, who played a role like that of the thought police in George Orwell's *1984*. 'Sell-outs' were identified by their critical thinking and their openness when they pointed out some of the gaps the liberation movement needed to fill. These people were too smart for the liking of the leadership. And one could also be declared a sell-out because of jealousy, ignorance, or tribalism. The decision as to whether you survived or not lay with the leaders. If you were declared a sell-out, the best that could happen to you was imprisonment. Otherwise your life could be terminated forthwith. It was very difficult for the intelligent or the creative. Such people could be sent to the front to die in battle or, if they were considered too dangerous as they might influence other people, they were either shot dead or spent the rest of the war in prison.

Coming back home was another painful journey. The celebrations were short lived as the reality began to sink in. All the fantasies of the struggle faded like dew. Although people sang and danced for the freedom fighters, the reality was that they had to start a whole new life in the independent country. Going back to the metaphor of the dog and the hunter, the latter took the prey into the house while the dog sat outside waiting for the bones. The hunter was celebrating with new friends who had not gone hunting with him and did not even know that the dog did the chasing. All the compliments went to the hunter, and the dog did not even exist in the eyes of the hunter's new friends.

The former fighters were shocked by this deceitful behaviour of their leaders, whom they had regarded as their comrades. Those who had survived the scrutiny of the thought police now faced new agonies. They were survivors and they now had to learn to survive again. They waited, hoping that the promises of the struggle would be actualised. They withdrew into oblivion until the 1990s when they came to realise that they had to organise themselves and act. At the same time, the leaders discovered that they had need of the former fighters again when they saw no one coming to their rallies. They asked the freedom fighters to fight their battles all over again. Serious cracks began to show, even among the fighters, as some agreed to this new call and some did not.

What is the future of the former freedom fighters? We carried out a survey to find out people's perception of us and the results were disturbing. The overall outcome was quite negative. The fighters seemed to be the people most feared by those liberated. The youth think that they are just cruel land grabbers. Even the elderly expressed concern over the former freedom fighters: 'The liberation guns have been turned against us.' However, these same people are clear that the role of the former freedom fighters is to defend the values of the liberation struggle – the equal distribution of the resources of the country, and to fight against corruption and exploitation of the people by their own. The future role of the fighters is very disturbing and hard to analyse. They no longer share the same vision and can probably be divided into three groups:

- those who have fused themselves into society and do not want to have anything to do with what is happening in the country. They do not even want to be identified as former fighters.
- those who are still in the forefront of re-educating the people involved in the farm invasions, as they see themselves as completing what they started in the bush – though they now lack a good strategy. And finally,
- those who are reorganising themselves, hoping to correct the image of the former fighters. They aim at creating rehabilitation programmes for the fighters and those who supported them during the liberation war.

The dilemma is how to bring the three groups together for the development of the new Zimbabwe for which so many sacrificed their lives.

Zimbabwe: The Past is the Future

The long way home: one man's story

Alexander Kanengoni

For me, the quest for land began in 1974 when I went to the war. It finally ended on an unlikely morning in January 2003 when the district land allocation committee in the small farming town of Centenary showed me a piece of land it had allocated to me. It had been a long and painful journey, a journey spattered with blood, a swollen river flooded with tears, a heart-rending story punctuated by the rattling sound of automatic gunfire, a sobbing account of fatal betrayals and unparalleled heroism, of miscarried childhoods, of mountains of shattered dreams and unfulfilled promises. It is an anguished story of people who walked away from each other because they were no longer friends; the story of a journey of a people and the strong relationship they have with their land.

The details of how the drama began and unfolded have been told many times. For me, it began with the Rudd Concession of October, 1888, an event that foretold the pain, blood and tears, which characterised the long and tortuous road to freedom. It was the document that Cecil Rhodes used to obtain the backing of Queen Victoria to occupy the country, and the circumstances surrounding its creation and signature left, for me, an enduring scar. Cecil Rhodes' representative, Charles Rudd, wrote it and Lobengula, king of the Ndebele people, signed it. In that treacherous document, Lobengula signed away the land and mineral rights of all 'Matabeleland, Mashonaland and other adjoining territories.' The immediate problem with the document was that it was legal and technical, and Lobengula was an illiterate man and certainly could not have understood its far-reaching implications. Quite frankly, there is no way he would have signed a document that not only gave away his land and mineral rights to foreigners, but also reduced him and his people to virtual squatters on their own land.

It is important to pause and take a look at the rather curious liberal school of thought that attempts to compare Cecil Rhodes, and the wave of people that he represented, with such movements as the Ndebele under Mzilikazi and his son, Lobengula, and the Shona who came from the

Great Lakes several centuries before. This perception is driven by local white liberals, like economist John Robertson and lawyer, Bob Stumbles. The fundamental point they choose to ignore is that Rhodes sought permission to invade from a metropolitan centre, London, and the whole effort was intended ultimately to further the imperial enterprise. When Mzilikazi escaped from Tshaka and settled in Matabeleland, he had no intention of benefiting the Zulu king. When the Shonas moved south, their journey was not, like Vasco da Gama's, to benefit some faraway kingdom which continued to claim their allegiance. When Rhodes' pioneers invaded we immediately became part of the British Empire.

The liberal perception is intended to legitimise colonialism. When Lobengula understood what he had done, he dispatched a personal letter to Queen Victoria repudiating the concession, demanding it be brought back to him so that he could destroy it. 'I have since held a meeting with my indunas,' he wrote to the queen, 'and they will not recognise the paper as it contains neither my words nor the words of those who got it . . .'

Unfortunately for the Ndebele monarch, it was too late. Queen Victoria had already granted Cecil Rhodes a charter to occupy the country. Different historians give different interpretations of the circumstances surrounding the events of that time. Some say Lobengula's letter never reached the queen, as some bureaucrats working in cahoots with Rhodes intercepted it and destroyed it. Others claim the concession itself was a mere cover because, even without it, Rhodes would have occupied the country. The bottom line is that the country was occupied on a premise of deception and lies. Further, the concession covered territory that was outside the jurisdiction of Lobengula. The Ndebele kingdom did not include Mashonaland and Manicaland.

Between the Rudd Concession of 1888 and the Lancaster House Agreement of 1979 lay a plethora of legal and statutory instruments that had one overriding intention, to consolidate the white man's grip on the land. The black person was systematically marginalised, pushed further and further from the fertile lands in the centre of the country to the arid and barren soils along the borders. These acts included the Land Apportionment Act of 1931, the Native Land Husbandry Act of 1951 and the Land Tenure Act of 1969. They all helped to confirm the centrality of the land issue.

The Lancaster House Agreement had a provision regarding land that prevented the Zimbabwe government from acquiring land for the first ten years of Independence to resettle blacks, except on a 'willing-buyer, willing-seller' basis – for which the British government would pay. The provision had several inbuilt assumptions. One was that a time might come when the acquisition would be compulsory if people with the land were reluctant to part with it. That time came with the promulgation of the Compulsory Land Acquisition Act of 1991. Another assumption was that once the 'willing-seller, willing-buyer' provision fell away, the British government might decide to stop funding the programme. This is precisely what happened in 1997. The stage was set and another violent confrontation was inevitable. Just as the 1896 Ndebele and Shona risings and the 1966-79 war were fought over land, so the critical disagreement between Tony Blair and Robert Mugabe would lead to a violent row over the same issue. Mugabe accused Blair of dishonesty and Blair charged back that the land, paid for in the first ten years, had largely benefited Mugabe and his friends. Meanwhile, the people waited with increasing impatience. While Blair had a point, the truth was that insufficient land was bought and the communal areas were becoming more and more congested.

The news that some villagers from Svosve Communal Land near Marondera had invaded an adjacent white commercial farm in 1998 reached me while I was on a business trip to Bulawayo, and I was not surprised. I had expected it to happen earlier than that. I come from a shaky and polygamous background. My father leased 80 hectares of land in Mount Darwin in the late 1950s, courtesy of some white man for whom he worked as a farm guard. My father did not know how the arrangement annoyed me – a white man suddenly seeming to do a black man a favour by giving him a piece of land in region 4! As we were five boys in our family, there would not be sufficient land for each one of us, with our families and animals. But my sister's situation was even worse. She is married and lives in Hwedza, very close to Svosve, and she has six boys. Each year, I watched painfully as her husband struggled to share his 15 acres with one more grown-up son until the land became indivisible. For a season or two we took the eldest son onto our farm until eventually, in 1993, he settled in the Dande Valley along the Zambezi River on the border where Zambia and Mozambique meet.

Some people argue that the government masterminded the farm invasions of the Svosve villagers. But to me the invasions were spontaneous. Even the large-scale invasions by the war veterans some time later, after the 2000 Constitutional Referendum, were not organised by the government. If anything, the government was actually in a dilemma as to how to deal with that bold move. The farm invasions by the war veterans were a direct response to the glaring attempt to reduce the land question to a non-issue in the emerging matrix of Zimbabwean politics. Fervent attempts were being made to create a new political premise without the land as an issue. And yet the land had always been an issue! If those attempts had succeeded, it would have been the second largest deception after the Rudd Concession.

The intentions of the monumental land reallocation programme were noble, but the implementation was fraught with corruption and rampant abuse. As the Nigerian president, Olusegun Obasanjo, conceded, there was no way an exercise on such a massive scale could be carried out without hiccups. But some of the hiccups were inexcusable. People like myself believed the invasions were a statement to highlight the people's hunger for land and that government would follow with a planned resettlement programme. Unfortunately, it was not always the case. I spoke with a farmer who had many properties, but was denied the chance to choose the one farm he could remain with because a cabinet minister wanted that farm. That was not excusable. One day, a friend whispered in my ear that a war veteran talking on television had amassed three farms in three different provinces. That, also, was not excusable.

I waited for over a year for a reply from the Department of Lands for my application for a piece of land. But nothing came. The waiting became increasingly agonising as the rainy season approached. After the rains had started I came across more and more people talking excitedly about activities on the land they had been allocated. What had become of my application? I decided to visit the Ministry of Land's head office where I had submitted my application. I was referred to the provincial office in Bindura, where I had indicated I wanted to be resettled, and where I now found hundreds of angry land-hungry people thronging the governor's office. That painful scene of angry men, and women – some with crying babies on their backs – all jostling at the governor's office, would repeat itself over and over again as I returned countless times to Bindura to follow up my application. The message was always the same: the application, together with thousands of others, was being attended to.

One day a junior officer advised me to go down to the district level and ask the land allocation people there whether there were any untaken plots and then return to Bindura with that information. That was how I finally ended up in the district administrator's office at Centenary, fidgeting uneasily in the chair, waiting for her to finish a conversation on the phone. She was a charming lady, who laughed more than she talked – something she must have developed walking the minefield of land allocation. She looked at me. Indeed, there was an untaken plot at Nyamanetsa Farm that I could consider taking up if I wished. She phoned the other members of her committee and that was how I got the land – as easily as that. I could not believe it. It was the biggest anticlimax of all time, as if all that blood, all those tears, all that pain, and distance covered were completely unnecessary.

An hour or so after the committee had left, I stood on top of the small hill overlooking the hundred hectares of land that I could now call my own. I burst into tears exactly the way I did on the day, 30 years before, when I started the journey at the railway station in Salisbury to go to the war. As the train pulled out of the station and sped away, my sister stood on the platform and her husband looked away to hide the tears in his eyes. And I knew long before the train disappeared from her sight she would break down, crying hysterically.

And now, standing alone on top of the small hill, I was crying for David, my best friend during the war, remembering his painful death in that horrible Rhodesian ambush somewhere near Bikita Mine at the height of the war. I was crying for Chipo, the disillusioned student teacher from Old Umtali and those torrid nights as we gasped and groped for each other before her death in a Rhodesian air raid at Chimoio. Not only did she give the war a human face, I staggered through it clinging to her painful memory. I was crying for my son, doing economics at the university, for coming home one day with a swollen and heavily bandaged head because of what I write in the papers. 'I told them my father is right about Mugabe and the land issue,' he declared proudly. How could a person have such total faith in another? I was crying for my late father and the few moments we transcended speech and talked without words. He saw the anguish in my eyes about a journey that looked destined to end in disaster. There was a reassurance in his old eyes that I could always come home to share the little that was there. I cried like a small child.

And then for the first time, I felt the weight of the AK rifle slung over my shoulder. Wasn't its purpose now over? Once again, I looked down at my piece of land. Yes, the war was over. Therefore, all arms must go to the armoury because the war was over. The journey too.

Zimbabwe: The Past is the Future

6

Environmental impacts of the fast-track land reform programme: a livelihoods perspective

Emmanuel Manzungu

Introduction

Since independence in 1980, land has dominated agrarian and political debate in Zimbabwe. There is not, however, and has never been, one single debate on the issue, though all have been heavily influenced by the moral question: whether a white minority should own the largest proportion of the most fertile land to the disadvantage of the black majority. The considerable international support for land reform in Zimbabwe has been based on the assumption that such disparities will be properly addressed. Ironically, the morality of the current reform process, defined along narrow racial lines, has provided the Achilles heel of the programme. The race card has been exploited to the detriment of the development of a holistic society-based political economy. The emphasis on 'race' has led to the neglect of other important issues. For example, the resettled black population has no more security today, in terms of land rights, than they had before independence. Indeed, some independent commentators argue that land reform is now being implemented within the context of a serious democracy deficit. It is said that the ruling class today holds all the cards, just as was the case during the colonial era, and the Fast-Track Land Reform Programme (FTLRP) was a political project to consolidate the power-base of the ruling class. We do not intend to pursue this debate here. Instead, this chapter will focus on environmental issues following the post-fast-track phase and consider the relationship between the environment and the livelihoods of the people who live off the land.

The Government of Zimbabwe embarked on the FTLRP in July 2000, after it had lost a referendum on the constitution in February of that year. Soon afterwards, some war veterans and landless people invaded some farms, beginning in Masvingo province.[1] This provided an opportunity for the government to recover from its defeat, and capitalising on the situation, they quickly devised what they called 'The Fast-Track Land Reform Programme'. This gave rise to much local and international publicity, but there has still been no cogent account of how or why the programme took place when it did. There is, however, no disputing the fact that the FTLRP has had a severe impact on the environment.

In this chapter we hope to illustrate that the environmental impact of the fast-track programme should be given the same critical emphasis as the quest for social justice – the latter being its ostensible basis, at least in state pronouncements. Concern for the environment, however, should not be considered a footnote to the so-called 'real issues' of allocating land to A1 or A2 farmers,[2] distributing crop inputs, determining crop prices or supporting the rehabilitation of irrigation schemes. Indeed, environmental issues entered the discussion as an afterthought. The government did not conduct environmental impact assessments as demanded by its own policy. It only belatedly produced environmental guidelines, which were not widely circulated, and were not followed because of the programme's chaotic nature.

Our general argument is that the human dimension of the FTLRP is critical and must be examined if we are to measure its success. It follows that an assessment of the environmental impact of the programme should focus on the livelihoods of ordinary people, and not just on economic indicators,[3] political pronouncements,[4] and statements about racial

---

[1] The government sponsored draft constitution contained clauses relating to land distribution. Rejection of the referendum caused consternation in government circles. The land invasions, which began soon afterwards, may have been voluntary expressions of frustration, or may have been prompted by the government itself. According to the ruling party, ZANU PF, the whites had urged voters to reject the constitution in order to hold onto their farms, hence the land invasions.

[2] The A1 model is meant to decongest communal areas while A2 beneficiaries are allocated a self-contained farm where they are expected to engage in commercial farming.

[3] Parameters such as number of households settled or increase in GDP or in export earnings do not mean much to ordinary people. Bond and Manyanya, (*Zimbabwe's Plunge* (2002). Durban: University of Natal Press, 41-2) report for example that increase in export earnings have not resulted in Zimbabwe attaining food sufficiency.

[4] The programme has been characterised by political demagogy with incessant propaganda campaigns, which have ignored the reality on the ground. It is frequently referred to as a resounding success with 330,000 households resettled under the A1 model and 54,000 under the A2 model. However, one equally frequently hears of plot uptake in the A2 as 30 per cent at best. The *Zimbabwe Independent* of 25 April 2003 reported that the Minister of Lands, Agriculture and Rural Resettlement, had issued a circular claiming that 11 million hectares of land had been acquired and that 210,000 and 14,800 settlers had been allocated A1 and A2 farms respectively. At the same time Zimbabwe's ambassador to South Africa repeated the 330,000 and 54,000 figures. The same paper reported that the government-controlled Early Warning System Network estimated that the 2002/3 season would see 1.3 million tonnes of maize being harvested while a more believable estimate by the Commercial Farmers Union put it at 600,000 to 700,000 tonnes. Given the state's extravagant claims in the past, it would be wise to choose the lower figures in both cases.

demographics, which are not, in themselves, criteria of success. People should not be marginalised or seen as tools in the development process. They should be able to participate fully in community decisions as well as enjoy their human rights and basic freedoms. In other words, development must entail the conferment on people of the capacity to access income, employment opportunities, educational and health facilities, and enjoy a clean, safe physical environment. These aspects will guarantee sustainable human development, that is, development which meets the needs of today's society without compromising the ability of future generations to meet their own needs.

Good governance is a precondition for human development. It ensures that political, social and economic priorities are based on a broad consensus and that the voices of the poorest and the most vulnerable are heard in the allocation of development resources. In Zimbabwe, good governance is the missing link in the country's socio-economic development. The United Nations Development Programme's (UNDP) Zimbabwe Human Development Report for 2000 focused on this theme. The country was seen as facing the twin challenges of building foundations for stronger democratic governance, as well as achieving sustainable human development – tasks that were considered more daunting than at any time since 1980. The FTLRP can be said to have broken environmental, political, social, economic, legal, and constitutional taboos. The common images associated with it relate to the absence of the rule of law, manifested in the lack of adequate compensation to those whose land was expropriated, violence (*jambanja*),[5] corruption,[6] unclaimed plots,[7] and barren croplands.[8] This is unfortunate, since environmental mismanagement, leading to environmental degradation, threatens the basis of human existence not only in Zimbabwe, but beyond its borders. Yet the environmental aspects have been under-reported and under-analysed. (We are defining environment not just in its narrow physical sense but also in its economic, social, and cultural aspects.)

---

[5] The programme was characterised by widespread violence related to the campaigns for the 2000 parliamentary and 2002 presidential elections.

[6] The *Sunday Mirror* of 16 March 2003 carried three reports on corruption related to the programme. The main story, 'Leaked report details abuse of govt scheme', alleged that senior government officials abused the Z$450 million Livestock Development Trust Scheme, administered by the Ministry of Lands, Agriculture and Rural Resettlement, which was set up to help farmers source and distribute livestock to communal, old and newly resettled farmers under both the fast-track and commercial farming settlement models. In a second report, a cabinet minister and a leading businessman with close association with ZANU PF were reported to be fighting over farm equipment left behind by evicted white farmers. The third was a follow up to a government report where senior government officials were alleged to have grabbed more than one farm each.

[7] As mentioned above, the figures for people actually taking up plots are far lower than claimed.

[8] Generally, cropping has been very low because of shortages of draught power and crop inputs among other things.

Convolutions of the land programme

During the initial stages of the discussion about land reform, the plan was to acquire five million hectares of agricultural land to relieve the pressure on the communal areas and correct the racial imbalance in the commercial farming sector. Economic, social, and cultural reasons were considered alongside the more visible political agenda. For economic reasons the government was to acquire only under-utilised land or that of absentee owners. Social or equity considerations were expressed through the one-man, one-farm policy. No farmer, white or black, would be deprived of land. There was a legal spin to this. First, land would be acquired within the legal and constitutional framework of the country. Second, compensation would be paid for improvements on the farm but not for the soil. For cultural reasons, farms adjoining communal areas would be preferred for resettlement to maintain the communal community's cultural identity.

In the early stages of the fast-track programme, there was a pretence at maintaining the rule of law, with the invasions onto commercial farms being merely interpreted as 'demonstrations' to force government to act on the land issue. The state characterised the invaders as 'trespassers'. But this moderate rhetoric was soon replaced by extremist political language, which boldly declared that land was being returned to its rightful owners, implying that all the present white landholders were illegitimately occupying the land they were on. Yet some of the farmers bought the farms after independence, and in some cases from the government itself.

It became clear that government would not be constrained by constitutional and legal considerations in its quest for a Third Chimurenga (revolution). Most farmers who challenged their removal and won court cases did not benefit from legal judgements. Instead, government and ruling party officials frequently asked, 'Where was the rule of law when the land was taken away from black people?' With that assertion all pretence at following the law was cast aside. What remained was a faint attempt to present the programme in constitutional and lawful terms, largely for propaganda purposes.

The extreme rhetoric produced extreme results. The FTLRP became associated with violent and illegal evictions, extortion, lack of compensation to those whose land was expropriated, as well as massive corruption – as shown in multiple farm ownership[9] by the well-connected, among others. Formerly productive farms ceased to function, and disruption of farming activities on undesignated farms became the order of the day.

---

[9] The *Zimbabwe Independent* of 25 April 2003 carried a story of A2 farms being leased out by well-connected individuals.

As the programme dragged on into its third year in 2003, the rhetoric shifted. For a short time, it was conciliatory and there was some dialogue between the government and white commercial farmers. The government intimated to South Africa and Nigeria, whose support they enjoyed, that some mistakes had been made. Indeed, in 2002, there had been an attempt to set up land audits. One of these was undertaken by the Ministry of Lands, Agriculture and Rural Resettlement, another by the Parliament of Zimbabwe, and a third by the Minister of Lands in the President's Office, Florence Buka. None of them have yet been published. However, a leaked version of the latter provided a damning picture of corrupt practices in land allocation. In February 2003, President Robert Mugabe announced that yet another land audit would be done.

But the twists and turns of the programme continued. Equity considerations seemed to have been abandoned as the Minister of Agriculture announced, in the first week of March 2003, that people who had fully used their land were eligible for more, so as to ensure food security. A week later, the Minister of Information again revised the goals and modalities of the programme. *The Herald*[10] quoted him saying that it was not about changing the complexion of the commercial farming, but about empowering people. In responding to allegations that some top government officials had more than one farm each, the minister did not deny it. He simply said this criticism was irrelevant. What was important was that 'we, the blacks,' acquired the eleven million hectares. He added that the programme should be given constitutional, legal, political, institutional, and cultural expression, implying that to that date, this had not been the case. The following is the first of two examples that indicate how the FTLRP was conducted:

1. *Letter addressed to the editor of the* Financial Gazette:[11]

    Sir, The Matetsi area in Matebeleland North province is characterised by harsh terrain, unreliable rainfall and high temperatures, making it suitable for wildlife and humans who are prepared to meet its challenges.

    In October last year my employer, who spent 20-plus years developing a successful game ranch, was given seven hours to vacate his home and two ranches that he had bought after independence in 1980.

    Besides the obvious negative effects this had on the owners and their 35 workers and families, the animals, which were benefitting from a feeding scheme, suddenly found themselves with very little food and water.

---

[10] 13 March 2003.
[11] 13-19 March 2003.

To date, none of the new settlers, many of whom are gainfully employed and hail from as far as Bulawayo and Victoria Falls, have moved to live on the properties.

Soon after the eviction, and up until now, the following has happened:

Only three of the 35 workers were retained (apparently on reduced wages and conditions).

The animal population suffered severely before the rains came – very little water was being pumped. Poachers of up to 10 in a gang were seen on the property and countless animals were snared. A total of 23 wire snares were removed from around a single waterhole.

One of seven operational borehole engines left on the properties was stolen and another vandalised beyond repair

An electric game fence is no longer operational after solar panels were stolen. The same fence had wire stolen off it, causing some animals to escape.

The new settlers who have apparently not been able to work on the property are now attempting to sell the hunting quota, since they do not have the capacity to conduct the business themselves.

I am neither politically active nor too religious. I am also neither white nor black, and I struggle to make sense of or see justification for this kind of land reform.

2. *Extract from a newspaper story 'UNDP calls for Second Land Conference':*[12]

... the UNDP resident representative, Victor Angelo, and French ambassador to Zimbabwe, Didier Ferrand, got first-hand experience of environmental destruction wrought by random resettlement when they visited the south-eastern lowveld at the end of the year. Their report stated, 'A tour of the commercial farms under designation and different stages of acquisition was characterised by glaring scenes of the wanton destruction of commercial agriculture infrastructure, vegetation, pastures and the decimation of livestock through poaching, snaring and killing of game by the settlers.

'The stealing of fences and the movement of livestock across former veterinary control zones has seen a foot and mouth disease outbreak in Mwenezi farms, depriving Zimbabwe of a lucrative export market to the European Union and other external markets.'

---

[12] The *Zimbabwe Independent*, 14 March 2003.

A theoretical interlude: the environment-livelihood's seamless web

The obvious starting point in discussing the environmental impact of the FTLRP is to define the word environment. Koos Neefjes[13] cites a definition put forward by non-governmental organisations (NGOs) and representatives of grassroots people from Central America:

> *Environment is both nature and society, which relate to each other and which coexist. In the environment we find forests, human beings, land, mountains, water, air, animals, etc., which are mutually inter-relating. This relationship can be good or bad. It is good when human beings can make adequate use of other environmental components, like water, forests, and air. It is bad when humankind has destroyed them (for example with deforestation or when a few people appropriate resources and thus endanger our survival and reproduction). That is why we need conservation, equity between human beings, and harmony between human beings and nature.*

Neefjes[14] goes on to make these among other points about the meaning of environment:

- *People depend on environmental resources.*
- *There is a connection between social development and natural resource conservation.*
- *Humanity has responsibilities for the balanced relationship between society and nature as well as responsibilities for the future of the natural resource environment and for future generations.*
- *Livelihood opportunities of poor, excluded, or deprived people are closely linked to questions of environmental sustainability.*

The above exemplifies the link between the environment and livelihoods; and the material relationship between environments, people, and their social institutions. The aim of any agricultural or development programme should be sustainable livelihoods that

> *... depend on the capabilities, assets (including both material and social resources) and activities which are all required for a means of living. A person or family's livelihood is sustainable*

---

[13] Neefjes, Koos (2000) *Environment and livelihoods: strategies for sustainability.* London: Oxfam Publications, 1.
[14] Ibid. 2-3.

> *when they can cope with and recover from stresses and shocks and maintain or enhance their capabilities and assets both now and in the future without undermining environmental resources.*[15]

As this chapter attempts to show, the environmental degradation, which is being caused by the FTLRP, will continue to impact on the livelihoods of people, directly and indirectly, and represents a threat to sustainability in the short and long term. Environmental degradation refers to the processes by which the life-sustaining functions of the biosphere are disturbed. It covers the totality of a wide range of interdependent processes occurring at a range of scales and in different places, which may include biodiversity loss; soil loss; depletion of wildlife, forests, and timber; contamination of plants and animals by synthetic chemicals; fisheries depletion; as well as salinisation and acidification of soils.[16] In sum, it can be said that environmental degradation results in environmental insecurity, which is best defined in terms of human insecurity. The points below present some characteristics of a people-centred definition of environmental insecurity.

- It is much more than the physical processes of environmental degradation; it includes the way the degradation impacts upon human welfare.
- It should be understood as a social problem because it impacts upon human welfare and is a product of human behaviour.
- It is about the risk to human health of infectious and traditional diseases such as malaria and tuberculosis; and waterborne diseases such as diarrhoea. Disease is related to population density, poverty and malnutrition, as well as environmental degradation.
- Water scarcity and poor water quality are two major causes of environmental insecurity.
- Poverty is an integral cause of vulnerability, and it is prevalent among women and children.[17]

In conclusion, this section shows that there are direct links between environment and livelihoods. Environmental issues, therefore, cannot be pushed into the background in favour of livelihood issues; neither should the former be seen as taking precedence over the latter. Yet it is important to stress that livelihood represents the sum total of economic, social and cultural issues as they relate to human welfare.

---

[15] Ibid. 82.
[16] Barnett, Jon (2001) *The meaning of environmental security: ecological politics and policy in the new security era*. London and New York: Zed Books, 14.
[17] Ibid. 17-18.

What is the environmental impact of the FTLRP? The following discussion is based on the broad definition of environment already given and appears under different, but complementary, sub-headings. The effects tend to be more pervasive than are discussed here for, as environmental problems impact on society, they have a domino effect. When discussing environmental damage, it is said that 'you can run but you cannot hide'.

Impacts of the Fast-Track Land Reform Programme

Physical impacts

The physical impacts of the FTLRP have to do with the allocation of fragile land for agricultural production and the general mismanagement of land and land-based resources. Fragile land is easily degradable due, for example, to the poor physical structure of the soil. Light sandy soils, land on steep slopes, and soils with a high water table tend to be fragile. Such land may, however, be used in a sustained way provided a high management regime is applied. Wetlands, which usually are ecologically fragile, can be cultivated in this way.[18]

The *jambanja* character of the allocation process adopted under the FTLRP has resulted in fragile land being brought under cultivation without the necessary conservation measures being put in place, a situation worsened by poor land husbandry practices, and the breakdown of environment protection enforcement structures. For example, in Mutoko district, some old resettlement areas established in the early to mid-1980s were converted to A2 models at the insistence of local war veterans. This resulted in land, previously zoned as non-arable, being brought into cultivation, predisposing it to environmental degradation. A combination of cultivating such fragile lands and the indiscriminate and widespread cutting down of trees – a common characteristic of the FTLRP – results in environmental problems. Vegetation cover, be it in the form of trees or grass, protects the soil against erosion. Damage to it worsens the well-documented environmental degradation story. While the following figures can be questioned, they remain a guide to illustrate the seriousness of environmental degradation:

- General soil loss was estimated to be 50–100 t/ha/yr while soil loss in cropped lands in average rainfall season was estimated to be 6–8 t/ha/yr.

---

[18] Owen, R. and K. Verbeek., J. Jackson and T. Steenhuis (eds) (1995) *Dambo farming in Zimbabwe: water management, cropping and soil potentials for smallholder farming in the wetlands*. Harare: University of Zimbabwe Publications.

- In bare uncropped lands and in pasturelands it is estimated to be 30–90 and 50 t/ha/yr respectively. This is against a background where sustainable soil loss was cited as 5 t/ha/yr.
- Deforestation was also severe.
- Each year land clearing for agriculture took out 60,000 – 70,000 ha.
- Fuel wood and construction account for 5 and 1 million tonnes of timber loss per year respectively.
- With the advent of Fast-Track Programme these figures can be expected to have grown exponentially since 11 million hectares was acquired.
- The effect of land degradation also extends to agricultural productivity directly. Loss of top soil leads to depressed crop yields, particularly in the smallholder sector.[19]

Campbell, Du Toit and Attwell[20] have underlined the importance of the relationship between land degradation and livelihoods in the Save catchment area in eastern Zimbabwe. Manzungu, Bolding and Senzanje[21] have made the same point. They argued that land degradation studies should be linked to water availability, with reference to siltation and sedimentation, which affect water resources upon which people depend both for domestic and agricultural purposes. Loss of soil cover increases run-off, thereby raising the possibility of flooding; this is becoming common in Zimbabwe and in other southern African countries. Cyclones Eline and Japhet, which hit the southern African region in 2000 and 2003 respectively, exacted a significant direct and indirect toll on human welfare. While the immediate cause was heavy rainfall, the lack of vegetation cover exacerbated the problem. The fact that Zimbabwe shares a number of river systems – the Zambezi, Limpopo, and Save – with neighbouring countries makes this an international problem. Shoko[22]

---

[19] Mudimu, G.D. (1996) 'Increasing Zimbabwe's smallholder agricultural output and food security: environmental and sustainability issues', in: G. D. Mudimu and R. Mabeza-Chimedza (eds) *Agricultural competitiveness, market forces, and policy choice: eastern and southern Africa perspectives and case studies*. Studen zur landlichen Entwicklug, 52, Munster-Hamburg:Lit Verlag, 336.

[20] Campbell, B.M., R.F. Du Toit and C. Attwell (2000) *The Save study: relationships between the environment and basic needs satisfaction in the Save catchment, Zimbabwe*. Harare: University of Zimbabwe Publications.

[21] Manzungu, E., A. Bolding and A. Senzanje (1999) 'Rethinking integrated water resource management in E. Manzungu, A. Senzanje and P. van der Zaag (eds) *Water for agriculture in Zimbabwe: policy and management options for the smallholder sector*. Harare: University of Zimbabwe Publications.

[22] Shoko, D. (2002) 'Small-scale mining and alluvial gold panning within the Zambezi basin: an ecological time-bomb and tinderbox for future conflicts among riparian states', in G. Chikowore, E. Manzungu, D. Mushayavanhu and D. Shoko (eds) *Managing Common Property in Age of Globalisation: Zimbabwean experiences*. Harare: Weaver Press. 67-85.

has hinted at the possibility of environmental problems emanating in Zimbabwe having wider implications as they can become ecological tinderboxes for future conflict among riparian states in the Zambezi basin.

Apart from quantitative reduction of water resources, water quality can also be affected by pollution arising from inappropriate use of chemicals. Many of the resettled farmers are poorly trained and have poor waste-disposal systems.[23] The latter is a real problem in newly resettled areas where there are no functional facilities for sanitation and drinking water. In such circumstances, bacterial contamination of water sources, which render the water unsafe to drink according to Zimbabwe and World Health Organisation standards, has been widely reported in Zimbabwe[24] and poses health risks through waterborne and water-related diseases such as diarrhoea, cholera and dysentery. This must be understood within a context in which the primary causes of disease and poor health in the region are mainly water related. Moreover, the diarrhoea death rate in Africa is the highest in the world at 17 per 1,000, schistosomiasis affects 28 per cent of the population, and malaria causes 800,000 deaths each year.[25] The FTLRP can be seen as exacerbating this situation.

In 1996, it was estimated that 2,5 million Zimbabweans had no access to safe water:[26] with only 64 per cent of the rural population having access to safe water compared to 99 per cent in the urban areas. A recent survey confirmed that water in the rural areas was largely unsuitable for human consumption due to bacterial contamination.[27] The overall situation has deteriorated in the last five years due to the country's severe economic problems, not improved by the withdrawal of donor assistance, and its change in emphasis from developmental to humanitarian aid (a far cry from the situation before FTLRP). Even this assistance is limited, with donors such as DANIDA, DFID and SIDA[28] who used to support poor people having ceased to do so. In

---

[23] Mukwashi, M.(2002) 'An overview of water quality problems in the Odzi sub-catchment' in E. Manzungu (ed) *The processes and dynamics of catchment management in Zimbabwe*. Harare: Save Africa Trust Publications.

[24] Moyo, N.A.G. and S. Mtetwa (2000) *Water quality management strategy for Zimbabwe*. Harare: Ministry of Rural Resources and Water Development.

[25] SADC Water Sector Coordination Unit (1998) *Regional Strategic Action Plan for Integrated Water Resources Development and Management in the SADC Countries, 1999-2004*. Maseru: SADC Coordination Unit. 46.

[26] Machingambi, M. and E. Manzungu (2003) 'An evaluation of rural communities' water-use patterns and preparedness to manage domestic water sources in Zimbabwe' *Physics and Chemistry of the Earth*. 28. ns. 20-27.1039-1046.

[27] Op.cit. ft. 22.

[28] Danish International Development Agency, Department for International Development (UK), Swedish International Development Agency.

addition, since 1980, the donor community financed the Rural Water and Sanitation Programme, the current reduction in funding, however, has resulted in poor maintenance of water supply facilities, forcing rural communities to revert to unsafe water sources. In urban areas such as Harare, increased squatting due to the FTLRP, seemingly with official sanction, will give rise to health problems. In addition, the Harare municipality is running out of foreign currency to purchase water-treatment chemicals; Bulawayo, the country's second city, is said to be facing the same problem.

Some environmental impacts are long-term: for example, climate changes resulting from the link between man's socio-economic activities and rainfall,[29] and between land-cover changes and rainfall.[30] Throughout the world there is an increasing awareness of the impacts of mismanaging the environment. Global warming is one frequently discussed issue. While it is far-fetched to imply the FTLRP will contribute to global warming, there is no doubt that poor land husbandry does contribute to climatic changes. De Groen and Saveninje have proposed that rainfall regimes in southern Africa are more affected by regional factors, including land management, than the faraway systems such as El Nino.[31] One can envisage a small but unwelcome contribution from Fast-Track Programme.

Socio-economic impacts

One of the rallying cries of the FTLRP was that since Zimbabwe's economy was agriculturally based, it was necessary that land be made available to the majority as a spur to economic growth, and that, in turn, this would improve the living conditions of most people. So far, this does not seem to have been achieved. The following points show some impacts of the FTLRP on agricultural production:

- Maize production plunged from 800,000 tonnes in 2000 and was expected to fall to 100,000 tonnes in the 2002/03 season
- Soya bean production plummeted by 100,000 tonnes in the last two years.
- Tobacco production was 236 million kg in 2000, 201 million in 2001, 165 million in 2002, and is expected to fall to 75 million in 2003, a development which has seen tobacco manufacturers turning to Brazil to replace Zimbabwe's quality tobacco.

---

[29] Makarau, A. (1999) 'Zimbabwe's climate: past, present and future' in E. Manzungu, A. Senzanje and P. van der Zaag (eds) *Water for agriculture in Zimbabwe: policy and management options for the smallholder sector.* Harare: University of Zimbabwe Publications.

[30] De Groen, M. and H. Savenije (1999) 'Do land use-induced changes of evaporation affect rainfall?' in E. Manzungu, A. Senzanje and P. van der Zaag (eds) op.cit. ft. 29.

- In 2002, wheat production fell to 150,000 tonnes from the normal deliveries of well over 300,000 tonnes in previous seasons, which represented a decrease of at least 50 per cent.
- The commercial beef herd shrunk by more than 600,000 head of cattle over the last two years, a significant part of which was breeding stock.[32]

There have been other repercussions. International animosity, not to land reform, but to the means by which it as been conducted has had negative consequences for the country. The programme has not received any international financial support. Travel and financial sanctions have been imposed on government ministers and certain senior officials by the USA and the European Union as an indication of their hostility to a system of governance in which law and human rights are ignored, as exemplified, in particular, in the FTLRP.

The economy has been negatively affected to the tune of 10 per cent, with inflation at 455 per cent in November 2003 and growing steadily. The political consequences of the FTLRP have also virtually forestalled any foreign investment in the economy. Shortages of practically all basic goods, motor fuels and certain manufactured goods are commonplace causing untold human suffering. It is estimated, for example, that some six million people were facing starvation in 2003. Allegations of politically motivated food distribution have not helped the situation,[33] nor has corruption, when maize intended for villagers has been sold. (It was, for example, alleged that the Deputy Minister of Youth, Gender and Employment Creation was implicated in selling Grain Marketing Board maize above the controlled price.[34])

The once promising tourism sector of the early 1990s recorded a significant decrease towards the end of the decade. This was poignantly illustrated by the fact that a few days after Zimbabwe, Mozambique, and South Africa had signed the Great Trans-frontier Park agreement, intended to create one huge sanctuary for wildlife between the three countries, and attract tourists, it was reported that financiers were withholding money for infrastructural investment on the Zimbabwe side. Worse still, the world-acclaimed Communal Areas Management Programme for Indigenous Resources (CAMPFIRE), which made local people custodians of wildlife, from which they would earn revenue from

---

[31] Op.cit. Makarau, ft. 29.
[32] Manzungu, E. (2003) 'Challenges of and opportunities for enhancing agricultural productivity through improved water utilisation in Zimbabwe's newly restructured agricultural sector'. Harare: African Institute for Agrarian Studies.
[33] For example, ZTV, 6 p.m. 7 March 2003.
[34] *The Daily News* 13 March 2003, 21 March 2003, 22 April 2003. *The Herald* 1 March 2004.

hunting concessions, was sabotaged by poaching.[35] This did not help to reduce the increasing poverty, which is in fact on the increase throughout the country.

No one can imagine the suffering of the 350,000 farm workers who lost their jobs as a result of the FTLRP. Mental anguish and sometimes the physical violence suffered by previous farm owners, workers and their families should be seen as devastating social impacts of the reform.

The same can be said for resettled families who were moved to make way for 'chefs', as reported in the leaked version of the land audit report written by Florence Buka. In Mutoko, irrigators in the Chiedza scheme who had been resettled in the 1980s were asked to relocate their homes to give way to yet newer settlers.

Cultural imperialism

The Fast-Track Programme has resulted in a marked cultural revivalism, with many actions being undertaken on the grounds of reclaiming the 'land of our ancestors'. This revivalism, however, has strong political undertones, is largely state-defined and enjoys generous publicity in the state-controlled electronic and print media. Justification for the FTLRP has tended to claim the endorsement of black ancestral spirits, with reference to the heroes and heroines of the First and Second Chimurengas. This explains why the programme was dubbed the Third Chimurenga which implicitly ties its exclusivity to the ruling party and their supporters.

There have been ironies, such as talk of repossessing the 'land of our forefathers'. Taken to its logical conclusion, this would mean that people would be resettled on their ancestral land. In reality, this has not happened. First, in Zimbabwe, unlike in South Africa, the concept of land restitution does not apply. As a result the state has claimed all the land in the name of the dispossessed and distributed it as it pleases. This explains why the FTLRP is pregnant with political patronage and party rhetoric, but short on families making spiritual reconnection with their ancestral land. In addition, the *jambanja* mode of operation has virtually precluded any such reunion.

There were other ways in which the FTLRP has reinforced cultural stereotypes, thereby contributing to a form of cultural imperialism. Chieftainships are being created, even in resettlement areas where there

---

[35] Poaching, particularly on the commercial farms, has been widespread particularly of small game. In itself this may not be a huge problem as stocks can be replaced with sound management. However, when rampant poaching is accompanied by the destruction of the indigenous miombo woodland, and the spread of foot and mouth disease, as well as uncontrolled fence-cutting, then the problem is likely to cause serious long-term damage to the environment.

were none.[36] Arguably, this is a return to the colonial era where there was an effort to create chiefs for every community. In addition, traditional leaders are now being entrusted with the management of commons, that is, natural resources which are commonly owned. Under the Traditional Leaders Act, for example, traditional leaders have now some power over land allocation. The Environment Management Act has empowered traditional leaders to declare certain areas suitable for environmental protection. Another example of traditional cultural revivalism is the concept of *zunde ramambo* (communal land administered by the chief). It is touted as an answer to drought, because local people, under a particular chief, till a common field, the proceeds of which will be distributed by the chief to the needy.[37] This romanticising of a glorious past is at odds with the reality on the ground. Communal land tenure, considered a bastion of traditional land tenure, is increasingly being privatised.[38] Despite the rhetoric, genuine traditional institutions are losing local legitimacy (although there are local variations) casting doubt on whether traditional institutions can be relied on as custodians of the commons, with people as obedient subjects of the chief.

Loss of biodiversity

Writers, Mudiwa[39] and Masiyiwa[40] among others, have argued passionately that developing countries are being undermined by developed countries under the current system of property rights through the direct exploitation of biological resources together with the trivialisation of local innovations and knowledge. Local communities suffer most in this regard, as they are directly affected by such exploitation or appropriation.[41] These authors note that the challenge facing developing countries is to draw up with an institutional framework that can ensure the following:

---

[36] Chikowore, G., E. Manzungu and F. Maphosa, 'Whither common property management in Zimbabwe?' in G. Chikowore, E. Manzungu, D. Mushayavanhu and D. Shoko (eds) op.cit. ft. 22, 193-201.

[37] Mararike, C. G. (2001) 'Revival of indigenous food security strategies at the village level: the human factor implications'. *Zambezia* 28:1.

[38] Mukamuri, B.B. (2000) 'Local institutions and management of indigenous woodland resources in Zimbabwe,' in P. Virtanen and M. Nummelin (eds): *Forests, chiefs and peasants in Africa: local management of natural resources in Tanzania, Zimbabwe and Mozambique. Silva Carelica*, 34.

[39] Mudiwa, M. 'Global or local commons? Biodiversity, indigenous knowledge and intellectual property rights. in G. Chikowore, E. Manzungu, D. Mushayavanhu and D. Shoko (eds) op.cit. ft.22, 173-191.

[40] M. Masiyiwa, 'Common property rights and the empowerment of communal farmers in Zimbabwe: institutional legal framework and policy changes under globilisation,' in G. Chikowore, E. Manzungu, D. Mushayavanhu and D. Shoko (eds) op.cit. ft.22, 15-30.

[41] Op.cit. ft. 20.

- Empowerment of rural communities to effectively manage their resources.
- Empowerment policies that do not contradict international rules.
- Ensure that rural communities of the country have a satisfactory share of benefits accrued from any genetically modified organisms (GMO) technology that uses resources from their country.

While these are noble ideas, the FTLRP has rendered such an initiative largely untenable due to uncontrolled environmental damage that has seen biodiversity (which existed in the former commercial areas and in other protected areas) being lost.

Conclusions

This chapter provides a brief summary of the environmental impacts of the Fast-Track Programme. We argue that environmental issues should be regarded in the same way as the quest for social justice, on which the FTLRP was predicated, and not seen merely as a footnote.

It was also argued that the human dimension of the FTLRP is a critical parameter that must be used to measure its success. To this end, assessing impacts on the livelihoods of ordinary people, who are vulnerable to life's shocks, is important. It is not enough to focus on the economic indicators, or to take political demagoguery at face value. It is suggested that the experiences of ordinary people, rather than those of government officials, should receive attention. In this endeavour, good governance should be regarded as part of the equation, since it is a precondition for human development. Its absence diminishes prospects for the country's socio-economic development.

Another point relates to the definition of environment as well as environmental degradation. For any headway to be made in understanding this subject, meanings must be taken beyond their narrow physical definition to include economic, social and cultural aspects. Even in the physical sphere, relational aspects should be emphasised. This has been the weakness of the few commentaries on environmental aspects of the Fast-Track Programme. There has been, for example, reference to felling trees, without linking that to such issues as soil degradation that threatens water resources (because of siltation and sedimentation), loss of soil fertility and loss of biodiversity.

There is a need for correct measures to be applied to reduce the environmental impacts of the Fast-Track Land Reform Programme. If left unchecked, environmental degradation threatens the livelihoods of all Zimbabweans, present and future, and has extra-territorial implications.

Land reform and farm workers

Lloyd M. Sachikonye

Land reform is normally undertaken for the purpose of equitable redistribution and poverty reduction. In Southern Africa, there is usually an emphasis on redressing the historical expropriation of the land of indigenous peoples. In Zimbabwe, land reform can be broadly divided into two phases. First, the slow but orderly phase between 1980 and 1997, when 3,6 million hectares was transferred from large-scale white farmers to 71,000 black small-farmer households. Second, the comprehensive but disorderly and controversial phase between 2000 and 2002 when 11 million hectares were confiscated from 4,000 white farmers and given to an estimated 127,000 small-farmer households and about 7,200 emergent black commercial farmers (according to revised figures that are much lower than exaggerated government figures of 300,000 and 54,000 respectively). This second phase marked the biggest property transfer in the history of Zimbabwe and the whole of Southern Africa to date. It is a phase that has led to chaotic land invasions, extensive food shortages, political power contests and diplomatic rifts. In combination, these represent a cocktail of factors which has made Zimbabwe's land reform complicated, controversial and exceptional. The consequences will be present and felt for years to come.

Employment insecurity and poverty

Prior to the land reform, there were about 320,000 farm workers on the commercial farms, supporting a population of about two million. They constituted about 25 per cent of the country's formal sector labour force. At the end of the reform period, between 180,000 and 200,000 farm workers had lost their jobs. The number of white commercial farmers shrivelled from 4,500 to about 600. Farm workers' incomes amounted to about Z$15 billion a year before reform, and it is estimated they have now declined to Z$2 billion a year. More than 75 per cent of those workers, who lost their jobs due to the eviction of white commercial farmers, have not received severance packages. Most farmers had difficulty in paying out the packages due to delay in being paid compensation for their land and property; even so, some were threatened by farm workers.

The impact of the loss of regular wage incomes has predictably been severe. Those farm workers who continue staying on farms have lost their permanent worker status and become seasonal or itinerant workers, who now survive on doing 'piece-jobs'. The new settlers have not provided employment opportunities on a significant scale. So it is clear that poverty amongst farm workers has been exacerbated, while destitution is on the increase. Land reform that does not incorporate the needs of farm workers and does not satisfy the criteria of equity and poverty reduction is, at least, questionable.

Tenure security and land access

Equitable land reform programmes should ensure that farm workers who are displaced find alternative employment opportunities, or at least have access to tenure security and land. Trade unions – and in Zimbabwe there is the General Agricultural and Plantation Workers' Union (GAPWUZ) – have insisted that displaced or retrenched workers should be provided with land to sustain their livelihoods. Yet, at the end of the reform period, less than five per cent of farm worker households had been granted land under the A1 model (which allows access to several hectares of land for subsistence and livestock production). Union demands for tenure security did not receive a positive response from commercial farmers before reform nor from government during reform. The denial of tenure security on farms or of access to land resettlement schemes elsewhere has been ultimately discriminatory against farm workers, making them more vulnerable than any other social group in the post-reform era. As already mentioned, some farm workers have stayed on farms as piece-workers, while others have drifted into squatter settlements or, more delicately, 'informal settlements' where access to land is limited or non-existent. Others may have drifted back to communal areas, from which they would have originally come. But the congested conditions in those communal areas make it difficult for them to eke out sustainable livelihoods there.

Land reform should address both tenure and welfare concerns of farm workers. It should not disclaim responsibility for consequences of displacement. Zimbabwe's land reform has made the vulnerability of farm workers more acute. Informal settlements have mushroomed near farming towns in, for example, Concession in Mashonaland Central, Macheke in Mashonaland East and Nyamandlovu in Matabeleland North.

Food security and farm workers

One of the assumptions behind land reform was that it would lead to enhanced productive capacity and increased food production. The first phase of Zimbabwe's land reform was orderly and took care not to undermine food security in the country at large or among the newly settled small farmers. Even before the second phase or 'fast track' reform programme ended in 2002, food shortages had become endemic – even within farming communities themselves.

Zimbabwe's land reform undermined arrangements that enabled farm workers to obtain cheap subsidised food through their employers. Compulsory acquisition of grain by the Grain Marketing Board worked against retention of stocks on farms for farm workers.[1] Their vulnerability has been partly mitigated by their growing dependence on food relief; organisations such as the Farm Community Trust of Zimbabwe (FCTZ) and Save the Children (UK) have provided such relief. Children have been particularly vulnerable, and supplementary feeding schemes have acted as the sole life-line for many. To complicate the situation further, the newly settled small farmers are themselves desperately short of food.

The attainment of food security is intimately tied up with the state of the economy. In situations of economic growth there are often sufficient foreign exchange reserves for adequate food imports. This was the case in Zimbabwe in the 1980s and 1990s, but it is no longer the case during the current deep economic crisis. Drought may have been a contingent factor in the 2001-2 and 2002-3 seasons, but it is not the sole factor in explaining food insecurity in what was once a 'breadbasket' in the region. Land reform should not unnecessarily undermine food security.

Farm workers, HIV-AIDS, health conditions and family structure

The relationship between land reform and HIV/AIDS may not be obvious at first sight. But, in a region that is an epicentre of the epidemic, its potential impact on land reform should be considered in any reform plan. Although the prevalence rate amongst the population in the 20 to 50 year age group is between 20 and 25 per cent, no consideration has been taken of this.[2] If about 25 per cent of the 200,000 new settlers are likely to have HIV/AIDS at present, or within the next five to ten years, then their land will be under-utilised, lie fallow or have new claimants to it. In general, there would not be maximum utilisation of the acquired land.

Amongst farm workers themselves, prevalence rates range between 25 and 27 per cent. These rates on farms and plantations appear higher

---

[1] A new piece of legislation in 2002 provided the GMB with authority to acquire maize on farms, and to prohibit private sales and retention of stocks. In commercial maize-growing provinces such as Mashonaland West, there were reported seizures of grain by the GMB on some farms.

[2] See the United Nations Development Programme (2002), *Zimbabwe Land Reform and Resettlement: Assessment and Suggested Framework*. Harare: UNDP.

than in surrounding rural areas and small towns. As parents die, the number of AIDS orphans on farms increases. It is estimated that in Mashonaland East province 16 per cent of children at farm primary schools in 1999 had lost one or both parents as a result of AIDS. These AIDS orphans are particularly vulnerable because the extended family system has come under severe stress due to the epidemic. They are often the last in the 'food queue'. Farm worker communities are increasingly less able to care for orphans as their own incomes dwindle or disappear, and as their future on farms becomes less and less secure. A survey of nearly 1,000 farm worker households in 2002 pointed to the phenomenon of 'child-headed households', and these constituted about 1.5 per cent of the sample.[3]

The wider impact of land reform in Zimbabwe has been the closure of most farm schools and clinics following the eviction of the white farmers. Very few of these basic social services are now available to farm worker households. The few that still exist are too far for impoverished and undernourished families to travel, as distances can range from five to 40 kilometres.

The family structure itself in farm worker communities is under great stress from the epidemic, evictions, and employment losses. There appears to be a large increase in instances of divorce and separation, and a growth in the number of female-headed households. Land reform should address, or at least plan for, the impact of HIV/AIDS and for changes in family structure and for the specific needs of women.

Participation, citizenship and migration

It is almost banal to observe that there are powerful social interests involved in the land reform process. There are those, like the landowners, who often resist it, and there are those, like politicians and potential beneficiaries, who press for it. In most instances, farm workers have not been a major force in land reform, nor have they been beneficiaries. In the Zimbabwean case they have been marginalised throughout the reform process.

The question of participation is nevertheless pivotal in land reform. It has a political dimension. Do farm workers actively participate in movements for land reform or are they passive actors? Are they identified

---

[3] Farm Community Trust of Zimbabwe (2003) *The Situation of Commercial Farm Workers after Land Reform in Zimbabwe.* Harare: FCTZ. also see Sachikonye, L. M. and O. Zishiri, (1999) 'Tenure Security of Farm Workers in Zimbabwe: A Research Report'. Harare: Friedrich Ebert Stiftung. Sachikonye, L.M. (2003) 'From Growth with Equity to Fast Track Reform: Zimbabwe's Land Question'. *Review of African Political Economy*, 96.

more with their land-owning employers than with those forces seeking change in land ownership? Under what specific constraints do farm workers operate? In an authoritarian setting such as that in Zimbabwe, where basic democratic rights are under threat, farm workers experienced intimidation and violence for associating with the opposition Movement for Democratic Change (MDC). Historically, they had few political rights and it was not until 1998 that they won the right to vote in local council elections. The Zimbabwean experience shows that there can be land reform in politically repressive conditions, suggesting that there is no necessary connection between reform and democratisation. But this raises the question of the sustainability of such reform.

Another major issue that land reform raises relates to migration and citizenship. Zimbabwe and South Africa have a significant proportion of migrant farm workers. In the case of Zimbabwe, about 26 per cent of farm workers trace their descent to migrant workers who originally came from Malawi, Mozambique or Zambia. They do not have land rights, and in the event of job losses they lead a precarious existence. It is unclear how the citizenship law that Zimbabwe introduced in early 2003, for workers from Southern African Development Community (SADC) countries, will benefit these landless migrant workers. It would have been more meaningful and sincere to introduce it before the reform, so that they could have had access to land rights. More generally, the way in which migrant workers could be integrated into land reform programmes is often ignored in planning.

The citizenship rights of white commercial farmers themselves were infringed by long delays in payment of compensation in a context of hyperinflation that eroded the amounts to be paid. Instructively, the government made an exception of farmers of European origin, for instance, French, German and Italian farmers who were, in theory at least, allowed to keep their farms. This suggested a strong punitive element in the land reform process as far as local white farmers were concerned.

New social relations: farm workers, new settlers and new farmers

Where land reform involves the resettlement of small farmers on former large-scale farms, they come into contact with farm workers 'with nowhere to go' or those in search of piece-jobs for survival. The small farmers or new settlers are now more powerful than the landless farm workers. Relations between the two tend to be infused with mistrust, jealousy, insecurity and apprehension. There is often an uneasy coexistence between them. The new settlers would like farm workers to 'clear off', vacate the housing on the farm and the small pieces of land that they previously utilised. The new settlers suspect, or allege, that the farm workers had once 'colluded' with white landowners to resist land reform. Sometimes there are clashes between the two sides. An additional source of tension between the two sides was the experience and memory of settlers' or initial squatters' looting of farm buildings and equipment, and farm houses, including those that belonged to farm workers.

Land reform that lacks strategic planning can lead to such conflicts on the newly acquired lands. In the Zimbabwean case, food shortages have flared into conflicts in some provinces due to an intense competition for access to food aid by the two social groups: the settlers and farm workers. In several provinces, non-governmental organisations (NGOs) have been challenged for giving preferential treatment to farm worker households rather than providing food aid also to the settlers on a non-selective basis. These conflicts over resources – land, housing, food, and so forth – are bound to persist. Rather than resolving land conflicts, the Zimbabwean reform seems set to generate a variety of land-based social conflicts.

It is not clear whether land reform was intended to encourage farm workers to seek employment opportunities on the new small farms and, if so, how conditions would be made attractive for them. It is also still unclear whether share-cropping and labour tenancy are new arrangements being encouraged on the acquired farms. Some, if not many, new settlers cannot fully utilise their new lands. A proper resettlement programme would take these features into consideration, providing negotiation and mediation services, as required.

Whither advocacy?

Prior to land reform, any advocacy to highlight the interests and problems of farm workers was a relatively straightforward matter. This was an historically marginalised, isolated and impoverished social group in need of visibility, assistance and solidarity. During the land reform process, it becomes much more complicated to put the interests of the farm workers at the centre of national, regional and global attention. The arguments for the interests and welfare of farm workers are also used by landowners against the concept of reform. Then there is the numbers game: are there more potential beneficiaries (the small farmers) than losers (the farm workers)? In the Zimbabwe instance, it was 127,000 settler households – and 7,200 black commercial farmers[4] – compared to 200,000 farm worker households![5]

---

[4] GOZ (2003) Presidential Land Review Committee (Utete Report). Harare.
[5] Commercial Farmers Union (2003) *The Current Status of Commercial Agriculture in Zimbabwe.* Harare.

Yet there is still an important role for advocacy to play. There is a continuing role for unions and NGOs. The plight of displaced farm workers needs to be expressed with a view towards generating a solution in the short and the long term. There is a humanitarian dimension here that cannot be ignored, even though the government may choose to look the other way for fear of embarrassment. There is also the rehabilitation aspect involving retraining farm workers, finding or creating new opportunities for them in, for instance, crop production, craft work, informal trades, and so forth. Finally, those few farm workers who remain on the farms and plantations continue to require attention and resources devoted to issues such as education and training, health care, and capacity-building at union level, in women's associations, youth groups, orphan-care, and HIV-AIDS awareness groups. For farm workers, 'the struggle continues', even after land reform and *jambanja* (violence).

Zimbabwe: The Past is the Future

The culture of party politics and the concept of the state

David Kaulemu

It is true of many things that the more they are needed the less readily are they available. Z. Bauman[1]

Introduction

Zimbabwe entered the new millennium under a national crisis. It is now a country deeply polarised and people feel they have to support either the Zimbabwe African National Union Patriotic Front (ZANU PF) or the Movement for Democratic Change (MDC). This polarisation threatens to exclude any sense of the common good, that is, the nation as a community of people mutually at the service of each other. National institutions and processes have been so politicised along party lines that their national character has been undermined.

Our crisis is due to the way leaders and ordinary people think and behave. There is a terrible poverty of imagination concerning the nature of the nation-state itself. Our enthusiasms, in the political parties that brought independence, blinded us to the need to establish national systems, institutions and cultural practices.

And so we suffer the effects of the disappearance of the state from our imagination and its replacement by party politics. Obfuscation of the distinction between the state and the party in the minds of leaders, professionals, and indeed of the people of Zimbabwe has placed us where we are today. Even opposition parties struggle to imagine truly national and inclusive systems and processes.

The limitations of impromptu seminars

Universities no longer have the monopoly of holding seminars on national issues. Weddings, funerals, family gatherings, church meetings, and other

---

[1] Bauman, Z. (1993) *Post-modern Ethics*. Blackwell: Oxford, 16.

social occasions have become opportunities for impromptu exchanges of views. Ordinary people discuss issues of governance, violence, intimidation, urban poverty, unemployment, scarcity of commodities and prices. Participants in these 'seminars' produce evidence to support their views and give vivid examples and analogies from the recent history of neighbouring countries. The participants know what they are talking about, and what they say makes a mockery of some of the seminars, workshops and public lectures I have attended at the University of Zimbabwe, which are often theoretical and removed from reality. Yet, some of the widely shared preconceptions used in these reflections have fundamental limitations and dangerous consequences.

Concepts are windows through which we view the world. As such they give a limited perspective. Many Zimbabweans worry about their society and the way it fails to provide basic social goods. Yet, their concept of the nation of Zimbabwe and their understanding of participation in politics is limited. They feel marginalised in one way or another. They want to contribute to the development of their nation and many of them – senior citizens – have contributed most of their lives to the national effort. Yet their dominant experience of politics is of being subjected to political harangues at rallies. Political affiliation has become more important than working for the health and the natural and peaceful growth of children and grandchildren.

The morality of social institutions and cultural practices can be judged by the way the weakest and most vulnerable members of society – such as young people and the elderly – are treated. The former are regularly hooked up into political divisions and fights and for the old there is no sense of retirement; no freedom from the political rallies and processes that are forced on them. By listening to these groups and observing how they live, I can only conclude that the country has failed them. Contemporary Zimbabwe demonstrates a severe degree of systemic and cultural cruelty and the source of this is our concept of society and the state.

Before independence, and the participation of blacks in local and national elections, people lived together as neighbours without problems. It is true the rivalries between nationalist parties in the 1960s generated hostility and violence. But they were but the seeds of what we have come to see since 1980. Elections have made neighbours into enemies open to harassment and violence. This 'discovery' needs explanation, for the Zimbabwe of today is a society of great human suffering. This is due to a concept of the state that undermines social solidarity and sympathy. If we conceptualise the nation state as favouring one section of the population and ignoring another, we will find that parents lose respect for the their children and children become cruel to their parents. Social solidarity and sympathy generally are undermined. The struggle for freedom becomes a nightmare.

The culture of party politics and the concept of the state

The nation-state is universal

Zimbabwe, as a nation, is a result of European imperialism, African tradition and nationalism, industrialisation and urbanisation. At the time of independence, in 1980, the people who had lived through the 'Rhodesian crisis' did not come from the same cultural or economic backgrounds. The ancestors of some had been part of the Munhumutapa kingdom, while others were offshoots of the *mfecane* movements from the south, the diaspora that followed the revolt against Chaka, or children of labour migrants during the Federation of Rhodesia and Nyasaland. Others came from Europe or Asia. The new nation had deeply divided interests, anxieties and aspirations. Rhodesia had built walls between whites, blacks and Coloureds. Blacks themselves were divided by tribe and economic standing. So the Zimbabwe of 1980 was not a closely knit community that shared the same historical experiences and values.

Yet, at the moment of independence, it was hoped that some stable and public system of rules, procedures and institutions would be established to meet the concerns and aspirations of all Zimbabweans. This system would be what we call 'the state'. The state would recognise and protect every individual as its citizen. It would distribute goods justly and without reference to tribe or race or gender. In return, all citizens would recognise and respect the state. Citizens would feel part of this larger political entity serving the common good. This entity would not belong to one section of society. It would not change when the government changed, but would continue to serve all citizens equitably. Procedures, for example, for acquiring a passport, birth certificate, citizenship, scholarship, or a job, would be the same for all. Basic human rights, such as freedom of expression or association, would not depend on membership of the ruling party.

The government is not the state, but is there to serve the state. It is made up of leaders elected for a limited time according to set procedures. When their time is over they go, but state structures remain. In a mature society, life goes on smoothly even if there is no government for a time. So there is a clear distinction between the state and the government, and the latter should not believe state structures are there to serve the narrow party interests of the government of the day. When leaders refuse to serve some citizens because they did not vote for them, they abdicate their responsibility. Citizens have a responsibility to respect established state structures, but they are also entitled to disagree with them.

The party is not the government

When a government, after elections, occupies state structures, it enters into a public arena. It takes on the job of dealing with national issues through publicly established procedures and processes. The political party that makes up the government does not occupy public space in this sense. Not all members of the ruling political party are members of government. Only those who are may make decisions about national issues. Confusion enters when some ruling-party members in Zimbabwe consider themselves to be part of the government and have used state structures for their own ends. National matters are taken to the ruling party's politburo or central committee for a decision when they should go to the elected government. Anarchy is the result. People who are not members of the government are making decisions through processes that are not accessible to public accountability. An example of this is the young man who recently went to visit his relatives in Gutu wearing an MDC T-shirt – a perfectly legal thing to do. Yet he, like so many, was forced to return to Harare in a hurry as the local ruling party had 'banned' the opposition party in this area. While the man escaped, his family went through a difficult time of questioning and harassment and had to pay a fine. Local party members confuse themselves with the government and ignore established state laws. It is only when state institutions are understood to be distinct from governments and parties that we can call ourselves a free society. Otherwise life becomes, in Hobbes's words, 'solitary, poor, nasty, brutish, and short'. We have seen this happening in our own country.

Privatisation of national state structures

National state structures are public and universal. When they are appropriated and monopolised by a private party or group of individuals, as with the man going to Gutu, the state is confused with the party or government. When private citizens use state structures to fulfil their private interests, the state becomes *privatised* or *particularised*. This is an illegitimate process. If a president or government uses the state as private property, then it abdicates from its public and moral responsibility of working for the common good. Some citizens then do not feel recognised and protected by the state. They feel alienated from their own state and this gives them reason to withdraw their allegiance.

Living a tragic paradox in present-day Zimbabwe

Recently, I addressed a meeting of religious leaders by default. Politicians from the two major parties had agreed to attend and debate national issues and particularly party political violence but they failed to come. This failure was symbolic of the disappearance of the sense of national common good whose main agent would be the state. ZANU PF considers it is the only legitimate ruling party in Zimbabwe and has systematically used state structures to reflect this. In the 1980s it appealed to Marxist-

The culture of party politics and the concept of the state

Leninist beliefs about the vanguard party and 'the dictatorship of the proletariat' to justify its position and it has also appealed to images of African traditional societies, which it sees as supportive of one-party rule. There are two consequences of this. By identifying itself with the state it makes any attempt at offering an alternative government to the electorate as tantamount to a criminal act. And also, opposition parties cease to trust state structures, which are no longer seen to operate for the benefit of all. The nation runs the risk of opposition parties appealing to forces and agents outside the legitimate constitutional parameters. The use of violence is often a result of such political closure and indeed it has become a national problem in Zimbabwe. It threatens to become part of our political culture and destroy the gains our independence brought. ZANU PF has included intimidation and violence as part of their political strategy and sometimes the MDC has responded with violence.

It is not difficult to see how violence became part of ZANU PF strategy. Ever since it engaged in the struggle for independence, ZANU PF has developed the structures, language, and agencies of politically inspired violence against its opponents. And, as Martin Luther King Junior has pointed out, violence has a logic; once it starts it is difficult to stop. Violence breeds violence and victims of violence become violent themselves. This is evident in individuals, families and communities. And it is Zimbabwe's experience too. The methods of violence developed during the War of Liberation have spread through our society. It has become part of our social and political language. Students, workers, ex-combatants, and even religious groups have used it. At independence, our society did little to rehabilitate itself from the habits of violence prevalent during the liberation war. We have assumed that violence is a tool that we can take up, use, and drop at any time. History has proved this is not so. It requires a sustained effort to relinquish it. We even celebrate political victory by beating up those we have defeated. ZANU PF has not been an exception, even though it once worked for a more democratic society.

When the MDC became a formidable political opponent, the ruling party felt threatened in its traditional strongholds, the towns and cities. ZANU PF lost the referendum on a new constitution in 2000 and met stiff competition in the parliamentary elections later the same year and also in the presidential elections of 2002. It was surprised and alarmed. It began to recruit people, especially unemployed young people, to enforce its rule. At the same time, in the mass media, the party systematically questioned – and continues to question – the legitimacy of the MDC, branding it a foreign-sponsored party, conveniently ignoring its origins in the ZCTU and the NCA. ZANU PF has consistently refused to acknowledge the MDC as a legitimate political entity whose task is to operate in Zimbabwe and aspire to rule.

The MDC, on the other hand, has declared ZANU PF illegitimate, claiming it 'stole' the elections and that it has the evidence to prove this. But the MDC uses the same confrontational language as its opponent. There is no evidence that it has developed a radically different political culture from ZANU PF. The MDC runs the danger of repeating the mistakes of ZANU PF – a party that feels strong when it uses the language of war. The MDC shows little sign as yet of shaping a different mould for the politics of Zimbabwe.

A nation state

Zimbabwe is referred to as a nation, a historical community. As such it may be understood to be a product of a shared life and a shared culture over a long period with its institutions the realisation of the ethical life of a nation. Yet, the development of Zimbabwe cannot be adequately explained in this way. Many Zimbabweans idealise the state as a closed community of people of the same origin, cultural values and historical experiences. Mudenge, for example, concludes his history of Zimbabwe in this way: 'Present Zimbabwe, therefore, is not merely a geographical expression created by imperialism during the nineteenth century. It is a reality that has existed for centuries, with a language, a culture and a "world view" of its own, representing the inner core of the Shona historical experience. Today's ... Zimbabweans have, both materially and culturally, much to build and not a little to build upon.'[2]

This way of understanding Zimbabwe excludes many people as not being part of the 'inner core' of the nation. Non-Shonas become secondary citizens who depend on their allegiance to the Shona historical experience for their membership of the nation. The legitimacy of the Zimbabwe nation is given by what Hegel would call the Shona 'ethical life'.[3] This downplays European imperialism and the political, economic and social contributions of non-Shonas in the creation of the nation. How can we talk about African nation-states without referring to the role of European imperialism? Mudenge tries, but he is not convincing. Yet, this narrow view of the nation-state is popular and influential. Its simplicity is attractive. Zimbabwe is taken to be a Shona nation state. It supports ZANU PF's claim that it is the only authentic voice of the Zimbabwe people.

---

[2] Mudenge, S.I.G. (1988) *A Political History of Munhumutapa c.1400 to 1902*. Harare: Zimbabwe Publishing House, 364.

[3] Taylor, C. (1979) *Hegel and Modern Society*. Cambridge: Cambridge University Press. Passim.

This view is clearly inimical to multi-party democracy. How can one national culture be concretely realised in two political parties? If one is authentic, the other is not. While ZANU PF seems to have used this view of the nation-state, the MDC appears to share it. It sees itself as replacing ZANU PF as the legitimate expression of the Zimbabwean ethical life. Each party has tried to convince people that the other party is not a legitimate part of the nation-state and people are morally required to reject the other party. We have not seen, in word or in deed, the acceptance by one party of the legitimacy of the other. Each defines the nation so narrowly that it excludes the other. And what is more depressing is the lack of any attempt to see the need for strong national structures that are party-politically neutral. It is difficult to imagine ZANU PF and the MDC collaborating in creating such structures even as they battle to occupy them. And yet this is what should happen.

Domination of the party-political realm

In our system, political leaders are very powerful and influential. The political realm dominates everything: economics, health, education, culture, and religion. Any advancement in one area is automatically interpreted in narrow party-political terms. So, a successful professional must declare his or her party-political allegiance in order to survive and make progress. Some businesses, academic enterprises, and other professional endeavours succeed or fail on this basis. The domination of the party-political realm has become so narrow that many professionals have to prostitute their abilities. Politics come into the allocation of housing, land, jobs, scholarships, food relief, security and dignity. Pressure has been put on universities, schools, newspapers, the Reserve Bank, and even private companies, to endorse specific party-political policies. Ministers and others who have tried to follow professional advice, as opposed to party policies, have lost their jobs.

The result is the systematic destruction of life outside politics and the undermining of the legitimacy and richness of life in other realms. It is not enough to be a peaceful citizen. The political realm is regarded as the only realm for real social existence. In Plato's language, business people, farmers, students, religious people, artists, sports persons, and many others are all *imitations* or *reflections* of politicians. Once these political leaders are in power, they try, as they are doing in Zimbabwe, to subsume all other realms under politics. The economic, social, academic, and cultural realms are systematically reduced to appendages of the political individuals, institutions, and practices. No one can survive without paying tribute to the dominant political forces. Even religious leaders, writers, artists and academics are forced to subsume their messages and vocations under some political goal in order to survive.

There is no life outside the political. Political leaders themselves feel this. Yet it is they who have killed it. No wonder they refuse to retire. What would they do? They have created a little hell on earth, where to quote Hobbes again, 'there is war of every man, against every man'.[4]

Political leaders and violence

Political leaders can easily cause political violence. They can also stop it. They are in a strategic position to influence the political atmosphere. So it is important for them to meet and discuss. Yet, because of the polarisation in party politics, many refuse to engage in dialogue with opposing parties. They invest more in their party than in their nation. This failure is a reflection of the tragic paradox we are witnessing in Zimbabwe.

The people who are the key to the resolution of major social, economic and political issues are not interested, have no time or are just cynical about the idea of genuine dialogue with others, especially those who oppose their views. Those who are interested in encouraging peaceful dialogue are without influence to do so. The churches and non-governmental organisations (NGOs) are being forced to take party-political positions instead of being peacemakers. National concerns have been abandoned in favour of party-political interests. This is tragic.

The sense of tragedy is deepened when we consider that those who could bring change have turned their refusal to take part in dialogue into a virtue. Political and religious leaders from outside Zimbabwe have tried to encourage dialogue between the two major political parties in Zimbabwe, without success.

Zimbabwe – a political tragedy

Looked at from a short-term perspective, Zimbabwe is a tragedy. Rhodesia was an apartheid state which formerly ended in 1980. It was ended amid high expectations of freedom for all, especially by the poor and marginalised. Zimbabwe became a legitimate nation with the potential to establish democracy as a system of governance and as a cultural practice. Prime Minister Mugabe's inaugural speech promised reconciliation between blacks and whites. It also captured the desire of all black communities to fully participate in the new dispensation. Independence would mark the end of all forms of discrimination: racial, tribal, gender, and religion. For the first time, we had a government that belonged to all. In many ways independence did bring the beginning of

---

[4] Hobbes T. (1968 edition) *Leviathan*, (ed.) C.B.Macpherrson. Harmondsworth: Penguin Books. Ch. 13.

democratic political structures and practices. The participation of blacks, women and youth in social, political and economic structures was evident. Schools, hospitals and clinics became open to all. Support for the liberation effort had come from many sides and people did not need party cards to prove this.

But the 'privatisation' of the national democratic process by the ruling party has led to the reversal of these gains. ZANU PF has failed to appreciate that its role in bringing liberation and democracy to Zimbabwe does not mean that it has a monopoly of what follows from this process. The ruling party wants to take all the credit for what has been done by many different people, organisations, and movements, some of which have no formal link with it. Many of these are ordinary Europeans, some of whom are now declared to be non-Zimbabwean citizens. Many do not belong to the Shona 'core'. The logical outcome of this attitude is to declare the party as more important than the government and state structures. The process can be seen, for example, in the criteria for choosing national heroes and the systematic elimination of government personnel who do not reflect the party position – judges, academics, teachers, and boards of directors of parastatals such as the Zimbabwe Broadcasting Corporation, the Grain Marketing Board, and Air Zimbabwe.

This process leads to intolerance not only of opposition parties, but of anyone who encourages pluralism. It even affects the party itself. Alternative voices within the party have been suppressed. This is the dire consequence of the Zimbabwean political situation: all social realms are reduced to the political, and that realm is constricted by violence and narrow party interests to the detriment of the development of a universal nation-state for the benefit of all. The major agent of liberation has turned itself into a tool for intolerance and oppression. This is the tragedy of Zimbabwe. It has been true also of other African countries. Liberation movements have not been the best agents for good governance.

We are coming to the end of one era and are on the threshold of another. The MDC represents the struggle with the era of ZANU PF. It represents a new sensibility, which has at least the virtue of refusing to privatise liberation and democracy. In this sense, it is open to pluralism. Many have identified the MDC with the youth, and ZANU PF with the older generation. But this is an oversimplification. It is an interpretation that says the youth do not care about history or about the land. Similarly, it says the old do not care about democracy. This is misleading. ZANU PF uses many youths in its campaigns. And again, many ZANU PF ex-combatants now belong to the MDC.

The real short-term tragedy of the MDC is that while it represents a new sensibility of democracy, it is itself deeply rooted in the cultural and political practices of the past. Some of the same youths and adults who used to be in ZANU PF and ZAPU (the Zimbabwe African People's Union) are now MDC. They are capable of challenging ZANU PF in elections, in the courts, and on the streets. But where is the evidence that they can challenge ZANU PF's political and cultural practices? Can the MDC move us into a true culture of democratic practice, which not only destroys old oppressive habits but positively builds a new thinking about the role of the state and its institutions? Can the MDC establish something more permanent than a successful political party? Does the present MDC have the vision, imagination, and will to do so? The tragedy of the MDC is that it has the right sensibility but the wrong political imagination and practice to draw from. On the question of party politics, the government, and the state, MDC members seem to make the same assumptions as ZANU PF. And this is why it has been difficult to banish violence from the Zimbabwe political scene.

Lessons for the future

In the long term, both ZANU PF and MDC represent two necessary sensibilities to the growth of Zimbabwe as a nation state. The injustices of the past must be dealt with. But they must be dealt with in the context of democracy and in the spirit of justice. The key to balancing these two essential sensibilities is the establishment of strong state structures, which are clearly distinct from – and provide guidelines and limits to – parties and governments. For this to happen, we must build truly national systems and procedures whose success does not depend on who is in charge and which party is in government.

Yet structures and systems alone are not adequate if people do not behave in ways that are appropriate to them. We must develop complementary national cultural practices that are compatible with our democratic structures. This will be achieved through allowing individual persons to cultivate specific democratic virtues and to discourage vices. We need a new concept of the state and its institutions. It is easy, in a politically polarised situation like the one in Zimbabwe, to blame all our economic, social and political woes on some evil, powerful people in our midst. But it is the responsibility of each citizen to build the culture of democracy. It is not so much our intentions as our imagination that has led us to where we are. We thought the arrival of Zimbabwe as a free nation would guarantee our freedom and growth. But we failed to recognise that the only guarantor of our freedom was a state that rises above the interests of individuals and groups to secure the common good.

Continuity and change in the Zimbabwean religio-cultural landscape in the era of HIV/AIDS

Paul H. Gundani

In the African world the religious is inextricably intertwined with the political, economic, ecological and other social forces. A people's world view constitutes the lens with which they interpret the world around them. In this paper, my contention is that the African worldview is religious at its core. The adoption of the term 'religio-cultural' in the title is a deliberate signpost about the religious core of our culture. We will examine the flux and shifts that are taking place within Zimbabwean culture in the age of HIV/AIDS. We interrogate the challenges and threats brought about by the new virus and target the changes that have occurred in peoples' attitudes regarding cultural institutions and practices of healing, inheritance and gender equity. We will find that some cultural practices have been radically altered, others have ceased to operate altogether, while still others have undergone a surprising revival. All of these responses show a vibrancy in culture when faced with the appalling challenge of the AIDS virus.

The irruption of HIV

Sometime in 1981, when Zimbabwe was barely two years old, medical scientists announced the discovery of a new human virus. They called it the Human Immunodeficiency Virus (HIV). As with any new virus, until its effects are visible, mention of it as a news item made little sense to people. It sounded like any other discovery associated with American sophistication. Rumours of the disease neither disturbed the regular revellers who patronised the trendy night clubs of Zimbabwe's towns, nor the popular beerhalls and shebeens that infest the 'locations' in the urban centres, and growth points in rural areas. The moral perversion associated with these places of entertainment was not affected by the trifling references to this new virus. The culture of promiscuity that had become entrenched, as a way of growing up, was not affected either. No urgency whatsoever was imposed by the consciousness of the new virus. This was partly because of its early manifestations in the USA, where it was associated more with drug peddlers and homosexuals than with heterosexuals. This made it easy for black people in Zimbabwe to dismiss AIDS as a white man's disease or a scourge amongst the few black men who, perhaps out of too much love for money, agree to be made 'wives' by white 'perverts'. Thus, the disease was added to the list of jokes that did the rounds in Zimbabwe. It became part of the new vocabulary for the urbanised ghetto people though it remained little known by the uneducated and conservative rural people. Little wonder then that a popular, but cynical, joke of the eighties portrayed a rural wife writing a letter to her husband working in town listing down EDZI (AIDS) as one of the commodities that she wanted her husband to buy for her. True to form, many a man, in their ignorance, continued to 'buy' the HIV from the sex market and took it to their wives as part of his marital obligations. Similarly, the younger generation of the eighties were cynical of HIV/AIDS and made a big joke of the acronym AIDS as something that referred to the 'American Idea to Discourage Sex'. And of course, in spite of the new virus, life went on.

As the nineties dawned, the government continued to behave as if nothing was amiss. One wonders whether the leadership was being given the right advice by the medical fraternity. It went on its daily business just as normal. The police continued to arrest women from the streets as soon as night fell, thereby insinuating that they were responsible for the spread of HIV/AIDS. Apart from violating women's freedom of movement and association, guaranteed in the constitution, such moves diverted the nation from making a moral decision that could have raised people's consciousness regarding the virus. The debates that gripped the nation tended to make HIV synonymous with *runyoka*, a sexually-transmitted infection that has traditionally been thought to be a punitive affliction affecting men who have sex with married women. The tendency of such vexatious debates was the reinforcement of the view that HIV/AIDS was not a disease that demanded a radical moral and behavioural change. One merely needed to know which women to avoid. Men could still continue in their promiscuous ways as long as they avoided married women. Looking back over the decades, one can surely say the people of Zimbabwe lost the opportunity for behavioural change, and continued the contagious moral laxity that was exacerbated by the migrant labour system and the concomitant economic differentials between male and female and between the rural and the urban. It was not just that personal freedom – and its responsibilities – were seldom discussed. But that matters of sexual morality were, and are, seldom aired outside the confines of the home. The axiom 'Chakafudza dzimba matenga' (what covers the house is the roof, that is, secrets are not discussed outside the family) applies to the sexual domain too. Sexual morality remains one of the exclusive matters that are only discussed by family members in private, and behind closed doors. There is an interesting dimension, however, to the liberation war. It brought about a revolution in terms of power relations and responsiblity. The 'freedom fighter' (*mukoma* – boy) had power over the parents (*vabereki*) even if he was a seventeen-year-old, and was talking to his elders. By virtue of wielding a gun, having the bravery to fight the white man, and the commitment to die for his country, 'mukoma' thrust upon himself the power to subvert social taboos, including matters pertaining to sexual morality. Culturally these were never matters for public consumption, but also in the new circumstances everyone feared to challenge the comrades (*vana mukoma*) over their sexual misdeeds. Hence, the liberation war introduced a new sexual permissiveness that was condoned but not officially sanctioned by the leadership or by the communities in which the 'freedom fighters' operated. The sexual licence that the 'comrade' allowed himself also applied, on a smaller scale, to the female freedom fighters, who generally operated in 'liberated zones'. In essence, Zimbabwe attained its political independence at a time when its values pertaining to sexual morality had been thoroughly shaken and were in need of healing. Unfortunately, the first years of independence afforded Zimbabwe little time to turn a corner before the irruption of HIV/AIDS.

The nation went to sleep as the virus quietly gnawed its way into its citizenry. The slumber affected not only civic society but also the nation's body politic. The shroud of mystery around HIV/AIDS was perpetuated by the government's desire to court investors during the nineties, the period of the Economic Structural Adjustment Programme (ESAP). Instead of coming out clean and appealing for outside help, the government of Zimbabwe concealed the growing HIV/AIDS statistics, fearing that investors would be driven away to safer havens. Our penchant to keep secrets about the ills in one's own home supported this attitude. Moreover, the medical fraternity was of little help in generating awareness about the virus, as it felt bound by the ethical and legal encumbrances of the confidentiality clause relating to a patient's medical condition. It tied their hands from divulging the condition of a patient even to a spouse or next of kin. The same is true for the cause of death.

Western scientific medicine has remained esoteric and confusing to ordinary citizens and the confusion has worsened with the advent of HIV. Let us suppose that a newspaper ran the headline; HIV/AIDS THE HIGHEST KILLER IN ZIMBABWE, it is unlikely that most readers would consider it a fair reflection of reality in the country. The level of denial in society is alarming. This denial syndrome is further buttressed by medical practice, which differentiates between the opportunistic diseases that cause the death of an HIV/AIDS patient. At funerals, relatives get comfort from medical certificates that only mention 'carcinoma sarcoma', 'cancer', 'meningitis', 'pneumonia', 'diabetes', or 'cerebral malaria' as the cause. That death certificates do not mention HIV/AIDS has the effect of perpetuating a sense of self-deception and of lulling relatives' alertness to the threat to life that the virus poses. A veil of denial and secrecy about the disease continues unabated and plays into the hands of socio-religious interests, as well as the deep cultural systems that prevail in Zimbabwe. It is these systems that primarily inform the conservative approach that the government adopted for so long with respect to HIV/AIDS. Many thousands had to die before the government decided to pass a law, in 1998, which made it mandatory for all workers in the formal labour sector to contribute towards an AIDS levy that was to be administered by the National AIDS Council (NAC).

Noble as the idea may be, questions and suspicions continue to abound regarding the efficiency (and relevance) of this national body. The first question is whether a body instituted by a government known for its failure to combat graft within its ranks, could ever be free from the virus of corruption. Why would it alone be free from nepotism and cronyism? No wonder allegations have already been made that funds, meant for the relief of people suffering from AIDS, were syphoned off and used for political purposes between 2000 and 2002. While such allegations were dismissed by the government as cheap politicking, the onus falls on it to deal firmly with cases of corruption. Secondly, the culture of patronage that Zimbabwe's leadership has become known for has fuelled the cynicism surrounding the founding of the NAC. The emphasis on political trust rather than professional competence, has damaged the credibility of many parastatal bodies in Zimbabwe. For this reason, mystery continues to surround the sacking of Professor G. L. Chavunduka as the first chairman of the council. How his political preferences may have interfered with the running of the NAC was never explained to the nation. Thus, its credibility continues to hang in the balance.

The effect of HIV/AIDS on Shona custom

In spite of the secrecy and fear that hover around the bereaved family at the time of death from HIV/AIDS, a veil of suspicion tends to direct the social customs as well as the rituals that follow the death. From the mid-nineties, when death from HIV-related diseases or from AIDS became common, many customs and rituals have undergone significant change.

(i) The *chigadza mapfihwa* custom

This is one of the customs most affected by HIV/AIDS. The *chigadza mapfihwa* inheritance system was generally understood to be a benign attempt to restore family cohesion in the wake of death and bereavement.

Hence, for a man who lost his wife, the natural replacement *(chigadza mapfihwa)* was deemed to be the sister or niece of the deceased wife. There were many reasons for this custom. First, it was much easier for the two families that had been bonded through marriage to continue the relationship smoothly. Moreover, if the union with the deceased wife was blessed with children, a natural bond between them and the new mother was envisaged – no matter what her age. While the mother-children bond continued between the children and the *chigadza mapfihwa*, the husband-wife relationship, which used to be latent, had to be formally upgraded and ritually activated after the *magadziro/kurova guva* (the spiritual homecoming) ritual. Invariably, the new mother was far younger than the husband, and sometimes even younger than some of the children that she was expected to mother. The *kugadza mapfihwa* custom was also favoured because it was considered to be an effective mechanism to deal with the distribution of the estate of the deceased's property. Allowing a situation where the husband would marry a foreign woman, that is, one who was completely unrelated to the children, was generally considered to be potentially precarious. The mere presence of a mother not related to the children was believed to create deep tensions in the family. It was also feared that the new mother would unfairly enjoy the material fruits created by the mother of the bereaved children at their expense. The new mother would also pull her husband away from the family of the deceased wife to her own. Further destabilisation was therefore the inevitable consequence of such a foreign union.

However, in this era of HIV/AIDS the custom of *kugadza mapfihwa* has been under serious onslaught. The custom is now viewed as a 'passport to death'. The Shona word *rushavashava* captures the dire consequences associated with this custom. The word can mean 'danger', very much as it can mean 'death'. When the Shona say, *Ah, zvinopinza rushavashava mumusha,* (something that brings danger/death in the family), that is synonymous with saying, *zvine ngozi* ('there is a retributive spirit, an *ngozi*'). The term *ngozi* not only carries the casual meaning of danger, but also brings into play a spiritual dimension whereby the spirit of a dead person takes vengeance against the culprits. In other words, the avoidance of this custom is in itself a conscious moral decision by the bereaved family not to drive their member into becoming a dangerous spirit for such an act would result in untold suffering and pain for the whole family.

(ii) The *kugadza nhaka* custom

Related to the *chigadza mapfihwa* custom is the *kugara nhaka* (wife inheritance after the death of a brother). In some Shona communities, the elder brother cannot inherit a wife of the deceased brother because he is viewed as a father who cannot at the same time be a potential spouse. It is only younger brothers who can inherit the wife of their late brother. This form of levirate marriage was also meant to maintain family stability in terms of the movement of the estate, as well as the purity of the clan. By virtue of being both virilocal and patrilocal, Shona marriage was meant to ensure that the bereaved wife would remain loyal to the family into which she had been married. In the face of the scourge of HIV/AIDS, however, most Zimbabwean families have abandoned the *nhaka* custom for the same reasons that apply in the case of *chigadza mapfihwa*. Moreover, in the case of *nhaka*, the one who inherits a wife could be married already. If the deceased died from an HIV/AIDS-related disease the greatest likelihood would be that the wife would also be infected. Through the *nhaka* system, the inheritor exposes not only himself to HIV infection, but also his own wife and any unborn children. This can lead to a chain of 'inexplicable' deaths in the family.

(iii) The *sara pavana* custom

While the *chigadza mapfihwa* and *kugara nhaka* customs are being eroded by the plague of HIV/AIDS, a related custom of installing a caretaker mother/father (*sara pavana*) appears to prevail, against the odds that are bedevilling the Zimbabwean family. In Shona custom, the *sara pavana* is formally installed at the close of the funeral proceedings. Traditionally, however, the office was meant to expire at the time when the *kugadza mapfihwa/kugara nhaka* has been settled, immediately following the *kurova guva* rituals. Throughout his or her term of office as *sara pavana*, one is expected to act as the 'shade' (*mumvuri*) to the children, who are in a state of bereavement. He/she gives the children a compassionate ear and assists them to manage the trauma of death and bereavement. He/she is also required to provide a link between the children and the rest of the family, so as to maintain their sense of belonging within the extended family. In this respect, the office of the *sara pavana* is bestowed on the person who can best serve the interests of the children. It is only bestowed after careful deliberation by the elders. The responsibilities that go along with the office cannot be treated in a cavalier and casual way. Thus the *sara pavana* is ultimately answerable to the family elders who, in turn, are accountable to the family ancestors, the real custodians of the family or clan. For that reason, the *sara pavana* office is both social and spiritual.

In the face of HIV/AIDS, the office of the *sara pavana* appears to be one of the viable cultural ways of helping the hundreds of thousands of orphans left behind by parents who have fallen victim to the pandemic. In its recent usage the *sara pavana* office has shed the marital potential that used to be associated with it. The *sara pavana* was normally a person of means and enterprise; one who would not live off the children's inheritance. Whilst the *kugadza mapfihwa* and the *kugara nhaka* customs were becoming more and more materialistic and are now viewed in a bad light, the *sara pavana* custom continues to carry the hope of the Shona family. In its pristine form, the custom was meant to embody the ideal of service. This Shona moral and ethical model, however, needs to be reinforced with some economic props. Since the majority of HIV/AIDS victims are in the economically productive bracket of 19 to 49 years, there is a high probability that most of them would not be able to leave substantial savings and property. Hence, the orphans left behind often have little to inherit. For this reason, the National Social Security Authority (NSSA) and the National AIDS Council (NAC) need to create synergies with family networks that continue to oversee the *sara pavana* custom. The estate of the deceased should be registered under the law, and the *sara pavana* should be encouraged to register with the chief and/or district administrator. The custom needs to be supported by law, so that the thousands of orphans left behind are not exploited and taken advantage of by unscrupulous relatives.

(iv) The *gata* custom

Another cultural practice that remains entrenched in the psyche of the people is the custom of seeking the service of a diviner (*n'anga*) after the death of a member (*gata*). This ritual is to establish the cause of death, and for the family to work towards the restoration of balance and harmony (*kutsigisa musha*). It is a process of restoring the dignity and respectability of the family and clan through ritual. The practice is carried out whether the family members have full or partial knowledge of the cause of death. Essentially, while HIV/AIDS could be acknowledged as the killer of X, the family regard the disease as merely a secondary cause. The primary cause has to be found, invariably, in the spiritual realm. A Shona proverb, *Mudzimu wakupa chironda wati nhunzi dzikudye*, ('The ancestral spirit that gives you a wound is sanctioning flies to feast on you') captures the decisive role that the ancestors are believed to play with regard to the aetiology of disease and death. The ancestors are believed to be the protectors of their progeny. They can, however, withdraw their protection out of anger resulting from the misdeeds of the living. The slightest cleavage between the living and their ancestors could be taken advantage of by enemies (*vavengi*) who are believed to be capable of using various spiritual agencies to destroy the family. It is this spiritual realm which the family tries to interrogate through the diviner (*n'anga*). Traditionally, the method which was most popularly used was the *hakata* (bone throwing), hence the term *gata*. Current practice is no longer restricted to the *n'anga*. Some families, especially those that have a long Christian background, go to consult independent church prophets (*vaporofita*) who use a variety of clairvoyant skills to interpret the cause of death and also assist in the *kutsigisa musha* rituals.

Consulting a *n'anga* (*gata*) or a prophet is similar to a post-mortem in the modern medical practice. Although it is carried out for all people who die, nobody seems to care about the use of the results afterwards. The report may well be delivered to the bereaved but often no follow-up is made. The original idea behind the *gata* ritual was for the family to adopt corrective measures by way of spiritual fortification, which often required the *n'anga's* involvement. A number of rites of affliction, atonement and reconciliation normally followed the consultation. Currently, however, nothing is done – save the cleansing rite preceding the distribution of the clothes of the deceased. In other words, the practice seems to have degenerated to the level of being merely symbolic routine. In some cases the tradition of consulting a *n'anga* is done out of respect for the elderly, who request the bereaved families to do so.

In the past, the *gata* custom demanded a follow-up, and violence often ensued, especially in cases where the *gata* process would have led to the disclosure of some people as being responsible for the death of the deceased member. Accusations and counter-accusations of witchcraft often followed such disclosures. The accusations invariably resulted in acts of revenge and a general situation of mayhem. In the process, relationships inside and outside the extended family were poisoned, or blood feuds between families or clans were created. Due to the potential divisiveness, violence, and bloody encounters associated with the custom, and in an attempt to suppress witchcraft accusations, the colonial government, supported by the missionaries, introduced the Witchcraft Suppression Act (1898). The enactment of this law, for more than a century, has transformed the *gata* custom in a radical way. For fear of being convicted before the law, the *n'anga* has been forced to avoid mentioning any names of persons in a way that could be interpreted as an accusation of witchcraft. The failure to disclose the person behind a death has, however, been viewed by the diviners as a way of blunting their contribution to society. In the belief that the colonial governments and the church had an ideological bone to chew with the African priests (*n'anga*), many Zimbabwean communities have resorted to the *tsikamutanda* practitioners in a vain attempt to deal with the HIV/AIDS scourge.

(v) *Tsikamutanda* and HIV/AIDS

Before the era of HIV/AIDS it was rare for young men and women to fall sick and die. In the event of such a tragedy, the whole village had to be 'smelt out' by the *n'anga*. The culprit, if found, was invariably ostracised. Before the colonial era, however, it is said that the culprit was either lynched, by being thrown headlong from a hill, or the witchcraft spirit was exorcised in a ritual that involved being taken around a sacred hill. Because of this practice there are some hills in the regions inhabited by the Shona that have the name *chavaroyi* (the hill of the witches). Due to the enactment of the Witchcraft Suppression Act, such practices became rare. They have, however, been transformed and are on the ascendancy as more and more young people die of AIDS.

Because of growing poverty in the urban areas, many people who are sick from HIV/AIDS-related diseases leave for the rural areas, where care from family members is readily available. There is also no monetary value attached to burial land, nor are there encumbrances such as the acquisition of a burial order before carrying out a burial. However, because of the high toll of HIV/AIDS casualties in every village in the country, there is a growing prevalence of the custom of inviting a diviner to smell out witches. Since this is a village-wide consultation, it is the village headman who calls the witch-hunter who is known as the *tsikamutanda*, after consulting the village elders. This is a specialist diviner in the art of smelling out witches. The whole village contributes money for their homes to be cleansed or for members to be exorcised of witchcraft.

In recent days, however, the *tsikamutanda* travel in groups and seem to constitute leagues. The explanation given for these leagues is that witchcraft is such a complex power that there is need for support systems in the attempts to eradicate it. Some forms of witchcraft are believed to have a much greater power than that wielded by the *tsikamutanda*. Stories abound that tell of cases where some *tsikamutanda* were killed while in the process of trying to incapacitate witchcraft forms. So the league of witch-hunters offers re-enforcement against the powers that they confront in their tour of duty.[1] There are, however, some top-notch *tsikamutanda* like Gaurani, who used to travel alone in Mashonaland East province in the late nineties.

The *tsikamutanda* tend to stay in a village for a relatively long period of time. They conduct their witchcraft eradication ceremonies at night. As they move from one end of the village to the other, a tense mood of expectancy builds up as people look forward to solving the puzzle behind the high death rate in their families. The *tsikamutanda* are known for plucking out evil agencies, which they kill in order to rid the community of witchcraft. Common in the era of HIV/AIDS seems to be the *chikwambo*, a form of malevolent force that is said to live on the blood of human beings. This force is believed to be acquired to enhance wealth for its owner. In the attempt to create such wealth, the owner has to be involved in nefarious activities so that he/she gets the blood for it, the only food that this being feeds on. The next most popular agency that the *tsikamutanda* are said to pluck out of people's homes is the *gona* or *nyanga* (magical horn). This is a form of evil energy that is also believed to live on people's blood, and therefore explains why some members of the owner's family, or outsiders, have to die regularly. The *gona/nyanga*

---

[1] Mr Matimati, interview at Chendambuya village, Headlands, 22 September 2000.

is believed to cause disease or death to families to which it is sent by its owner. The commonest explanation for the deaths occurring in the villages, however, is bewitchment, carried out especially by old women, who are said to make nocturnal trips in the villages. These women are believed to belong to three groups: those believed to be possessed by a spirit of an ancestor who was a witch (*ane shavi rokuroya*); those who were taken through a process of apprenticeship; and finally those who got into the practice involuntarily through ritual incision (*vakatemerwa nyora*) performed on them by an older relative when they were young.[2]

In recent years, those accused of witchcraft by the *tsikamutanda* are usually banished from the village.[3] If allowed to remain, depending on the *tsikamutanda's* diagnosis, they are taken through a cleansing/exorcism ritual. The most unfortunate scenario in rural Zimbabwe, however, is that it is the elderly women and widows who are usually referred to as witches.[4] Claud Mararike, of the Sociology Department at the University of Zimbabwe, seems to confirm the resilience of this belief when he says, 'It is a stigma dating back to the time of our forefathers and it would be difficult to remove.'[5] Ironically, it is the elderly women in rural Zimbabwe who shoulder most of the burden of attending to the victims of HIV/AIDS and who look after the orphans that are left behind. This fact has been well illustrated by a television programme, *Lifelines*, that ran on Zimbabwe Television (ZTV) from 2000-2003. It was produced by Sr Tendai Makonese O.P. on behalf of the Zimbabwe Catholic Bishops' Conference and looked at the social conditions of people, especially the poorest.

Whilst the activities of the *tsikamutanda* are supposed to bring relief to communities that are ravaged by HIV/AIDS, the opposite seems to be achieved. Their activities leave behind only a trail of fear, suspicion and reprisal. The witch-hunts cause both physical and mental suffering to those widows identified as witches. The cases cited by Rodrick Mukumbira illustrate the point very poignantly. They come from the village of Mawabeni in Matabeleland South.

Case 1

Sinikiwe Nkosana, 47, is homeless after being smelt out for causing the death of her own husband. Her husband died last July in what people in her village, in Mbalabala, 60 km south of Bulawayo, termed 'suspicious circumstances'. She is now living in a squatter camp next to the railway station in Bulawayo. 'Everyone knows that my husband had many other

---

[2] Interview: Mrs A. Chikuvire, Farm no. 244, Lancashire,Chivhu. 9 December 2001.
[3] Rodrick Mukumbira, 'Shock treatment for widows as pandemic ravages Zimbabwe', in *Africa News*, No. 72.
[4] Ibid.
[5] Ibid.

women partners and that he brought the disease home.' She says, 'I was surprised when the tsikamutanda said that I had bewitched him and that I was a danger to the other villagers if I was allowed to remain in the village.' Nkosana, whose only two children have also died of HIV/AIDS-related illnesses, says she was given one hour to leave the village by her in-laws and was not allowed to carry anything. 'Even my in-laws had turned against me. They only allowed me access to a few clothes. I have lost everything I accumulated in my lifetime. ...[6]

Case 2

For Ntombana Mlalazi, a 62-year-old widow, life will never be the same again. Branded a witch in January 2001, following a string of deaths in her village ... she now has to bear the scars of this title. Her face and right arm are now permanently disfigured – a result of an exorcism ceremony ordered by the local headman of her area to clear the place of witchcraft. 'People are dying and tsikamutanda said I was responsible,' she says tearfully. 'They made me crouch over a bucket with boiling water and covered me with a blanket. When I cried that the steam was hurting me I could hear the tsikamutanda saying the demon was leaving me.' She says she was freed from the blanket 10 minutes later and her face and right arm were already scalded. A good Samaritan arranged that she be carried to hospital where she spent two months.[7]

That no arrests were made in either case, particularly in the case of Mrs Mlalazi who was admitted to hospital, says much about the extent to which the belief in witchcraft is entrenched in Zimbabwean society. This is in spite of the Witchcraft Suppression Act amendments of 1989, which make it illegal to either accuse someone of practising witchcraft or to solicit someone to name witches. Moreover, the belief in witchcraft has effectively clouded the people's understanding of killer diseases such as AIDS. The old women and widows have been reduced to scapegoats by a culture that not only continues to be highly patriarchal, but also has failed to rise to the moral challenges demanded by the current era of the deadly disease. Local efforts to counter the ravages of HIV/AIDS are bound to fail as long as they are informed by a patriarchal ideology. Below, we consider one other local community endeavour sponsored by the traditional leadership, but different from the forays associated with the *tsikamutanda*.

---

[6] Ibid.
[7] Ibid.

(vi) Virginity tests and the prevention of HIV/AIDS

As more and more people in Zimbabwe continue to die from HIV-related diseases a number of communities in Zimbabwe are forced to dig deep into their culture for solutions. Chiefs and other traditional leaders, including *masvikiro* (spirit mediums), as the repositories of African indigenous knowledge systems, have come up with some measures that encourage changes of sexual behaviour in order to prevent the infection. In some cases, the traditional leadership is receiving significant co-operation from rural district council staff as well as from Western health professionals. One such strategy that traditional leaders seem to agree on as an effective prevention of infection is the reintroduction of virginity testing of girls. In recent years, the most vocal leader behind this strategy has been Chief Naboth Makoni of Makoni district. He has found ready support from other chiefs, especially those of Hurungwe district in Mashonaland West. The latter are more radical as they call for 'compulsory virginity tests for girls'.[8] Whilst the Hurungwe virginity testing programme is still at an initial stage, Chief Makoni's programme has been under way since 2001. Thousands of girls in the Makoni district have already undergone, and continue to undergo, such tests. Many media houses have followed the tests with keen interest. Below we capture some findings from both the electronic and print media.

In a report on 22 July 2002, *The Sunday Mail* referred to a party that Chief Naboth Makoni hosted in honour of about 2,000 girls who had passed virginity tests. 2,007 girls presented themselves for the test and most of those who passed were between the ages of 12 and 18, followed by those between 19 and 25. The smallest group represented was aged from 25 to 30 – only five 'girls' in this category turning up for tests.[9]

Apparently, another test was carried out at the end of that year. A report by the South African Broadcasting Corporation read as follows:

> In Zimbabwe, about two thousand young women from the Makoni district, east of Harare, passed virginity tests at the weekend. They were told that tribal authorities in the region would regard any attempt by a man to touch a woman above her wrist as rape. The girls and women, aged between 12 and 25, were examined by nurses, women elders and tribal princesses as part of an attempt to prevent the spread of HIV/AIDS. Makoni, which is on one of Zimbabwe's busiest transport routes, is one of the worst affected areas in the country. There are a large number of prostitutes who offer their services to passing truck drivers.[10]

---

[8] *The Weekend Tribune*, 25-26 January 2003.
[9] *The Sunday Mail*, 22 July 2001.
[10] http://www.sabc.co.za/

Chief Makoni's virginity tests have no doubt attracted unprecedented interest, as a report on 22 October 2002, by Eugene Soros, of *World Press Review*, illustrates. The report describes a community festival to celebrate female virginity, following a virginity test that had attracted 5,000 girls.

> It is a serene Saturday morning at Osborne Dam, in Manicaland, Zimbabwe, and hundreds of men and women are already waiting for the biggest festival celebrating female virginity Zimbabwe has ever seen. The assembled crowd mills about in a constantly shifting sea of colour, bedecked in festive veils, orange turbans streaked with violet, and yellow boubous splashed with blue. Finally, just as the impatient crowd begins to get restless, Chief Naboth Makoni calls the proceedings to order.
>
> The party begins in earnest. Spectators clap and dance, women ululate. Participants celebrate the virgins' chastity in traditional songs. After a week of being chaperoned by the elderly women, the girls are ready for the next challenge: finding a fitting husband. The festival has attracted 5 000 girls. By the time they leave, each will have received a certificate of their virginity.[11]

> According to Chief Makoni, the practice of virginity tests was in existence before the colonisation of Zimbabwe. He resolved to revive the practice and the festival in 2001 as a means of curbing the spiralling rate of HIV infection in Manicaland province, where his district is located. Surveys carried out in the area have shown that half of all women attending maternity clinics were HIV positive.[12] At the festival held in October 2002, Chief Makoni appealed to parents 'to keep a shorter leash' on their children. 'You must be ashamed of yourself', he said, 'if your daughter does not have a virginity confirmation certificate, because the whole village will scorn you.'[13]

> At an earlier festival, held in 2001, Chief Makoni had reacted sharply against other preventive methods encouraged in the country. He lashed out at the dishing out of condoms to young people arguing that: 'Guns are only given to soldiers ... Our children do not need condoms. They need education. Let us stop condom distribution to our children, this way we will win'.[14]

---

[11] E. Soros, 'Virgins, Potions, and AIDS in Zimbabwe' in http://www.lehigh.edu/
[12] *HIV Update International*, 20 December 2001.
[13] Ibid.
[14] *The Sunday Mail*, 22 July 2001.

Virginity in Zimbabwean culture

Among the Shona people, female virginity was highly valued by the family into which any woman would marry. A girl's virginity was well guarded before marriage. Although testing girls for virginity was not the norm in traditional Zimbabwe, as the late Peter Sibanda of the Zimbabwe National Traditional Healers' Association (ZINATHA) correctly observed, elderly women in the village had the responsibility of overseeing the virginity status of the girls in the entire village.[15] In other regions, the girl's virginity was tested before marriage. However, the celebration of virginity was conducted after, and not before, marriage. As E. Gundani and P. H. Gundani argue, 'virginity symbolised sexual purity and moral unadulteration', in the Shona society.[16] Virginity was a profound source of pride to the girl's family at the time of marriage. If she was a virgin, then the bridegroom's family had to arrange for the payment of a cow to her parents over and above the *danga* (the *roora* cows) that her family settled for. This cow is called *chimandamanda*. It was, and continues to be, slaughtered for consumption at a festival to be held at the bride's home. At this ceremony, the families of both the bride and groom, their relatives, friends and members of the neighbouring community celebrate the bride's virginity. This ceremony was very important for the bride's family as it put them on respectable moral ground in the community. Consequently, failure to hold the *chimandamanda* ceremony became a source of embarrassment for the bride's family.

In those communities where virginity tests were administered on the girls, all those who had attained the age of puberty were targeted. Elderly women regularly examined them in the presence of family aunts. The latter were considered to be the custodians of family values.

> *Due to the communitarian character of the Shona life, and the gender specific roles attached to family members, it was much easier for aunts to monitor contacts between the girl child and the male members of the community. The times to fetch wood and water, to go for the night dance and to go to bed were closely monitored by aunts and elderly females in the community. Most of these activities were also conducted in groups, and never singly. Equally, the girls' bedroom, nhanga, was jealously guarded from male visitors.*[17]

---

[15] E. Soros, op.cit. ft.11.
[16] E. Gundani and P.H. Gundani, 'Virginity tests of girls in Makoni district, Zimbabwe: Implications for HIV/AIDS prevention, sexual and reproductive heath and rights of the girl child', unpublished paper presented at the Amanitari Conference on the theme: The African Women's sexual and reproductive health rights: prosperity through empowerment, Johannesburg, 4-7 February 2003.
[17] Ibid.

Implications of the reintroduction of virginity tests in contemporary Zimbabwe

The reintroduction of virginity tests in Shona communities today can be interpreted as one of the many unintended results of the ill-fated ESAP that the Government of Zimbabwe experimented with from 1991 to 1996. The International Monetary Fund and World Bank sponsored the programme aimed at, *inter alia*, the liberalisation of the economy and the withdrawal of state subsidies in the social service sectors such as health and education. The hasty withdrawal of state contributions in these areas has left a lacuna that calls upon communities and families to be innovative. The health system, in particular, has been the hardest hit in the post-ESAP era. In the light of the high toll that the HIV/AIDS pandemic continues to claim, communities have been forced to revert to those traditional institutions and practices that offer some potential for social recovery. For this reason, virginity testing was deemed to offer an effective prevention method against HIV infection. The attempt is not only driven by nostalgia for a mythical past, but also by the desire to fight a disease that has run rampant and continues to pose a serious threat to the family unit and, inevitably, the whole Zimbabwean society.

The traditional leaders in the Makoni and Hurungwe districts are apparently clear that sexual behaviour is at the core of the matter as far as HIV/AIDS is concerned. In their world view the woman is the foundation of the family and her moral and sexual integrity forms the basis for its well-being. The Shona idiom *musha mukadzi* (the wife makes a home) bears provenance to this world view. Hence, the appeal for the chastity of the girl child. Virginity testing and certification has, therefore, become a way of discouraging premarital sex, with the hope that HIV-free families will be founded. The initiative in Makoni and Hurungwe districts should also be viewed as an attempt by some elements of the civil society, in this case traditional leadership, to recover the space which had for long been lost to the central government. This moral-retrieval system apparently resonates with the conservative value systems that prevail in the rural areas of Zimbabwe. This explains its popularity. Traditional leaders are reasserting their power and moral authority and, incidentally, discrediting the government's treatment of the HIV/AIDS crisis. The government's policies are seen in the work of the Zimbabwe National Family Planning Council (ZNFPC), which regularly visits schools and local clinics distributing condoms to all and sundry. We have already mentioned Chief Makoni's broadside against this practice: 'Guns are only given to soldiers...'[18] Chief Makoni's reference to education appears to point to a

---

[18] *The Sunday Mail*, 22 July 2001.

critical area of deficiency in the government's programmes to fight HIV infection. Mbuya Chikamhi Machire of Hurungwe also sees education as critical for the empowerment of the girl child. She supports virginity tests for girls, but it is not clear whether she sees it as secondary to education. In the *Weekend Tribune* she is quoted as saying, 'There is no way women can talk about being empowered without being educated. In my area, early pregnancies are an obstacle, hindering the young girls from continuing with their education, yet modern women can only be emancipated through the pen.'[19] In their desire to re-arm their communities in the fight against HIV/AIDS, traditional leaders seem too eager to stamp out the moral decadence that is perpetrated mostly by men.

It is this which women's organisations find deficient in the initiatives by Chief Makoni and the chiefs and councillors in Hurungwe. Women and men who are socially conscious of the rights of the girl child scorn virginity testing. Moreover, the silence of the traditional leaders regarding the sexual status of boys makes the practice a mere patriarchal, gender-biased gimmick to maintain and further reduce girls and women to sex tools. The practice rings hollow and desperate, considering the apt comments that Eugene Soros made after attending the ceremony at Osborne Dam in October 2002.

> *Chief Makoni expects the festivals to encourage parents to keep a shorter leash on their children. Perhaps so, AIDS workers retort, but men spread HIV more often than women. And in Zimbabwe, as elsewhere, male infidelity is often explicitly or tacitly sanctioned. In some parts in Zimbabwe, a bride is advised not to ask where her husband has been if he spends the night out. Worse, a deteriorating economy and a brutal famine have led increasing numbers of young girls to offer sex in exchange for food.*[20]

This comment raises a serious question on the need to have a holistic approach to the challenge of HIV infection through a deliberate linkage of the following factors: (a) the respect for the girl child's rights, (b) the formulation and implementation of a policy of women empowerment, and (c) the encouragement of a culture that respects autonomy in the determination of sexual choices for both female and the male members of the society. Clearly, the introduction of virginity testing rings hollow in a society where no mechanisms are put in place to control the sexual behaviour of the boy child. It is ironical and curious that the girl child, who in the Shona culture has no power over sexual and reproductive matters, is made the subject and agent of change towards the envisaged

---

[19] *The Weekend Tribune*, 25-26 January 2003.
[20] E. Soros, op.cit. ft.12.

new moral and sexual order. In spite of the facade of moral renewal associated with the practice, virginity testing fails to address the fundamental issues of gender equity pervading Zimbabwean society in the twenty-first century.

The major weakness in the programme lies in the fact that it does not question the patriarchal myth embedded in the idiom *musha mukadzi*. Through virginity testing and the certification that is done publicly, the woman that the programme purports to protect is made more vulnerable to HIV-infected men who lurk in the woods waiting to pounce on some virgin girl in search of 'cleansing'. Furthermore, the programme falls short of ensuring an HIV-free marriage union. Noble as it may seem, preserving the girl's virginity does not guarantee her from being infected immediately she marries. In this regard, Petudzai Nyanhanda's comment is insightful. She is a member of the steering committee of the International Community of Women Living with HIV/AIDS. When asked about the festival's potential to help fight HIV/AIDS in Zimbabwe, she pointedly replied, 'The Virgin Mary should marry virgin Peter.'[21] Comments like these tell a story of the slow change taking place in the Zimbabwean culture, in contradistinction to the views of people such as Chief Makoni and Mbuya Machire. Change is constant in the life of any society, and present wherever there is a deliberate attempt to resolve apparent contradictions existing in a community.

Finally, the implications of virginity testing in Zimbabwe cannot be discussed outside the Zimbabwean constitutional arrangements regarding gender equity. Until recently, it was commonly believed that the constitution of Zimbabwe was clearly against all forms of discrimination, and that it provided an adequate framework for the emancipation of women. Since 1982, when the Legal Age of Majority Act was passed, the judiciary was also viewed as the agent of transformation regarding gender equality and non-discrimination. Thus, the 1999 Magaya v Magaya case[22] shook the nation's confidence in the constitution.

In this case, Vernia, the eldest child from the first wife in a polygamous marriage, claimed ownership of her deceased father's estate – including a house and other property. The Community Court magistrate, however, held that she could not be appointed heir as she was a woman, and since she had half-brothers. The applicable customary law in Zimbabwe only recognises the eldest male heir to succeed to the status of the deceased. 'In terms thereof, both the property and the responsibilities of the deceased – in particular, the duty to support surviving family dependants – are inherited.'[23] Vernia contested this view of the law by appealing to

---

[21] Ibid.
[22] ZS 16/2/99 and SC2 10/98.
[23] Ibid.

the Supreme Court. Her argument was that strict application of African customary law of succession had caused untold suffering to many widows and dependants, and that African customs were, like everything else, dynamic and capable of adapting to social change.

The Supreme Court ruled in favour of Vernia's half-brother, arguing that the anti-discrimination clause in the constitution of Zimbabwe, Section 23(3), excluded subjects that fall under 'customary laws'. In addition, the Supreme Court noted that the applicable customary law did not apply to matters such as 'adoption, marriage, divorce, burial, devolution of property on death or other matters of personal law'. In defence of the full bench ruling, Justice J. A. Muchechetere held that it was 'prudent to pursue pragmatic and gradual change'. He also argued that matters of law reform were complex and were best left to the legislature.[24]

The ruling by the Supreme Court was received with consternation by women's organisations, legal experts and all progressive citizens. They accused the Supreme Court judges of having failed to effect the change, which they had apparently endorsed.[25] They also called for additional constitutional protection in order to fully protect women's human rights and gender equality. Since 1999, however, the government of Zimbabwe has not moved towards making any legislative amendments that provide for non-discrimination in all circumstances. The reaction by Welshman Ncube, an expert on constitutional and family law, is acutely relevant to our discussion on culture and virginity testing. With respect to the Magaya v Magaya case he said: 'We are desirous of getting out of the quicksand of tradition, but we can't. We try to get rid of the ghosts of the past, but we can't exorcise them. They keep haunting us.'[26]

Virginity testing seems to be another case where Zimbabweans continue to be haunted by the ghosts of the past. There is a high probability that the explicit discrimination that the virginity testing practice espouses is legally acceptable, as it may fall under customary law. Would such gender-biased practices be excluded from the anti-discrimination clause in the constitution? However positive such practices may appear to those who subscribe to a conservative view of culture, the long-term dangers in them seem to outweigh their short-term usefulness. As Maryse Fontus says, 'If gender discrimination is allowed in the sphere of family and personal law, including decisions about marriage, childbearing and child custody, much of women's lives will be reduced to second-class citizenship.'[27]

---

[24] J. Robb and J. Cassette, 'Customary law of primogeniture upheld in Zimbabwe', October 1999 in http://www.derebus.org.za/
[25] Ibid.
[26] 'Zimbabwe must act to reassert equality', in http://www.crlp.org/ 30 June 99.
[27] 'Zimbabwe's women lose most rights', in *The Times-Herald* Record (Rockland County, New York, USA); in http://www.ilga.org/

Whilst Zimbabwe's short-term future lies in the political maturity of its leadership and its citizenry in resolving the current political crisis that the country is reeling under, its long-term future as a healthy nation will depend on the degree to which its leadership and citizenry show moral and ethical maturity in fighting the HIV scourge. Resorting to the past without a clear focus on the future will not be the salvation for Zimbabwe. That future surely rests in a careful synthesis of our age-old traditions, many which are blatantly discriminatory towards women, with modern legal codes, which enshrine equal rights for all.

Conclusion

What seems clear is that when a society is under the onslaught of an external or internal threat, it mobilises all its cultural resources in varied and, sometimes, contradictory ways. It is also clear that community leaders will utilise the cultural and moral space that is available in order to come up with local solutions to a given threat, without necessarily waiting for guidance from central government. When this happens, however, the tendency is to dig deeper to retrieve some of the values and customs that were once effective in dealing with what may be deemed to have been similar threats in the past. The biggest problem with this approach, however, is the partisan – if not mythical – lenses that the interpreters of such a past wear. The perceived solutions may thus fail to match the complexity of the threat that the society is trying to eradicate. Nevertheless, the efforts and initiatives that the society undertake in the endeavour to fight the threat, provide the context for changes to occur in a people's culture. This continues to be true also for Zimbabwean culture since the irruption of HIV/AIDS. Cultural change can take many forms. It can be retrograde or progressive, depending on the factors that give impetus to it. While community or government leaders may be keen to initiate and manage change, culture change does not always lend itself to official management.

Zimbabwe: The Past is the Future

The Zimbabwe economy 1980-2003: a ZCTU[1] perspective

Godfrey Kanyenze

Introduction

The dual and enclave economy Zimbabwe inherited at independence (1980) was shaped by the ideology of 'white supremacy' that characterised the pre-independence period, 1890-1980.

On the one hand it reflected a high level of development with a relatively large and diversified formal sector as shown in Table 1.[2]

At independence, agriculture, manufacturing and mining accounted for almost half the gross domestic product and 53.1 per cent of formal employment. There was no overwhelmingly dominant sector as is often the case in African economies. The manufacturing sector contributed the most (25 per cent) to GDP, exceptional by sub-Saharan African standards. And the share of manufacturing output to GDP continued high in the period 1980-89, averaging 23.3 per cent, while the corresponding figure for sub-Saharan Africa was 10.4 per cent. Apart from its relative size, the manufacturing sector was diversified, consisting of some 1,260 separate units producing 7,000 different products. Agriculture in most sub-Saharan African countries averaged 31.6 per cent of GDP during the period 1980-89 while in Zimbabwe it was 12.2 per cent for the same period. The relative strength of the economy was also reflected in the fairly broad export base, with agriculture accounting for 41 per cent of export earnings in 1984, followed by manufacturing (32 per cent) and mining (27 per cent).

Yet the dual structure of the economy lay in the co-existence of a non-formal relatively backward and underdeveloped sector, the sphere of 70 per cent of blacks, with this formal relatively well-developed and

---

[1] The Zimbabwe Congress of Trade Unions.
[2] Calculated from the *Quarterly Digest of Statistics*, CSO (various issues). Agriculture includes hunting and fishing, finance includes insurance and real estate, mining includes quarrying, distribution includes hotels and restaurants, and transport includes communication.

Table 1: Structure of Gross Domestic Product and employment by sector for selected years (GDP at constant prices)

Sector	1980	1985	1990	2000	1980	1985	1990	2000
	per cent of GDP				per cent of Employment			
Agriculture	14.0	17.6	14.8	18.4	32.4	26.3	24.3	26.3
Mining	8.8	4.7	3.9	3.9	6.0	5.3	4.8	3.6
Manufacturing	24.9	20.7	20.5	17.4	14.7	16.0	16.7	14.7
Electricity	2.2	1.9	2.5	2.1	0.7	0.7	0.8	0.9
Construction	2.8	2.2	2.9	2.2	4.1	4.4	5.7	4.3
Finance	6.3	7.6	8.4	11.0	1.2	1.5	1.5	2.8
Distribution	14.0	14.1	15.2	16.9	6.9	7.7	7.9	8.4
Transport	6.6	5.9	5.5	8.3	4.4	4.8	4.4	3.5
Public Administration	9.0	6.8	5.7	3.3	7.5	8.6	8.0	4.7
Education	5.2	6.1	5.9	7.2	3.4	8.1	8.9	11.3
Health	2.2	1.6	1.5	1.0	1.5	1.9	2.0	2.3
Domestic Service	2.0	2.0	1.6	1.4	11.2	9.5	8.8	8.3
Other Services	5.4	3.5	3.6	5.1	4.3	5.3	6.1	9.0

diversified sector. The enclave nature of the inherited economy derives from this fact. This formal sector had a growth momentum of its own, relatively isolated, like an enclave, from the non-formal sectors (informal and communal). The communal sector was developed as a reservoir of cheap labour for the formal sector and to meet some of its food requirements. In this sense the communal sector is partly linked to the formal sector through the labour and commodity markets. Yet it too is an enclave in that the majority of the households rely primarily on subsistence production and on traditional methods of allocating resources, while the formal sector relies predominantly on the market for resource allocation. So the non-formal sector, trapped in low productivity and a low-income cycle, is peripheral to the formal economy. The performance of the formal sector is determined by external market forces with regard to the export of primary goods and the importation of capital and intermediate goods for industry. Because of these external links, the formal sector does not depend on the non-formal sectors for its growth.

The process of creating a capitalist economy in Zimbabwe centred on the acquisition of land from blacks for whom it was their means of production and livelihood. The Land Apportionment Act (1931) and the Land Tenure Act (1969) allocated 18 million hectares (the former Tribal Trust Lands, now Communal Areas) to blacks – 95 per cent of the population – and an equal amount to around 6,000 whites who were just 4.5 per cent in 1969. The remaining two million hectares became game reserves and government land. White farms ranged between 500 and 2,000 hectares. Blacks were relegated to the agro-ecological zones with poor soil and unreliable rain while their white counterparts occupied prime land. By the time of independence, the communal areas were overcrowded with 700,000 families despite the estimation that their safe carrying capacity was 275,000 families[3] (In sharp contrast, in white farming areas an estimated 60 per cent of the land was either unused or under-utilised.[4] Table 2[5] traces the distribution of land by natural region and land use during the early 1980s.

Clearly, large-scale commercial farms, which were predominantly white owned, were located in the prime agro-ecological regions I and II, while communal areas were mainly located in the poorer natural regions IV and V.

Table 2: Distribution of land according to Natural Regions: per cent

Natural Region	Large-scale commercial land	Communal areas	Small-scale commercial land	Other land	Total
I	63	18	1	18	100
II	74	21	4	1	100
III	44	39	7	10	100
IV	27	49	4	20	100
V	35	46	1	18	100
Total	40	42	4	15	100

---

[3] Riddell Roger C. (1979) 'Alternative Development Strategies for Zimbabwe', in *Zimbabwe Journal of Economics*, 1:3.
[4] Stoneman C. (1988) 'The Economy: Recognising the Reality' in Stoneman C. (ed.), *Zimbabwe's Prospects: Issues of Race, Class, State and Capital in Southern Africa*. London: Macmillan Publishers. Riddell, op.cit.
[5] GoZ (1982) *Transitional National Development Plan*, Table 11.2: 67.

This inequitable distribution of resources led to inequitable income distribution. Table 3[6] summarises this situation.

Table 3: The distribution of income by race

Group	Proportion of population	Share of wages & salaries
African	97.6	60.0
Europeans	2.0	37.0
Coloured	0.3	2.0
Asians	0.2	1.0

An estimated 3 per cent of the population controlled two-thirds of gross national income.[7] The World Bank found that, at independence, black incomes were one-tenth of those of whites, with the wage differential as high as 24 (times for whites as for blacks) in agriculture.[8] The differential stood at 7.3 in manufacturing and the lowest was 3.5 in the financial services. The observed trend was that the lower the average skill level in a sector, the higher the average wage differentials between black and white.

The relative diversity of the economy has been presented as a strength. Yet the predominance of agriculture and mining, accounting for 68 per cent of total export earnings in 1984, was a point of vulnerability, given the dependence of the two sectors on exogenous factors. Weather patterns and commodity prices lie outside the control of governments.

The manufacturing sector presented its own contradictions. The import substitution industrialisation strategy, which had performed well during the sanctions period (particularly during the period of fastest growth, 1966-74), was already showing signs of severe stress by 1980. All easy and moderately hard industrialisation had been exhausted by 1975.[9] The deliberate policy of compressing imports to contain the balance of payments situation left capital stock in an obsolete and depleted state. The manufacturing sector itself became a net user of foreign exchange. Although it contributed 32.1 per cent of export earnings in 1984, it accounted for 90.6 per cent of imports during the same year.

Furthermore, the high level of protection created a monopoly structure. Single firms produced 50.4 per cent of manufactured products, 20.6 per

---

[6] GoZ (1981) National Manpower Survey. Vol. 1.
[7] Stoneman, Colin and Lionel Cliffe (1989) *Zimbabwe: Politics, Economics and Society.* London: Pinter Publishers.
[8] World Bank (1987) *Zimbabwe: A Strategy for Sustained Growth* (2 vols). Washington D.C: World Bank.
[9] Green, Reginald H. and Xavier Kadhani (1986) 'Zimbabwe: Transition to Economic Crisis, 1981-1983: Retrospect and Prospect', in *World Development,* 14: 8, August.

cent involved two firms and 9.7 per cent came from three firms. This trend shows that 80 per cent of goods produced are monopoly or oligopoly products.[10] This structure was further exacerbated by the concentration of production in the two major towns, Harare (accounting for 50 per cent of all manufactured products) and Bulawayo (accounting for 25 per cent). Above all, the economy in 1980 was war-ravaged and hence required a substantial inflow of resources for reconstruction and rehabilitation. National ownership of the economy was very low, with over two-thirds of invested capital in foreign hands.[11] Such a structure inevitably created pressure on the balance of payments. The government's five-year development plan lamented that between 1980 and 1983, as much as $300 million was remitted abroad in the form of dividends and profits.[12]

The first decade of Independence: 1980-90

The new government was hardly given any time to settle in. Even before it was sworn into office, the nation was engulfed in nation-wide strikes emanating from 'a crisis of expectations'. The government responded by promulgating the Minimum Wage Act of 1980. The employers' response was to retrench workers, and the government, realising the benefits of higher wages were being eroded, responded with the Employment Act of 1980, aimed at forestalling unwarranted retrenchments and making the remuneration of casuals double that of permanent employees.

The government approached the wider issues of incomes policy by constituting a commission of inquiry, under the chairmanship of Roger Riddell, in September 1980 to look at incomes, prices and conditions of service, with a view to correcting inherited anomalies. The Riddell Commission Report recommended the introduction of a minimum wage linked to the Poverty Datum Line (PDL). On the basis of this inquiry, the government linked minimum wages to the PDL until 1982. There followed three years of drought during which the government felt constrained to abandon its expansionary incomes policy and adopt a stabilisation programme in 1983. This effectively restricted the movement of wages.

But in the first two years of independence the economy experienced a major boom as a result of the opening up of the economy, the end of the war, renewed access to international aid and borrowing, favourable terms of trade, good weather conditions, excess capacity, and increased aggregate demand arising from agricultural and wage incomes. Real Gross Domestic Product (GDP) grew by 11 per cent in 1980 and 10 per cent in 1981.

---

[10] Ndlela, Dan B. (1984) 'Sectoral Analysis of Zimbabwe Economic Development with Implications for Foreign Trade and Foreign Exchange', *Zimbabwe Journal of Economics*, 1:1 (July). United Nations Industrial Development Organisation (1986) *The Manufacturing Sector in Zimbabwe*, Vienna, UNIDO.
[11] GoZ (1986), *First National Five-Year Development Plan*, 1986-1990, Vol. 1 (April).
[12] Ibid.

The boom of the first two years of independence resulted in the introduction of liberal policies on foreign exchange allocation, remittance of dividends and profits and an expansionary incomes policy that were to contribute towards macroeconomic instability in the subsequent period. Even during the boom, these liberal policies led to the deepening of the current account deficit from $74m in 1979 to $157m in 1980 and $440m in 1981. The capital account followed very much the same trend, moving from a surplus of $174m in 1979 to a deficit of $44m in 1980 before returning to a surplus of $134m in 1981. The economy showed other signs of over-heating in 1981, with the rate of inflation rising from 7 per cent in 1980 to 14 per cent in 1981.

Government had banked on the US$2.2 billion that had been promised at the Zimbabwe Conference on Reconstruction and Development (ZIMCORD) donors' conference in March 1981. Only a fifth of the promised funds had been disbursed by the end of 1984.[13] To meet its obligations, government borrowed indiscriminately, especially from non-concessionary commercial sources, with short maturity periods and high interest rates. As a result, total debt rose markedly from US$786 million in 1980 to US$2,304 million in 1983.[14] The debt service ratio, which represented 1.3 per cent of export earnings in 1979, had risen to 25 per cent by 1983, generating additional pressure on the balance of payments.

While the budget deficit amounted to 8.5 per cent of GDP in 1980/81, it fell to 6.6 per cent of GDP in 1981/82 before rising thereafter. For the period 1982/83-84/85, the budget deficit averaged 8.7 per cent of GDP. Due to security commitments in Mozambique and at home, expenditure on drought relief, and because social services were sustained, the budget deficit remained high during the 1980s. By the end of 1982, it was clear that the crisis was deep-seated and therefore required intervention. In response, the government adopted a 'home grown' stabilisation programme, which had the following elements:

- devaluation of the Z$ by 20 per cent on 9 December 1982 and thereafter tying it to a trade weighted basket of undisclosed currencies;
- introduction of new incentives for exports;
- restrictions on new non-concessionary foreign borrowing from 23 March 1983;
- balance of payments controls (27 March 1984) through a) temporary suspension of remittances of dividends and profits; b) temporary reduction of emigrants' settling allowances; c)

---

[13] World Bank (1985) *Zimbabwe: Country Economic Memorandum, Performance, Policies and Prospects*, 3 Vols. Washington D.C.

[14] World Bank (1993) *World Debt Tables: External Finance for Developing Countries*. Washington D.C.

acquisition of blocked external securities pool; and d) sharp cutbacks on foreign exchange allocations in each year until the second half of 1985;
- price and wage controls through cuts in subsidies and increases in administered prices (from May 1982); wage freeze (January 1982) and thereafter the adoption of a wage restraint policy;
- restriction on government credit expansion; restriction on new recruitment by government (1983/84);
- contraction monetary policies through increases in interest rates, restriction on domestic credit expansion and increased liquidity ratios (from February 1981);
- a major increase in central government revenues (they rose by about 10 per cent of GDP between 1979/80 and 1983/84) through both increases in taxes and a shift from quotas to tariffs; and
- increases in the controlled prices of key food items and utility and rail tariffs.[15]

The programme had elements of the orthodox stabilisation programmes implemented elsewhere. However, the use of the exchange rate as an instrument for stabilisation was not accompanied by a liberalisation of the trade regime and the removal of price controls, as is the case with orthodox stabilisation and adjustment programmes. The Zimbabwean government rejected the option of liberalising trade and foreign exchange allocation. The 18-month IMF standby agreement reached on March 24 1983 initially supported the stabilisation programme. This was subsequently suspended following the measures adopted (see the fourth measure in the stabilisation package outline above) in March 1984. The adoption of a stabilisation programme produced angry reaction from civic society groups, and especially trade unions. These groups questioned the claims by government that this was a 'home grown' programme.

As a result of the implementation of the stabilisation programme, the current account deficit improved from -Z$533 million in 1982 to -$101million by 1984, before deteriorating again to -Z$149.3 million in 1985. The outcome emanated from the severe reductions in normal allocations of foreign exchange in 1982, 1983 and 1984 and compressed domestic consumption, which curtailed the demand for imports. It was also facilitated by the improvement in exports arising from the depreciation of the exchange rate and the introduction of export incentives. The marked fall in the current account deficit recorded in 1984 was partly due to the temporary suspension of remittances of

---

[15] Davies R. and D. Sanders (1988) 'Adjustment Policies and the Welfare of Children: Zimbabwe, 1980-1985', in Cornia Giovanni, A. Jolly, Richard and Stewart Frances (eds), *Adjustment with a Human Face: Protecting the Vulnerable and Promoting Growth*. New York: UNICEF and Oxford: Oxford University Press, Vol. 2. World Bank (1985) op.cit. ft. 13.

dividends and profits and the temporary reduction of emigrants' settling allowances (measures adopted in March 1984).

The worsening of the current account deficit in 1985 resulted from increased demand for imports arising from the return of favourable weather conditions. This also reflected increased global allocation of foreign exchange for importers. With real GDP averaging only 1.9 per cent growth during the Transitional National Development Plan (TNDP) period (1982/83-84/85), against the Plan target of 8 per cent per annum, and employment growing at an annual average of only 0.4 per cent during the same period, it is clear that the TNDP targets were not met. Such a performance is way below the population growth rate of 3.1 per cent per annum in the 1982-92 period. Whereas Gross Fixed Capital Formation peaked at about 20 per cent of GDP in 1982, it collapsed to around 12 per cent of GDP by 1985, compared to the TNDP targets of 23 per cent by 1984/85. The TNDP planned to resettle 162,000 families during the 4-year period, but this was not achieved. By the early 1990s, only 52,000 families had been resettled and 64 per cent of these were resettled during the first 4 years of independence.

Following the expiry of the TNDP in 1985, the government launched its First Five Year National Development Plan in April 1986, covering the period 1986-90. During this plan period, the projected annual rate of real growth was revised downwards from the 8 per cent of the TNDP to 5.1 per cent. The projected investment to GDP ratio remained as under the TNDP, over 20 per cent. The number of families to be resettled was reduced from 162,000 under the TNDP to 75,000 by the end of the Plan period.

The economy grew at an average annual rate of 4 per cent during the period 1986-90, close to the target growth rate of 5.1 per cent, while employment grew at an annual average rate of 2.7 per cent during the same period. This employment performance was inadequate to absorb new entrants into the labour market, with the labour force growing at close to 3 per cent per annum.

Whereas the current account improved considerably during the period 1986-88, it deteriorated in 1989 and 1990. Following the initial improvement, factor payments abroad were resumed at the beginning of 1986. To deal with the deteriorating situation of the current account, government reduced foreign currency allocations. Consequently, the real value of the 1986 allocation amounted to only about 35 per cent of its 1981 value. Following additional reductions in the foreign exchange allocation in 1987, the real value of the 1987 allocation was only 30 per cent of its 1981 level. The adoption of such contractionary measures was induced by the bunching up of debt repayments, which reached a peak with a debt service ratio of 33 per cent in 1987. As a result, pressure mounted on the government to reschedule its debt obligations. The desire

The Zimbabwe economy 1980-2003: a ZCTU perspective

to maintain credit-worthiness resulted in government honouring its obligations, but it came at high cost, measured in terms of the imposition of a price and wage freeze, which resulted in workers in the leather and shoe sector going on strike. While it was easy to effect a wage freeze, commodity prices went up, to the dismay of the ZCTU, which complained that its members were being sacrificed.

After peaking in 1987, the debt service ratio declined to 23.5 per cent by 1990. Some improvement in foreign exchange allocation was achieved after 1987, resulting in the real value of the 1990 allocation rising to about 40 per cent of its 1981 value. Using import compression to stabilise the balance of payments took its toll on imports, adversely affecting investment and capacity utilisation. During the period 1986-90, the budget deficit remained high, averaging 9.8 per cent of GDP.

As was the case with the social sector, post-independence government policy focused on redressing the inherited inequalities in the allocation of land. The major focus of agricultural policy was to achieve equity and efficiency gains among smallholders through the reallocation of land, the development of marketing infrastructure and marketing services and the re-orientation of research and extension services towards them.

During the period 1980-84, 35,000 households were settled by government on approximately 2 million hectares of land.[16] As a result of this redistribution, real agricultural output grew at around 4 per cent per annum up to 1987, with much of that growth emanating from the small-scale producers. The share (in value terms) of crop sales through marketing authorities from communal areas increased from 5.9 per cent in 1980 to 22 per cent in 1988. Rukuni and Eicher[17] suggest that the development of infrastructure in small-scale farming areas also helped, observing that until 1984, about 22,000 kilometres of communal area roads had either been constructed or reconstructed. Moyo[18] marshalled evidence that suggests an increased role of the small-scale and communal sector in marketed grain. In the case of maize, for instance, deliveries to the Grain Marketing Board (GMB) from the communal areas rose from 3.6 per cent in 1979/80 to 36.5 per cent by 1984/85, while those from the small-scale farming sector rose from 2.7 per cent to 5.8 per cent during the same period. A panel survey of resettled farmers initiated in 1983 suggests that the well-being of resettled households improved dramatically over the years.[19] The success of Zimbabwe's agricultural

---

[16] Central Statistical Office (1998) *Poverty in Zimbabwe*. CSO, July. 9.
[17] Rukuni, M. and C.K. Eicher (eds) (1994) *Zimbabwe's Agricultural Revolution*. Harare: University of Zimbabwe Publications.
[18] Moyo, S. (1987) 'The Land Question', in I. Mandaza (ed.), *Zimbabwe: The Political Economy of Transition, 1980-86*. Dakar: CODESRIA.
[19] Kinsey B.H. (1999) 'Land Reform, Growth and Equity: Emerging Evidence from Zimbabwe's Resettlement Program,' in *Journal of Southern African Studies*, 2, 173-196.

policies was widely celebrated, to the extent that the whole question of land redistribution was shelved.[20] This 'success' was built on achieving a balance between support for the white commercial farmers, who were still responsible for producing the bulk of agricultural output, and nurturing the peasant farmers.

During the late 1980s, however, growth in agriculture stagnated, resulting in some analysts wondering whether the expansion of much of the period was a one-off development achieved by transferring technologies and services to previously marginalised areas.[21] It has been argued that most of the land where the new settlers were settled had either been previously put to little agricultural use or had been abandoned through the hostilities of the 1970s and early 1980s. The provision of credit and extension services to the new farmers played a role in the agricultural expansion of the early 1980s. From its inception, the resettlement programme made provision for accessing credit, for both seasonal purchases of crop inputs and the build up of cattle for draught power and commercial sale. A Resettlement Loan Fund was set up in 1981 under the Agricultural Finance Corporation (AFC). This scheme was replaced a year later by the Resettlement Credit Scheme (RCS), under which the settlers had an automatic right to loans from the second to the fifth year of their resettlement, irrespective of their repayment record. As a result, in 1983/84, 60 per cent of settlers had accessed loans.

The number of small-scale farmers receiving AFC/RCS lending increased from 21,000 in 1981 to almost 94,000 by 1987 and the real value of loans increased six-fold. By 1987, smallholder farmers accounted for nearly half of the total lending by the AFC, a marked change from the prevailing situation at independence, when virtually all loans went to the large-scale commercial sector. Most of the loans to the small-scale sector were short-term to enable the farmers to purchase improved seed, fertiliser, agro-chemicals and other inputs. Medium term loans were also provided to enable the farmers to buy cattle, and on a limited basis, to acquire tractors and farm machinery.

However, following three years of consecutive drought (1982-84), loan repayments became poor, such that by the mid-1980s, the average indebtedness of resettlement farmers was estimated at 40-55 per cent of average net farm income. The AFC responded by tightening its lending policy to the resettled farmers, beginning in 1987, only extending credit to farmers who did not have outstanding debts. As a result, AFC lending to small farmers plummeted to a clientele of less than 25,000.

---

[20] Moyo, op.cit. ft. 18.
[21] See, for instance, C.K. Eicher (1995) 'Zimbabwe's Maize-based Green Revolution: Preconditions for replication'. *World Development*, 23: 5, 805-17.

A similar trend emerged with respect to the provision of public sector agricultural marketing services, particularly those provided by the Grain Marketing Board (GMB). At the time of independence, the GMB had only three depots in the communal areas, implying that farmers in these areas incurred substantial transportation costs to access GMB depots. Following independence, additional depots were established, even where they were not cost effective. During the bumper harvest of 1985/86, new collection points were created. The importance of these collection points is underscored by the fact that over 60 per cent of deliveries went through them.[22] The number of depots in communal areas continued to increase until 1989. Thereafter they remained stagnant. The number of collection points, which were temporary in nature, declined sharply from 135 in 1985, to 42 in 1989 and only nine by 1991. In the absence of an increase in private sector marketing channels, this meant limited access to markets by smallholder farmers.

Some analysts have argued that the slow-down in resettlement also reflects the changing political economy, with influential lobbies pushing government to put more emphasis on tackling the racial aspect of the large-scale sector.[23] Moyo argues that, by the mid-1980s, there was a growing international consensus – and local acceptance – that there was really no 'land question' considering Zimbabwe's success in agricultural production. This notion of success was buttressed by the country's ability to generate and export surplus grain and meat during normal years, and to maintain food self-sufficiency during the three consecutive years of drought (1982-84). Moyo[24] contends that this issue of 'success' was effectively used to wish the land question away. Mumbengegwi[25] also argues that the 'success story' emanated from an impression that there should be continuity with the colonial era so as to sustain the 'success', and the government should not tamper too much with the existing structure of agriculture. He observed that '... where equity issues are pitted against efficiency arguments, it is the former that usually suffer; and this is what appears to have happened.'[26] This attempt at maintaining the status quo while at the same time realising the need for some radical change characterises the treatment of the agricultural sector in the national plans adopted by government. Herbst argues that the interests of the white farmer where already covered by the Lancaster House Constitution, which spelt out the land issue was to be resolved on a 'willing seller/willing buyer' basis. According to Herbst, 'The white farmers

---

[22] Moyo, op.cit. ft. 18.
[23] World Bank (2000) 'Zimbabwe: Interim Strategy, 2000-1'. Draft November.
[24] Moyo, op.cit. ft. 18.
[25] Mumbengegwi, C. (1987) Continuity and Change in Agricultural Policy,' in Mandaza (ed.) op.cit. ft. 18.
[26] Ibid. 210.

were surprised to find the ship of state going in the general direction that they favoured, and were then faced only with the task of constructing information buoys so that the government did not go – in their view – off course.'[27] These buoys involved drumming up the importance of the large-scale farming sector and the importance of keeping it intact. For Moyo, '...for the time being, the social forces that initially fuelled the overt struggle around the 'land question' are themselves temporarily dissipated.'[28]

Herbst further argues that the realisation by the bureaucracy of the challenges involved with resettlement, building infrastructure, roads, clinics, and schools, the involvement of several Ministries and government departments, all made for a slow resettlement process. For instance, the provision of water services was crucial, given that 91 per cent of the resettlements were in areas without adequate water. He contends that it was this realisation that resettlement was no quick-fix that resulted in the focus on redeveloping the communal areas themselves by focusing on changing the land-use patterns in these areas, an issue also raised by Moyo.[29] Herbst observes that newspaper coverage of the land question tapered off after 1982, at a time when the resettlement programme was slowing down substantially during the drought period.[30] Co-operating partners were also leaning towards this focus on the communal areas themselves.

Another issue that allowed the 'land question' to take a back seat was the absence of countervailing pressure. The National Farmers Association of Zimbabwe (NFAZ), which represented peasants, was weak. The other farmers' organisation, the Zimbabwe National Farmers Union (ZNFU), represented small-scale commercial farmers, and its interests were more inclined to those of the Commercial Farmers Union (CFU), the voice of the large-scale commercial farmers. Towards the end of the 1980s, the CFU criticised the resettlement programme, arguing that it was targeting the wrong people. It argued for the resettlement of master farmers and graduates of agricultural institutions who had proven or potential ability. Thus, when the land debate resurfaced in 1989, it was the political leaders who spearheaded it in preparation for the general election due in 1990.[31]

In addition, some studies have suggested that the improved sales from communal areas hide a highly skewed situation. Chipika and Amin[32]

---

[27] Herbst, J. (1990) *State Politics in Zimbabwe*. Harare: University of Zimbabwe Publications, 57.
[28] Ibid. 198.
[29] Ibid.
[30] Ibid.
[31] Ibid.
[32] Chipika, J. and N. Amin (1994) 'A Sectoral Analysis to Peasant Differentiation and Food Security in Zimbabwe'. Open University and University of Zimbabwe Working Paper No. 3, Dec.

found that the three high rainfall provinces of Mashonaland West, East, and Central accounted for about 70 per cent of maize in surplus years and up to 90 per cent in drought years. Even in these areas, a high level of differentiation exists, with 75-90 per cent of households having incomes below their rural poverty datum lines. According to Moyo, less than 20 per cent of the peasantry benefited from the 'success' even though these were from areas with quality land.[33] Moyo[34] and Mumbengegwi[35] concur that this regional differentiation sharpened the contradictions within the agrarian structure. It is important to keep in mind that the communal farmers made inroads in labour-intensive, low-skill crops (mainly staple food) such as maize, cotton and sorghum. Export crops like tobacco, tea, coffee, and sugar remained under the control of large-scale farmers.

Following the onset of drought and recession, the government abandoned its expansionary policies of the first three years of independence and adopted a stabilisation programme in 1983, which effectively took the country on a more conservative economic route. According to Herbst,[36] by 1988, the government had only resettled 42,000 families on approximately 2,6 million hectares. By the mid-1990s, an additional 20,000 households had been resettled. Government policy was informed by the desire for gradualism, arguing that '...while the inherited economy, with its institutions and infrastructure, has in the past served a minority, it would be simplistic and, indeed, naïve to suggest that it should, therefore, be destroyed in order to make a fresh start. The challenge lies in building upon and developing on what was inherited, modifying, expanding and, where necessary, radically changing structures and institutions in order to maximise benefits from economic growth and development to Zimbabweans as a whole.'[37] Thus, 64 per cent of the households that had been resettled by the mid-1990s were resettled during the first five years of independence. The original plan of government was to resettle 162,000 families during the period of the Transitional National Development Plan (1982/83-84/85). The First Five Year National Development Plan (1986-90) intended to settle 15,000 families annually – a total of 75,000 families between 1986 and 1990.

So, attempts at redressing the anomalies of the past were abandoned, following a period of drought (1982-84), world recession during the same time, and the resultant balance of payments problems. The economy came to be managed on a reaction-to-crisis basis. Throughout the first decade of independence, Zimbabwe did not pursue a comprehensive

---

[33] Moyo, op.cit. ft. 18.
[34] Moyo, op.cit. ft. 18.
[35] Mumbengegwi, op.cit. ft. 19.
[36] Herbst, op.cit. ft. 27.
[37] GoZ, (1982) Transitional National Development Plan, 1982/83 – 1984/85, Vol. 1 (November).

development strategy. The measures taken treated the symptoms, not the real causes, of the problems, which were of a structural nature. During this period, civil society groups hardly participated in the design and implementation of policy.

What constrained the adoption of a radical agenda?

Independence had been won on the basis of a compromise settlement, which effectively limited the extent to which the new government could implement a radical agenda. The Lancaster House Agreement had safeguards to protect the interests of the white community. In the words of Mugabe, '...even as I signed the document [Lancaster House Agreement] I was not a happy man at all. I felt we had been cheated to some extent ... that we had agreed to a deal that would to some extent rob us of the victory that we had hoped to have achieved in the field.'[38] In particular, the Bill of Rights, through its provision on 'Freedom from Deprivation of Property', provided a ten-year period of protection for private property. Land redistribution was to be based on a 'willing-buyer, willing-seller', basis, with the British government providing 50 per cent of the cost of acquiring the land.

Furthermore, the experiences of Mozambique, where Mugabe's ZANU was based, had taught them the dangers of adopting a radical approach. In that country, there was an exodus of white skills at a time when the black population did not have adequate skills to fill in the gap. In addition, given the balance of global forces, the adoption of such an approach would also affect the flow of international aid and capital and influence trade. Aid was also being used as a political weapon against governments that went against the grain of western thinking. For example, it is estimated that Zimbabwe lost some US$40 million in US aid for voting against the USA invasion of Grenada and for abstaining against voting on the Soviet shooting of a South Korean airliner.[39] At a farewell luncheon for the outgoing USA ambassador in April 1986, a speech read on behalf of the then Minister of Foreign Affairs attacked US policy on Angola and declared that Zimbabwe will not be controlled by any power. This precipitated a walkout by former USA President, Jimmy Carter, and USA officials attending the function, and suspension by the USA of its aid to Zimbabwe.[40] The IMF and World Bank continued to pressurise Zimbabwe to pursue more market-oriented policies, especially liberalising its trade regime.[41]

---

[38] Quoted in Mandaza, I. (ed,.) (1987), *Zimbabwe:The Political Economy of Transition, 1980-86*. Dakar: CODESRIA. 38.
[39] Sibanda, Arnold (1988) 'The Political Situation', in Stoneman Colin (ed.), op.cit. ft. 4.
[40] Ibid.
[41] Stoneman, Colin (1989) 'The World Bank and IMF in Zimbabwe,' in Campbell. Bonnie K. and J. Loxley (eds), *Structural Adjustment in Africa*. London: Macmillan Publishers.

The presence of a hostile neighbour, South Africa, also acted as a deterrent against the adoption of a radical approach. Hanlon[42] shows how South Africa destabilised its neighbours. He reports that at the time of the ZIMCORD donors' conference in March 1981, South Africa gave Zimbabwe one month's notice that it would not renew the bilateral trade agreement that had been in force since 1964. At the same time, South Africa stopped renewing contracts for Zimbabwean migrant workers and started sending them back home. An estimated 40,000 workers, and remittances worth about Z$25 million per year, were affected. Further, it is estimated that by March 1981 300,000 tonnes of Zimbabwean goods were stranded at South African ports. The technicians who had been seconded to Rhodesian Railways by South Africa were withdrawn and, on 4 April 1981, 24 diesel locomotives that had been leased to Rhodesian Railways were also withdrawn. Since the Beira-Mutare oil pipeline was not yet operational, the slowing down of goods from and to Zimbabwe (locomotive diplomacy) created fuel shortages in August 1981.[43] When this approach failed, South Africa changed strategy, ending its railway embargo in November 1981, and even leased 26 locomotives to its neighbours. To maintain Zimbabwe's dependence on it, South Africa used Renamo to attack the Beira-Mutare corridor. Faced with such destabilisation, Zimbabwe sent its troops to Mozambique to guard its trade routes at high cost. Under pressure like this, Zimbabwe adopted a cautionary, reconciliatory strategy.

More fundamentally, the forces calling for radical change were weak and ill organised, while those preferring the status quo were well organised locally, with powerful international links. In the ruling party, socialism was still being debated, with those opposed to it in the dominant position.[44] Government's plans reflected a contradiction in that while espousing radical rhetoric, they also were rooted in the status quo. In the words of Stoneman, post-independence plans '…were more matters of elucidating the pleasant ends desired than setting out the means for getting to them.'[45] Most unfortunately, the budget was not framed from the priorities set out in the development plans. As government itself noted, '…the present budgetary system was neither designed, nor is it easily adaptable, to meet the demands for planning, programming and budgeting required by Government's commitment to comprehensive planning.'[46] In fact, the budget was crafted in a veil of secrecy, with

---

[42] Hanlon, Joseph (1988) 'Destabilisation and the Battle for Reduced Dependence', in Stoneman,. op.cit. ft. 4.
[43] The oil pipeline was opened on 19 June 1982.
[44] Sibanda, op.cit. ft. 39 ; Mandaza, op.cit ft. 38.
[45] Stoneman, Colin (1988) 'The Economy: Recognising the Reality', in Stoneman (ed.), op.cit. ft. 4, 53.
[46] GoZ (1982) *Transitional National development Plan, 1982/83 – 1984/85*, Vol. 1 (November). 46.

parliament's role reduced to rubber-stamping. Even line Ministries were marginalised in its preparation. Worse still, the private sector and civil society were only 'consulted' through pre-budget meetings with Ministry of Finance officials, and their inputs were not taken seriously.

Within this tight framework, the government adopted a conservative programme that largely promoted the status quo. The inherited structures remained almost substantially unchanged, while government added a few state-owned corporations and provided social services. Radical rhetoric was only used to pacify the people. Thus, Lehman found that '...while in public he has espoused the arguments and rhetoric of the radical group, in private Mugabe has favoured the implementation of more orthodox policies.'[47] This view is supported by a US bank official who is reported to having observed that business '...seem to be impressed by and satisfied with Mugabe's management and the increased level of understanding in government of commercial considerations ... I feel it is a political pattern that Mugabe give radical, anti-business speeches before government makes major pro-business decisions or announcements.'[48] We may conclude with Nyawata that '...the rhetoric of politicians is a poor guide to a country's economic policy.'[49]

As a result, the aspirations of the people were largely abandoned '...as the African petit bourgeoisie (the ruling elite) began gradually to find access to the same economic and social status as their white counterparts so, too, did it become increasingly unable to respond effectively to the aspirations of the workers and peasants.'[50] These contradictions come out clearly with respect to foreign investment. Whereas on the one hand government was suspicious of foreign investment, at the same time it sought to attract it. In the words of Stoneman, '...the juxtaposition of socialist aims and the need for investment produces the bizarre implication that foreign capital may be attracted to help achieve such a revolution.'[51]

At the same time, the World Bank and IMF sustained pressure on the government. For example, it refused to sign an agreement for an extension of the export revolving fund in 1987 until measures were taken to liberalise trade. The World Bank's perseverance paid off with government adopting investment guidelines in April 1989 that marked a major shift in its policy. The establishment of the Zimbabwe Investment Centre in mid-1989, a move designed to create a 'one-stop' investment

---

[47] Lehman, H.P. (1990) 'The Politics of Adjustment in Kenya and Zimbabwe: The State as Intermediary', in *Studies in Comparative International Development*, 25: 3, 53.
[48] Quoted in Hanlon, op.cit. ft. 42, 35.
[49] Nyawata, Obert, I. (1988) 'Macroeconomic Management, Adjustment and Stabilisation,' in Stoneman Colin (ed.), op.cit. ft. 4, 115.
[50] Mandaza, op.cit. ft. 32. 51.
[51] Stoneman, C. (1988) ft. 4. 55.

window, followed this. When government signed the World Bank's *Multilateral Investment Guarantee Agency Convention* (MIGA) in September 1989, and in June 1990, signed the USA's *Overseas Private Investment Corporation (OPIC) Agreement* to reassure investors, it was already clear the game of hide-and-seek was up.

While there was general consensus on the need for reforms, there was no agreement on the form the reforms were to take in order to boost depressed investment, streamline inefficient labour regulations, and restructure the economy to achieve growth with equity, promote exports, and create employment.

The Economic Structural Adjustment Programme (ESAP): 1991-95

When it became clear that the economy was not generating sufficient jobs, especially in the context of depressed investment, government adopted a more market driven reform programme, ESAP, in 1991. Civil society was not consulted in the design of ESAP and most resented the programme. Even within government itself, the issue was not subjected to debate, and was largely confined to the Ministry of Finance.

The key objectives of ESAP were as follows:

- achieve GDP growth of 5 per cent during 1991-95
- raise savings to 25 per cent of GDP
- raise investment to 25 per cent of GDP
- achieve export growth of 9 per cent per annum
- reduce the budget deficit from over 10 per cent of GDP to 5 per cent by 1995
- reduce inflation from 17.7 per cent to 10 per cent by 1995

To achieve these key targets, the government started to liberalise trade and the financial and labour markets in line with the prescriptions of the World Bank and IMF. Price controls, subsidies, and other regulations were abandoned. Yet while the government implemented the standard stabilisation and adjustment measures, it did not stabilise its accounts as recommended. The issue of missed targets, with respect to the budget deficit, became one of the areas of perennial dispute between the government and the international financial institutions. As the IMF put it, '... a strengthening of fiscal policy, combined with an acceleration of public enterprise reforms, were prerequisites for Zimbabwe's return to its targeted adjustment path and the continuation of Fund support ...'.[52] Following lack of real progress in this area, the IMF suspended disbursement of funds under the Enhanced Structural Adjustment Facility

---

[52] International Monetary Fund, 1993: *World Economic Outlook*, Washington D.C, May. 1.

(ESAF) in September 1995 and put Zimbabwe on a shadow programme for the next six months. Since then, the relationship between Zimbabwe and the IMF has been on/off, culminating in the withdrawal of the Fund in 1999. Because of the government's failure to address the issue of public spending, some observers (mainly from business) have argued that ESAP itself did not fail; the government failed to implement it.

However, much as the government did not adhere to fiscal discipline, there were other more fundamental problems with ESAP, which go to the very design of these programmes. There were no broad based consultations on ESAP: it was largely imposed from above and so there was no national ownership of the programme. The performance of the economy under ESAP was dismal. Real economic growth decelerated from an average annual rate of 4 per cent during the period before ESAP (1985-90) to 0.9 per cent during the ESAP period. Employment grew at an annual average rate of 2.4 per cent during the period 1985-90 and slowed to an average annual rate of only 0.8 per cent during ESAP, way below the growth rate of the labour force at 3 per cent per annum. Inflation rose by an annual average rate of 27.6 per cent during the period of ESAP, compared to 11.6 per cent during the period 1985-90. The real earnings index, which averaged 100.6 during 1985-90, plummeted to an average index of 75.7 during the period of ESAP. The budget deficit deteriorated from 10 per cent of GDP at the onset of ESAP to 12.2 per cent by 1995. The target of reducing the budget deficit to 5 per cent of GDP by 1995 was far from achieved.

ESAP aimed at reducing subsidies to public enterprises from $629 million in 1990/91 to $40 million by 1994/95. The actual performance of these enterprises deteriorated during ESAP, with losses amounting to $2 billion in 1993/94 and $1.8 billion in 1994/95. The Grain Marketing Board, ZISCO, the National Railways of Zimbabwe, the Cold Storage Commission, and Affretair accounted for the bulk of the losses, which emanated from management inefficiencies and poor restructuring strategies. To finance the high budget deficit, government resorted to borrowing. As a result, debt outstanding rose sharply from 42.5 per cent of GDP in 1990, peaking at 82.6 per cent in 1993 before declining to a projected 66.9 per cent in 1995. The objective of ESAP with respect to the debt service ratio was to reduce it to below 20 per cent, yet it averaged 27.5 per cent during the period 1991-5. Whereas interest payments accounted for 12 per cent of government expenditure in 1990/91, this had risen to 22 per cent by 1994/95. This has had the effect of constraining government's discretionary expenditure, resulting in real declines in social expenditure, especially on health and education.

By restructuring incentives in favour of tradable rather than non-tradable goods, ESAP favoured the production of cash crops relative to food crops. During the 1980s, the government imported maize only in

1984/85, while during the 1990s the staple crop had to be imported each year except for 1990/91, 1994/95 and 1997/98. 1990/91 was before ESAP and so virtually the whole decade – and especially the ESAP period – was a time of a food deficit. Thus, by restructuring incentives in favour of cash crops, ESAP effectively transformed the economy from a food surplus to a food-deficit position.

Although the performance of the economy during the period 1991-95 cannot be wholly attributed to ESAP (there was a severe drought in 1992 and lack of fiscal discipline on the part of government), many of the outcomes can be traced to the policy prescriptions of the programme. The combined effect of high budget deficits, depreciating exchange rates, decontrol of prices, removal of subsidies, and poor supply response due to drought, delivered high levels of inflation. It rose from 15.5 per cent in 1990 to a peak of 42.1 per cent in 1992, before falling to 22.3 per cent and 22.5 per cent in 1994 and 1995. In the face of loose fiscal policy, this necessitated the maintenance of excessively high interest rates, which remained above 30 per cent for the period under review. The liberalisation of trade resulted in some de-industrialisation. While the manufacturing sector accounted for 20.5 per cent of GDP and 17 per cent of formal sector employment on the eve of ESAP in 1990, by 1995 the respective shares had declined to 18.8 per cent (12.7 per cent by 2000) and 15 per cent (14.7 per cent by 2000). The liberalisation of the labour market made it easy to retrench without paying meaningful compensation and the liberalisation of the financial sector resulted in the marginalisation of small-scale entrepreneurs, owing in part to the prevailing punitive interest rates and lack of collateral security. The *Structural Adjustment Participatory Review Initiative* (SAPRI) involving the government, the World Bank, and civil society, in a joint review of ESAP analysed the impact of the liberalisation of trade, the financial market, agriculture, the labour market, and the minimalist state on the economy. The findings show that the adverse impacts outweighed the limited positive ones, as suggested by the overall impact on poverty.

A study by the Central Statistical Office[53] found that the incidence of poverty had increased from 40.4 per cent in 1990/91 to 63.3 per cent by 1995/96.[54] The incidence of extreme poverty (households that cannot meet basic food requirements) increased from 16.7 per cent to 35.7 per cent during the respective periods. Similarly, the 1995 *Poverty Assessment Study Survey* (PASS) of the Ministry of Public Service, Labour and Social Welfare found that 61 per cent of households lived in poverty and 45 per cent in extreme poverty. Levels of poverty were higher in rural areas (75 per cent of households) than in urban areas (39 per cent of households). The incidence of poverty was found to be higher in

---

[53] CSO (1998) op.cit. ft. 16.

female-headed than male-headed households with levels of poverty of 72 per cent and 58 per cent respectively. The Social Development Fund, that was meant to provide safety nets to mitigate the adverse impacts of ESAP, failed for various reasons: its late design as an add-on, its poor resource base, and the failure to target the deserving poor. In the words of the World Bank, 'The SDF appeared to have been tacked on to ESAP more as an afterthought than as an integral part of the overall program.'[55] In this context, the social costs of adjustment were not mitigated at all. As the Bank further observed, ESAP '... entailed considerable pain but little visible gain'.[56] 'Unless the programme is seen to be generating benefits for everybody in Zimbabwe, it might not be possible to follow through with and maintain the momentum of many of the recent policy changes. This will require dealing more effectively with poverty and with the social dimensions of adjustment.'[57] The failure of ESAP to redress the inequalities inherent in the Zimbabwean economy meant that the majority of the people could not take advantage of the opportunities offered. This constituted a major impediment to the success of reforms.

A World Bank 'performance audit' of ESAP concedes:

> *The concerns ... go beyond the issues of pace and design: the comprehensiveness of the program seems a fundamental issue, especially given the objective of reducing poverty. Given the highly dualistic nature of Zimbabwe's economy (where the white minority dominates formal sector economic activity and owns two-thirds of high potential land, and the black majority is concentrated in rural, communal areas and the urban informal sector), it would appear that some basic questions were not explicitly addressed at the outset. First, would ESAP, predicated on the formal sector acting as an engine of growth create sufficient jobs, quickly enough, to address the serious problems of employment? ... Even realisation of the most optimistic scenarios for formal sector growth will not provide a quick solution to the unemployment problem.*[58]

In this regard, we may conclude with Kapoor, 'Given the weak implementation capacity in African economies, ... structural adjustment programs, in general, have unrealistic expectations about how fast adjustment can occur; consequently, the political costs of

---

[54] Here, the incidence of poverty is measured in terms of the number of households (and not people) whose incomes cannot meet the basic requirements for living.
[55] World Bank (1995) *Performance Audit Report: Zimbabwe Structural Adjustment Program*, Operations Evaluation Department, June. 23.
[56] Ibid. 10.
[57] Ibid. 18.
[58] Ibid. 11.

speedier implementation are also often underestimated.'[59] The emphasis of ESAP was, as in other SAPs, on 'getting prices right' and there was therefore over reliance on 'free markets'. But successful exporting requires 'the upgrading of export infrastructure, the provision of export finance, and the development of market intelligence.'[60] Export growth requires more than just depreciating the exchange rate. Lessons from South East Asia suggest that industrial development requires a strategic role of the state in guiding and leading the market through provision of incentives to those productive sectors offering the best returns (picking winners).

More importantly, the failure to consult other social partners hindered progress. In the words of the World Bank, 'The Zimbabwe case demonstrates the importance of popular ownership and participation throughout the process of adjustment. An open, transparent dialogue can help generate realistic expectations, reduce uncertainty, and contribute to a unified sense of national ownership for reforms.'[61] This consultation did not happen and, as the World Bank[62] found, ESAP was highly unpopular. The experiences with ESAP fit easily into the UNDP's analysis of market-driven outcomes the world over:

- jobless growth (growth that does not expand employment opportunities);
- ruthless growth (growth associated with increasing inequality and poverty);
- voiceless growth (growth in the absence of democracy or empowerment);
- rootless growth (growth that withers cultural identity); and
- futureless growth (growth that squanders resources needed by future generations.[63]

After some years in denial, the World Bank eventually admitted that ESAP had failed. Addressing the First Forum of the Structural Adjustment Participatory Review Initiative (SAPRI), on 2 September 1999, Tom Allen, the Resident Representative of the World Bank, admitted so much. He attributed its failure to the following:

- growth needs to be inclusive – 'Partial deregulation *without* a restructuring of the dual economy creates social tensions and not enough jobs';

---

[59] Ibid. 3. Kapil Kapoor was the chief economist of the World Bank in Harare during the period of ESAP.
[60] Ibid. 4.
[61] Ibid.
[62] UNDP (1996) Human Development Report, New York: UNDP and Oxford: Oxford University Press.
[63] Ibid.

- social sector expenditures need to be protected and targeted measures to deal with poverty should not be seen as 'add ons' but as an integral part of the programme;
- state intervention is necessary – 'getting the prices right and making markets work better are important, but these need to be complemented with measures to ensure that the 'unequal' balance of power of those who can readily engage in the market and those who cannot, does not lead to dangerous levels of social tension'; and
- national ownership is critical.

Although the Fund has moved much more slowly than the Bank, it is increasingly reforming its operations. In the light of the Asian crisis, even the IMF has changed its position, arguing vigorously for regulation of financial markets and calling for a new International Financial Architecture.[64] The IMF is increasingly talking about the need for good governance, national ownership of programmes, etc. In September 1999, at their annual meetings, the Fund and the Bank adopted a new Poverty Reduction and Growth Facility (PRGF)[65] that is supposed to be:

- country-driven, with the broad participation of civil society, elected institutions, key donors, and relevant International Financial Institutions (IFIs);
- developed from an understanding of the nature and determinants of poverty and the links between public actions and poverty outcomes;
- recognising the importance of rapid economic growth in sustaining poverty reduction;
- an oriented toward achieving outcome-related goals for poverty reduction.

Although most welcome, this initiative suffers from the following limitations:

- participation of civil society is subject to the discretion of governments;
- the PRGF is still based on the same orthodox macroeconomic framework; and
- while the Poverty Reduction Strategy Papers (PRSP) are prepared in a participatory manner, the PRGF itself is taken as given and is therefore not open for discussion. Participation has focused on the social issues, taking the macroeconomic framework as given (see for instance AFRODAD (2003), for an analysis and critique of PRSPs in ten African countries).

---

[64] See Finance and Development, IMF, Sept. 1999.
[65] PRGF will replace ESAP.

Onset of the Crisis: 1996-2003

Following the end of ESAP in 1995, there was indecision in terms of policy. The government made it abundantly clear that the term 'ESAP' should be discontinued. They realised ESAP was extremely unpopular and civil society in particular resisted it. It was not until April 1998 that a new economic policy, the Zimbabwe Programme for Economic and Social Transformation (ZIMPREST), was announced; however, the programme was supposed to run from 1996-2000, and so was already two years behind schedule when it was launched.

Although ZIMPREST emphasised the need for fiscal discipline on the part of the government, for parastatal and civil service reform, as well as stakeholder participation in the design of policies, this call was not heeded. ZIMPREST also identified – as critical to development – improvements in the quality of democratic institutions, the pursuit of good governance, and elimination of corruption. It sought to achieve an average annual GDP growth rate of 6 per cent, 42,200 new jobs in the formal sector per annum, per capita income growth of 3.4 per cent, and consumption growth of 4.4 per cent. To achieve the minimum target growth, the government was expected to reduce the budget deficit from 10 per cent to under 5 per cent of GDP, reduce inflation from over 20 per cent to a single digit level by the year 2000, achieve higher levels of savings and investment (an average of at least 23 per cent of GDP), export growth of at least 9 per cent per annum in US$, and raise the health budget from the average allocation of 2 per cent of GDP to at least 2.5 per cent. ZIMPREST's policy document warned that '...slippages in one area can have a profound impact on the success of actions in other areas'.[66]

It is now generally agreed that the events that precipitated the current crisis can be traced to the year 1997. As the World Bank observed, 'The unexpected and rapid deterioration of the economy since mid 1997 forced Bank assistance to Zimbabwe to be flexible and responsive, and has consequently differed from what was envisaged in the Country Assistance Strategy (CAS) dated May 1, 1997.'[67] What is often missing in analyses of the current crisis is its link to the hardships of ESAP and general failure over the years to articulate and translate the wishes of the majority into practical programmes. There are even heroic attempts at suggesting that ESAP was in fact on course, that the crisis is all about government's failure to rein in its expenditures and carry through civil service and parastatal reforms.[68] So it is essential that the crisis is examined within a historical perspective for its underlying causes to be correctly spelt out.

---

[66] GoZ (1998) ZIMPREST Policy Document. 7.
[67] World Bank (2000) Zimbabwe: Interim Strategy, 2000-1. Draft November. 2.
[68] See for instance government's policy documents on ZIMPREST, 1996-2000 and the Millennium Economic Recovery Programme (MERP), 2000-2001.

1997 was the turning point because it was the year civil society groups agitated visibly for their rights, which had been eroded under ESAP. In 1996, the longest and most acrimonious public sector strikes since independence occurred, especially involving health workers and teachers. And in 1997, 232 strikes were recorded, the largest number in any year since independence. Because of the widespread nature of these strikes and their high levels of mobilisation, the Employers' Confederation of Zimbabwe (EMCOZ) agreed with the ZCTU to hold a summit before negotiations with workers commenced. Both EMCOZ and the ZCTU realised the erosion of workers' purchasing power (inflation) was largely due to the imprudent fiscal policies of the government. The first of a series of joint meetings was held in March 1998, and the series helped reduce the number of strikes in subsequent years. This is illustrated in Table 4:[69]

Table 4: Strikes: 1991 to 2000[70]

	Jan	Feb	Mar	Apr	May	Jun	Jul	Aug	Sept	Oct	Nov	Dec	Total
1991												5	5
1992	1	2	2	0	1	3	1	0	1	0	0	3	14
1993	5	2	3	3	3		1	0	3	3			23
1994	2												2
1995	2	2	1	6	4	4	6	12	8	9	11		65
1996				12	9	6	8	3	4	13	7		62
1997	3	3	6	7	19	18	28	16	22	98	5	7	232
1998	6	9	21	9		20	3	3	16	10	5	17	119
1999	6	28	5	14	8	4	11	6	13	19	17	17	148
2000	5	12	14	8	16	12	10	22	10	9	12		130
Total	30	58	52	47	51	61	60	59	73	148	50	44	733

As a result of their disenchantment with lack of political space for civil society participation, and with lack of transparency and accountability, civil society groups came together and formed the National Constitutional Assembly (NCA) in May 1997. This marked the major turning point in relations between the state and civil society. For quite some time, war veterans had been complaining about being left out of the political landscape, to which the President would respond by

---

[69] Ministry of Public Service, Labour and Social Welfare, 2001.
[70] Ibid.

challenging them to compete with others for consideration. During the first half of 1997, the war veterans organised themselves and demonstrated to put their case forward. At first, the government ignored them. But then the demonstrations became increasingly raucous, culminating in the war veterans interrupting the President's speech at Heroes' Acre in August 1997. The demonstrations had become too loud and dangerous to ignore. The President reached an agreement with the war veterans in November 1997 whereby each of the estimated 50,000 ex-combatants was to receive a one-off gratuity of Z$50,000 by 31 December 1997 and a monthly pension of Z$2,000 beginning January 1998. Since this was not budgeted, the government sought to introduce a war veterans' levy, but workers rejected this through demonstrations organised by ZCTU. The government had to resort to borrowing to meet its new obligations.

Following the massive depreciation of the Z$ in 1997, agriculture input costs soared, undermining the viability of producers, who in turn demanded that the producer price of maize be raised. Millers then hiked prices by 24 per cent in January 1998 and the consequent increase in the price of maize-meal triggered nation-wide riots during the last week of the month. The government immediately intervened by introducing price controls on all basic commodities. The exchange rate was fixed at Z$38 to the US$.

In August 1998, the government sent Zimbabwean troops to the Democratic Republic of Congo (DRC) to help put down rebels, who were on the point of taking Kinshasa. The cost of involvement in the DRC was estimated at US$33 million a month. At the beginning of 2000, just before the referendum on the government's proposed new constitution, civil service salaries were increased by 69 to 90 per cent. Since there was no budget for such salary increases, the government had to borrow more money to meet this expenditure.

When Zimbabweans rejected the government proposed constitution in the referendum of February 2000, the government deliberately encouraged the occupation of farms by war veterans and other pro-government elements. This followed accusations by the government that white farmers had provided transport for their workers to vote against the proposed new constitution. From the chronology of developments, it is clear that the land invasions were a vendetta against the white farmers for openly supporting and facilitating the opposition. Realising that its support base was dwindling, government embarked on the fast-track land resettlement programme. Since then, there has been a breakdown in the rule of law and the period before, during and after the June 2000 parliamentary elections was characterised by violence and intimidation. 'Project money' was disbursed at ZANU PF rallies as a way of attracting voters. Since the Ministry of Gender, Youth and Employment Creation was disbursing the money, it was obviously public money from the national budget. The impact of these political decisions was particularly acute with respect to the budget deficit. It progressively deteriorated from 5.5 per cent of GDP in 1998 to 24.1 per cent by the end of 2000. The deficit had been targeted to decline to 3.8 per cent by the end of 2000. Domestic debt, which stood at Z$24.5 billion in 1995 shot up to Z$347 billion by end of 2002. The country accumulated arrears on its foreign debt repayments in 1999, which rose to US$1.3 billion by December 2002. Again, politically motivated violence characterised the period before, during and after the March 2002 Presidential elections, whose result, the re-election of President Mugabe, was highly contested.

Against this background, the relationship between Zimbabwe and its development partners deteriorated such that the country earned itself a high-risk profile (pariah status), resulting in the acute shortage of foreign currency. The breakdown of the rule of law and the anti-western rhetoric led to the relationship between Zimbabwe and the powerful western economies reaching an unprecedented low level. As a result, a thriving parallel market emerged, which virtually became the only port of call for seekers of foreign currency.

Clearly, the performance of the Zimbabwean economy is at odds with the general trend in the rest of the world. The global economy grew in real terms by 2.5 per cent in 1998, 2.8 per cent in 1999, 4.7 per cent in 2000, 2.2 per cent in 2001, 2.8 per cent in 2002, and a projected 3.2 per cent in 2003 and 4.1 per cent in 2004. World inflation is on a downward trend. Global inflation averaged at 1.6 per cent in 2003 and a projected 1.8 per cent in 2004.

Even Africa is experiencing similar good economic fortunes. Whereas real output grew at an annual average rate of 1.2 per cent during the period 1991-94, it accelerated to an average annual rate of growth of 3.9 per cent during the period 1995-98. Real economic growth for Africa improved from 2.8 per cent in 1999 to 4.9 per cent in 2000 and 4.3 per cent in 2001. While 26 African countries achieved growth rates above the 'traditional' 3 per cent in 2000, the number increased to 37 in 2001 and 40 in 2002. Inflation in Zimbabwe was at 198.9 per cent in December 2002 and rose to 623 per cent in January 2004. In comparison, inflation in Africa as a whole averaged 12.6 per cent for the same period. As for SADC, growth averaged 2.6 per cent in 2003 and inflation 15.3 per cent. The latter is projected to decline to 8.1 per cent in 2004. These considerations all reinforce the conclusion that Zimbabwe's current economic crisis (cf. Table 5) is self-inflicted: it is closely tied to the deteriorating conditions of domestic governance. The timing and persistence of the economic plunge is closely linked to the deteriorating political environment since late 1997.

Table 5: Key Economic Indicators, 1995-2003[71]

	1995	1996	1997	1998	1999	2000	2001	2002	2003*
Real GDP (%)	0.2	9.7	1.4	0.8	-4.1	-6.8	-9.5	-14.7	-14.0
Per Person Real (1990) GDP US$	235	220	180	90	55	42	32	28	26
Inflation (%)	22.5	21.7	18.9	31.7	58.5	55.9	71.9	133.2	365
Savings/GDP %	22.4	16.9	10.3	18.0	19.3	12.1	0.8	4.3	4.3
Investment/GDP (%)	25.3	17.4	18.8	22.3	17.1	13.5	10.3	8.9	8.5
Budget deficit / GDP (%)	-12.2	-7.7	-8.2	-5.5	-7.7	-24.1	-8.2	-13.8	>14.0
External payment arrears US$m	-	-	-	-	109.0	471.1	762.7	1333.3	-
Domestic debt Z$bn	24.7	33.2	31.4	44.2	77.6	162.1	194.1	345.8	590.9
Foreign debt US$m	4001	4141	4117	3841	3285	3164	3180	4503	-
Export growth (%)	13.8	12.6	-2.9	-20.6	-0.1	14.3	-28.5	-10.8	-5.3
BOP US$m	44	4	-739	-283	9	-166	-197	-1182	-825
Employment growth (%)	-1.9	2.8	5.6	-0.1	-2.3	-5.9	-0.6	-	-

Virtually all economic indicators point to a downward trend, beginning in 1997. This downturn is particularly acute in more recent years. Total external debt increased from US$3.1 billion in 1991 to almost US$5 billion by 1997, before falling to US$3.5 billion by 2000. This decline reflects the drying up of traditional sources of external finance following the fall-out with the IMF and subsequent withdrawal of development partners. Thereafter, it rose slightly to just over US$3.7 billion by 2002 and to about US$4 billion by end of November 2003. As shown above, Zimbabwe accumulated external repayment arrears of US$109 million in 1999, rising to US$1.3 billion by end of 2002. The total external debt to GDP ratio averages 62.9 per cent during the period 1991-2002, while the debt service ratio averages 24.8 per cent during the same period. The World Bank argues that debt repayment difficulties are likely to occur when the debt service ratio is within the 20-25 per cent range. As at end of 2002, Zimbabwe's debt service ratio of 31 per cent is way

---

[71] Selected Economic Indicators, the Reserve Bank of Zimbabwe, Jan 2003. Asterisk* denotes estimates; BOP is Balance of Payments.

above the World Bank's threshold. The country's debt service obligations for 2002, at US$508 million, are way above the budgetary allocations for health and education.

Domestic debt rose sharply from Z$24.7 billion in 1995 to Z$345.8 billion by 2002 and Z$607.1 billion by December 2003. Over time, there has been a marked shift in the composition of domestic debt as government increasingly resorted to short-term instruments. Whereas short-term treasury bills accounted for 3.9 per cent of the total debt in 1990, their share rose to 53.4 per cent in 1995, 88.1 per cent in 1999 and 94.5 per cent by December 2000. In December 2000, government undertook to restructure domestic debt towards longer-dated maturities. By December 2002, reliance had shifted towards 2-year treasury notes, as opposed to 90-day treasury bills. Of the Z$607.1 billion domestic debt as at 5 December 2003, 94.6 per cent is in the form of short-term treasury bills (Z$574.5 billion), 2.4 per cent in government stocks (Z$14.6 billion) and 3 per cent was overdraft from the Reserve Bank (Z$17.9 billion). The predominance of short-term instruments reflects difficulties encountered in issuing longer-term instruments in a highly inflationary context (see RBZ, 2002). Risk-averse investors shunned the issue of stocks given the attendant uncertainty related to high levels of inflation, leaving treasury bills as the only available option. With an estimated 44 per cent of total expenditure or 14 per cent of GDP in the 2001 national budget going towards interest repayments alone, substantial resources are tied up in servicing the debt. In his monetary policy statement of 18 December 2003, the new Governor of the Reserve Bank, Gideon Gono indicated that several ideas were being considered to deal with the domestic debt overhang, namely:

- issuance of a zero-coupon bond, which investors purchase at a discount and on which they received no interest over the tenure of the bond, only the full amount after a five year period; and
- converting the domestic debt into foreign debt. Friendly countries would issue foreign currency denominated bonds in the international capital markets, which would be sold to the Reserve Bank, and the local currency used to pay off the domestic debt, while the foreign currency would be used to pay off part of the foreign debt or meet required imports.[72]

Clearly, therefore, Zimbabwe is in a serious debt crisis, with far-reaching implications.

---

[72] RBZ (2003) *Monetary Policy Statement*, Issued by Dr. G. Gono, Governor, Reserve Bank of Zimbabwe, 18 December. 46-48.

Attempts at addressing the Crisis

Since the advent of the current crisis, there have been numerous attempts at resolving it. Some were spearheaded by civil society, while others were from government. As far back as 1995, the ZCTU came up with its 'Beyond ESAP Study'. One of the suggestions in the ZCTU proposals was the establishment of a consultative forum for stakeholder dialogue and consultations. In October 1996, the ZCTU facilitated a tripartite study visit of the National Economic Development and Labour Council (NEDLAC) of South Africa. Following this initiative, the three parties (ZCTU, the Ministry of Public Service, Labour and Social Welfare, and EMCOZ) started working on how to create a similar initiative in Zimbabwe. At the same time, the business sector was contemplating the creation of something similar.

The President's Office took over the initiatives and started co-ordinating the process. It was agreed that the new forum, to be called the National Economic Consultative Forum (NECF), would comprise organised labour, business, NGOs, academia, and government. At the launch of the forum on 9 July 1997, it became clear that the representation on the forum was on individual basis, and not institutional, a development that was contrary to the agreed position. When the ZCTU sought clarification on the matter, the government was not ready to compromise, so the ZCTU withdrew from the forum and boycotted its first conference held on 22 January 1998. The ZCTU organised a two-day stay-away in March 1998, calling for the removal of the increase in sales tax of 2.5 per cent to fund the war veterans' package and the development levy. A stalemate led to employers approaching the government in August 1998 to forestall further stay-aways and, as a result, the Tripartite Negotiating Forum (TNF) was formed in September 1998. The TNF reached the following agreement:

- to remove the development levy with effect from 1 January 1999;
- to remove the 2.5 per cent increase in sales tax with effect from 1 November 1998;
- to defer the 15 per cent tax on pension funds pending further studies;
- to increase the tax threshold to Z$2,000 per month, implying that those earning up to that level would be exempted from paying income tax; and
- to increase the bonus free component from Z$1,100 to Z$2,000 with effect from 1 November 1998.

Towards the end of September 1998, fuel prices were hiked by 67 per cent, increasing inflation. Irked by the erosion of the packages agreed in the TNF, the ZCTU organised a stay-away in November 1998 and threatened weekly stay-aways on Wednesdays. The TNF was quickly reconvened to discuss the fuel situation among other issues. The government admitted that there was a lot of corruption at the state-owned fuel procurement organisation, NOCZIM, and promised to it clean up. Yet nothing was done. Realising that the government was not prepared to deal with the underlying causes of economic decay, fiscal indiscipline, and bad governance, the ZCTU and at least 40 other civic groups organised a Working People's Convention at which they agreed to form a 'broad based movement for change'. This movement, which was named the Movement for Democratic Change (MDC) was officially launched in August 1999. After the launch of the MDC, the political landscape of the country was never the same again. The ruling party, realising the massive support the MDC had, resorted to terror tactics. The turning point was the February 2000 referendum, which amply demonstrated that the political pendulum was swinging in favour of the opposition.

As the economic crisis deepened, the TNF was reconvened in October 1999 to explore the possibilities of developing and signing a binding Social Contract. On the 19 January 2000, the three social partners signed a Declaration of Intent, which outlined the obligations of the parties. The ZCTU withdrew from the negotiations, citing lack of seriousness on the part of government as evidenced by the continued violence. However, following the 70 per cent increase in fuel prices of June 2001, the ZCTU organised a two-day stay-away in July, which resulted in the reconvening of the TNF. The parties agreed on national minimum wages for agriculture, and industry and commerce based on the June 2001 Poverty Datum Levels of Z$4,000 and Z$8,900 respectively. The parties also agreed to negotiate viable prices with producers since price controls had failed. But, even as the negotiations were going on, government slapped price controls on all basic commodities. As with the controls introduced in 1998, these too failed and instead created shortages, which resulted in a thriving, parallel market. Ministry of Industry and International Trade officials were openly castigated by the President for supporting a negotiated approach to price controls. They were seen as being sympathetic to 'profiteering' firms.

Meanwhile, the social partners under the TNF, realising that the problem was political, agreed to go on a retreat to discuss what they termed the 'political risk factor'. The three social partners, labour, business and government were requested to prepare detailed position papers on the 'political risk factor'. What emerged after the synthesis of the positions is the Kadoma Declaration, which highlighted the need to restore relations with development partners, the rule of law and good governance. The declaration was not signed, however, following misunderstandings between the government and labour over continued violence, and especially the facilitation of a rival trade union body, the Zimbabwe Federation of Trade Unions (ZFTU).

In the 2003 national budget statement, the Minister of Finance and Economic Development, Herbert Murerwa, observed with respect to price controls,

> *Efforts to protect the consumer from spiralling prices are being undermined by price controls that focus mostly on the final product, ignoring developments affecting inputs into the production process. This has affected production viability and the sustainability of the controlled price levels. As a result, the real costs to society have been high and include the following:*
>
> - *Shortages of critical basic commodities on the formal market. Where these are available, they are not easily accessible to the majority of the poor since they are not traded openly.*
> - *A thriving parallel market for basic commodities, where the price is much higher than the controlled price. This is the market where a significant part of our population is sourcing basic commodities. The beneficiaries of the price controls are, therefore, the speculators and dealers and not the targeted vulnerable groups.*
> - *Production of lower quality products as producers are forced to 'shave inputs' in order to maintain profit margins against a backdrop of rising input costs.*
> - *Loss of employment opportunities as companies downsize production capacity in view of viability problems accessioned by unsustainable price control levels.*[73]

In a move that contradicted the budget statement, the government published Statutory Instrument (SI) 302 of 2002 on Control of Goods (Price Freeze) Order on 15 November 2002. The SI extended the list of items covered by the price freeze, which was for a period of six months. During the TNF meetings that commenced in December 2002, the government tried unsuccessfully to have stakeholders buy into the idea of a price and wage freeze, an issue taken up below. In his address at the opening of the 52nd ZANU PF central committee meeting in Chinhoyi on 11 December 2002, the President attacked business and blamed it for hyperinflation: 'While many manufacturers and traders want to blame it on production costs, it is clear that the consumer is being ripped off, abused and taken advantage of by avaricious heartless business people, several of whom would want to politicise production processes in sympathy with white landed interest.'[74]

---

[73] Ibid. 14-15.
[74] *The Herald*, 12 December 2002, 1.

In an attempt to go it alone, the government launched its Millennium Economic Recovery Programme (MERP) early in 2000. MERP is an 18-month programme that was supposed to run concurrently with the Millennium Budget announced on 21 October 1999. Its vision is to mobilise all stakeholders – government, business, labour, and civil society – to implement a set of measures designed to restore macroeconomic stability. MERP builds on the fiscal policy adjustment targets under ESAP (1991-95), ZIMPREST, and the Millennium Budget announced on 21 October 1999.

Five principles are outlined in MERP:
- the prime responsibility for the implementation of the programme is with government and stakeholders;
- it commits itself to use market forces in the allocation and pricing of goods and services, with limited government intervention;
- where required, direct market interventions will be for a limited duration and confined to resolving the market distortion: market institutions will be developed to allocate resources efficiently;
- costs of adjustment will be equitably shared amongst social groups; and
- the programme will use balanced and flexible strategies to resolve macroeconomic imbalances.

MERP is presented as a continuation of the commitments and targets of ESAP and ZIMPREST, without 'problematising' these programmes. In the sections that evaluated ESAP and ZIMPREST – and in the one that draws lessons from the first decade of reforms – the problems are presented as a failure of implementation. MERP argues, 'Implementation of the two previous reform programmes (ESAP 1 and II) lacked both co-ordination and commitment at all institutional levels resulting in the missing of targets by wide margins.'[75] Delays in rationalising the civil service, privatisation, and commercialisation are presented as the 'culprits'.

The issue is going beyond 'sequencing' problems, to the very design of these programmes. The targets set are quantitative, not qualitative, and it is important to focus on qualitative, human-centred indicators, which reflect the ultimate goal of development. In the design of MERP, the recovery programme contends, 'in addition to the policy measures on economic structural adjustment which government has been implementing since 1990, the design of the current programme regards broad macro-economic stabilisation targets agreed with international co-operating partners, including those contained in the millennium budget, as essential parameters'.[76] This flies in the face of the principle of stakeholder participation and national ownership of programmes.

---

[75] GoZ, (2000) *Millennium Economic Recovery Programme 2000-2001*. 63.
[76] Ibid. 16: 3.1.

As was the case with ZIMPREST, MERP has largely been ignored. The target of MERP, as that of the 2000 budget, was to reduce the budget deficit to 3.8 per cent of GDP. MERP sought to allocate at least 25 per cent of total expenditures to capital projects. However, in the millennium budget, the capital budget was allocated 8 per cent of total expenditures, down from 11 per cent in 1999. The capital budget amounted to 4 per cent of total expenditures in 2001, 8.1 per cent in 2002, 10 per cent in 2003, and 11.3 per cent in 2004.

In his address to parliament in August 2001, the President announced that government was now implementing a ten-point strategy, which was agriculturally driven. But the strategy remained largely a mystery, with the then Minister of Finance and Economic Development, Simba Makoni, insisting that MERP was still alive. Statements from the Ministry of Finance suggested that the government was pursuing a market-friendly strategy that eschews controls, while pronouncements from the President indicated that controls were in effect. That in itself clearly showed the extent of policy contradictions within government and the existence of two diametrically opposed views on how to manage the economy.

In a move to project a problem-solving approach on the part of government, the new cabinet after the parliamentary elections of June 2000, incorporated technocrats. But it soon became clear that they could not change the wheels of government and two of the leading ones, from whom much was expected, Nkosana Moyo and Simba Makoni, resigned in frustration. After the presidential elections of March 2002, a new 'war-cabinet' was unveiled on 24 August 2002, ostensibly to defend the government's position.

All these efforts at addressing the crisis foundered because they dared to suggest a course of action at odds with the preferences of the President. The presidential approach is that the current crisis is emanating from efforts by the west to re-colonise Zimbabwe. This position sees businesses as part of the problem because they formed cartels that are profiteering at the expense of the people; it is articulated in the MERP document and in the ZANU PF manifesto, and has characterised most of the President's speeches. In MERP, the crisis is seen in the context of 'deleterious effects of neo-imperialist machinations aimed at limiting national sovereignty over the redistribution of national assets such as land in favour of indigenous Zimbabweans. These machinations are aimed at frustrating national efforts to transform the Zimbabwean economy so that it cannot reach higher levels of development as well as withstand acts of economic destabilisation.'[77] The challenge is seen as 'the development of a capacity to break the current siege imposed by co-operating partners who are withholding much needed development assistance, mainly for political

---

[77] Ibid. 13: 1.3.

reasons. This international antagonism has been accompanied by well-orchestrated negative publicity intended to scare away foreign investments.'[78] Profiteering and unfair business practices and business cartels are also identified as part of the problem. MERP argues that well-meant economic reforms such as liberalisation have been 'exploited by crime syndicates and corrupt businesses who illegally externalise funds, destabilise foreign exchange markets through speculative behaviour which in some cases is foreign inspired in order to frustrate economic stabilisation efforts by government. Amidst these challenges, the Zimbabwean people have proved to be very resilient. The country is united under a visionary leadership.'[79]

This position sees the country as engaged in a war and sees violence as a useful tool in dealing with discontent; it sees price and other controls as the only way of dealing with the crisis. It is in this context that the President, in a direct rebuttal of his finance minister's stance, labelled those calling for the devaluation of the Z$ enemies of the State. The ruling party has reduced the whole issue to land, and hence its slogan that 'Land is the economy, and the economy is land'. In other words, it exonerates the mismanagement of the economy on the basis that the people did not have what matters: land. Asked in an interview with *The Sunday Mail* of 19 January 2002, what they are planning to do about the deepening crisis the Minister of Information, Jonathan Moyo, stated that there was no need to develop new policies. What needs to be done is already in the ZANU PF manifesto. He went on to blame bureaucrats for not implementing the manifesto.

The policies flowing from this position have been a disaster. The closure of the bureaux de change at the end of November 2002, and the new policy that directs exporters to surrender all foreign currency to the Reserve Bank and get reimbursed at the official exchange rate of Z$55 to the US$ has backfired. Table 5 opposite shows the weekly inflow of foreign currency during 2002.

Foreign currency inflows dropped massively following the measures announced in the budget statement of 14 November. The land reform programme experienced its own problems, such as multiple claimants to one piece of land, lack of inputs (the input scheme required Z$60 billion, yet the 2003 budget only allocated Z$12.5 billion to it) and the drought. Given this scenario, the focus on 'Land is the economy, and the economy is land' is problematic. It exacerbates the crisis in the short term. To make matters even worse, the deal with Libya to provide fuel faltered, with petrol and diesel queues part of everyday life until recently. Most parastatals are reportedly in dire straits, requiring urgent assistance

---

[78] Ibid. 1.4.
[79] Ibid. 14: 1.7.

Table 6: *Official foreign exchange inflows (US$ million): 2002*[80]

Week ending	Inflows
May 31	11.7
June 14	13.8
June 21	11.6
June 28	15.0
July 5	10.7
July 12	18.0
July 19	15.5
August 2	16.5
September 13	14.1
September 27	18.5
October 4	12.3
October 11	14.9

at a time when resources are hard to obtain. The measures announced in 2003, whereby exporters surrender all their foreign exchange earnings to the Reserve Bank, have resulted in serious viability problems, especially in the mining sector. Most tellingly, during its annual close down in December 2002, industry issued an ultimatum that some firms may not re-open after the festive season.

With businesses on the brink, the CZI cobbled together a last gasp economic recovery paper, which was presented as a matter of urgency to Acting President Simon Muzenda at the end of December 2002. The document is entitled 'Government and Business Partnership on Key Economic Issues' and is dated 20 December 2002. In the proposal, business offers to support government's agrarian reform, in return for an active partnership with government (including regular meetings with the President). The proposal insists on consultations on key issues as part of confidence building. To make the deal attractive, business offered to regulate itself on the basis of a Position Charter, to pursue price management (as opposed to controls), to raise off-shore lines supported by export earnings, to minimise foreign exchange leakages, to proportionately reduce prices when the exchange rate has been reduced and stabilised, and to share notes with other key stakeholders such as TNF. The main issue in the proposal is the suggestion on export incentives.

---

[80] Unpublished data.

The first 50 per cent of exporters' earnings would be exchanged at the official rate of Z$55 to the US$, while the second 50 per cent would be the favourable rate of Z$800 to the US$. For mining, a higher rate of Z$1350 to the US$ is proposed for the second 50 per cent. To raise the stakes, the president of CZI, Anthony Mandiwanza, reportedly threatened to resign from his post at the CZI if these last-ditch measures are not implemented.[81]

These efforts coincided in December 2002 with the reconvening of the TNF. A technical sub-committee of the TNF went on a retreat to develop a draft Prices and Incomes Stabilisation Protocol in January 2003, which was the basis for subsequent negotiations. The three social partners officially signed the protocol on 30 January 2003. The proposal was that prices would be managed on a viability basis and wages and salaries would be negotiated by 28 February 2003 for the period up to June 2003, the proposed date of expiry of the protocol. In addition, the protocol called on the social partners to negotiate minimum wages based on an updated Poverty Datum Line (PDL). For its part, the government pledged to reduce the deficit to 11 per cent of GDP and inflation to 96 per cent amongst other steps. Labour and business also acquired obligations under the protocol.

Apart from the Prices and Incomes Stabilisation Protocol, the TNF also agreed to sign and put into effect the Kadoma Declaration and the Declaration of Intent signed in January 2000 on what has to be done to deal with the 'political risk factor'. This included among other things the restoration of the rule of law and good governance, the depoliticisation of public institutions, and the restoration of relations with development partners. Clearly, therefore, the TNF's position was that the precondition for sustained stabilisation and recovery lay in addressing issues of governance and pursuit of mutually agreed economic policies. Because of its strong political overtones, it is not surprising that the TNF's recommendations were largely ignored since it dared to define a path at loggerheads with the position of the President.

Apart from the Protocol and the Kadoma Declaration, the TNF also came up with immediate measures to resuscitate the economy, including the readjustment of the exchange rate from Z$55 to the US$ to Z$824 to the US$, which was adopted by government. On the 19 February 2003, the Productivity Centre and Movement were launched under the auspices of the TNF. On the basis of the request by the TNF for the Ministry of Finance and Economic Development to come up with short-term measures to deal with the crisis, government launched the National Economic Revival Programme (NERP) in February 2003. In its preamble, NERP acknowledges that 'the country is facing severe socio-economic

---

[81] Following discussions in the TNF, the idea of multiple exchange rates has been replaced by a single inflation-consistent exchange rate of Z$700 to the US$.

challenges'.[82] It contends that the crisis has been compounded by the existence of 'a hostile external and domestic environment, arising from our detractors' opposition to our Land and Agrarian Reform Programme' and sanctions.[83] This external focus of the diagnosis of the causes of the crisis is also reflected in paragraph 10, which argues, 'Furthermore, the negative perceptions of our detractors and their portrayals of our land reforms internationally have dented the country's image. Confidence in the economy is at its lowest ebb as a result, adversely affecting private investment and tourism.'[84] This diagnosis is at variance with that in the Kadoma Declaration, and indeed in the TNF, which focuses on issues of governance, suggesting that the causes of the crisis are internal.

NERP correctly observes that coupled with poor export performance, there has been a failure to provide adequately for fuel, electricity, food, drugs, spares, capital, and equipment. The document notes, 'if not urgently addressed, foreign exchange unavailability will lead to national instability and pose a threat to national security'.[85] NERP points out that the manifestations of the crisis as characterised by economic decline, external arrears, unemployment, worsening poverty levels, high growth of money supply, and related hyperinflation and acute shortage of foreign exchange.

As a way forward, NERP endorsed the principles already agreed at the TNF level, such as price management, based on ensuring:
+ increased viability of companies to sustain production; and
+ protection of consumers through guaranteed availability and affordability of products.

It also adopted measures to give incentives to exporters and to attract remittances from Zimbabweans abroad. The multiplicity of prevailing commodity support schemes, were collapsed into a uniform Export Support Scheme. The 50:50 arrangement whereby exporters retain 50 per cent of export earnings and surrender the other 50 per cent was retained.

The other immediate measures identified by the TNF to revive the economy included the introduction of a Production and Export Facility with government availing through the Reserve Bank Z$50 billion and another Z$50 billion coming from the financial and banking sector as agreed under the TNF. NERP endorsed the dual interest rate policy announced by the Reserve Bank in November 2002. It made the following additions:
• narrowing the high spreads between deposit and lending rates;

---

[82] GoZ (2003) NERP, 1.
[83] Ibid. 2.
[84] Ibid. 3.
[85] Ibid. 1.

- reviewing upwards deposit interest rates to encourage savings;
- reviewing upwards rates on consumption and speculative activities; and
- reviewing the proliferation of service charges levied on depositors.

NERP undertook to put in place commercialisation processes for public enterprises by March 2003 and set quantifiable performance targets. This objective was agreed in the TNF and was inserted into the Prices and Incomes Stabilisation Protocol as part of the obligations of government. It was agreed that once these were established, the TNF had to endorse the programme and monitor its implementation.

Paragraph 135 of NERP states, 'In future, fuel prices will be reviewed within magnitudes determined through the Tripartite Negotiating Forum.'[86] However, this was violated. On 25 February 2003, government unilaterally announced a fuel price hike of almost 100 per cent, followed by another of over 200 per cent on 15 April 2003. Irked by the continued unilateral decisions of government, ZCTU demanded the reversal of the latter increase and organised a three-day stay-away from 23-25 April 2003. At the same time, ZCTU announced that it had withdrawn from the TNF until the fuel price hike was reversed. The business sector also raised its disquiet with the violation of the Prices and Incomes Stabilisation Protocol, especially considering that fuel is a significant input in the production process and hence its cost affects all other prices. In a bid to pacify labour, government and business met on 24 April, the second day of the stay-away, and agreed to introduce new minimum wages. Business only agreed to the new minimum wages on condition that the price controls were lifted, which was granted. However, ZCTU rejected the new minimum wages, arguing that they were now outdated being based on January Poverty Datum Levels. The government announced that apart from the basic commodities that would remain under price controls, all other commodity prices were decontrolled. Since then, the TNF has not sat again and the relationship between the State and the ZCTU remains strained.

Yet another attempt at resolving the crisis arises from the appointment of Dr Gideon Gono as the Governor of the Reserve Bank in December 2003 and the launch of his monetary policy statement on the 18th of that month. Like the 2004 budget statement, the new bank policy emphasises the need to stabilise the macro-economy, pledging to reduce inflation to 170-200 per cent by end of 2004. The monetary policy statement also focuses on the need for prudential regulation of the financial sector. A new auction system for foreign exchange was introduced to commence in mid-January 2004.

---

[86] Ibid. 40.

While much has been said with regard to monetary policy, there has been a tendency at the official level to over-emphasise its effectiveness as a tool of economic stabilisation. The foreign exchange auction system, with its lower and upper ceilings within which the exchange rate fluctuates, has reduced the parallel market rate that applied up to December 2003, but it will not stabilise the macro-economy on its own. The limitation of the auction system is that it aims at mopping up foreign exchange that was not flowing through the official channels, without addressing the supply of that foreign currency. Furthermore, in the absence of a complementary fiscal policy, it is not possible to achieve macro-economic stability. As with past attempts, economic policies on their own will not achieve sustainable outcomes if they are not combined with an attempt to resolve the political crisis. A settlement between the two main parties, ZANU PF and MDC, is the only way of creating a political environment that promotes stability, recovery, and growth. As things stand, it is expecting too much to put faith in 'technocratic' solutions.

The way forward

It is clear that a political settlement between the major political parties is a prerequisite for the return to normalcy in Zimbabwe. Various attempts at resolving the crisis have hitherto failed. The underlying causes of the crisis lie in the failure to bring into the mainstream of the economy the majority of the people. Since independence, government policies failed to address the inherited dual (separate) and enclave (isolated) economy. This is underscored by the fact that an estimated 85 per cent of Zimbabweans are living below the poverty line. Clearly, therefore, the economy is not benefiting the majority of the people.

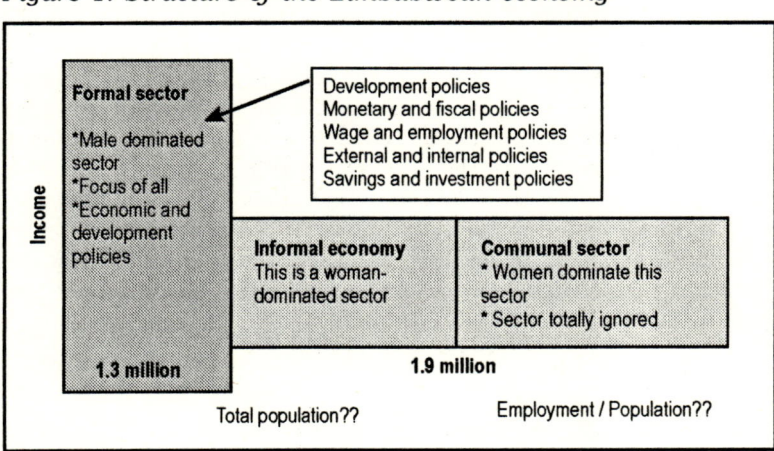

Figure 1: Structure of the Zimbabwean economy

| Income | Formal sector
*Male dominated sector
*Focus of all
*Economic and development policies | Development policies
Monetary and fiscal policies
Wage and employment policies
External and internal policies
Savings and investment policies |
|---|---|---|
| | | Informal economy
This is a woman-dominated sector | Communal sector
* Women dominate this sector
* Sector totally ignored |
| | 1.3 million | 1.9 million |
| | Total population?? | Employment / Population?? |

By focusing on the formal sector, which is male-dominated, past policies have neglected the non-formal sectors that accommodate the majority of the population, and especially women. They have therefore reinforced the inherited dual and enclave structure of the economy. This has resulted in a highly skewed distribution of resources.

It is therefore necessary to incorporate the hitherto excluded sectors and groups (women, children, youths, and people living with disabilities) into the mainstream of the economy. This can be achieved by:

- economic empowerment through access to land, capital and appropriate technology and entrepreneurship;
- building infrastructure(roads, electricity, water, etc.) in hitherto disadvantaged areas;
- strengthening the capacity of local government and government structures to deliver requisite services;
- focusing on people, the ultimate goal of development, and not merely on achieving growth (human-centred development policy): this approach prioritises the attainment of basic social and economic rights, such as the right to food security, health, education, housing, reliable transport, water and electricity;
- internalising the source of growth (shifting from debt-driven or externally driven growth strategies) through economic empowerment; and
- broad-based community participation in decision-making, implementation, monitoring and evaluation processes.

While land redistribution has occurred, it has not empowered the beneficiaries to utilise the land productively through provision of inputs. It is necessary to depoliticise the land redistribution exercise by appointing a Land Commission to spearhead the redistribution programme and correct the new anomalies created as the politically privileged grabbed highly productive land and acquired several farms.

In order for economic policy to benefit the marginalised, it is necessary to establish aninstitutional framework for stakeholder participation in decision-making, implementation, monitoring and evaluation, along the lines of the National Economic Development and Labour Council (NEDLAC) of South Africa. The existing National Economic Consultative Forum (NECF) suffers from a lack of institutional representation and has therefore been reduced to a talk shop. NECF was established as the current crisis was starting in 1997, and has generally presided over the demise of the economy. Its various resolutions have not made any meaningful change in policy direction.

Travails of opposition politics in Zimbabwe since Independence

Eldred Masunungure

'The hardest lesson of my life has come to me late. It is that a nation can win freedom without its people becoming free.'
Joshua Nkomo[1]

Introduction

Politics is fundamentally about power, its capture, maintenance and loss. In one of his seminal works, *The Anatomy of Power* (1983), John Kenneth Galbraith wrote 'Modern society is in equilibrium, more or less, between those who exercise power and those who counter it, ... power creates its own resistance.'[2] Where you have a party in power, all things being equal, you are likely to have countervailing centres of power in opposition. At Zimbabwe's independence, in an atmosphere of virtually unrestrained euphoria, ZANU PF captured power and has maintained it ever since. However, in the last four years, the ruling party has faced the real prospect of losing power. Its response has been vicious. Power created its own resistance.

I wish in this chapter to study the fate of opposition politics in Zimbabwe. One disclaimer should be made at the start. Opposition politics are not the same as organised opposition parties. Opposition politics is broader and more inclusive. While it may be organised, it may also be unorganised (even disorganised), informal, anomic or irregular. Stayaways, mass actions, demonstrations, and the actions of civic associations are all part of opposition politics. The history of Zimbabwe since independence shows us that ZANU PF can tolerate opposition politics only to the extent that they do not threaten its hold on power. To understand the deep dynamics of opposition politics we need to use the concept of Zimbabwe as a 'party-state'.

---

[1] Nkomo, Joshua (1984 and 2001) *Nkomo: The Story of My Life*. Harare: SAPES Books.
[2] Galbraith, J.K. (1983) *The Anatomy of Power*. Boston: Houghton Mifflin.

The party-state and its historical baggage

The thesis of this chapter is that opposition politics in Zimbabwe, reaching back before Independence in 1980 and up to the present, has been in travail. This has been essentially because of the capture of the state by successive ruling parties: the Rhodesian Front under UDI (1965-79) and since 1980, the ruling ZANU PF party. The state has successively been used, or abused in the service of the ruling party.

In his analysis of parties in communist political systems, Amos Perlmutter observed:

> *The vanguard role ascribed to the Communist party in Marxist-Leninist ideology produces, in practice, a political system in which the party is sovereign, acting as the chief arbiter of values, authority relations, institutional arrangements, political practices, and policy. ... From its place at the pinnacle of politics, the party acts as integrator by setting public policy and assuring that other institutions follow through faithfully with its implementation. Although these functions of direction, arbitration, and integration may be carried out more or less successfully in specific instances, they are always and everywhere a function that is in principle the preserve of the party and is thus the essential content of its role as political vanguard. When a ruling communist party is not successfully performing such functions, the political system is almost always in a clear state of crisis.*[3]

In the 1970s, ZANU/ZANLA was commonly described as a Marxist-Leninist party, and the West and its media propagated a view of Robert Mugabe as a dedicated Marxist. In 1977, the party declared Marxism-Leninism as its official ideology: 'ZANU is guided by the Marxist-Leninist Principle. ZANU aims to achieve a socialist revolution.'[4] During the struggle, ZANU PF learnt the important lesson of constructing and managing an effective political organisational structure so as to ensure the party's hegemony in society and politics. Makumbe comments:

> *The political organisation of ZANU ... assumed the eastern bloc format, complete with a central committee and politburo. With regard to the development and differentiation of political institutions, however, ZANU PF has been very thorough in ensuring that it dominates virtually every political institution in Zimbabwe. This has had the effect of stifling all political*

---

[3] Perlmutter, A. (1982) 'The Party in Uniform: Toward a Theory of Civil-Military Relations in Communist Political Systems', *American Political Science Review*, 76:4, 779.

[4] Tarter, J.R, (1983) 'Government and Politics' in H.D. Nelson (ed.) *Zimbabwe: A Country Study*. Washington, D.C: American University, 215.

> *actors that are not part of that political party.... Attempts have been made to ensure that organised social and economic interests either conform to the dictates of the ruling party or, at least, organise themselves within its ideological framework.*[5]

The public's response to the party's quest for hegemony can be described in two words: subordination and quiescence. Serious opposition, especially where organised, was seen as a challenge that must be contained, swallowed, infiltrated, manipulated and controlled at all times. Consequently, the various bureaucratic institutions gradually underwent a process of professional subordination to the dictates of the party. The party and its interests became virtually indistinguishable from those of the state. In the first decade of independence, the party progressively gained supremacy over the organs of the state. In *The Story of My Life*, Joshua Nkomo observed the dominance of the ruling party over the official structures of government including the cabinet of which he was a part:

> *I had once asked him (Prime Minister Mugabe) directly: 'What is the supreme organ in Zimbabwe?'. He had answered: 'the supreme body in Zimbabwe is the central committee of ZANU PF, my party'.*[6]

Nkomo critiques the party-state system as it operated then:

> *The underlying problem was that Zanu ministers – sixteen out of the twenty-two of the cabinet – regarded their party central committee as more important than the cabinet or parliament itself. This was unconstitutional, and in practice it was dangerous*[7] *... the Zanu central committee kept the real decisions in its hand*[8]. *...Zanu central committee had taken over the functions of the cabinet and of parliament.*[9]

In short, what Nkomo was describing was the nature of a party-state, *any* party-state, in which, by definition, the question of alternation in power, or transfer of power from one party to another, does not arise. This is the political psychology that ZANU PF absorbed and it is most pronounced during election seasons. In the run-up to the April 1995 elections, ZANU PF chairman for Manicaland province and also senior cabinet minister, Kumbirai Kangai, threatened civil servants who might support an opposition party:

---

[5] Makumbe, J. (2003) 'ZANU PF: A party in transition?' in R. Cornwell (ed.) *Zimbabwe's Turmoil: Problems and Prospects*, Monograph No. 87. Pretoria: Institute for Security Studies, 34 and 35.
[6] Nkomo, Joshua (2001) op.cit. ft. 1, 3.
[7] Ibid. 223.
[8] Ibid. 227.
[9] Ibid. 229.

> [He] said civil servants should always bear it in mind that there is nothing Government does that does not come from the party. 'No one should say: "I work for the Government and not for the party." If you hear any civil servant saying that in this area, please let me know so that I may approach the ministry he works for so that he is removed from Manicaland.'
> ... He said those civil servants were receiving fat salaries, but were biting the very hand that feeds them.[10]

In the run-up to the 2002 presidential election, Parliament's Speaker and Secretary for Administration in ZANU PF, Emmerson Mnangagwa, reportedly informed his party's conference in December 2001 he was setting up a party 'election command centre with the power to fire anybody in a parastatal or government department "if they are a hindrance to our victory".'[11] In crisis politics, the ruling party almost always feels insecure and often reacts rabidly against any real or perceived threats.

The party-state must also be understood in the context of the culture of the liberation war from which it largely sprang. Political culture flows from three streams: traditional political culture, the colonial authoritarian inheritance and the liberation-war legacy.[12] All three were authoritarian and reproduced authoritarianism.

A spiral of authoritarianism

The liberation war was spearheaded by two political movements: the Zimbabwe African National Union (ZANU) and the Zimbabwe African Peoples Union (ZAPU), together with their military wings, the Zimbabwe National Liberation Army (ZANLA) and the Zimbabwe Peoples Revolutionary Army (ZIPRA). The two guerrilla movements were not structured democratically. Authoritarian militarism was the chief and common feature of the liberation war. Civic activist Brian Kagoro writes that the movements 'paid scant attention to issues of individual and civic rights in fashioning their vision of a liberated Zimbabwe' and both advocated an implacable internal unity.[13] The liberation struggle was fraught with intense intrigues, factionalism, violent purges and assassinations, a feature that Masipula Sithole captures in the phrase

---

[10] *The Herald*, 14 January 1995.
[11] *The Daily News*, 8 January 2002.
[12] Masunungure, E. (1997) 'Political Culture and Democratic Governance in Zimbabwe'. Paper prepared for the Democracy and Governance in Zimbabwe Project, Department of Political & Administrative Studies, University of Zimbabwe, (forthcoming).
[13] Kagoro, Brian (2003) 'The Opposition and Civil Society', in R. Cornwell (ed.) *Zimbabwe's Turmoil: Problems and Prospects*, Monograph No. 87. Pretoria: Institute for Security Studies, 10.

'struggles within the struggle'.[14] There was a lot of witch-hunting, intimidation and torture, 'enemies' within being summarily dealt with. The ZANU President and Commander-in-Chief of ZANLA, Robert Mugabe, captured the *modus operandi* of ZANLA when he chillingly warned:

> *The ZANU axe must continue to fall upon the necks of rebels when we find it no longer possible to persuade them into the harmony that binds us all.*[15]

The 'struggles within the struggle' were particularly acute during the 'Badza-Nhari' rebellion in 1974 and the very serious 'ZIPA moment' in 1975-76. ZIPA (the Zimbabwe Peoples Army) represented the unity of the armed forces of ZIPRA and ZANLA and, most crucially, it sought to supplant the political leadership of both ZAPU and ZANU – from the very outset, ZIPA disowned and denounced the 'old guard' political leadership, specifically Joshua Nkomo, Ndabaningi Sithole and Robert Mugabe. It also denounced the 'old guard' military leadership of ZIPRA and ZANLA. ZIPA was the closest to being an opposition movement, though it existed outside the context of the state, and the manner in which it was ruthlessly dealt with gives us some insight into the general attitude of the old guard when it finally captured state power. Massive force was unleashed upon real or imagined ZIPA leaders and their 'Vashandi'[16] adherents and sympathisers. Many lives were lost in these purges. At the first post-independence ZANU PF Congress held in 1984, Robert Mugabe explained how ZIPA was liquidated:

> *This exercise [of crushing ZIPA and its Vashandi influence] was followed by a politicisation programme in the camps. We warned any person with a tendency to revolt that the ZANU axe would fall on their necks: Tino tema nedemo [Shona for 'We will axe you'] was the clear message.*[17]

The overall effect of the war of liberation was that it had, according to Jonathan Moyo, 'a deep socio-psychological impact on both its targets and its perpetrators'.[18] It is this sub-culture of intolerance, terror,

---

[14] Sithole, Masipula (1999) *Zimbabwe: Struggles-within-the-Struggle (1957-1980)*, 2nd ed., Harare: Rujeko Publishers.
[15] Moore, D. B. (1990) The Contradictory Construction of Hegemony in Zimbabwe: Politics, Ideology, and Class in the Formation of a New African State. PhD thesis, University of York. 201.
[16] 'Vashandi' (Shona for workers) was an ideology based on Marxism-Leninism in which the workers were to be the vanguard of the revolution. In this context, the workers were themselves the soldiers/guerrillas.
[17] *Zimbabwe News*, January 1985.
[18] Moyo, J.N. (1992) *Voting for Democracy: Electoral Politics in Zimbabwe*. Harare: University of Zimbabwe Publications, 12.

intimidation and fear that was reproduced in the post-independent era. On this theme, Kagoro argues, the hegemonic approach of the two liberation movements

> ...gave rise to a legacy of repressive and monolithic state politics in the post-colonial politics that was suspicious and intolerant of notions of pluralism and independent associational life. Pluralism and dissent of any kind have often been characterised as anti-revolutionary and therefore divisive.[19]

Makumbe echoes:

> As a movement engaged in armed struggle against a strong state, ZANU effectively became commandist and regimentalist rather than democratic in its operations and management style. Thus, although the various party structures claimed to engage in and encourage participation and the active involvement of party members in decision-making processes, the militarist approach tended to brook no dissent.[20]

The armed struggle and the manner in which it was prosecuted instilled in both the leaders and their supporters a militaristic conception of political processes and this has exercised a heavy burden on post-colonial Zimbabwe. The Economist Intelligence Unit commented as early as 1983 that 'the political experience learnt in fighting a seven-year guerrilla war is leading to increasingly repressive measures and an increasing authoritarianism'.[21] Jonathon Moyo wrote that 'democracy cannot exist in an environment where violence and fear dominate the political process. Something needs to be done with Zimbabwe's political culture.'[22] Writing in 1997, this author also pointed out that 'far from political independence representing a sharp break with the past, [it] was more [a] continuity. ... In fact, the historical continuities are remarkable and impressive if only they were not so negative.'[23] With reference to the enduring influence of the liberation war Makumbe also argues, 'Evidence abounds that on entering the corridors of power, the former liberation movement failed to transform itself into a democratic political party. The guerrillas have still not taken off their uniforms; they have not yet laid down their guns.'[24] The main difference since

---

[19] Kagoro, B. (2003) Ibid. ft. 13.
[20] Makumbe, J. (2003) op.cit. ft. 5, 34.
[21] The Economist Intelligence Unit (1983) London, 9.
[22] Moyo, J.N. (1992) op.cit. ft. 18, 3.
[23] Masunungure, E. (1997) op.cit. ft. 12, 13.
[24] Makumbe, J. (2003) op.cit. ft. 5, 33.

independence is that the ruling class now has all the coercion inherent in a state to tame or liquidate its real or imagined enemies. It is in this sense that Sithole and Makumbe are right in asserting that 'the fate of the opposition was decided during the war of liberation in the 1970s'.[25]

Phases in opposition politics

I divide the history of political opposition in post-independence Zimbabwe into three phases: (i) before the Unity Accord of 1987 when it was dominated by PF-ZAPU, (ii) from 1987 to the formation of the MDC in 1999 when opposition was fragmented, though ZUM made a powerful showing for a while, and (iii) the present period of opposition led mainly by the MDC. The first and the third phases bear striking resemblance to each other: both were characterised by the existence of a real organised opposition with a potential to capture power. In both cases, the reaction of the party-state was to violently liquidate the source of countervailing power. The one difference was that the victim in the first phase, (PF-ZAPU), in the end allowed itself to be swallowed up by the ruling party. So, in the third phase, PF-ZAPU is an integral part of the machinery for the liquidation of the MDC. A distinctive characteristic of the second phase was that opposition politics was virtually in limbo, struggling to define its role. It was characterised by anarchy and fragmentation within its ranks, though civil society organisations began to find their feet at this time.

1. The pre-Unity Accord phase

This was a period of extreme tension and friction that later transmuted into dissident activity. PF-ZAPU was a towering voice and constituted the real, though subdued, opposition in the first two Parliaments of Zimbabwe. Three parties won representation in the 1980 independence elections (February 27-29), with ZANU PF gaining 57 seats in the House of Assembly, PF-ZAPU 20 and Bishop Abel Muzorewa's United African National Council (UANC) three. ZANU PF's campaign slogan was: 'ZANU PF started the war of liberation and only ZANU PF can end the war.' This served to remind people to vote for ZANU PF or else they would re-ignite the war. The slogan carried the further message that only ZANU PF was entitled to rule. To this day, this attitude of entitlement to rule, by virtue of having 'delivered' independence, has endured as part of ZANU PF's core thinking. The results of the election were as follows:

---

[25] Sithole, M. and J. Makumbe, (1997), 'Elections in Zimbabwe: the ZANU PF Hegemony and its Incipient Decline' in *African Journal of Political Science*, 2:1, (122-139) 134.

Table 1: Results of Common Voter Election to House of Assembly, 1980

Party	Number of seats	Percent of votes	Number of total votes
ZANU PF	1,668,992	63.0	57
PF-ZAPU	638,879	24.1	20
UANC	219,307	8.3	3
ZANU	53,343	2.01	0
Other five parties	69 008	2.6	0
TOTAL	2,649,529	100.00	80

(a) The White Opposition.

The Lancaster House agreement of 1979 allowed the whites the temporary respite of voting on a separate roll and they duly voted overwhelmingly for the Rhodesian Front (RF), the party that had led pre-Independence Rhodesia into obduracy and war. With 20 seats in the new parliament the whites, to the chagrin of the new ZANU PF government, tried to constitute themselves as an opposition under the British-oriented parliamentary system. Mugabe was incensed. He argued that

> *The RF gave the impression that the rights of whites in Parliament must be represented through a political party. That dimension is serious and dangerous, because if a party representing whites in Parliament is in opposition, the impression given is that whites as a community are in opposition to the Government because the Government is predominantly black. That is a situation we do not want and cannot allow to be perpetuated.*[26]

So the intolerance of ZANU PF in government to opposition politics was evident at a very early stage. Despite the anger of ZANU PF, Moyo noted, 'In practical terms the RF turned out to be a very skilful opposition party in Parliament.'[27] In the 1985 white election, the RF, which had earlier changed its name to the Republican Front, and then renamed itself the Conservative Alliance of Zimbabwe (CAZ), soundly defeated its rivals. It was an affirmation of the supremacy of white conservative philosophy and a subscription to the Smith notion of 'white national unity' – the campaign theme in the election. ZANU PF was disgusted and interpreted it as a rejection of the reconciliation it had extended to the

---

[26] *The Herald*, 4 April 1981.
[27] Moyo, J.N. (1992) op.cit. ft. 18, 19.

whites. Emmerson Mnangagwa, then Minister of National Security, fumed, 'while whites had the right to vote as they wished, they did not have the right to deceive us; their vote showed us that they desire to reassert the stupid philosophy of white supremacy which we defeated five years ago.'[28] Mugabe himself bitterly alleged:

> The vote cast by the majority of the white electorate has shown us that the trust we placed in whites and our belief that they were getting reconciled to the new political order was a trust and belief that was not deserved.... [Whites] have spilled the blood of thousands of our people.... The vote has proved that they have not repented in any way.[29]

The result of the white roll election was the last nail in the coffin of organised white opposition politics. ZANU PF proceeded to put in motion the constitutional requirements for erasing organised white politics in the Zimbabwe Parliament. The Constitution of Zimbabwe Amendment (No. 6) Act abolished the twenty reserved white seats and allocated them to party loyalists and a few whites deemed sympathetic to ruling party.

(b) PF-ZAPU as an opposition party

Inside and outside the House of Assembly, real opposition to the ZANU PF government emanated from its nemesis, PF-ZAPU. However, its role as an opposition party was compromised by its being part of the government of national unity, set up by Mugabe in the desire for reconciliation in 1980. The cabinet consisted of eighteen members of ZANU PF, four from PF-ZAPU and two whites. The PF-ZAPU leader, Joshua Nkomo, became Minister of a pruned Home Affairs portfolio,[30] was demoted to minister without portfolio in January 1981, and was ejected from the cabinet in February 1982 on allegations of sponsoring dissident activity in the western part of Zimbabwe. Two other PF-ZAPU ministers were removed with Mugabe accusing Nkomo and his party of having been like a 'cobra in the house'.[31] Then came the Gukurahundi.

In seeking to explain the weakness of the opposition in Zimbabwe, the late Masipula Sithole isolated the 'Gukurahundi policy,' adopted in 1979, as one of the key factors. For him, Gukurahundi, 'the rain that washes away the chaff from the last harvest', was the decisive moment in the treatment of opposition forces just before and after independence. '[It]

---

[28] Ibid. 20.
[29] Sithole, M. (1986) 'The General Elections: 1979-1985' in I. Mandaza (ed.) *Zimbabwe: The Political Economy of Transition.* Dakar: Codesria (75-97) 92.
[30] Nkomo at one time complained that he felt like an 'ornament' in the coalition after nine senior PF-ZAPU officials were detained without his knowledge, even when he was in charge of Home Affairs, which included the Zimbabwe Republic Police (see Tarter, J.R. (1983) op.cit. ft. 4, 211).
[31] Tarter, J.R. (1983) op.cit. ft. 4, 212.

was a policy of annihilation, annihilating the opposition (black and white)'.[32] To him, the moment of Gukurahundi catapulted Mugabe and his party to power in the 1980 election. More crucially, Gukurahundi was an integral facet of the liberation war logic outlined above. Expressions like 'muvengi' ('enemy') and 'pasi naye' (literally 'down with', meaning 'kill') were part of this ideology, which has exercised a firm hold on ZANU PF's dealings with the opposition ever since. The policy was gradually extended into the structures of the state once the party had consolidated its hold on power.

In the first, and perhaps well into the second, independence decade the party did not trust the structures and personnel it inherited to implement this policy against its enemies. This explains the formation of the commandist youth and women's wings of the party, mostly led by former combatants or collaborators and imbued with a paramilitary organisational culture and style of operation. Also, when the dissident activity broke out in Matebeleland, the government did not trust the newly integrated and professionalised (under the British Military Advisory Training Team) Zimbabwe National Army (ZNA) to counter the threat. Instead, it invited North Korea to create a Fifth Brigade from former ZANLA combatants, whose operational command was separate from that of the ZNA. Sithole writes, 'The Fifth Brigade was commonly referred to as *gukurahundi* with pride by its sponsors, and with resentment and fear by the recipients of the evil storm in Matabeleland.'[33] Of the continuities between pre- and post-independence Zimbabwe, the Gukurahundi philosophy is clearly one. It is the buckle that connects the violent side of the armed liberation struggle to the violent side of independent Zimbabwe. The philosophy filtered from the party to the state reaching its maturation in the form of the Third Chimurenga from February 2000. By then, the party and state had become fused and virtually indistinguishable. When the party and its leadership became angry, the state became equally angry and reacted on behalf, and often at the behest, of the party and its leadership. *Gukurahundi* is now an embedded mindset in the party/state and for as long as this persists opposition politics in Zimbabwe will be in travail. It is black Zimbabwe's version of white settler authoritarianism and so a legacy of a brutal colonial political tradition. Welshman Ncube wrote in 1991, 'From about the beginning of 1983 the people of Matebeleland experienced once again military and political terror hardly distinguished from that inflicted on the people of Zimbabwe by the Rhodesian State.'[34] Puzzled by the

---

[32] Sithole, M. (2000) 'In Search of a Viable Democratic Alternative in Zimbabwe'. Paper prepared for the Democracy and Governance in Zimbabwe Project, Department of Political and Administrative Studies, University of Zimbabwe, (forthcoming) 8.
[33] Ibid. 9.
[34] Ncube, W. (1991) 'Constitutionalism, Democracy and Political Practice in Zimbabwe' in I. Mandaza and L.M. Sachikonye (eds), *The One-Party State and Democracy: The Zimbabwe Debate*. Harare: SAPES Books, 162.

continuities in the 'culture of repression' from the Rhodesian era into independence, Ncube speculated that

> .... the repressive political and legal culture of Rhodesia was so entrenched as to acquire a momentum of its own and thereby independently impose itself upon the new leadership which had to rely on Rhodesia's bureaucratic and security personnel under whose auspices the 'culture of repression' originated and developed.[35]

The war against dissident military activities, however justified from a public order and national security standpoint, also provided hawks in the ruling party with a golden chance to liquidate PF-ZAPU as an opposition party. Jonathan Moyo observed, 'Some ZANU PF leaders viewed these developments as an opportunity to eliminate Nkomo and his party from political opposition through non-political means.'[36] Moyo stressed that

> At any rate, the dissident activity provided an opportunity for the ruling ZANU PF government to remove PF-ZAPU as an obstacle to the establishment of a legislated one-party state in Zimbabwe. The outcome of this opportunity did not materialise, however, because PF-ZAPU, and especially its supporters, remained resilient to ZANU PF pressures ...[37]

All evidence suggests the ruling ZANU PF's almost congenital intolerance of opposition politics in general, and of electoral political competition in particular. This was starkly and tragically revealed in the aftermath to the 1985 general elections. The results were as follows:

Table 2: 1985 Zimbabwe Common Roll Results

Party	Number of valid votes	Percentage of total votes	Seats won
ZANU PF	2 233 320	77,2	64
PF-ZAPU	558 771	19,3	15
ZANU-Ndonga	36 054	1,2	1
UANC	64 764	2,2	0
NDU	295	0,01	0
NFZ	81	0,003	0

---

[35] Ibid. 160.
[36] Moyo, J.N. (1992) op.cit. ft. 18, 25.
[37] Ibid. 27.

Compared to the 1980 elections, the ruling party had in fact increased its parliamentary representation from 57 to 64 and PF-ZAPU had its share drop from 20 to 15. Instead of celebrating its electoral success, ZANU PF went on an orgy of violence, outraged that PF-ZAPU had challenged it in the elections. Masipula Sithole captures this well when he observed:

> The irony of the 1985 election ...was the almost unbelievable reaction of many ZANU PF supporters, mainly women and the youth in the urban areas. A few days after the news of the victory, they went on a rampage, beating up and evicting members of minority parties from their houses. Whole families and their belongings were thrown out on the streets during the cold July weather, and several people were killed in [this] post-election violence.[38]

In this orgy of violence, the police stood by and watched, betraying that they were under strict instructions not to intervene. This 'watch and do nothing' approach has become the Zimbabwe Republic Police's (ZRP) trademark reaction to political violence instigated by the ruling party. Perhaps the ZANU PF supporters were 'demonstrating', as President Mugabe was later to say in reference to the post-2000 farm invaders. It was not until the fourth day, and after government ministers had intervened, that the police started to disperse the violent crowds of party youths and women. Ncube commented on this post-election violence and its implications:

> The practice and perpetuation of all this political violence is important because it has demonstrated virtually the total absence of a culture of democracy embracing tolerance of opposing views as expressed through a multi-party democracy. However, what is worse is that the mass 'mobs' appear to have received express and/or tacit encouragement from the political leadership. Worse still was the behaviour of law enforcement agencies who seemed disinterested in upholding the rule of law.[39]

PF-ZAPU's 'crime' was to have swept all the seats in the two Matebeleland provinces, though it was certainly not such a formidable threat on a national scale. However, even before the 1985 election, intolerance and intimidation were directed towards the main opposition party. Prime Minister Mugabe's election campaigns were marked by thinly veiled threats to those contemplating voting for the opposition. He was reported

---
[38] Sithole, M. (1986) op.cit. ft. 29, 92.
[39] Ibid. 164.

as asking a rally in Bulawayo, 'Where will we be tomorrow? Is it war or is it peace? Let the people of Matebeland answer this question.'[40] At one point he again likened ZAPU and its leader to 'a cobra in a house. The only way to deal effectively with a snake is to strike and destroy its head.'[41]

But ZAPU survived and so did its head, Joshua Nkomo. When ZANU PF saw that force was failing to eliminate the opposition it resorted to a political formula: unity talks between the two parties. On 22 December 1987 a Unity Accord was announced. This accord has been variously interpreted, but PF-ZAPU's rank and file believe their party surrendered. ZANU PF had long yearned for a one-party state. The absorption of PF-ZAPU appeared to pave the way for this long-cherished dream. Moyo noted, 'for Mugabe and his party, the merger ... ended a complicated exercise in removing PF-ZAPU as an obstacle' to this dream.[42] 'Mugabe had effectively destroyed the only viable opposition that had remained after the attainment of national independence in 1980.'[43] Mugabe himself put it this way: 'United ZANU PF has the potential ... to develop into that sole party to which all Zimbabweans can and should lend their membership and support. ... Any attempt to form any new political parties for the future is a long step backwards.'[44]

2. From the Unity Accord to the birth of the MDC

ZANU PF proceeded to construct the institutional framework for a legislated one-party state. It created the Ministry of Political Affairs (later the Ministry of National Affairs) for this purpose and housed it at the party headquarters in Harare. This ministry was later disbanded but its function was continued through the Ministry of Youth Development, Gender and Employment Creation. So, after the Unity Accord and the removal of the reserved white seats in 1986, there was no credible opposition. The formation of the Zimbabwe Unity Movement (ZUM) in April 1989 was the fly in the ointment. In October 1988, Mugabe spearheaded the expulsion of Edgar Tekere, his one time close ally, from the party. Tekere had spoken out against corruption by the 'vampire class' in ZANU PF and he claimed democracy in Zimbabwe was in the 'intensive care unit'. He went on to campaign in the 1990 general and presidential election against the one-party state, and this became the key issue in the 1990 elections.[45]

---

[40] Ibid.
[41] Nkomo, Joshua (2001) op.cit. ft.1, 2.
[42] Moyo, J.N. (1992) op.cit. ft. 18, 30.
[43] Makumbe, J. (2003) op.cit. ft. 5, 35.
[44] Mugabe, R.G. (1989) 'The Unity Accord: Its Promise for the Future', in C. Banana (ed.) *Turmoil and Tenacity: Zimbabwe 1980-1990*. Harare: The College Press, 354-5.
[45] Jonathan Moyo argues that the 1990 elections became a matter of 'voting for democracy' the title of his book. Op.cit. ft. 18, 2.

(a) The Zimbabwe Unity Movement

Tekere's expulsion turned out to be a strategic mistake for ZANU PF. Many who joined ZUM were actually defecting from the united ZANU PF, disgruntled by a series of intra-party scandals, quarrels and factional politics. The 'Willowgate scandal' was the most notorious and cost the party dearly in terms of support and credibility. Moyo commented:

> ...by the ninth anniversary of independence in 1989, ZANU PF had lost seven politicians of ministerial rank and one deputy minister. All of these politicians fell because they were found not only to have been corrupt but also to have engaged in illegal activities. The toll on the ruling party was heavy.[46]

This was one of ZANU PF's darkest hours and it was precisely at this moment that Tekere formed his party. In political terms the timing could not have been more perfect. ZUM's formation was an instant hit with the electorate, especially in the urban areas. Moreover, ZUM was a national phenomenon; it could not be accused of being a regional party, an accusation that stuck to Sithole's ZANU-Ndonga. The reaction of the party-state was initially one of disdainful arrogance. ZUM was dismissed as 'the joke of the year' with Mugabe promising that ZUM 'will zoom itself into doom'. But then the reality of ZUM's support finally hit them and there was palpable panic. The ruling party started presenting ZUM as a divisive and reactionary force, of being a 'front for Rhodesians' wanting to re-colonise Zimbabwe[47] and of receiving funding from apartheid South Africa. The draconian instruments of the state, crafted by the colonial regime, were unsheathed to clamp down on the activities of the party. ZUM promised that if elected in 1990, it would 'promote the complete rejection of a one-party state in Zimbabwe and secure a multi-party democracy'.[48] In taking this position, ZUM defined a clear policy difference from the ruling party. The view, expressed by Deve and Goncalves in 1994, that 'opposition parties have failed, in the view of many, to present the Zimbabwean public with major, coherent policy alternatives, concentrating instead on individuals and technical aspects governing the conduct of an election',[49] could not be ascribed to ZUM in 1990. The reaction of the party-state was, as in 1985, to unleash violence upon ZUM. The army played a subdued role, if any, in this violence but the same cannot be said for the Central Intelligence Organisation (CIO). Many Zimbabweans had already come to associate the CIO as an appendage of ZANU PF. Though there were many incidents

---

[46] Ibid. 35.
[47] The same accusations were to be made against the MDC as a way of discrediting it with the electorate except that the West – especially Britain and the USA – had replaced South Africa as the source of MDC funding and 'mischief'.
[48] Moyo, J.N. (1992) op.cit. ft. 18, 39.
[49] Deve, T. and F. Goncalves, May 1994, *Whither the Opposition in Zimbabwe?* SAPEM, 7:8, 10.

of electoral violence, the best known involved the CIO and ZANU PF militants shooting and seriously injuring a prominent ZUM candidate, Patrick Kombayi, who was contesting against Vice-President Simon Muzenda in Gweru. The culprits were arrested, prosecuted and convicted, but the President soon pardoned them, further entrenching a culture of impunity dating back to the Gukurahundi excesses. The 1990 election campaign starkly confirmed ZANU PF's intolerant and violent side. Mugabe himself articulated this during the campaign, 'ZANU PF was merciless in dealing with the opposition,' he said and this statement, according to Anthony Masendeke et al., became a slogan in the party campaign.[50] He urged people to 'get rid of ZUM at all costs,' that people must not listen to 'small, petty little ants which we can crush,' and that if whites 'rear their ugly terrorist and racist heads by collaborating with ZUM, we will chop that head off'.[51] Gory advertisements were part of the campaign. One featured a vehicle with a threatening voice saying: 'This is one way to die. Another is to vote for ZUM. Don't commit suicide, vote ZANU PF.' An even more insensitive one showed a coffin and a grave with a comment, 'AIDS kills, so does ZUM. Vote ZANU PF.' Public protest later forced the ruling party and ZBC to remove this advertisement.

What was ZUM's political base? The uprooted and disillusioned youth were a ready recruitment ground, so was the frustrated intelligentsia and the middle class generally. To Kagoro, ZUM's formation 'was the earliest indication of a serious generational disjuncture between the nationalist leaders and the non-combatant generation of young Zimbabweans'.[52] ZUM's political base was to be the same catchment area as the MDC's. In both cases, the University of Zimbabwe (UZ) was a hotbed of opposition politics and the barometer of change in the national psyche. In a large sense, ZUM politics led to the first closure of UZ in October 1989 while MDC politics led to the banning of political (read opposition) activities on the UZ campus in 2000. ZUM posed a respectable and stout resistance to the ruling party particularly if one takes into account the unequal playing field and the infancy of the party. A noteworthy characteristic of ZUM was the national challenge it posed to ZANU PF. After fielding 102 candidates[53] out of the 120 constituencies, it garnered a respectable 23 per cent of the votes in the parliamentary

---

[50] Masendeke, A.F., M.U. Mafico, and P.T. Chitopo (1991) *Report on the 1990 General and Presidential Elections: Masvingo and Manicaland Provinces*, University of Zimbabwe, Department of Political and Administrative Studies, Election Studies Project, Occasional Paper Series, 1 (3).
[51] Mhlaba in Laakso, L. (1999) 'Voting Without Choosing: State Making and Elections in Zimbabwe', University of Helsinki, Department of Political Science, *Acta Politica*, 11, 140.
[52] Kagoro, B. (2003) op.cit. ft. 19, 13.
[53] There were also last minute withdrawals by six candidates, some of whom resigned and even joined or rejoined ZANU PF. One such candidate, Farai Takavarasha told a ZANU PF gathering 'like a prodigal son, he was coming back to the fold' (in Laakso 1999, 136). The UANC contested only 14 seats while ZANU (Ndonga) contested 9.

elections and 22 per cent in the presidential election. Thanks to the unfairness inherent in the 'winner-take-all' electoral procedure, ZUM managed to win only two seats. However, the significance of the ZUM challenge lay elsewhere. The 1990 presidential election was the first direct presidential election in the history of Zimbabwe and Tekere and his ZUM had challenged Mugabe and his ZANU PF party. Commenting on this, Sithole writes:

> *Although he lost ... Tekere's challenge to Mugabe, and ZUM's challenge to ZANU PF, broke the myth of invincibility. This is the contribution which Tekere and ZUM made at a critical hour in Zimbabwe's political development, when the country faced the real possibility of a one-party state.*[54]

Mugabe had to cancel his trip to Namibia's 1990 independence celebrations so as to campaign for his and his party's political survival. But then ZUM strangely disintegrated, generating many conspiracy theories about its formation and the role played by its leader. The most popular 'thesis' was that Tekere was planted by the ruling party, and the CIO, to destabilise opposition parties. Edwin Nguwa, then Secretary General of Sithole's ZANU (Ndonga) fully subscribed to this line of thinking:

> *ZUM was a trick. Tekere was supplied by ZANU(PF) to weaken and retard the growth of the opposition. ... The important point is that the plan to destabilise the opposition by supplying it with leaders worked.*[55]

More weight to this CIO/ZANU PF conspiracy thesis came from Daniel Sithole,[56] former ZUM Secretary for Foreign Affairs in the 1990-95 Parliament who declared in February 1995:

> *Tekere betrayed and cheated us and the nation – he was never an opposition cadre. In actual fact, Tekere never left ZANU PF from the beginning. All this time he was serving ZANU PF by trying to destroy the opposition parties.*[57]

(b) The Forum

Opposition parties approached the 1995 elections with narrow and muddled aims. ZUM and the UANC proposed a merger in January 1994

---

[54] Sithole, M. (2000) op.cit. ft. 29, 18.
[55] Ibid. 41.
[56] Daniel Sithole was at one time a ZANU PF Provincial Chairman in Manicaland who resigned after the expulsion of Tekere from the ruling party.
[57] Makumbe, J. and D. Compagnon (2000) *Behind the Smokescreen: The Politics of Zimbabwe's 1995 General Elections*. Harare: University of Zimbabwe Publications, 11.

but this was widely dismissed as a 'marriage of convenience' and it collapsed within eight months. ZUM was now a shadow of its former self. Tekere himself was accused of serious leadership and organisational deficiencies. Sithole claimed that 'up to its eventual demise ZUM operated from wherever its leaders happened to be'.[58] Defections from ZUM gave birth in 1991 to the Democratic Party, led by medical doctor Emmanuel Magoche, who resigned in 1993 for 'personal reasons' handing over to insurance professional Davison Gomo. During the latter's long study leave in the United Kingdom, chartered accountant Wurayayi Zembe was acting president before becoming substantive president. Apart from its rapid leadership turnover, the Democratic Party suffered the fatal weakness of being perceived as a tribal (Karanga) party. It may have been incidental, but all its presidents hailed from Masvingo, and were suspected of being close to Edison Zvobgo, the ZANU PF godfather of Masvingo politics. The suspicion was therefore that the DP was a mere front for Zvobgo. Like its parent, ZUM, the DP was never of more than nuisance value to the ruling party. It became well known, though, for its principled stance of boycotting 'bogus elections' conducted on an uneven playing field. When another opposition party, the Forum Party of Zimbabwe (Forum) was formed in 1993, some DP members defected to it. There was also another feeble attempt to bring all opposition forces under one canopy called the United Parties (UP) under Bishop Muzorewa after he re-entered politics – he had retired in favour of the pulpit. UP, founded in September 1994, was meant to be the equivalent of the ZANU PF Unity Accord but it failed to make any mark. The travails of the opposition, though largely originating from the machinations of the party-state, were also self-inflicted. The case of the Forum Party is illustrative of the chaos, anxieties, selfishness and general lack of focus within opposition ranks. The Forum was founded in March 1993 out of two political pressure groups, the Harare-based Forum for Democratic Reform Trust and the Bulawayo-based Open Forum. The former patron of the Trust and also former Chief Justice, Enoch Dumbutshena became its President while another retired judge, Washington Sansole, was his deputy. Many hailed the Forum's formation as representing the opposition's salvation. It was considered able to pose a real challenge to the ruling ZANU PF. It had substantial support among intellectuals, the middle class and the business community and other frustrated achievers, was able to mobilise financial resources, and had a clear and well-articulated political programme. Sithole was later to comment:

> *The initial asset of this party was the reputation of the two former Justices in the era of human rights. Although its*

---

[58] Ibid.

> leadership was not young, its apparent wisdom seemed to attract many young professionals. Moreover, the Forum aroused the curiosity and interest of many personalities from the old guard nationalists under rustication such as James Chikerema, Michael Mawema and Enos Nkala. Further, the Forum attracted some support in the white community, which had withdrawn from direct political involvement after independence. These two developments proved to be a liability rather than an asset.[59]

The hopes pinned on the Forum soon proved misplaced. Forum leaders and members had no battle experience in the rough and tumble of Zimbabwe politics and were certainly no match for ZANU PF's tried and tested political tricks. Further, although Forum was prepared to negotiate about co-operation with other parties, it was never interested in either merging or forming a grand alliance with them. Forum wanted to maintain its identity. Autocratic tendencies soon crept into the party. Dumbutshena, who increasingly saw himself as its soul and life-blood, appointed James Chikerema, former chairman of the externally-based Frolizi in the 1970s war of liberation, and Patrick Kombayi, former ZUM executive leader and ZUM candidate in the 1990 elections, into high positions in the party hierarchy. This was done without consultation with his colleagues. He also later unilaterally ruled out a merger with ZUM when the negotiations had reached an advanced stage. All hell broke loose in March 1994. A founding member of Forum, Joshua Cohen, who was the party's Labour and Transport Secretary, together with 21 others, publicly accused the leadership of tribalism, racism and dictatorship, pointing out that some members of the party's National Executive Council (NEC) were appointed and not elected, that the party had been hijacked by politicians like Chikerema and Kombayi and that the leadership was replacing employees in the Harare Forum office with those from their own tribes.[60] The 22 'musketeers' were expelled from the party with Chikerema accusing some of the 'gang of 22' of being agents of ZANU PF and the CIO. In another twist, the Forum's national chairman, Agrippa Madhela, accused Chikerema and other former Frolizi members of trying to hijack the party and denounced the allegations that the 22 expellees were infiltrates as 'total nonsense'. He went further by warning that the unity of the party should not be compromised by an intolerant leadership bent on arrogating itself the right to hire and fire.[61]

Things fell apart in May 1994. In a leadership dispute, Secretary-General Themba Dlodlo 'dismissed' Dumbutshena at a meeting in Harare. Dumbutshena, in turn, said the meeting had been unconstitutional and

---

[59] Sithole, M. (2000) op.cit. ft. 33, 22.
[60] *The Daily Gazette*, 12 March 1994
[61] *The Sunday Gazette*, 27 March 1994.

obtained a court order barring Dlodlo from assuming the interim leadership. In June 1994, a vote of no confidence in Dumbutshena and Sansole was passed for violating party rules, co-opting members into the NEC and for expelling members. Both Dumbutshena and Sansole refused to relinquish their positions. In July 1994, Dlodlo formed his own party, the Forum Party for Democracy, along with Agrippa Madlela and their disciples. The last nail in the Forum coffin was when the leadership cancelled unity negotiations with the United Parties leading to six members of the NEC resigning leaving the party in disarray with Dumbutshena and Sansole as the only significant founding members and with its original support having withered away. The sad story of the birth, life and death of Forum was typical of opposition politics. In significant respects, opposition parties dug their own graves and they were deep dishonourable ones. Both within and between opposition political parties there seemed to be the Hobbesian 'state of nature,' that is, the war of each against all. They appeared to be more aggressive in attacking each other than in directing their combined firepower at ZANU PF. Zembe of the DP summarily dismissed the Forum saying, 'Forum was sponsored by white liberals who hand-picked retired Dumbutshena for its leader.' For its part, ZANU (Ndonga) saw Forum as a 'badly infiltrated party' with its secretary-general saying, 'Forum is elitist. It is never understood by the workers and peasants of Zimbabwe.'[62] Even Ian Smith castigated the opposition parties for being too disorganised and fragmented. Just before the 1995 elections, he lamented, 'If [the opposition parties] do not unite, this will only show that they are extremely unintelligent.'[63] Forum and ZANU (Ndonga), were the only two significant opposition parties to participate in the parliamentary elections of April 1995. The other eight parties decided to boycott the elections following a resolution made at a meeting of opposition parties in Harare in February 1995 under the umbrella of Zimbabwe Multi-Party Consultative Conference. It demanded that the uneven playing field be levelled first, failing which they would boycott the elections. Therefore, in participating in the elections, Forum and ZANU (Ndonga) were accused of betraying the opposition cause.[64] The two parties only managed to field candidates

---

[62] See ibid. And, as if to confirm its elitist and white-aligned tag, Forum launched its election campaign at the Harare Sports Club where about 65 people attended, 'the majority being elderly middle class whites'. The Sports Club is located in downtown Harare, away from high-density urban dwellers and the rural masses.

[63] *The Herald*, 13 April 1995.

[64] ZANU PF appears to have been embarrassed somewhat by the boycott. Mugabe himself complained: '...what we had hoped would be country-wide election fight is not to be. Fifty-two of our candidates are uncontested and have already become winners. All that loud and 'bullyish' talk of Muzorewas, Dumbutshenas and Sitholes that they will throw out the ZANU PF government was it, after all, this hollow?' (*People's Voice* (1995) 19-25 March).

in 65 of the 120 contested seats, and did not field candidates against each other in those constituencies where one or the other had a greater chance of winning. As it turned out, only the Chipinge-based ZANU (Ndonga) managed to win two seats. The other 118, of which only 63 were contested, went to ZANU PF. After Forum's electoral defeat, Dumbutshena relinquished leadership of the party to his deputy, Sansole. So ended another attempt at opposition. Yet the Forum did make a contribution in 'democratisation by litigation'. Inspired by the legal training of its top leadership, it fought many legal and constitutional battles in the courts and won some of them, such as the nullification of mayoral elections in Bulawayo and Harare in 1996.

(c) Independents in politics

The second decade of Independence was largely a period in which there were no viable opposition parties but there were individuals who stood for parliament as independents. This phenomenon haunted the ruling ZANU PF. The best known of the independents was Margeret Dongo. She had been a ZANU PF Member of Parliament in the 1990-95 parliament, but in 1995 the ZANU PF Politburo refused to nominate her for the elections. She defied the party and ran as an independent but controversially lost. Her petition to the courts for a re-run was allowed and, in the by-election, she beat her opponent by a 3:1 margin. There were no independent candidates in the 1980 and 1985 common roll elections but there were twelve in the 1990 parliamentary elections, all unsuccessful. In 1995, the number rose to 29 and their votes rose from 9,478 votes in 1990 to 62,085 in 1995. The 'independent candidates' phenomenon had a contagious effect on local municipal elections, where some of the candidates contested and won both council and mayoral elections against ZANU PF. This development was significant politically in that even individuals now had the self-confidence to challenge the ruling party. It demonstrated that though ZANU PF remained omnipresent, it was no longer omnipotent. More importantly, it was a harbinger of an incipient opposition movement, which started under the organisational name of the Movement of Independent Electoral Candidates (MIEC), under Dongo's chairmanship. MIEC metamorphosed into a political party in December 1998 and called itself the Zimbabwe Union of Democrats (ZUD) with Dongo as its President. A year later, the fissure disease infected ZUD when its secretary-general Kempton Makamure split from the party. He accused Dongo of a lack of transparency and formed his own party, the Transparency Front. ZUD members, in turn, accused Makamure of having been a ZANU PF agent. It was yet another testament to the immaturity and capacity to self-destruct apparently embedded in opposition politics.

What the development of 'independent candidates' illustrated was a huge organisational void to which the lost sheep in ZANU PF and other disaffected citizens could turn for shelter. In 1997 (two years before the formation of the opposition MDC), this author made the following observation:

> ... at the psychological level, many Zimbabweans are not, or are no longer ZANU(PF) 'at heart'. There is considerable ambivalence on this matter. The political society appears to be in a transitional phase in terms of partisan affiliations such that though many Zimbabweans may feel disenchanted with the ruling party, they are yet to find a satisfying 'political home' in the organisational form of a viable alternative party.[65]

By the late 1990s, Zimbabwe was ripe for a more robust opposition party. The 'hitherto mammoth and monolithic party began to show cracks [as early as] the latter part of the 1980s'.[66] Solidarity at the elite level within the ruling party was melting away as a result of intra-party criticisms, challenges and other centrifugal forces. The standard reaction of the party to these tendencies was to expel or suspend such critics as happened with Tekere (1989), Dongo (1995), Lawrence Mudehwe (who also defied the Politburo and contested and won the Mutare mayoral election in 1996) and Dzikamayi Mavhaire (suspended in 1996 for saying 'Mugabe must go' in parliament). The elite fissures in the ruling party opened up political space for both formally organised and latent opposition in civil society.

(d) Civil Society: manifestations of opposition politics

Another development that arose from the vacuum of political opposition was the growth of surrogate opposition forces within civil society. The best known of these are the Zimbabwe Congress of Trade Unions (ZCTU), the National Constitutional Assembly (NCA), the Zimbabwe Human Rights Association (ZimRights) and the Catholic Commission for Justice and Peace (CCJP). And there were other manifestations of opposition to government in the form of anomic expressions of political anger and discontent. All of these were responded to in the usual ZANU PF fashion. In November 1995, ZimRights organised a demonstration against police brutality. A diverse spectrum of concerned groups including opposition politicians, civic organisations, university students and lecturers joined in. The demonstration degenerated into violence and looting in Harare when it was hijacked by a group of youths, who ran amok throwing bricks, overturning and burning eight government vehicles, in 'an

---

[65] Masunungure, E. (1997) op.cit. ft. 12.
[66] Sithole, M. and J. Makumbe (1997) op.cit. ft. 25, 134.

unprecedented show of anger at the state'.[67] After the demonstration, 'Mugabe threatened to ban all demonstrations, labelled local human rights groups "gangster" organisations, and warned that they would "be ruthlessly dealt with"'.[68] Less than a year later, the 'worst national strike in Zimbabwe's history' took place when the civil service, under the direction and leadership of the Public Service Association, engaged in a two-week work stoppage that paralysed virtually all essential services. In response, the Public Service Minister, acting typically in a commandist governing style, issued a two-day ultimatum to the strikers to return to work. They did not, and were sacked *en masse* – about 7,000 of their jobs were advertised for replacements. President Mugabe arrogantly but recklessly announced that he welcomed the opportunity to trim the civil service, 'We don't take kindly to illegal strikes. Already the public service is far too large.'[69] The government, under pressure to end the crippling strike that cost the nation over US$80 million, later gave in to the strikers' demands.

Strictly speaking, the PSA strike was not politically inspired but it clearly had political overtones. Brian Raftopoulos commented that 'the strike represented a rebellion from a central arm of the state.'[70] The Economic Structural Adjustment Programme (ESAP) of the early 1990s, instead of improving, actually worsened the living conditions of Zimbabweans to a point that they felt alienated from the government. Though the strike adversely affected the average citizen, there was enormous public sympathy for the strikers. The PSA strike was also a further demonstration that the party-state was not invincible: its capitulation to the demands of the strikers was additional evidence that it was vulnerable – that, after all, the 'owl had no horns'. More evidence of this vulnerability emerged in mid-1997 when the Liberation War Veterans Association organised threatening demonstrations against the government, the ruling party and the President himself. They demanded compensation and political recognition for the role that they played in liberating the country. The President initially stood firm, but the war veterans would not be deterred and they besieged the ZANU PF headquarters, holding hostage senior politburo officials. The President relented. He promised, and later paid, more than 50,000 ex-combatants large unbudgeted one-off gratuities and a monthly pension until death. The payments were estimated at Z$7billion, (then US$700 million) and forced the government to borrow heavily in the domestic money market.

---

[67] Sithole, M. (1998) 'Political Violence: The Zimbabwe Experience' in Seminar Report: Political Violence in South Africa, Konrad Adenauer Stiftung, 54.
[68] Thiis, O. and G. Feltoe (1998) *Zimbabwe* in H. Stokke et al. (eds) *Human Rights in Developing countries Yearbook 1997*. The Hague: Kluwer Law International, 386.
[69] *The Herald*, 26 August 1996.
[70] Raftopoulos, Brian (2000) 'The Labour Movement and the Emergence of Opposition Politics in Zimbabwe' in *Labour, Capital and Society*. 33:2, 269.

Many analysts attribute the subsequent, prolonged economic meltdown to this capitulation. The victory of the war veterans had its own contagious effect on other civic groups, notably the ZCTU.

(e) The Zimbabwe Congress of Trade Unions

The ZCTU was a child of the party-state that desired to see a united and cohesive labour body affiliated to it. The government facilitated the formation of one labour centre out of the six that existed at independence, and in the early 1980s, the ZCTU was 'effectively a wing of the ruling party'.[71]. It was dependent on the state for political patronage so that when the ruling party abolished the twenty reserved white seats in 1987, 'the ZCTU leadership made an urgent appeal to be included in the new parliament, as an interest group within ZANU PF'.[72] The ZCTU president, Geoffrey Mutandare, felt 'the ZCTU should be represented on the decision-making bodies [of the state and party so as to] 'put across the view, sentiments and attitudes of the working people of Zimbabwe'.[73]

It was not until a new leadership emerged in 1988 that efforts were made to wean the ZCTU from the state. To Raftopoulos, by 1990, 'the labour movement had moved from being a pliant wing of the ruling party to a more autonomous critical force, which had begun to make broader societal alliances, in an attempt to link the issues around economic policy to problems of governance.'[74] When the ZCTU held its extraordinary congress in 1988 at which it severed all ties with the ruling ZANU PF party, the latter smelt a rat. The new ZCTU Secretary General, Morgan Tsvangirai accused the ruling party of being in an ideological crisis and of being insecure, and the Labour Minister, John Nkomo, asked, 'How can ZCTU [say] the government is insecure? Are they trying to form another government?'[75] ZANU PF could not envisage its own child operating outside the framework of the ruling party. Mugabe expressed it this way: 'Trade unions are free to discuss political issues and refer their recommendations through the proper channels. We do not want to see a situation where the ZCTU becomes a political party.'[76]

Tsvangirai started to build his political profile at about this time. On 4 October 1989, University of Zimbabwe students went on strike to commemorate their 1988 anti-corruption demonstrations. Tsvangirai issued a statement in support of the students' action and he was promptly arrested together with the student leaders. He was kept incommunicado for a week without access to a lawyer and stood accused of 'attempting

---

[71] Raftopoulos, Brian (2000) op.cit. ft. 70, 260.
[72] Ibid.
[73] *The Sunday Mail*, 25 October 1987.
[74] Raftopoulos, Brian (2000) op.cit. ft. 70, 265.
[75] *The Sunday Mail*, 7 August 1988.
[76] Ibid. 27 November 1988.

to bring about the downfall of Government through unconstitutional means ... and that he was acting under external influence'.[77] The High Court acquitted him on 18 October 1989, but the state immediately re-arrested him claiming that he was recruited by the apartheid South African National Intelligence Service to, among other things, facilitate the unconstitutional overthrow of the government. On 24 October 1989, the High Court again threw out the state's case and ordered his release. Kagoro ascribes Tsvangirai's rise in politics to these episodes:

> Arguably, this attack raised Morgan Tsvangirai's profile in the public eye. His resilience earned him the respect that would later serve as political capital in his ascent in the broader civic movement and the Movement for Democratic Change (MDC). The state thus unwittingly turned Morgan Tsvangirai into a national figure as well as its most avowed opponent.[78]

In 1992, the state introduced an amendment to the Labour Relations Act, deregulating labour relations, so as to be consistent with the demands of ESAP. The ZCTU was aggrieved and organised an anti-ESAP demonstration on 13 June 1992. The police banned the demonstration and suppressed it 'using very crude force'.[79] Six unionists were arrested and charged under the infamous Law and Order Maintenance Act but the High Court acquitted them and affirmed their constitutional right to assemble and demonstrate. The state-controlled paper, *The Herald*, expressed the opinion that the ZCTU seemed to be 'in conflict with the Government and the ruling party.'[80] So, by the time the war veterans demonstrated against the party-state, the ZCTU was an autonomous body and it confronted the state head-on with respect to its measures to fund the war veterans' payments. Because these funds were not budgeted, the government proposed to raise the money through a 5 per cent war veterans levy. The ZCTU called for a nation-wide strike for 9 December 1997 to express the workers' outrage at the proposed levy as well as heavy taxation and the skyrocketing cost of living. The government initially pretended to be unmoved, but barely a week later the President withdrew the war veterans levy at a ZANU PF annual conference, ostensibly because the 'people's representatives had rejected it,' not because of the ZCTU's threatened action. Sensing the uncompromising public mood, parliament had also threatened not to approve the proposed levy, which it said imposed an unbearable burden on taxpayers. As Laakso wrote, 'The workers had shown that there was a limit to the power of the executive.'[81]

---

[77] Kagoro, B. (2003) op.cit. ft. 19, 17.
[78] Ibid.
[79] Ibid.
[80] *The Herald*, 23 June 1992.
[81] Laakso, L. (1999), op.cit. ft. 52, 92.

The President's withdrawal of the hated levy did not assuage the labour organisation; it insisted that other 'unfair' and onerous taxes (including a 5 per cent 'development levy' and a 15 per cent tax on pension profits) be removed. The ZCTU had also moved into more general governance issues, like transparency in budgetary decisions, that to them had a direct bearing on their human welfare. The strike was described as the most successful in Zimbabwe's history, attracting massive support from across the socio-economic spectrum, including employers. Even the Zimbabwe Police Commissioner acknowledged the unprecedented success when he lamented:

> ...I note with surprise that for the first time since independence in this country we have all institutions – banks, stores, the industry and farms – being closed and urged to go out and demonstrate.[82]

The active involvement, or at least discrete connivance, of employers with their traditional rivals, labour, was unprecedented. The government saw something akin to an triangular 'axis of evil' – 'an unholy alliance between the ZCTU, employers and white commercial farmers, who have been angered by the government's designation of farms,' as the Home Affairs Minister put it.[83] For some analysts, however, 'The general strike marked a convergence of views among a cross section of Zimbabwean society that the growing economic crisis could only be dealt with by addressing the issue of governance.'[84] Soon after the general strike, there was an assassination attempt on Tsvangirai.

The government steadfastly refused to talk to the ZCTU and the confederation organised a two-day job stayaway in March 1998,which was described as the most effective job action in the country's history, crippling virtually all economic activities and costing the economy an estimated Z$1 billion (approximately US$90 million at the time). The insouciant government did not back down. It hardened its position with Mugabe and his ministers announcing that henceforth they would treat the ZCTU as an opposition party intent on the downfall of the government. There was a campaign to demonise the union leadership by pointing out their lack of liberation war credentials, a theme that Mugabe has resorted to when under severe threat. Mugabe warned Tsvangirai and Sibanda, 'The freedom that you have came from the people, from ZANU PF and those who chose to fight while you stayed behind enjoying everyday comforts.'[85] There was even news about the government planning to de-

---

[82] The *Financial Gazette* 11 December 1997.
[83] Laakso, L. (1999), op.cit. ft. 51, 92.
[84] Raftopoulos, B. (2000) op.cit. ft. 71, 271
[85] *The Sunday Mail*, 22 February 1998.

register and ban the ZCTU.[86] In his 1998 May Day speech, Tsvangirai denied that he had political ambitions or that the ZCTU was involved in politics, 'The only politics we are involved in is the politics of the stomach.'[87]

The strike of March 1998 elicited no positive response from the government and the labour body threatened to organise another job stayaway, this time for five days. The ZCTU leadership toured the urban centres, addressing huge rallies, seeking a mandate for the proposed action. Without exception, this was overwhelmingly endorsed – many workers were in fact now calling for an indefinite strike. Mugabe remained unyielding and obdurate and continued lambasting the ZCTU at every available opportunity while 'advising' the workers to fight with their employers, and not the government. His intransigence was making the urban masses restless and he risked an urban revolt. The President then agreed to meet the ZCTU. The meeting, the first in three years, took place in July 1998. The Labour Minister subsequently announced that the government was going to scrap the 2.5 per cent increase in sales tax, monitor prices of basic foods, 'study' the impact of the unpopular pension tax on the workers but retain the development levy. The ZCTU was not appeased; it rejected the concessions and again threatened to embark on the five-day stayaway while simultaneously calling for dialogue with the government and specifically with the President. The captains of industry and commerce, knowing the catastrophic implications of the threatened strike, requested and were granted an urgent audience with the President, at which they reportedly told him bluntly that the mass job action would destroy an already ailing economy. The President then ordered his officials to arrange an urgent tripartite meeting of government, employers, and labour to discuss various economic issues but focussing on the labour demands. This meeting was held on 2-4 September 1998 but did not seem to yield much, for in November the ZCTU organised another successful mass stayaway demanding salary increases and that the government should suspend the 67 per cent increase in fuel prices. Thereafter, it was reported that the CIO had launched intense investigations into the labour body's funding, especially foreign funding.

The strike of 9 December 1997 marked a watershed in state-labour relations. The rejuvenated ZCTU managed to weave together a formidable coalition of anti-government forces, all of which in one way or another felt injured by the policies of the government. The momentum of this resistance continued into 1998, a nightmare year for the government. Though unconnected to the ZCTU, Harare witnessed another outburst of people's anger in the form of the food riots of 19-22 January that

---

[86] The *Zimbabwe Independent*, 13-19 March 1998.
[87] The *Financial Gazette*, 4 June 1988.

erupted mostly in the high-density suburbs. The riots later spread to other towns, forcing the government to summon both the army and air force to support the police in quelling the looting and threat to life, limb and property. At least eight people died, ten were wounded and a lot of property damaged. Predictably, the government blamed the spontaneous explosion of anger on the ZCTU and opposition parties but Dongo was closer to the truth when she said, 'The stomach organised and co-ordinated these food riots. Hungry people need no one to organise them to look for food.'[88] These food riots mark the intersection between 'stomach politics' and national politics, underlying the fact that bread and butter (or sadza and meat) issues are governance issues as well. The riots were repeated in October 2000 and the police and the military again combinined efforts to crush the politically threatening riots.

(f) The National Constitutional Alliance (NCA)

Once the ZCTU had weaned itself from the paternalism of the party-state, the labour movement sought allies and joint action with similarly aggrieved members and groups within civil society. This was a logical and inevitable outcome after the ZCTU had defined the plight of its members in political terms. This explains its engagement with another organisation, the National Constitutional Alliance.[89] The NCA grew from an amalgam of disparate groups and individuals who considered that the 1979 Lancaster House Constitution was defective and had outlived its usefulness. It comprised a diversity of civic organisations, professional associations, churches, trade unions, student organisations, human rights groups, and other groups and individuals, particularly intellectuals and journalists.[90] The NCA was first set up in May 1997 but officially launched in January 1998. The ruling party saw it as a potential threat, if not an incipient political opposition. The traditional way of dealing with such a threat was to eliminate or neutralise it, or co-opt its agenda or its leadership. The government's fears were understandable, as the leaders of the NCA were almost all associated with some anti-government position, notably the ZCTU. At the core of the NCA's argument was that a bad constitution led to bad governance and bad governance led to the people's suffering. As the NCA put it: 'We strongly believe that the current socio-economic problems we face as a nation are a result of a constitutional

---

[88] Sithole, M. (2000) op.cit. ft. 33, 56
[89] This section on the NCA is largely based on my paper entitled 'Constitution-Making in Zimbabwe: the Role of Non-State Actors' in I. Mandaza (ed.) *The Constitution Making Process of 1999/2000 in Zimbabwe.* Harare: SAPES Trust (forthcoming).
[90] Brian Kagoro describes the NCA as 'the largest and most effective civic coalition in the whole of Zimbabwean history. It has managed to build membership structures in every province and constituency within Zimbabwe. By February 2000, it had 700 institutional members and 100,000 individual members' (op.cit. ft. 19, 88, endnote 20).

crisis arising out of the shortcomings of our present constitution.'[91] On the question of a new constitution for Zimbabwe, the NCA occupied high moral ground and put the party-state on the defensive. It forced the issue from the systemic agenda (where it had been since independence) onto the institutional agenda of government. The NCA initiative was initially ignored by the state but at the ZANU PF annual conference in December 1997 calls for a new constitution were made. As Sachikonye observed, 'It is not unlikely that the ZANU PF congress resolution later that year on constitutional reform was partly a response to this growing pressure from civil society and elsewhere.'[92] Ibbo Mandaza, a member of the Constitutional Commission that was later established by government, confirmed this: 'What is not in dispute is that the NCA's initiative towards a new constitution for Zimbabwe did provide the impetus for the State's response, in the form of a Constitutional Commission.'[93] At the December 1998 ZANU PF conference, Mugabe, 'agreed in principle and pledged government support to expedite possible reforms to the Zimbabwe constitution'.[94] In April 1999, the President duly appointed a Constitutional Commission, '...to inquire into and carry out a comprehensive review of the present Constitution and to make appropriate general and specific recommendations for consideration by the President.'[95] The NCA disagreed with both the membership and process of the government-initiated-constitution-making process and put in motion its own parallel process. The 400-member Constitutional Commission comprised all members of parliament (virtually all ZANU PF, and others who were mostly from the ruling party or its sympathisers. Consistent with the unilateralist thinking of ZANU PF, the national constitution making process was thought of as an essentially ZANU PF affair. The President himself articulated the party-driven approach in March 1998, a year before the appointment of the CC. He contended:

> *The procedure, which all along I thought we would adopt, is one which would first enable our party at the provincial and then at the Central Committee level to address the matter and come to some initial conclusions on the various aspects of the constitution needing amendment. The views of other organisations can be sought and collected in the process, but only for consideration by us and in comparison with our own.*[96] *(My emphasis.)*

---

[91] *Agenda*, 2:1, 1999, 9.
[92] Sachikonye, L. (2000 a) The Consultative Process in Constitution-Making in Zimbabwe, Paper presented at the conference on Constitution-Making Process in Southern Africa, Harare, 26-28 March, 4.
[93] Ibid.
[94] *The Sunday Mail*, 7 February 1999.
[95] Statutory Instrument 138A of 1999.
[96] Cited in Sachikonye, L. (2000 a) op.cit. ft. 92, 4.

The Commission's Draft was submitted to a referendum in February 2000 and was rejected by 55 per cent to 45 per cent on a 20 per cent turnout. The rejection of the Draft was the first electoral defeat suffered by the ruling party. It marked a turning point in the politics and governance of the country. Thereafter, it was to be all-out war against real and perceived enemies, specifically against the NCA and the newly formed Movement for Democratic Change (MDC).

3. The Movement for Democratic Change (MDC)

The MDC owes its parentage to both the ZCTU and the NCA. There was overlapping leadership in the two organisations with the ZCTU Secretary General, Morgan Tsvangirai, being at the same time the NCA Chairman. By January 1998, the ZCTU appeared to be irrevocably on a political path. At its Special General Council meeting held on the 30th of that month a resolution was passed as follows:

> *When workers cannot earn a living wage and decent working conditions through industrial action at the workplace, they will go beyond the shop floor and bring their issues in the national stage, thus politicising the issues. When in addition the Trade Unions have been marginalised and cannot successfully address these issues through National Reforms in a government that has abandoned the desire to engage in national politics, the only recourse is action at national level.*[97]

The solid alliance with the NCA, the largest civic coalition, meant the labour movement was now in a strategic position to take a leading role in opposition politics. Thus, it was not surprising that in February 1999, the ZCTU spearheaded a National Working People's Convention to 'critically analyse issues through discussion based on the society's views and experiences, and identify together how best to improve the current situation for the betterment of every Zimbabwean'[98] Sibanda chaired the Convention in his capacity as ZCTU President. The broad-based Convention resolved to build a consensus on the formation of a 'vigorous and democratic political movement for change'. This was followed in May 1999 by another convention at which the ZCTU was mandated to facilitate the establishment of a political party. Sibanda explained the position of the ZCTU at a rally of an estimated 15,000 applauding workers when he said:

> *Government has always accused us of harbouring political ambitions, but that was not so until we were pushed to the*

---

[97] Raftopoulos, B. (2000) op.cit. ft. 70, 274.
[98] Ibid.

> wall. [We] were left with no choice but to be masters of our own destiny. In Zambia, the labour movement told the then government that enough was enough and brought a new government that they are still in control of. We are ready! We want things to be better in reality.[99]

In pursuit of this mandate, the labour organisation held a special congress in August 1999 at which it was unanimously agreed to form the party, which was finally born on 11 September 1999. Sibanda, provided the philosophical and moral (and biblical) justification for the move:

> For how long shall we wait for the biblical Moses to deliver us? ... Throughout history, from deep within our culture, there are times when people take back the power they have entrusted to their leaders, demonstrating firmly that power comes only from the people, and entrust that power to new leaders.... Today we are here to fulfil a promise because in 1980 we removed the Union Jack here [Rufaro Stadium], so we are here to remove the ZANU PF government.[100]

The newly born movement made judicious use of the structures of its parents, the NCA and the ZCTU, as it penetrated the hitherto rural strongholds of ZANU PF with the active support of some white commercial farmers and rural-based public service workers like teachers, nurses and agricultural extension officers. In the run-up to the referendum of February 2000, the NCA and ZCTU vigorously campaigned together for the 'No' vote. The reaction of the party-state was vicious. Never before had Mugabe, his party and government, been defeated so soundly and on a national scale and so near another electoral contest, the 2000 parliamentary elections. Mugabe himself appeared to take the defeat with humility, even thanking whites for shrugging off the political apathy they had shown since 1985. However, this was soon followed by well-orchestrated, party-driven and government-assisted violent land invasions and on a national scale. White commercial farmers, who had actively worked for the 'No' vote by providing crucial logistical and financial resources, were the direct targets of the land seizures. In an about-turn from his statesmanlike speech in February 2000, Mugabe had, by April the same year, put on his warrior attire and verbally assaulted the whites in uncompromising terms, 'Our present state of mind is that you (whites) ... really behaved as enemies of Zimbabwe. Our entire community is angry and that is why ... the war veterans [are] seizing land.'[101] He reiterated this message even more forcefully in

---

[99] *The Standard*, 3-9 May 1999.
[100] Ibid. 12-28 September 1999.
[101] *Business Day*, 19 April 2000.

December 2000, 'The white man is not indigenous to Africa. Africa is for Africans. Zimbabwe is for Zimbabweans. Our party must continue to strike fear into the heart of the white man, who is the real enemy.'[102] The state-sponsored violence was thus ratified by the state President himself.

ZANU PF has used the white factor to mobilise the rural political support that was fast waning in the face of a concerted campaign by the MDC and its strategic allies. The ruling party, in the face of real danger to its twenty-year hold on power, crafted a total counter-strategy with violence as the chief weapon. The strategy was total in the sense that it was not only manifested in physical terms but also centred on a propaganda assault on the MDC and on its real and presumed sympathisers. ZANU PF became a paramilitary machine. The war veterans, marginalised from independence until 1997, were now an integral part of ZANU PF and were in the forefront of the land invasions and the violence against the opposition forces. ZANU PF youths were enlisted as militias and deployed to re-enact the role they had played during the Gukurahundi scorched-earth campaign in Matebeleland. The youth militia was given official recognition in the form of a national service training programme, which was ostensibly meant to inculcate a sense of patriotism, discipline and hard work, teaching them entrepreneurial and vocational skills. Human Rights Watch, however, observed that 'the activities of youth militia who have been deployed to communities suggest that they have received military training and instruction in torture'.[103] Formal state structures, that are supposed to be non-partisan and professional were co-opted in the service of the beleaguered ruling party. Most prominent among these were the Zimbabwe Republic Police, the army, the CIO and the Zimbabwe Broadcasting Corporation.

The strategic objective was in all cases to destroy the human, organisational and financial infrastructure of the MDC and its alleged accomplices. The white farmers were at the top of the list. Land invasions motivated by genuine land hunger were not new; they had been a perennial irritant since independence and often led to illegal settlers 'squatting' on commercial farms. The government had always insisted on the forcible removal of such settlers. By 1998, the situation had become untenable with some impatient and frustrated villagers forcibly settling themselves in Mashonaland and Matebeleland provinces. 'We are tired and we are not asking for land anymore, we are taking it,' one villager declared.[104] What was new in the post-referendum period was that they were orchestrated by the party-state. As Raftopoulos notes, 'The difference with the occupations that ensued in March (2000) was the central role of

---

[102] Reproduced in *This Day*, 10 November 2003.
[103] Human Rights Watch, 6 June 2003, *Under a Shadow: Civil and Political Rights in Zimbabwe*. New York.
[104] *The Zimbabwe Mirror* 31 July-6 August 1998.

the state in the logistics and violence that accompanied it.'[105] This state-sanctioned policy aimed to achieve a cluster of political objectives: to appease the land hungry electorate, to decimate the opposition and to re-gain the party's rural support base in preparation for the long season of elections in 2000 and 2002. Raftopoulos writes, 'In political terms, the occupations became a frontal assault on opposition politics, effectively violating the personnel and structures of the MDC in its growing rural campaign, and cordoning off large areas of the rural constituency from opposition politics.'[106] The party-state engaged in a carefully orchestrated campaign of violence, intimidation, harassment, rape, assaults and even murder, all directed, not at the opposition in general, but specifically at the MDC. Thus in the run-up to the June 2000 parliamentary elections, more than 30 people were reportedly killed, mostly MDC members, and approximately 18,000 others were victims of a myriad of human rights violations.

A distinctive quality of the MDC was that it was a new party in almost every sense. It was not a breakaway party nor was it founded by rebels from existing parties. It was born out of civil society's struggle against the party-state. Its leadership was therefore not tainted through previous associations with other parties. The MDC was a new party, with a new leadership and with a new agenda. The new agenda was to change the way Zimbabwe was governed, as captured in its imaginative slogan, *Chinja Maitiro* ('Change your ways'). The MDC caught the imagination of most Zimbabweans, especially the urban youth, workers, and middle and professional classes. It was particularly popular throughout Matebeleland, as it filled a political and psychological void that had been in existence since PF-ZAPU was swallowed by ZANU PF in 1987. Since the MDC stormed onto the political scene, Zimbabwe has for all practical purposes become, not so much a multi-party as a 'highly competitive two-party system'.[107] Certainly, the Zimbabwe Parliament has become a two-party parliament. All attempts to liquidate the MDC, or at least emasculate it, have so far met with very limited success. They have certainly failed in the urban areas and would have failed in the rural areas had the party-state not fenced off and sealed these areas from opposition encroachment.

Fifteen parties entered the parliamentary elections in June 2000, but it was clear that the real contest was between the ruling ZANU PF and the nine-month-old MDC. The campaign was characterised by unprecedented levels of violence and intimidation in virtually all parts of the country and according to the European Union Observer Mission,

---

[105] Raftopoulos, B. (2000) op.cit. ft. 70, 277.
[106] Ibid.
[107] Sachikonye, L. (2000b), 'Just a Victory', SAPEM, 6 July.

the bulk of the violence was attributable to ZANU PF. In its assessment, 'The evidence showed that between February and June ZANU PF was engaged in a systematic campaign of intimidation aimed at crushing support for opposition parties.'[108] The Report continued:

> Key groups of the electorate whom Zanu PF deemed to be opposition supporters were targeted by war veterans and other party supporters operating from bases on white-owned farms they had invaded, from militia camps in other rural areas and from government and party offices in rural towns. Farm labourers on white-owned farms across the country were threatened and abused, forced to attend party meetings and taken off to re-education camps. Thousands of incidents of assault, torture, abduction and rape were recorded. Several prominent MDC organisers were murdered.[109]

Also targeted were teachers, nurses and other civil servants. Up to 7,000 teachers fled their homes, forcing 250 primary and secondary schools to close. The EU Observer Mission noted that in many rural areas 'the levels of intimidation by Zanu PF were so intense as to make it virtually impossible for opposition parties to campaign'.[110]

A Report by the Commonwealth Observer Group made a similar assessment:

> The campaign was not peaceful. There was violence, intimidation and coercion in many parts of the country, especially in rural areas, both against ordinary voters and against candidates and party supporters. All parties share responsibility. There were incidents where opposition parties carried out acts of violence. But it would appear that most of the violence was directed against the opposition parties, especially the Movement for Democratic Change. These violent acts included murders, rapes and beatings and the ransacking and burning of houses of opposition members and supporters.

The Commonwealth Report goes on to describe the distinctive character of the 2000 electoral violence.

> As in many elections, there were occasions when violence was the result of unplanned clashes between groups of party supporters. But for the most part it appears to us that the

---

[108] European Union, 4 July 2000, *Report of the EU Election Observation Mission on the Parliamentary Elections which took place in Zimbabwe on 24th and 25th June 2000*. Harare-Strasbourg, 15.
[109] Ibid.
[110] Ibid. 16.

> violence which disfigured this campaign was employed systematically as part of a strategy to diminish support for the opposition parties.[111]

In all these instances of violence and intimidation it was the ruling party and the state that were instrumental. The repression was methodical and systematic. Whites were particularly targeted. But so were farm labourers, teachers, nurses and civil servants working in the rural areas. ZANU PF was actually boastful about its activities. 'We should not be blamed when we hit back. The area of violence is an area where ZANU PF has a very strong, long and successful history.'[112] The polling days were surprisingly peaceful and orderly with few incidents of intimidation and violence. The EU teams 'rated the polling process as good or very good in 84 per cent of their reports, an impressive performance by international standards'.[113] The counting process was also generally rated to be satisfactory and procedures for the count were assessed to have been followed in a proper manner. This is crucial given the perception in Africa that what counts in an election is not who votes, but who counts the votes. The results of the parliamentary election nearly surprised ZANU PF out power. In a voter turnout of about 50 per cent, ZANU PF won 62 seats (and 48 per cent of the total vote), the MDC 57 seats (and 46 per cent of the votes) and ZANU Ndonga won one seat in its traditional stronghold, Chipinge. In one analysis of the results, there was found to be a correlation between reported acts of violence and the performance of ZANU PF. One report stated that 'the ruling party obtained its highest votes in those constituencies where its supporters carried out terror campaigns.'[114] Indeed, the MDC failed to win any seats in the provinces of Mashonaland Central and East, areas that witnessed some of the worst intimidation and violence. Sachikonye notes that the MDC commanded the majority of the seats in the largely rural provinces of Manicaland, Matebeleland North and South and adds, 'In relative terms, there was less political violence and intimidation in these three provinces.'[115] There was also an apparent urban/rural divide: most of the opposition to the ruling party came from the working and middle-classes in the urban areas while its support was largely from the poorer and less educated rural electorate. This was more than a class factor. It reflected the genesis of

---

[111] Commonwealth Secretariat, March 2002, *Report of the Commonwealth Observer Group: Zimbabwe Presidential Election 9 to 11 March 2002.* London.
[112] The ZANU PF Information and Publicity Secretary quoted in *The Herald* 2 October 2000.
[113] EU. op.cit. ft. 108, 18.
[114] Zimbabwe Election Support Network, 2000, *Report on the 2000 Parliamentary Elections: Zimbabwe,* Harare, 33.
[115] Sachikonye, L. (2000b), op.cit. ft. 107, 5.

the MDC arising out of organised civil society. Sachikonye comments that 'the outcome of the elections in social terms pointed to the pivotal role of civil society in contributing to the shifts in Zimbabwean politics. Clearly, civil society is stronger and better organised in urban centres than in dispersed villages in the countryside.'[116]

How did the President react to the MDC's performance? As after the February 2000 referendum, Mugabe was at first conciliatory. This was in sharp contrast to the aggressive and combative rhetoric he poured out during the campaign. He again harped on the theme of national unity 'across race, tribe, ethnicity, across regions, across class' and declared that the results 'bind us all, loser and winner'. He indicated his willingness to work with the new-look parliament. For his part, the MDC leader, Tsvangirai, though emphasising the impact that intimidation and violence had had on the electorate, nonetheless grudgingly accepted the results and promised to work constructively with the government. Sachikonye described the 2000 elections as 'indeed a turning point in Zimbabwe's political landscape'.[117] With 57 of the directly elected seats, the MDC became the first significant opposition party within parliament. 'Something seismic has happened in Zimbabwean politics,' Sachikonye observed.[118] From a 'good governance' standpoint, a major aspect of the re-configured parliament was that the ruling party can no longer run roughshod over the national constitution. The opposition has sufficient representation to block constitutional changes. Compared to the sixteen constitutional amendments rammed through parliament in the first twenty years, not a single one has been enacted in the last four years. This probably explains the avalanche of presidential decrees passed under the Presidential Powers (Temporary Measures) Act whose effect in some instances has been to amend the constitution in subtle ways. Sachikonye observed that for the first time, Zimbabwe now had a shadow cabinet as well as a fully-fledged official opposition party. This meant its full participation in all aspects of parliamentary work, especially in the all-important parliamentary committees. Theoretically, the heavy presence of the opposition promised to make the Fifth Zimbabwe Parliament a much more dynamic institution than its predecessors. Indeed, despite being novices, and in some instances exhibiting glaring political immaturity, the MDC has significantly transformed the quality of parliamentary debates and parliamentary processes.

By winning 46 per cent of the total vote, the MDC had by far exceeded the new threshold of 5 per cent needed for a party to be eligible for

---
[116] Ibid. 6.
[117] Ibid. 5.
[118] Ibid.

crucial public funds. This was the first time an opposition party was entitled to access public funds under the Political Parties (Finance) Act. The Act was amended in 2001 to outlaw foreign funding of political parties in a move that was clearly designed to target the MDC. The party had to resort to litigation to obtain the first tranche of funding due to it, after it became evident that the ruling party would use subterfuge to block and or delay the disbursement. With adequate funds, the MDC could strengthen and prepare itself for the presidential elections. Both the MDC and ZANU PF knew very well that the election in 2002 was going to have 'all the makings of a political epic'.[119] Despite having expressed willingness to work with the opposition, ZANU PF nevertheless proceeded to put in motion measures to prevent the MDC consolidating itself in preparation for the 2002 presidential elections. There was a lull inpost-election violence but it was only the calm before the storm. Tables 3 and 4 tell a greater part of the story. This time, there was no pretence of any distinction between party and state organs. Through covert and overt means, legal and illegal mechanisms, party and state organs and personnel, ZANU PF mobilised all resources, material and symbolic, organisational and ideological, human and financial, to mount a ferocious campaign against the MDC and its domestic and international supporters and sympathisers.

Table 3: Average number of selected politically motivated human rights violations (Excluding commercial farm violence): 2000-2001

	14 February to 26 June 2000: per month	27 June to 7 December 2000: per month	1 January to 30 June 2001: per month	1 July to 30 November 2001: per month
Killing	8	1	2	5
Physical assaults	569	176	192	548
Detention/ abduction	142	9	70	35
Assault threats	439	33	199	805
Death threats	567	10	71	73
Property offences	263	74	66	360
Displacement	>2000	57	174	>4000

---

[119] Ibid. 6.

Table 4: *Affiliation of perpetrator for all reported politically motivated human rights violations*

	14 February to 26 June 2000	27 June to 7 December 2000	1 January to 30 June 2001	1 July to 30 November 2001
Bodies affiliated to government*	94,5 %	93,2 %	88,7 %	92,1 %
Others/unknown**	5,5 %	6,8 %	11,3 %	7,9 %

* ZANU PF supporters, 'war veterans,' CIO, police, army
** including MDC

Source: Amani Trust, Network of Independent Monitors (South Africa) and Physicians for Human Rights, *Analysis of Zimbabwe Presidential Election March 9th and 10th 2002*, 15 March 2002, 9.

The following were part of the opposition's Odyssey on the road to the 2002 elections:
- Violence and intimidation on an unprecedented scale – see above Tables.
- Severe restrictions on freedom of association and expression, most epitomised in the draconian, and probably unconstitutional, Public Order and Security Act (POSA) of January 2002. Some clauses of the Act outlaw meetings of more than two people without police authorisation four days in advance. Others outlaw any criticism of the president and provide long jail terms for anyone 'usurping the functions of government' or being critical of the police, army, or economy. Amani Trust et al. commented, 'It is notable that in some of the first invocations of POSA, MDC meetings and their organisers were targeted, with violence against them by security forces justified through the act.'[120] Indeed POSA amounted to a state of emergency without one being declared.
- Denial of opposition coverage and exposure in the public media whether print or electronic. According to Amani Trust et al, 'The public media are the almost exclusive domain of the ruling party, with more than 90 per cent of all campaign coverage being given to the ruling party. Opposition parties are constantly attacked in the public media with no opportunity to reply.'[121] The preliminary report of the SADC Parliamentary Forum Election Observation Mission concurred: 'There was lack of access to the public media

---
[120] Amani Trust et al. (2002), Analysis of Zimbabwe's Presidential Election 9 and 10 March 2002. Harare. 10.
[121] Ibid. 13.

by political parties other than the ruling party.'[122] Coupled with this were attacks of various kinds on the non-state media. The attacks include the sabotage in January 2001 of the printing presses of the only independent daily newspaper, *The Daily News*, the petrol bombing of its offices and repeated arrests of reporters and editors. 'Death threats, assaults and warnings by government ministers and state officials against journalists and private sector media became commonplace in 2001.'[123] In all these efforts, the objective was to completely cut out the opposition MDC from its constituency and the public as a whole.

- Systematic disenfranchisement of possibly millions of Zimbabwean by, for example, the government's refusal to allow postal voting by its citizens based abroad (estimated at one million and predominantly MDC supporters), internal displacement consequent upon the 'fast track land reform' (estimated at about one million), government's insistence for the first time in a presidential election that people were to vote in their constituencies, proof of residence in order for one to register, etc. Also included in this systematic and massive disenfranchisement were descendants (often third and forth generation) of migrants who originated from neighbouring and other foreign countries and these were mostly whites, farm workers, and urban-based domestic workers. They suddenly lost their citizenship on the spurious grounds that they had not renounced their right to citizenship of a country they knew little or nothing about. The rationale for this was political; to undermine the political base of the opposition as these descendants were perceived to be real or potential opposition sympathisers.
- Constant amendments to the electoral laws throughout the presidential election campaign, all meant to constrain the chances of an MDC victory. One such presidential decree (Statutory Instrument 41D of 2002) was introduced just three days before the poll – reintroducing electoral changes that had been struck down by the Supreme Court. This meant, in effect, that the President (himself a contestant) overturned the Supreme Court.[124]

---

[122] SADC Parliamentary Forum Election Observation Mission, 2002, *Zimbabwe Presidential Elections 9-10 March 2002*, Harare, 13 March 2002. 4.
[123] Amani Trust (2002) op.cit. ft. 120, 13.
[124] This was to be one of the issues raised in the MDC's case challenging the freeness and fairness of the presidential election result. Jeremy Gauntlet, the MDC's lawyer, argued in part: 'The elections were stifled at best because the president, one of the contenders, became the rule maker' (BBC News, <http://news.bbc.cp.uk/go/pr/fr/-/2/hi/africa/3236053.stm>)

- The misuse of public resources and funding of political activities. Amani Trust et al commented: 'While it is hard to quantify in exact monetary terms, the ruling party blatantly uses public resources and tax payers' money to run its campaign. This includes the use of air-force helicopters and other government transport to get to and from rallies, the use of the public media including state television and newspapers as free advertising for the ruling party candidate, and the abuse of drought relief or tax payer-funded food as provisions at rallies'.[125]

The cumulative impact of all the above was to create a very difficult playing field for the opposition. It was the most chaotic, controversial and tension-filled election in the country's history. And it was a defining moment for Zimbabwe to determine whether it was going to move forward or regress.[126] As it turned out, the incumbent was re-elected in a result that reflected the deep polarisation of the electorate, the sub-region and indeed the international community. Mugabe received 56 per cent of the valid vote, Tsvangirai 42 per cent for and the balance was shared among the three other inconsequential contestants. The voter turnout was 55 per cent, 22 per cent above that recorded in the 1996 presidential election. Most local election observers and some of their international counterparts, including the European Union and the Commonwealth, declared the election neither free nor fair. However, many African and some Third World groups endorsed the poll as free, fair and a legitimate expression of the peoples' voice. It must be acknowledged that the voter turnout could have been considerably higher had the urban electorate been catered for as were the rural voters. The number of polling stations was increased in the rural areas (the ruling party's power base) and significantly reduced in the urban areas (the MDC's stronghold). The SADC Parliamentary Forum Election Observation Mission reported, 'The reduction of the number of polling stations in urban areas had a major impact on the elections. This was particularly so in Harare and Chitungwiza where tripartite elections were held. It resulted in congestion with some people spending more

---

[125] Amani Trust (2002) op.cit. ft. 120, 12.
[126] *SAPEM*, a Harare-based Southern Africa publication, commented on the controversy surrounding the election and how crucial this election was:
'[I]t was a controversy that epitomised the importance of the process itself, as for many Zimbabweans this election was not just an ordinary act of exercising the constitutional right to choose a leader. Indeed, the stakes were high. It was an election that right from the beginning , was set to change the complexion of Zimbabwean society. It was a choice between radical change and a gradual, conservative change.' (14: 9, 2002, 3).
Writing in the same magazine, Fernando Goncalves described the election 'an epic election in which for the first time in the 22 years of Zimbabwe's independence, President Mugabe faced the most serious challenge to his continued stay in power' (5). It was, 'the closest contest ever witnessed in Zimbabwe's post-independence history.' (6).

than 48 hours in queues because of their sheer determination to vote.'[127] Thus although a large number of people voted, 'a significant number of the electorate was unable to vote as a result of logistical, administrative and other impediments'.[128] In Harare 'the voting process was excruciatingly slow'. It is fair to say that all this was part of a deliberate strategy to disenfranchise as many opposition voters as possible, and these were largely in the urban centres. It is notable that of the total votes cast, over 73 per cent were from the countryside. A further breakdown shows that the voter turnout in the government stronghold of Mashonaland Central was 69 per cent; in the opposition stronghold of Harare it was about 46 per cent. 'The significantly low numbers in the opposition strongholds are mainly due to reduction of polling stations in urban areas by 40 per cent, and procedural delays in voting there.'[129]

Despite winning the ultimate prize, the presidency, there has been no let up in the party-state's assault on the opposition and its perceived allies. For instance, on 18 and 19 March, 2003, the MDC organised a mass stayaway to protest declining economic and political conditions in the country; the stayaway had a 60 per cent success rate. Not unexpectedly, 'it also triggered a severe government backlash against political activity in the country'.[130] A combination of state security forces and ruling party militia was deployed to 'teach' MDC activists a violent lesson. This violent stance was escalated in the run-up to two parliamentary by-elections held in Harare at the end of March 2003 where, as before, the MDC was prevented from undertaking normal campaign activities and its supporters were detained, beaten and harassed. Human Rights Watch commented, 'The reaction of the government and the security forces during these weeks illustrated a clear and systematic repression of MDC activists, which amounted to a criminalization of political affiliation.'[131]

The reality of the emergence of a viable opposition party in Zimbabwe is now beyond dispute. The question is, what will be the fate of that opposition? It is hard to predict, but it is illuminating to turn to Alfred Stepan, an eminent scholar of democratic transitions, and particularly his essay, 'On the Tasks of a Democratic Opposition',[132] where, he says that in an eroding authoritarianism, the opposition has five tasks. These

---

[127] SADC, op.cit. ft. 122, Statement 3.
[128] Ibid.
[129] Mair, S. and M. Sithole, (2002) *Blocked Democracies in Africa: case study of Zimbabwe*. Harare: Konrad Adenauer Foundation, 11.
[130] Human Rights Watch op.cit. ft. 103.
[131] Ibid.
[132] Stepan, A. (1993) 'On the Tasks of a Democratic Opposition', in L. Diamond and M.F. Plattner (eds) *The Global Resurgence of Democracy*. Baltimore: Johns Hopkins UP, 61-69.

are: resisting integration into the regime; guarding zones of autonomy against the regime; disputing the regime's legitimacy; raising the cost of authoritarian rule; and, creating a credible democratic alternative. Stepan argues that the more effective the regime's control of the polity, the less the opposition is able to perform these tasks. The corollary is that when the regime's grip on the polity weakens, for whatever reason but chiefly because of the erosion of elite cohesion, the opposition chances of success are enhanced. It is fair to say the MDC has so far performed the five tasks rather well.

What made opposition politics a viable enterprise after twenty years of groping in the dark? Previously, the fatal malady of opposition parties was their tendency to go it alone and jealously guard their own turf, no matter how small and denuded that was. The other fatal tendency was towards fragmentation. Apart from PF-ZAPU, most other political parties spawned rebellious offshoots that soon withered away. Some of the differences were frivolous and based on personality clashes at the leadership level; few had anything to do with ideological or policy differences. With monotonous consistency, all Zimbabwe opposition parties went the same route and were afflicted by the same disease: Muzorewa's UANC, Sithole's ZANU-Ndonga, Tekere's ZUM, Magoche's DP, Dumbutshena's Forum and Dongo's ZUD. They could not see the bigger picture beyond their own organisational existence. 'Everyone wants to be leader of that united party,' opposition leader Dongo herself confessed,[133] adding that:

> There is no culture of power sharing where the best from each party comes into the new party in a different role. They go to these meetings with preconceived ideas of maintaining the positions they occupy in their parties, even the name.[134]

One distinctive feature of opposition politics until the formation of the MDC was its chaotic, if not anarchic, character and its the lack of organisational capacity. However, the EU Election Observation Mission on the 2000 Parliamentary elections was quite impressed by the MDC's vibrancy despite its lack of public funding.[135] It could also be averred that at the end of the second decade of independence, Zimbabwe was ripe for serious opposition politics, resulting from a complex mix or confluence of factors. ESAP, for instance, was a clear godsend for the opposition. Whatever its presumed merits in the economic realm, it was

---

[133] Sithole, M. (2000) op.cit. ft. 33, 25.
[134] Ibid.
[135] EU, op.cit. ft. 108, 15.

a political disaster for the party-state. What Jeffrey Herbst observed in 1990 could have been written for Zimbabwe in the late 1990s:

> At the very least, political life will become much more difficult for African leaders who attempt to reform their economic systems without structurally adjusting their politics. Some leaders may find the necessary political changes so unattractive that they actually balk at the economic reforms being suggested. The real losers in structural adjustment may be African leaders themselves.[136]

The fact is that Zimbabwean politics since independence has been anchored in patronage and such politics can only thrive when there is a large public sector. One of the impacts of ESAPs – intended or otherwise – is to shrink the public sector and thus also shrink the scope for patronage. Sachikonye observed that 'the country's economic crisis is also the reason why ZANU PFs hegemony has largely been eroded'.[137] Without patronage, political clients melt away.

By 1995, poverty levels – not necessarily ESAP-induced – had risen to alarming levels even by official statistics. Popular discontent also rose, as the EU Election Report found out

> In recent years, its [ZANU-PF's] popularity has declined. Economic recession, high inflation, rising unemployment, petrol shortages, power cuts, corruption and mismanagement have produced a groundswell of discontent.[138]

The 'groundswell of discontent' translated into the de-legitimisation of the party-state and conditions fertile for opposition politics. In short, by the mid-1990s the social discontent was available for mobilisation. Zimbabwe's economic adjustment programme created, by default, the objective conditions that made opposition politics a viable enterprise. ZANU PF's answer to the new threat has already been described, i.e. the total strategy whose visible form was the physical violence directed at perceived and real members of the MDC. Another facet of this strategy was ideological, a reaction that seems to fit very well into what the late Nigerian political scientist, Claude Ake called 'defensive radicalism'.[139] In his *Revolutionary Pressures in Africa*, Ake explains what he means:

---

[136] Herbst, J. (1990) The Structural Adjustment of Politics in Africa, World Politics, vol. 18, no. 7, 949-958, 957.
[137] Sachikonye, L. (2000 b) op.cit. ft. 107, 6.
[138] EU, op.cit. ft. 108, 4.
[139] Ake, C. (1978) *Revolutionary Pressures in Africa*. London: Zed Press, 92.

> It is an attempt at mystification. It is the assumption of a
> radical posture and the use of this posture as a cover for
> containing revolutionary pressures and for maintaining the
> status quo.[140]

It manifests itself in: (a) increasingly radical rhetoric against imperialism even among the most reactionary African leaderships; (b) a verbal commitment to some form of socialism and the rejection of capitalism; (c) policy statements to justify extensions of public ownership; (d) a militant attack on inequality; (e) policy statements explaining curbs on the operations of foreign capital; and (f) the show of being friendly with socialist countries.

Ake explains that defensive radicalism is not simply something that occurs because some African leaders happen to have decided on defending the status quo by means of ideological mystification. Rather, it is an objective necessity of the African situation. 'African leaders have to make a show of being on the side of the masses.'[141] In fact, in a large sense, defensive radicalism can be seen as a substitute to force, which the leaders cannot always rely on to maintain their rule. 'Defensive radicalism is the only way of connecting with the aspirations of the masses, of joining their side so to speak, of plausibly acting as their champions.'[142] There are not many concepts that illuminate Zimbabwe's political economy more than that of Ake's defensive radicalism. This is particularly so in the post-referendum period. As the threat of losing power became more real and imminent, ZANU PF shifted its ideological position to the left of centre. Its rhetoric became unambiguously anti-imperialist, pro-socialist and pro-masses leading to the high profile abandonment of ESAP at the end of 2001. In the 2000 elections, the ruling party's campaign slogan was: 'Land is the economy and the economy is land.' Mugabe never missed an opportunity to speak on the land question in aggressively revolutionary terms. Raftopoulos noted that Mugabe 'repeatedly emphasised *the land* as the sole authentic signifier of national belonging.'[143] At the time of writing, the reigning slogan, captured in many of the government's jingles on the state media declares that 'Our land is our economy', and its 2003 annual conference had the theme 'Total Land Use for Economic Turnaround and Prosperity.' Raftopoulos, without referring to the concept, articulates the ideological *modus operandi* of defensive radicalism in Zimbabwe:

> ...Robert Mugabe has consolidated his support in the Southern
> African region by articulating the land question in Zimbabwe

---

[140] Ibid.
[141] Ibid. 93.
[142] Ibid.
[143] Raftopoulos, B. (2000) op.cit. ft. 70, 279.

> as part of a broader regional, and indeed, continental struggle against a colonial legacy. As the broad socialist alliance that brought ZANU PF to power in 1980 has unravelled, Mugabe has distilled his survival message into an essentialist Africanist position, symbolised by a life and death struggle for land.[144]

Mugabe and his party-state were consciously and assiduously projecting a virulent anti-imperialist stance clothed as Pan-Africanism and themselves as the unwavering champions of this dogma. While appealing for popular support at home, they also appealed for Pan-African unity and solidarity in Southern Africa, the African continent and in the Black Diaspora.

The future of opposition politics in Zimbabwe

In a highly fluid and volatile political milieu, it is impossible to predict what the future has in store. At the beginning of this chapter, we said that opposition politics is not necessarily consituted by organised political parties. It is a much broader canvass that encompasses many oppositional anti-state activities that have a political bearing. What this means is that the future of opposition politics is not necessarily the future of the MDC. Opposition politics preceded the MDC and will outlast it. Given the political culture and history of authoritarianism, that was reinforced by the liberation war culture, and given that culture changes slowly through the process of political socialisation, we can only conclude that for the foreseeable future the life of opposition politics in Zimbabwe will be dark. Defensive radicalism, most recently displayed by the party-state's withdrawal from the Commonwealth, will continue to constrain and restrict opposition political space. The withdrawal itself was probably to unshackle the party-state from any obligations to conform to the principles embodied in the Harare Declaration. When this is read against the backdrop of the sustained assault on the independent media and the stance of the 'restructured' top judiciary, it is difficult to be sanguine about Zimbabwe's opposition politics. Worsening the plight of opposition politics is the Machiavellian manoeuvre by the party-state to immobilise the leader of the main opposition party, Morgan Tsvangirai. Two treason trials hang over his head. As each is extremely serious, one carrying the death penalty, he was forced to surrender his travel documents and is thus virtually in internal exile, unable to travel outside the country to articulate his party's position or counter the demonisation campaign orchestrated by the party-state and its media. In addition, as the

---

[144] Ibid. 285.

Travails of opposition politics in Zimbabwe since Independence

opposition leader, he is under constant surveillance by state security agencies and this has the intended effect of seriously constraining him.

It is clear that almost all routes for organised opposition politics have been blocked, and it is likely that opposition politics will take a more unorganised and anomic tendency. Anomie is a phenomenon that occurs when organised channels of expression and dissent are absent. Almond and Powell explain:

> *Anomic groups are the more or less spontaneous groups that form suddenly when many individuals respond similarly to frustration, disappointment, or other strong emotions. They are flash affairs, rising and subsiding suddenly. Without previous organisation or planning, individuals long frustrated may suddenly take to the streets to vent their anger as a rumour or new injustice sweeps the community or news of a government action touches deep emotions. Their actions may lead to violence, but not necessarily.*
>
> *Particularly where organised groups are absent or where they have failed to obtain adequate representation of their interests in the political system, smouldering discontent may be sparked by an incident or by the emergence of a leader, and it may suddenly explode in unpredictable and uncontrollable ways.*[145]

If Zimbabwe was ripe for a more cohesive and credible opposition party by the end of the 1990s, it can also be said that the failure of this party (the MDC) is most likely to open the floodgates for opposition politics in its anomic forms. The tragedy is that anomic politics, by its very nature, is anarchic politics. In a country besieged by a syndrome of crises, desperate and fast deteriorating conditions of living, and where there are no legitimate avenues for venting mass discontent, it is almost inevitable that the bottled-up anger will explode with ghastly consequences for everyone. Some analysts share this pessimistic prognosis. For instance, Kagoro sees several challenges facing the MDC in the post-presidential election period. One is 'street credibility':

> *There were expectations that if Mugabe stole the election there would be an uprising by the masses. The MDC leaders seem to have expected the masses to initiate this uprising, whereas the masses looked to the MDC leaders to do so. There is thus a crisis of leadership in the alternative movement. .... However, if the MDC leadership is indecisive on this matter, it will lose*

---

[145] Almond and Powell (1998) *Comparative Politics Today*. Scott, Foreman and Company: Boston, 68.

> street credibility as the crisis in Zimbabwe worsens. The ambivalence has been met with brutal attacks against MDC MPs by state security agents and the militia. There is a sense of frustration among MDC supporters that may fuel spontaneous, riotous conduct. .... *The MDC has also not been as effective in demonstrating its continuing relevance to the people's strongly felt needs in the present situation.*[146] *(My emphasis.)*

The MDC leadership itself appears helpless about the resolution of the Zimbabwe crisis and is as frustrated as its restless power base. This was most evident at the recent conference held by the MDC at which Morgan Tsvangirai betrayed this disillusionment. He told his supporters, 'We have tried appeasement. We have tried to reduce the tension during the last quarter of this year [but] we have realised they [ZANU PF] are not sincere,' and warned that the party would organise mass action against Mugabe and his party.[147] Organised mass action has been tried before and has elicited a poor response from the public who are increasingly threatened by the state's retribution. But it still leaves the door wide open for disorganised mass action, anomic political action. Cataclysmic changes seem inevitable, and the next few years will be decisive.

---

[146] Kagoro, B. (2003) op.cit. ft. 19, 24.
[147] SABC, 21 December 2003.

12

The onslaught against democracy and rule of law in Zimbabwe in 2000[1]

Geoffrey Feltoe

The rule of law has been under attack for some time in Zimbabwe, with the year 2000, particularly, seeing a ferocious and unrelenting offensive. It was a year characterised by widespread violence, threats, intimidation and lawlessness. Scores of people were killed and large numbers of people were injured or had their property destroyed. Many of the people affected were completely deprived of the protection of the law. In the aftermath of this violence, fear spread throughout the country.

Most of this violence resulted from the farm invasions orchestrated by the Zimbabwe government and the campaign by supporters of the Zimbabwe African National Union (ZANU PF), the ruling party, against the main opposition party, the Movement for Democratic Change (MDC). In a whole series of court cases, government officials admitted that the farm occupations had been carried out illegally. Nonetheless, the government saw fit to mount a virulent propaganda attack against the judiciary, particularly against white judges.

The violent intimidation of opposition party supporters prior to the 2000 parliamentary election period subverted the entire democratic process by preventing people from exercising their vote freely. Few of the perpetrators of this violence were charged and later the government cynically granted amnesty to most of them.

---

[1] This paper treats in detail of the year 2000. The onslaught it describes continued unabated in the years 2001, 2002 and 2003. The reader can find details of these years at <http://www.lrf.co.zw>www.lrf.co.zw> under special reports: 'Justice in Zimbabwe.'

What will emerge from this paper is a terrifying picture of a corrupt and increasingly unpopular regime[2] that is prepared to promote violence ruthlessly to maintain power.[3] In its propaganda campaign, political opposition is depicted as tantamount to treason, and the ruling party does not hesitate to discard the rule of law whenever it gets in the way of its political machinations. In its desperate bid to cling to power, the regime continues to take actions that are devastating an already extremely weak economy and plunging its people into ever-greater impoverishment and destitution.

The rule of law

The rule of law is an essential foundation of any democratic system of governance. It is a complex concept, but its core aspects are straightforward. It requires that power be exercised in accordance with the law and disallows the arbitrary use of extra-legal power. It requires that everyone should be equally subject to the law and that no one should be above the law. It requires that the law enforcement agencies and the courts should enforce and apply the law impartially. Finally, it requires that the law should protect everyone equally against illegal action causing harm.

The Zimbabwe government has claimed that adherence to the rule of law would have prevented meaningful land reform. It has maintained that the property laws were designed to protect minority land rights at the expense of the majority and that the judges, particularly the white judges, were interpreting these laws to give maximum protection to vested property rights. It has argued that the white commercial farmers were bound to rely on these laws to prevent proper land reform.

Yet it is clear that radical land reform could have been achieved within the framework of the law and without the destructive chaos and lawlessness that has accompanied the government-orchestrated farm invasions and

---

[2] According to *The Political Opinion and the Crisis in Zimbabwe Survey*, a public opinion survey commissioned by Helen Suzman Foundation of South Africa and published in October 2001, 74 per cent of Zimbabweans want Mugabe to quit. It was also estimated in this survey that if the presidential election was held at the time the survey was published the leader of the MDC, Morgan Tsvangirai, would win by 62 per cent to 38 per cent for Mugabe. According to the survey Mugabe was seen by most people as the major obstacle to improvement in the country. A branch of Gallup Poll in Zimbabwe carried out this survey. Some analysts, however, have cast doubts on the reliability of this survey, suggesting that its methodology is flawed and the questions were compiled in a biased fashion.

[3] During the 1980s ZANU PF mercilessly smashed ZAPU during the *Gukuruhundi* era, killing thousands of people in the process, most of whom were civilians. See *Breaking the Silence Building True Peace* (1997) joint report of the Catholic Commission for Justice and Peace in Zimbabwe and the Legal Resources Foundation, Harare. See also Welshman Ncube; *State Security, the Rule of Law and Politics of Repression in Zimbabwe* (1990).

its 'fast-track' land grab. Whilst it is true that the commercial farmers had used the legal system in the past to retard the progress of land reform, government could have overcome any attempts by the commercial farmers to block or obstruct necessary land reform in the future by passing appropriate laws and making sure that the prescribed procedures were scrupulously followed. Additionally, there probably would have been far less resistance on the part of commercial farmers to land reform if government had not suddenly decided, in February 2000, that it would pay compensation only for improvements on expropriated land.[4]

The political and economic environment

Up to the year 2000, ZANU PF was politically dominant in Zimbabwe. This was particularly so after the Zimbabwe African People's Union (ZAPU), led by Joshua Nkomo, was absorbed through the unity agreement of 1988. ZANU PF strongly believed that it had a right to rule in perpetuity because it had liberated Zimbabwe from colonialism. It was intolerant of political opposition. Up to 1990, the official ZANU PF policy was to have a legislated one-party state. When in 2000 a new 'upstart' political party, that had been formed only in September 1999, threatened its stranglehold on power, it reacted in a predictable way.

At the beginning of the year 2000 the Zimbabwean economy was in a complete mess. The government was largely responsible for this. Runaway spending, uncontrolled borrowing and rampant corruption had produced mountainous debt, spiralling inflation and sky-high interest rates. The government was squandering large sums of money in the Democratic Republic of the Congo to prop up the Kabila regime. There was a huge budget deficit. The climate for commercial business was extremely hostile and many businesses were failing or contracting, thereby swelling the ranks of the (then) conservatively estimated 50 per cent unemployment rate. The cost of living was rising and poverty was rapidly spreading.[5]

---

[4] The last minute amendments to the draft constitution of the Constitutional Commission to the land provisions created the impression that no compensation whatsoever would be payable for expropriated land if Britain did not honour its 'obligations' to pay into a resettlement fund. Before this amendment the draft constitution required the payment of just and equitable compensation but went on to draw from the South African Constitutional provisions requiring there to be an equitable balance between the interests of the public and of the landowner and that certain criteria be taken into account, such as the history of ownership and the current use to which the property was being put. However, there was an incredibly vague additional criterion not to be found in the South African Constitution, namely the resources available to the acquiring authority in implementing the programme of land reform. Later the Land Acquisition Act was amended to allow government to pay such compensation over a number of years.

[5] According to 1998 Central Statistical Office figures, 63.3 per cent of Zimbabweans were poor and 47 per cent were very poor, whereas in 1991, 40.4 per cent were poor and 16.7 per cent were very poor. In October 1998 the (then) Minister of Finance stated that 75 per cent of Zimbabweans were poor and 47 per cent were very poor. Poverty in the rural areas is far more acute.

There were recurrent fuel shortages and frequent power cuts. International financial institutions had withdrawn financial support because of the inability of the government to fulfil its fiscal obligations.

By the end of the year the economic situation was nothing short of a disaster. The violence had driven away investors and tourists, and unemployment had risen to about 55 per cent as more and more businesses closed. Poverty was spreading at an alarming rate. However, in the delusional world of ZANU PF, government was not responsible for this state of affairs. It was claimed the poor state of the economy was due to the falling prices on international markets for primary commodities and to vindictive measures applied by some western governments and international institutions to try to reverse Zimbabwe's quest to achieve economic equity by its land-reform programme.[6]

Government response to the referendum outcome

The pivotal event of the year 2000 was the rejection of the government-sponsored draft constitution by 54 per cent of the voters in February. This sparked off a series of extreme responses from government that have all but destroyed the rule of law and have had ruinous consequences for the country. Based on its previous electoral support, the ruling party confidently expected the electorate to endorse the draft constitution. It threw its full weight behind it and the state-controlled media gave saturation coverage to those campaigning for the approval of the draft. On the other side, a coalition of non-government organisations – the National Constitutional Assembly, and the recently established opposition party, the MDC – campaigned for a rejection.[7]

Before putting it to the people, the government made various changes to the draft. The most important related to land. The amended provision provided that the government would not be obliged to pay compensation for land it expropriated for resettlement if the former colonial power (Britain) failed to provide funds for such compensation. It was believed that this amendment would ensure that at least rural voters would vote heavily in favour of the draft.[8]

---

[6] See President Mugabe's State of the Nation Address reported in full in *The Herald* on 21 December 2001.
[7] Its main objection to the draft was that it did not properly reflect the wishes of the people, especially in relation to eliminating the inordinate concentration of power in the hands of the Executive President.
[8] The land issue figured prominently during the exercise to draw up a new constitution for Zimbabwe. In its advertising campaign for a 'YES' vote in the referendum, the Constitutional Commission executive paid particular attention to the land issue. Using racist and politically inflammatory language, it accused reactionary and racist whites and other 'sell-outs' of opposing the draft constitution because they did not want land reform. It alleged that persons opposed to the draft constitution were sell-outs and puppets of their colonial masters.

The ruling party was thus badly shocked by the rejection of the draft.[9] Initially, President Mugabe seemed prepared to accept the outcome, but this was only the calm before the storm. Within days large-scale farm invasions began. There was also a welter of recriminations against a whole variety of targets. There were vitriolic attacks on whites, especially white farmers, and against the MDC. In mid-March the president said: 'Those who try to cause disunity among our people must watch out because death will befall them.'[10] In early April, he said the whites were determined to fight against ZANU PF and that they would not win. If they aligned themselves with the MDC they would be treated as MDC and would never win the election.[11] Other members of the ruling party also made inflammatory statements against the MDC and the whites.

The involvement of war veterans

The conditions for a major escalation of violence in Zimbabwe were created by the ruling party's fateful decision to co-opt the war veterans for their election campaign. Those same war veterans who were fanatically loyal to the ruling party were later to execute the farm invasions. The ruling party announced that the war veterans would help with its election campaign and initially allocated them Z$20 million for this purpose.[12] In mid-March, one of the leaders of the National Liberation War Veterans' Association, Andrew Ndlovu, threatened to use violence to overthrow the MDC if it won the upcoming parliamentary elections. He said that the war veterans would never allow the country 'to go back to Smith' and that if it did they would 'declare a military government'. He noted that the war fighters had arms caches all over the country. 'We will get arms from government armouries. We are a reserve army and we have the right to use the arms to defend the government of ZANU PF. We will invade military camps just as we have gone to the farms.'[13] This statement did not attract any public condemnation from the ruling party and no criminal charges were laid against Ndlovu for these utterances. However, some leaders of the war veterans who organised farm occupations and the campaigns of violence

---

[9] Some rejected it because of objections to its contents, but many probably rejected it to protest against the disastrous state of the economy that they attributed to gross mismanagement and corruption by ZANU PF.
[10] *The Daily News*, 17 March 2000.
[11] *The Herald*, 8 April 2000.
[12] The Chairman of the War Veterans Association, Dr Chenjerai Hunzvi, immediately complained that this amount was inadequate.
[13] *The Daily News*, 16 March 2000.

faced criminal charges or were accused of engaging in other disreputable conduct.[14]

The farm invasions

In all these sad scenarios, the government pretended that it did not order, organise or take part in these farm invasions. It claimed that the invasions were a spontaneous manifestation by the people desperate for land and a peaceful protest against the rejection of a constitution that contained a provision allowing government to acquire white farm land without compensation. The president said he would not intervene in the invasions as long as the war veterans remained peaceful.[15] Later in March 2000, he said, 'There have been very few cases of violence, but if the farmers start to be angry and start to be violent, then of course they will get that medicine delivered to them. And it can be very, very, very severe, but we don't want to get there.'

---

[14] Andrew Ndlovu is a rehabilitated former anti-dissident who fought to destabilise Zimbabwe during the mid-1980s. He operated as a dissident in Matabeleland until he received an amnesty in 1987. He is alleged to have been involved in the kidnapping and murder of four tourists. He is also alleged to have been involved in a number of murders of District Development Fund workers and committed a number of rape cases. Dr Chenjerai Hitler Hunzvi has been tried on criminal charges of fraud in which he is alleged to have defrauded the War Victims Compensation Fund of $361,620. Although he was acquitted by the High court of these charges because the State failed to prove its case, the judge said that Hunzvi had been up to some mischief or no good, as there were a number of unsatisfactory features in his evidence and conduct. He has also appeared in court on a charge of defrauding war veterans companies of $3 million. Serious allegations have also been made that he had misappropriated funds from the ex-combatants' company, Zexcom. At one stage it was reported that the police said they were keen to interview him in connection with allegations of fraud. Hunzvi's Polish ex-wife has alleged that Hunzvi used to beat her when they were married. Before the June 2000 Parliamentary election, his surgery in a high-density suburb in Harare was allegedly used as a torture centre. In the lead up to the Bikita West by-election in January 2001, allegations have been made that Hunzvi participated in the petrol bombing of some MDC vehicles and that he, personally, beat some alleged MDC supporters.
Mr Joseph Chinotimba was recently charged with attempted murder arising out of an incident on 13 October 2000 in Harare, where he is alleged to have shot twice his next-door neighbour, a female member of the MDC, seriously injuring her (*The Sunday Mail* 15 October 2000). The fact that he was on bail facing this serious charge did not stop him from taking part in a protest against the Supreme Court judges and actively campaigning for ZANU PF in two by-elections.

[15] Speaking in a CNN interview Mugabe said, 'We did not order the war veterans to occupy land. They did it entirely on their own, but we can talk to them and we can advise them. As long as the occupation is peaceful and there is no seizure of any property on the land or any violence, it amounts to a mere demonstration and to the extent that it is a mere peaceful demonstration, we will not intervene. The government has not intervened and if that is encouragement, well let it be, but we haven't actually organised it in that physical sense.' The interview was published by *The Sunday Mail* and broadcast by ZBC. Information Minister Chen Chimutengwende described as 'absolute rubbish' allegations that the war veterans' actions were incited by the government. He said, 'Those who voted 'NO' (in the referendum) complicated the matter. It's now leading to these invasions and I can only see more of the invasions.' The *Mail and Guardian* 2 March 2000.

It is quite clear that these farm invasions were planned and orchestrated by the leadership of ZANU PF. There is overwhelming evidence that high-ranking party members were actively involved in this campaign, together with intelligence and army personnel.[16] The farm invasions formed an essential part of a political strategy to combat the growing influence of the MDC and to win back rural support by using the promise of land resettlement. The government also used the land issue to try to deflect attention away from other pressing problems, such as the dire state of the economy and widespread corruption within government.[17]

A few days after the referendum results there were large-scale, synchronised invasions of farms countrywide.[18] The rapid expansion of the process required considerable pre-planning and logistical support and it was clear there was substantial government involvement. The farm occupiers were transported in an assortment of government vehicles.[19] Once in place, the occupiers received monthly payments and regular food supplies delivered in government vehicles. Government ministers and other high-ranking ZANU PF politicians and local party officials linked up with war veterans during this process. Only a small number of the invaders were actually war veterans. Most were far too young to have taken part in the liberation struggle and probably participated primarily because they were unemployed, although some did so because they wished to obtain land. There is no doubt that government condoned and supported the invasions once they were underway.

---

[16] See *Who is responsible? A preliminary analysis of pre-election violence in Zimbabwe* (A report compiled by the Zimbabwe Human Rights Non-Governmental Organisations Forum) 20 June 2000.

[17] Veteran politician James Chikerema has said that the farm invasions were organised and orchestrated and that the President, desperate to counteract the support for MDC, had hired Hunzvi to use war veterans to intimidate the electorate. The war veterans being used were on the criminal fringe and its leadership has court cases pending. The President, he asserted, was using the land issue as a decoy to divert people's attention away from the corruption and misrule of the government. (These remarks were made in an interview published in *The Daily News* on 28 April 2000.) Jerry Grant, vice-president of the Commercial Farmers' Union, which represents most of Zimbabwe's commercial farmers, said, 'I'm shell-shocked. I just can't believe a government can behave in this manner.' He said the government, which had blamed whites for its referendum defeat, orchestrated the invasions. 'The word is out that this is punishment for the whites for rejecting the constitution,' he said. 'It is orchestrated at the highest level. There are government and party vehicles involved in delivering (the invaders).' Grant said white farmers had been subjected to 'serious intimidation'. 'The police are aware of this and they're still doing nothing about it. They've had an instruction from the top not to interfere.'

[18] Invasions of white-owned farms first began at the end of February and, within a few hours, over the weekend of 26-27 February 2000, groups of 'war veterans' had occupied farms in Mashonaland East, Mashonaland West, Mashonaland Central, Masvingo and Manicaland provinces.

[19] These include District Development Fund vehicles, Air Force vehicles and various other vehicles with government number plates.

Despite several court orders ordering the eviction of farm invaders on several occasions, President Mugabe declared that government would not drive the farm invaders off the farms until the land issue was resolved. In his perception, the invaders were the vanguard of a land revolution. This was necessary to complete the goals of the War of Liberation.[20] High-ranking government officials, including a minister and a governor,[21] publicly stated that only ZANU PF supporters would be settled on the land that had been acquired. This showed clearly the political objective of this exercise. Settlement on the land was to be used to reward party loyalists such as the war veterans and their supporters, and to induce members of the opposition to defect to ZANU PF.

In early April 2000, the president said no white commercial farmer would be chased away from Zimbabwe as long as he or she wanted to stay in the country and share land with the landless blacks.[22] But as time went on the anti-white rhetoric intensified and, in ZANU PF propaganda, the white farmers became the enemy of the people. The numbers of expropriations of white commercial farms was drastically increased as the government implemented its 'fast-track' resettlement programme. By the time of the ZANU PF congress in December 2001, the president was really on the warpath against the white farmers.

He declared a racial war against whites in general, in these terms: 'Our party must continue to strike fear in the heart of the white man, our real enemy.'[23] In his State of the Nation address, the president claimed yet again that the thousands of war veterans and landless peasants had 'spontaneously moved on to commercial farms to demonstrate their determination to see government effect a speedy resolution to the land question'. It was this that had 'prompted government to deal with the land issue decisively by adopting the fast-track land-reform programme'.[24]

Court rulings in relation to farm invasions

The High Court decisions

When the farm invasions started, Augustine Chihuri, the Commissioner of Police, ignored them. The police, he said, could not act because the

---

[20] See for instance *The Herald*, 9 June 2000.
[21] Minister Gezi and the Governor of Matabeleland North, Obert Mpofu, respectively.
[22] *The Herald*, 8 April 2000. It should be pointed out that many white farmers bought the land after 1980. Assurances were given that their property rights would be secure. During earlier land redistribution programmes, a number of these farmers had been given certificates of no interest in acquiring the land.
[23] The *Zimbabwe Independent*, 15 December 2000. The number of whites in Zimbabwe in 2000 was somewhere in the region of 70,000 among 12.8 million blacks. This speech was made just a few days after war veterans had killed another white farmer.
[24] *The Herald*, 21 December 2000.

The onslaught against democracy and rule of law in Zimbabwe in 2000

matter was political.[25] On 17 March, the Commercial Farmers' Union (CFU) obtained a High Court order, from Judge Paddington Garwe, declaring the land invasions illegal and ordering the police to evict unlawful occupiers within 24 hours.[26] This order was made with the consent of all the parties, including Dr Chenjerai Hunzvi, leader of the war veterans, and the police.

In his affidavit in connection with this case, Dr Hunzvi categorically denied that he had been involved in organising or encouraging farm invasions.[27] Yet, in an interview at the beginning of March, he had said that it was within the rights of the former combatants to invade the farms. He said they were bitter about the fact that white farmers had engineered the rejection of the draft constitution that contained a provision for state acquisition of land without compensation.[28] He went even further and played a very active role in the later invasions. By December, Dr Hunzvi was no longer engaging in any dissimulation. He warned of more confrontation with the farmers. He said he was not talking to farmers because dialogue had broken down and he didn't think it was going to resume. 'We are now fighting for our land and whosoever is killed, it's tough luck,' he said.

Leaders of the war veterans changed their earlier stance and publicly proclaimed they would not obey Judge Garwe's court order, but instead would intensify the programme of farm occupations. The police did not attempt to comply with the order, claiming that the issue was a political one and that it would be impossible, dangerous and counterproductive to do so.[29]

The attorney-general then applied for a variation of the order on behalf of the police. He argued that after it was issued, the police realised that they had insufficient resources to effect the evictions. It would be ill advised for the police to intervene in a situation that was so charged with political and racial overtones. The land distribution and ownership

---

[25] *The Herald*, 29 February 2000. Later, on 13 January 2001, the Commissioner of Police cast off any thin cloak of political neutrality he had worn previously. He publicly announced, 'I support ZANU PF because it is the ruling party.' See The *Daily News*, 16 January 2001.

[26] *Commercial Farmers' Union v Commissioner of Police & Ors* HH-3544-2000. The High Court also ordered that in taking action to evict the illegal occupiers, the police commissioner and his officers were to disregard any Executive instruction, if that instruction prevented the police from effecting the evictions. The Executive deliberately misinterpreted this to mean that they had been ordered not intercede to assist in the process of ending these illegal farm occupations.

[27] He said, 'I must categorically state that I am not and was not responsible for the occupation of the farms.' *The Standard* 19-25 March 2000.

[28] *The Herald*, 1 March.

[29] The Minister of Information, Chen Chimutengwende said, 'I don't know what the police will do on this issue, it is a very serious political matter.' He questioned whether the courts could give orders to Mugabe and the Commissioner of Police.

201

pattern in Zimbabwe was iniquitous and it needed to be remedied in the shortest possible time. He further argued that it would not promote the rule of law to enforce an inequitable ownership structure through the application of brutal state power.

Judge Chinhengo[30] characterised the invasions as illegal and of a riotous nature. The Commissioner of Police, had a clear duty, he said, to enforce the consent order and to afford commercial farmers the protection of the law enshrined in the constitution. If there were laws that stood in the way of more equitable land redistribution, parliament could change the laws. Whilst the laws remained in existence, however, the courts had the duty to enforce those laws. In the opinion of the judge, police intervention was unlikely to ignite an already explosive situation. Where the executive had acted on the previous farm invasions, the invasions had ended.

Yet the farm invasions continued and the police continued to take no action. On 19 April, the High Court held Dr Hunzvi in contempt of court for failing to comply with an earlier High Court order barring him from inciting war veterans to invade farms.[31] The judge, however, postponed the passing of sentence until 5 May[32] on condition that Dr Hunzvi complied with the initial court order and that he took steps to assist the CFU to ensure peaceful evacuation from the occupied farms.

The Supreme Court decisions

The CFU brought two actions in the Supreme Court. In the first, in mid-September 2001, it challenged the legality of the entire resettlement programme. In the second, brought at the end of October, it complained that government had failed to follow the correct procedures for acquisition specified in the laws it had passed.

In the first case the CFU argued that the laws upon which the state was relying to carry out its programme of land acquisition were unconstitutional.

Before the Supreme Court could hand down its decision in the first case, the CFU felt obliged to bring a second action, because the government was not complying with legally prescribed procedural requirements in carrying out its fast-track resettlement programme. In this second case, the respondents were the ministers involved in carrying out the resettlement programme and the provincial governors. The respondents consented to the order handed down by the Supreme Court, acknowledging

---

[30] *The Commissioner of Police v The Commercial Farmers' Union* HH-84-2000. This judgment was handed down on 13 April.
[31] *The Herald*, 20 April. The CFU had applied for an order sentencing Hunzvi for contempt of court, but conditionally suspending the sentence on condition that he complied with the court order.
[32] On 5 May 2000 the court granted an application by the CFU to further postpone this matter to allow Dr Hunzvi further time to comply with the order.

the illegality of the programme. They were ordered to stop implementing it until the procedural prerequisites had been followed. The court also ordered the police to remove from farms all persons who had unlawfully entered the properties or had breached the peace on the occupied farms.[33]

The Supreme Court then gave its judgment in the first case:[34] 'There is no dispute that a programme of land reform is necessary and indeed essential for the future peace and prosperity of Zimbabwe.' It was expected, however, that the resettlement would be carried out in conformity with the law. The government had enacted the necessary laws but had then failed to comply with its own laws.

It went on to observe that the government was 'unwilling to carry out a sustainable programme of land reform in terms of its own law' [section 16A of the constitution].[35] The settling of people on farms

> has been entirely haphazard and unlawful. A network of organisations, operating with complete disregard of the law, has been allowed to take over from government. War veterans, villagers and unemployed urban people have simply moved onto farms. They have been supported, encouraged, transported and financed by party officials, public servants, the CIO and the Army. The rule of law has been overthrown in the commercial farming areas and farmers and farm workers on occupied farms had consistently been deprived of the protection of the law.

The Supreme Court declared further that farm occupations amounted to unfair discrimination. Various government officials had announced that only ZANU PF supporters would be resettled on the land. This amounted to unfair political discrimination against farmers who were believed to be supporters of an opposition party. If ZANU PF party branches or cells or officials are involved in the selection of settlers and the allocation of plots, the exercise degenerates from being an historical righting of wrongs into pure discrimination.[36] The displacement of thousands of farm workers of foreign origin who were lawful permanent residents also amounted to unfair discrimination. And forcing farmers

---

[33] *Commercial Farmers' Union v Minister of Lands, Agriculture & Rural Resettlement* Supreme Court case S-314-2000.
[34] *Commercial Farmers' Union v Minister of Lands, Agriculture and Resettlement* Supreme Court case S-132-2000.
[35] It is relevant to note here that Article 14 of the African Charter of Human and People's Rights provides that the right to property must be guaranteed and must 'only be encroached upon in the interest of the public need or in the general interest of the public and *in accordance of the provisions of appropriate laws.*' (Emphasis added.)
[36] If the government had had a serious intention to allocate land on a non-politically partisan basis it would have set up a Land Commission that would have distributed expropriated land on the basis of need and not on the basis of party political affiliation.

and farm workers to attend political rallies violated their right to freedom of association and assembly.

The Supreme Court ordered the respondents[37] to comply with the High Court and Supreme Court orders, made with the consent of the parties, in terms of which government was ordered to comply with the law. It also forbade the minister involved to take further steps to acquire land. However, it postponed the operation of this interdict for six months to enable the ministers to produce a workable programme of land reform and to enable the Minister of Home Affairs and the Commissioner of Police to satisfy the court that 'the rule of law has been restored in the commercial farming areas.'[38]

It is difficult to understand this delay. Once the court had decided that the resettlement exercise was unconstitutional, one would have expected the court to order it to stop until a proper programme was in place. What the court was doing was allowing the government to continue with an unconstitutional process while taking steps to make it constitutional.

In the first land case to come before the Supreme Court after his installation as acting chief justice [No 55, May 2001], Justice Chidyausiku tried to pick holes in the previous Supreme Court decision [S-132-2000]. He ruled there was no constitutional requirement that government must put in place a land-reform programme before acquiring land in terms of the Land Acquisition Act. There was no such requirement provided for in the constitutional provision relating to acquisition, namely, section 16.

It was only in the compensation provision, section 16A of the constitution, that reference was made to a land reform programme. Thus, the issue of a programme only became relevant with reference to compensation. He also sought to cast doubt on the Supreme Court's interdict on the minister about acquiring land for redistribution under the powers given to him under the Land Acquisition Act. The four other Supreme Court judges disagreed with this reasoning, holding that sections 16 and 16A are inextricably inter-linked and one could not separate compulsory acquisition from compensation. A land reform programme was a necessary prerequisite for acquisition of agricultural land for resettlement.

ZANU PF attacks the judges

Given the political aims of its sponsored land invasions, the government was not prepared to allow the courts to interfere. It simply ignored the

---

[37] The Ministers involved in the resettlement programme, the Minister of Home Affairs, the Commissioner of Police and the President.

[38] The court does not set out how it will enforce this order, and what steps will be taken if a workable programme is not produced and the rule of law is not restored on commercial farms. The CFU would presumably have to return to court and ask the court to fine the government and the police in contempt.

court rulings to evict farm invaders and to comply with the required legal procedures. It proceeded to mount vicious verbal attacks upon the judges, and stage-managed a series of protests by the war veterans against them, culminating in the invasion of the main courtroom of the Supreme Court just before the court was due to sit. The war veterans vowed they would force the judges to resign. In early December 2001, the permanent secretary in the Ministry of Justice, Legal and Parliamentary Affairs disclosed that he had received a report that the war veterans and supporters of ZANU PF were planning to attack judges at their homes to force them to resign.[39]

The Minister for Information in the President's Office led this campaign, accusing the Supreme Court, particularly the chief justice, of being biased in favour of the white landowners at the expense of the landless majority. He called upon the chief justice to resign.[40] ZANU PF members of parliament urged government to set up a commission of inquiry to investigate the judges. The Minister of Justice, Legal and Parliamentary Affairs joined in this campaign, attacking a number of the white judges and suggested that their appointment had been ill-advised.[41]

On a number of occasions President Mugabe denounced the white judges. Speaking at the ZANU PF congress on 14 December he went further and disowned the courts. Referring to the land issue he said, 'The courts can do what they want. They are not courts for our people and we should not even be defending ourselves in these courts.' The purpose of these constant attacks was to discredit the judiciary and create the impression that the judges were deliberately obstructing the equitable redistribution of land. They were also intended to intimidate the judges into becoming more compliant and ruling in favour of the executive.[42] When the judges continued to manifest their independence, the government appointed four judges who had connections with the ruling party.

The chiefs attack the chief justice

In January 2001, many chiefs,[43] who as traditional leaders wielded considerable influence in their local areas, joined in the attack upon the

---

[39] He said he had handed over the matter to the police. 'It is a very sad development because the judges are defenceless.' He had been receiving calls from Supreme Court judges, who were concerned about their security, after receiving many threats from the war veterans. *The Daily News*, 14 December 2000.
[40] *The Financial Gazette*, 2-8 November 2000.
[41] *The Herald*, 29 November. Two out of the five Supreme Court judges are whites and four out of nineteen High Court judges are white. All the white judges were appointed by government after 1980. Gubbay was appointed as Chief Justice in 1990.
[42] In January, the UN Special Rapporteur on the Independence of Judges and Lawyers expressed concern about threats against judges in Zimbabwe. He said: 'Threats and intimidation of independent judges and their institutions will necessarily be seen as attacks on the rule of law, which is the very foundation of a democratic state'.
[43] The government appoints Chiefs.

chief justice and called for his resignation. Showing remarkable disregard for the concept of separation of powers, one of the chiefs said, 'Justice Gubbay is working against the same government that gave him the job and pays his salary. He must be fired. When a person is employed, he must serve the interests of the employer and if he fails to do that he must be fired.'

The judge president attacks the chief justice

In the same month, the head of the High Court, Judge President Chidyausiku, joined in the attacks upon the chief justice by publicly accusing him of bias in favour of the white commercial farmers. He said the chief justice had started the controversy by his public remarks in 1991, in which he criticised a proposed constitutional amendment that sought to remove the power of the courts to determine the fairness of the compensation payable for land acquired for resettlement. These comments, said the judge president, gave an implicit assurance to the white commercial farmers that if they sued the government after being evicted they would win their cases. In effect, the judge president accused the chief justice and the Supreme Court of having pre-decided all cases brought by commercial farmers in the farmers' favour.

This accusation is unfounded. The Supreme Court decided against the commercial farmers in a case in 1996.[44] In this case, some commercial farmers appealed to the Supreme Court against the decision by Judge Chidyausiku.[45] The judge had ruled designation of land for acquisition did not amount to acquisition and that farmers were not entitled to compensation in terms of the constitution. The Supreme Court agreed with this judgment and dismissed the appeal.[46]

The two other decisions by the Supreme Court on land resettlement have been dealt with above. In one case, the government consented to the order handed down. In the other, the first order granted by the Supreme Court was merely one that had been previously granted by the consent of government in cases in the High Court and the Supreme Court. In respect of all these orders, there could be no question of bias against government because the government agreed to the orders. It is only in respect of the second order of the Supreme Court that any allegation of

---

[44] *Davies & Ors v Minister of Lands and Agriculture & Water Development* 1996 (1) ZLR 81 (S).
[45] *Davies & Ors v Minister of Lands, Agriculture and Water Development* 1994 (2) ZLR 294 (H).
[46] It should also be pointed out that the Supreme Court has decided in favour of government in a number of other property related disputes. These include *Hewlett v Minister of Finance & Anor* 1981 ZLR 571 (S); *May & Ors v Reserve Bank of Zimbabwe* 1985 (2) ZLR 358 (S); *Nyambirai v NSSA & Anor* 1995 (2) ZLR 1 (S) and *Chairman, Public Service Commission & Ors v Zimbabwe Teachers' Association* 1996 (1) ZLR 637 (S).

bias might be relevant. This was the one that interdicted the government from continuing with acquisition and resettlement until a proper plan had been put in place and the rule of law had been restored on the farms.

Having adjudged the government scheme not to be constitutional, however, the court then gave the government considerable leeway by suspending the interdict for six months. It is difficult to see any legal basis for the judge president to take issue with these decisions by the Supreme Court. The government had conceded the illegality of the farm invasions and had consented to the order relating to those invasions. In regard to the nature of the programme, the Supreme Court fully accepted that a programme of land reform was essential for future peace and prosperity. What it could not accept was the unplanned, chaotic, politically biased and violent nature of the current fast-track 'programme.' Again it is difficult to see to what aspects of this the judge president could object. For instance, he surely could not be in favour of the violent assaults and killings that had been taking place.

In his stinging attack upon the Supreme Court the judge president also raised the issue of the setting aside of one of his judgments by the Supreme Court. After the Supreme Court had, with the consent of the government officials involved in the case, ordered the eviction of farm occupiers, a number of the persons facing eviction had sought to bring a class action in the High Court to oppose their eviction. The judge president granted a provisional order suspending the Supreme Court judgment and allowing the occupiers leave to bring their class action in the Supreme Court. The Supreme Court then set aside this order on the basis that the Judge President had no power to suspend a Supreme Court decision.

Technically this is correct. Only the Supreme Court can set aside its own decision. The Judge President complained that this decision breached the right of the occupiers to be heard before a decision affecting them was taken. However, when the Supreme Court had made its order with the consent of the government, the occupiers had not commenced their action and there was no way in which they could have been heard before the decision. If the matter was to be reopened the correct procedure was for the occupiers to apply to the Supreme Court to set aside or suspend the carrying out of its order so that the occupiers could be allowed to present their arguments on why the order should not be carried out.[47]

---

[47] It is apparent that the Judge President completely misunderstood the ruling by the Supreme Court. It ruled that the Judge President could not grant leave for a class action to be instituted *in the Supreme Court*, as a class action can only be instituted in the High Court. In his attack upon the Supreme Court, the Judge President complained that the Supreme Court had wrongly ruled that the High Court has no jurisdiction to grant leave to institute a class action. The point is that the High Court only has jurisdiction to grant leave to institute a class action *in the High Court*.

Resignation of the chief justice

The unrelenting attacks on the judges took their toll. The government forced the chief justice to retire well before his term of office expired[48] and applied enormous pressure on the remaining judges to follow suit. The ZANU PF members of parliament passed a vote of no confidence in the Supreme Court and the Minister of Justice visited the remaining Supreme Court judges to encourage them to resign.

An agreement was finally reached between government and the chief justice about his early retirement. Chief Justice Gubbay agreed not to oppose the appointment of an acting chief justice and the government agreed not to interfere with the judiciary or make further attempts to unlawfully remove any of the remaining judges. The government also withdrew all demeaning statements previously made by officials about Judge Gubbay.

Dr Hunzvi immediately said the war veterans would not recognise this agreement and would intensify their efforts to kick out the whole Supreme Court bench and white High Court judges. He said the war veterans would use violence to achieve this if necessary.

Were there any alternatives to land invasions?

During the colonial occupation of Zimbabwe, the white occupiers forcibly dispossessed the indigenous people of Zimbabwe of their land, taking the fertile land for themselves. Before the year 2000, the pattern of land distribution in Zimbabwe was highly inequitable and land reform was urgently required.[49] From 1980 to 1990, entrenched provisions in the constitution protected land rights and made it very difficult for the government to bring about meaningful land re-distribution.[50] Nonetheless, with financial assistance from various governments, including Britain,[51] from 1980 until 1999 government acquired

---

[48] *The Herald*, 3 February 2001.
[49] About 4,500 white farmers own 11 million hectares of Zimbabwe's prime agricultural land. The total white population of Zimbabwe constitutes about one per cent of the total population. About one million blacks occupy 16 million hectares, in far less fertile and more drought-prone areas. The communal farming areas occupied by black farmers are congested, and the land is over farmed. The white-owned farms are typically large, mechanised estates using modern farming methods. In the communal lands farming is carried out on a small-scale basis and provides subsistence for the farmers, or a small cash crop. In a CFU publication entitled *Facts on Land and Present Situation, April 2000*, it is stated that CFU members occupy 20,7 per cent of the total land holding in Zimbabwe of 39 million acres.
[50] These required the government to pay full market price for expropriated land. The payment had to be made in foreign currency, if the owner of the property requested this. This obviously made it expensive for government to acquire land.
[51] The British government has provided somewhere in the region of £44 million towards the land resettlement programme.

3,8 million hectares of commercial farmland and resettled 71,000 families.[52]

Many of the early resettlement programmes were not successful due to inadequate planning and failure to provide proper infrastructures and agrarian support systems. Corruption also crept in as high-ranking members of the ruling party acquired sizeable quantities of farm land and were granted leases on land made available after existing leases were cancelled, by government, on all leased state land.[53] The commercial farmers also used the failure by the government to follow the procedures, laid out in the acquisition legislation, in order to obstruct and delay acquisition for resettlement.

What seemed a suitable framework for planned resettlement was finally put in place in September 1998. Agreement was reached at an international donors' conference on a programme of resettlement based on a policy framework document produced by the government. This envisaged a planned and properly implemented resettlement programme with donor funding for the necessary infrastructure to support the resettled farmers.[54] As preconditions for funding, the donor community obviously required that the programme be transparent, that it would benefit those in need of land, and that compensation be paid for acquired land. Two months later the government simply abandoned the programme, claiming lack of donor support.[55]

So in mid-2000 the government decided to embark on its fast-track resettlement programme. Within a matter of months, and without any proper planning and preparation, and also just prior to the rainy season, it acquired five million hectares of commercial farmland, mostly without following the proper procedures for acquisition.[56] It proceeded to settle 46,111 families on 2,5 million hectares of this land. In a speech, President Mugabe, in effect, admitted that the infrastructure for large-scale

---

[52] Government also owned 300,000 hectares of former commercial farmland, which had not yet been allocated for resettlement. There were also sizeable quantities of land that could have been acquired as derelict land.
[53] An opposition party MP, Margaret Dongo, revealed in parliament in March 2000 that 272 State-owned farms had been leased to high-ranking civil servants and members of the ruling party.
[54] Initially, under this scheme, a limited number of properties would be acquired and various resettlement schemes would be tested. A planned resettlement programme would follow.
[55] In November 1998 the government proceeded to issue large numbers of acquisition orders but then could not proceed with these acquisitions because the Administrative Court ruled that government had not complied with proper procedures.
[56] In the case of *Commercial Farmers' Union v Minister of Lands, Agriculture & Rural Resettlement* Supreme Court case S-314 2000 of the Supreme Court pointed out that, 'All the indications are that the government has overreached itself in terms of the numbers of farms listed, both from the point of view of the financial resources available, and of the administrative capacity not only to handle the acquisition exercise, but also to cope with the very large burden that will be thrown upon the Administrative Court'.

resettlement on the huge quantities of acquired land had not been put in place. He said that before the onset of the rainy season in 2001 government would resettle landless people on the remaining 2,5 million hectares. It would then put in place the necessary infrastructure and support systems.

Given the current parlous state of the economy and the lack of donor support, it was highly unlikely that government would be able to provide the support systems needed to allow peasant farmers to make anything like full use of previously productive farms. Dumping landless peasants and their families on acquired farms without the necessary support systems can hardly be seen as a sensible method of solving the problem of inequitable land distribution in Zimbabwe.

The land invasions themselves caused havoc on the commercial farms.[57] On some farms infrastructure such as tobacco barns and irrigation equipment was destroyed. Farm animals were stolen or slaughtered for the pot. There was extensive poaching of wild animals on game ranches. Huge areas of woodland were indiscriminately cut down. Many farmers were ordered not to plant tobacco or wheat. Where planting had occurred, some of the crops were pulled up so that the occupiers could plant maize. Several farmers were killed and the farm occupiers made constant threats of violence towards farmers and their families, which caused a number of farmers to abandon their land. Some occupiers simply invaded farmhouses and ordered the farmers to leave immediately or be assaulted or killed.

Later on in the year, land occupations became a chaotic free for all with many different groups engaging in a wholesale scramble for land, whether it had been designated for resettlement or not. There were incidents of army and air force personnel stopping farmers from planting. Eventually the government announced that the army would be used to assist in the resettlement exercise by transporting people to the farms on which they were to be resettled.

All of these sad activities drastically affected agricultural production for the 2000-01 season. This led inevitably to shortages of commodities such as wheat and to a substantial reduction in foreign exchange-earning crops such as tobacco. The situation had high adverse consequences for an economy that was already in terrible shape. There were also some downstream effects of the chaos on the commercial farms. Suppliers of agricultural equipment and farm inputs such as seed and fertiliser suffered a drastic reduction in business. Banks that had loaned large sums to commercial farmers were faced with writing off debts. More

---

[57] By December 2000 more than 1,700 commercial farms had been occupied, disrupting production of tobacco and other crops.

than 250,000 farm workers[58] who lived with their families (constituting a total population of over one million) on the farms that were expropriated were displaced and rendered destitute.

If the government had wished, it could have brought about radical land reform without unleashing lawlessness throughout the country. On several occasions during the year 2000 regional leaders, and the international community, sought to broker deals that would have allowed the Zimbabwe government to engage in organised resettlement. Under these proposals land would have been acquired in more manageable quantities and there would have been substantial donor funding for the essential support systems for the resettled farmers. Given the disastrous state of the economy, it was clear that the government would be unable to afford the large amounts of money needed to support resettled farmers. Yet, time and time again, the government spurned such proposals. In December 2001, the United Nations Development Programme (UNDP) recommended that the government abandon its fast-track resettlement exercise in favour of a more limited and planned donor-funded programme. The UNDP understood the unsustainable and destructive nature of the fast-track land grab. Again the government rejected this proposal.

The state propaganda agencies continually proclaimed that the rule of law was a capitalist doctrine invented in western Europe and is designed to protect property rights. The doctrine was then imported into Africa during colonial times and the propagandists claim it now stands in the way of equitable redistribution of land stolen by force from the indigenous people during colonial occupation. What is clear from the analysis above is that equitable land redistribution could have been achieved in Zimbabwe without abandoning the rule of law and deliberately letting loose forces of lawlessness. Government could have used the law to overcome resistance by commercial farmers to necessitate land reform. If government had passed appropriate laws and had followed the procedures laid down in those laws, the courts would have upheld these measures, and unnecessary friction between the executive and judiciary could have been avoided.

The land grab was not, as government would have it, a continuation of the liberation struggle to bring about economic emancipation for the majority. Instead it was a campaign of violent lawlessness primarily motivated by political considerations. The way in which land was being allocated clearly establishes this. Land was used to reward supporters of the government and to induce others to join the ruling party. War veterans are also allocating land to themselves and their supporters as a reward for their service to the ruling party.

---

[58] It is estimated that the total number of farm workers on all the commercial farms is about 450,000.

The political terror campaign

In the period leading up to the June 2000 elections, violence, threats and intimidation were used extensively to coerce people into voting for the ruling party.[59] The first targets of the terror were white commercial farmers known to be associated with the MDC. The white farmers killed during the early stages of this campaign were known MDC supporters.[60] Using bases on farms, the occupiers started conducting a reign of terror against farmers and farm workers to ensure they would not support the

---

[59] In its report issued on 4 July 2000 the European Union Election Observation Mission on the Parliamentary Elections made these observations, 'The election campaign was marred by high levels of violence and intimidation. Most areas of the country were affected. The evidence showed that between February and June, ZANU PF was engaged in a systematic campaign of intimidation aimed at crushing support for opposition parties. Key groups of the electorate, whom ZANU PF deemed to be opposition supporters, were targeted by war veterans and other party supporters operating from bases on the white-owned farms they had invaded, from militia camps in other rural areas, and from government and party offices in rural towns. Farm labourers on white-owned farms across the country were threatened and abused, forced to attend party meetings and taken off to 're-education' camps. Thousands of incidents of assault, torture, abduction and rape were recorded. Several prominent MDC organisers were murdered. Other key groups that were targeted by ZANU PF included teachers, nurses and civil servants. More than 7,000 teachers fled their homes, forcing 250 primary and secondary schools to close. In campaign speeches, ZANU PF leaders seemed to sanction the use of violence and intimidation against political opponents and contributed substantially to the climate of fear that overshadowed the election campaign. Calls for peaceful campaigning and efforts to restrain party supporters, including war veterans, were often ambiguous. The police frequently witnessed violence and intimidation, but appeared to be under instructions not to intervene.

MDC supporters were also engaged in violence and intimidation, but the degree of their responsibility for such activities was far less. Moreover, MDC leaders were clearer in their condemnation of violence. The levels of violence and intimidation varied from one part of the country to another. In some areas, notably in the main urban centres, relatively normal political campaigning continued. In many rural areas, however, the levels of intimidation by ZANU PF were so intense as to make it virtually impossible for opposition parties to campaign.' EU Provincial Co-ordinators, making their own assessments of the campaign after three weeks in the field, all referred to intimidation and violence as a major factor in the election, and attributed responsibility for it overwhelmingly to ZANU PF. Further corroboration of ZANU PF's prominence in violence came from the number of incidents reported to EU Observer teams in the field. Out of 250 incidents recorded, ZANU PF supporters were alleged to be the perpetrators in 68 per cent of cases; MDC supporters in 7 per cent of cases; and other perpetrators including war veterans in 18 per cent of cases. Studies, made by other independent organisations, supported these results. In analysing the cases of some 13,000 people affected by political violence, the Amani Trust, an NGO, found ZANU PF supporters and government officials to be responsible for approximately 93 per cent of violence; and MDC and other non-governmental supporters for 2 per cent of violence.'

In its report published on 11 July 2000, the Commonwealth Observer Mission also accuses the ZANU PF party of being the aggressors in most of the pre-election violence, and condemns the government for allowing a reign of terror during the election campaign. It also criticises the police for inaction in the face of the violence.

[60] The MDC had attracted strong support amongst some white commercial farmers. Those farmers had facilitated meetings by the MDC and NCA to rally the opposition against the constitutional draft.

MDC. War veterans forced farm workers to attend numerous lengthy 're-education' sessions during which suspected supporters of the MDC were beaten or made to renounce their membership of the MDC.[61]

During the farm invasions the police offered little protection to the embattled farmers and farm workers. When they did occasionally intervene, they were accused of being MDC supporters or of obstructing the land reform programme. One police officer who investigated an assault upon a white farmer was killed by suspected war veterans a few days later. Some police officers were transferred to other stations because they had tried to offer protection to the persons being unlawfully attacked. None of the murderers of the white farmers have been punished for their crimes, despite the fact that the police know the identities of some of the suspects.[62]

Militia forces of ZANU PF spread the terror campaign to the communal areas, using the farms as bases. They also established bases at growth points and other places. Gangs of ZANU PF thugs roamed the rural areas assaulting and intimidating actual or suspected supporters of the MDC. In the worst affected areas it was too dangerous for candidates of opposition parties to organise and campaign for the parliamentary elections. Attacks on members of opposition parties resulted in the deaths of one prospective MDC candidate, the brother of another and at least 33 supporters of the MDC and other opposition political parties.[63] The terror campaign was also directed against teachers and nurses in the rural areas as these people were perceived as possible supporters of the MDC and were likely to have political influence over others.

Torture centres were set up on farms and in towns and people were forcibly taken there and subjected to the most appalling forms of abuse. One such centre was established at the surgery of Dr Hunzvi in a high-density suburb of Harare. The terror campaign was extended to towns and cities. Thousands of people were assaulted or tortured or had their houses and possessions burnt. At least ten women were raped. Over

---

[61] According to the Commercial Farmers Union, 430 people have been hospitalised and 2,400 assault cases have been reported since February, mostly against black farm workers. There were 1,490 death threats, 70 per cent of them against the workers.

[62] The police finally arrested one person in connection with the murder of one farmer, Mr Stevens, but the prosecutor withdrew the case for want of evidence. Stevens was taken away from a police station and was executed in the presence of another white farmer. In the case of the murder of another farmer, Mr Olds, the attackers sustained injuries during the gun battle with Olds before he was killed. The police had visited these injured persons in hospital and must, therefore, know the identities of the attackers.

[63] Only in one of these 35 cases of murder is anyone facing trial. Three persons, including the notorious war veteran, Biggie Chitoro, were arrested in July in connection with the torture of an MDC supporter that led to his death. They have been charged with murder and have been in custody since then awaiting trial. (Editor's note: He was released sometime in 2001, allegedly to spearhead again a new wave of violent political campaign for the 2002 Presidential elections.)

10,000 Zimbabweans, mostly rural people, fled into town to escape the violence. According to the Amani Trust, a non-governmental organisation that chronicled the incidents of political violence from mid-February 2000 onwards, some 35,000 politically motivated criminal acts[64] occurred prior to the elections in 2000. It found that ZANU PF supporters committed over 90 per cent of these crimes.[65] The state-controlled mass media prominently reported all instances of alleged violence by MDC, but ignored or played down violence perpetrated by ruling party supporters.[66]

Politicians of the ruling party and their supporters made statements indicating that the parliamentary ballot would not be secret and that stern action would be taken against people who voted for opposition parties. War veterans threatened reprisals if people in any areas voted against the ruling party. War veterans also threatened to use violence in the event of the opposition winning the election, to ensure that it would not rule the country. In some areas, the war veterans and their supporters went around confiscating national identity cards from people to prevent them from voting, as people were obliged to produce these cards before they could exercise their votes.[67]

Although the polling itself took place in relatively peaceful conditions, the preceding violence and threats had severely compromised the holding of free and fair elections by preventing campaigning in some areas and intimidating voters.[68]

Amnesty for perpetrators of political violence

In early October, the President saw fit to grant an amnesty to those who kidnapped, tortured and assaulted people, and destroyed houses and

---

[64] The violations include 2,500 assaults, the destruction or serious damage to more than 1,100 properties, the displacement of over 10,000 people, and the illegal detention or kidnapping of about 600 people. There were also thousands of other human rights violations, such as: death threats, assault threats, interference with the rights to vote, to associate, and to express opinions.
[65] It found that ZANU PF supporters committed 91.2 per cent of the crimes.
[66] See *Elections 2000 The Media War* produced by the Media Monitoring Project of Zimbabwe 41-48.
[67] *The Daily News*, 15 June 2000.
[68] In its report issued on 4 July 2000 the European Union Election Observation Mission on the Parliamentary Elections reached the conclusion that, 'The scale of violence and intimidation in the run-up to the campaign and during the election period marred the final result. The government failed to uphold the rule of law and compromised law enforcement agencies'.
It also said that the election process was legally flawed and affected by violence and intimidation. 'As a result, the term "free and fair" was not applicable to the Zimbabwe polls..
The Commonwealth Observer Mission reached similar conclusions, observing in its report published on 11 July 2000, that 'the violence and threats impaired the freedom of choice of the electorate'.

other possessions.[69] Those who committed murder or rape were not given amnesty.[70] The amnesty meant that all criminal investigations and criminal proceedings in respect of these crimes had to be abandoned. This highly regrettable amnesty created the impression that political violence will be condoned and those responsible for such violence will not be punished. This gave encouragement to the perpetrators to engage in further violence and, in fact, some of those who benefited from the amnesty have violently attacked some of those who reported them to the police.

As supporters of the ruling party committed most acts of political violence, it is they who have mostly benefited from the amnesty. But, the amnesty has effectively deprived thousands of Zimbabweans of their right to criminal justice through the courts. These include victims of appalling torture and violence who have suffered permanent disabilities and serious psychological trauma, and victims whose entire properties have been destroyed.

Attempting to block constituency challenges

Following the June 2000 parliamentary elections, the MDC commenced proceedings to have the results set aside in 38 constituencies, mostly because of the use of violence, but in some cases because of other irregularities such as bribery.

In early December 2000, just a month before the challenges were to be heard, the president sought to prevent the courts from invalidating any of the election results on the grounds of corrupt or illegal practices. Purporting to act in terms of his powers under section 158(1) of the Electoral Act [*Chapter 2:01*], the president 'validated' any corrupt or illegal practices committed during the June 2000 elections and deemed those practices not to be violations of the Electoral Act. This was a complete subversion of the legal process and a total elimination of protection of the law. In the preamble to those regulations, the president proclaimed that the elections were 'held under peaceful conditions . . . the people who voted did so freely' and the outcome of the election

---

[69] Clemency Order No. 1 of 2000 published on 6 October 2000.
[70] The fact that the Amnesty does not include those who have murdered and raped is not significant, given the use, by the President, over the years, of his right to pardon, so as to ensure that those who have murdered on behalf of the State do not serve jail sentences. No persons have been arrested, let alone prosecuted, for the murders of MDC officials and supporters despite the fact that in some cases the alleged culprits are known. For instance, two MDC party workers were killed when their vehicle was petrol-bombed. Eyewitnesses have identified the two alleged assailants but the police have taken no action against the named persons.

'represents a genuine and free expression of the people's will'. Those assertions flew in the face of a large body of evidence to the contrary.[71]

The challenges brought by the MDC were dismissed as frivolous and vexatious. The president maintained that those legal actions placed intolerable burdens on the elected members of parliament concerned, the registrar-general, and the courts, but he totally ignored the intolerable burden imposed upon candidates and members of opposition parties because of the pre-election violence. He further maintained that those actions undermined political stability and the democratisation process. He concluded that it was necessary to take those steps in the interests of peace, security and stability. Nothing can be further from the truth. In any democratic country, candidates will be given the right to challenge electoral results based on alleged widespread political violence or corrupt practices. No one can have any confidence in any electoral process that disallows challenges to the results on those grounds. The credibility and legitimacy of an electoral system is negated by a denial of a right to challenge results on the grounds of alleged fundamental breaches of electoral laws.

The MDC brought a case in the Supreme Court in which it has challenged the constitutionality of those regulations. At the end of January 2001, the Supreme Court unanimously decided that those regulations were unconstitutional. It found that those regulations violated the right of candidates to seek legal recourse when election results are challenged on the grounds that the elections were tainted by corrupt and illegal practices.

Post-election violence

Despite the widespread violence used against opposition parties before the June parliamentary elections and the use of the land issue, the MDC took 57 seats from ZANU PF. Previously, the opposition had had only three seats in Parliament. ZANU PF won 62 seats. The MDC captured all the cities and major towns and it won almost all the seats in Matabeleland constituencies.

The ruling party was profoundly shocked by the outcome of the June elections. In his usual fashion, the president looked for scapegoats to blame. White farmers and whites in general were singled out. The MDC

---

[71] See the following: Statement of the National Democratic Institute (NDI) Pre-Election Delegation to Zimbabwe issued in Harare on 22 May 2000; Amnesty International report entitled *Zimbabwe Terror tactics in the run-up to parliamentary elections June 2000*; the report of the European Union Election Observation Mission on the Parliamentary Elections dated on 4 July 2000; the Report of Commonwealth Observer Mission published on 11 July 2000; the Report of International Rehabilitation Council for Torture Victims dated 4 June 2000.

was repeatedly attacked as being a party that was led by whites and a front for the protection of white property rights. It was depicted as being sponsored by 'Western imperialist governments' who wanted to protect the economic interests of the white minority.[72]

Immediately after the election results were announced, the army was deployed in the high-density suburbs of Harare, together with the police, supposedly to stop any violent reaction to the election results. These units went around terrorising and beating up unarmed civilians.[73] In October 2000, after food riots in Harare, the army was again deployed. Again many unarmed civilians were beaten, including an MDC member of parliament and some of his family members.[74] In early November, when the students at the University of Zimbabwe attempted to stage a protest in support of salary demands by lecturers, the police and later the army descended upon them, tear gassing students in residential halls and meting out brutal punishments in the form of beatings with whips.[75]

The MDC had threatened to engage in mass action to force President Mugabe to resign. The government prepared to crush civil unrest by establishing a National Reaction Force. This consisted of army and police personnel. The plan was that army personnel would be drawn from sections of the army likely to show fanatical loyalty to the President. The police personnel would be given military-style training. When it was formed, it was this unit that was used against the students in early November. The Commissioner of Police publicly stated that any mass action would be crushed with ruthless force, depicting such action as an uprising against the legitimate government.[76] The Minister of Home Affairs has also threatened to deal ruthlessly with the MDC and civic organisations calling for mass action and mass protests against government.[77]

At the end of September 2000, government announced that war veterans were to become a reserve force of the army. Whereas previously the war veterans had operated as an informal militia force to terrorise the opposition, they were now being given formal status to operate as a partisan force on behalf of the ruling party. The war veterans were also given office accommodation at a large government building in Harare, from which they could organise and co-ordinate their activities.

---

[72] The whites were not the only targets of the President's anger. On 4 May, the President attacked the black middle class in cities. These people had now become white-blacks who wanted nothing to do with those who liberated the country and brought equality. According to the President, the residents of Mbare (a high-density area in Harare), especially those of foreign ancestry, had no totems and hence their support for MDC.
[73] *The Daily News*, 12 July 2000.
[74] Ibid. 18 and 20 October and *The Herald*, 17 and 18 October 2000.
[75] *The Daily News*, 7 and 8 November 2000.
[76] Ibid. 1 December 2000.
[77] Ibid. 14 December 2000.

In late December 2000, one newspaper reported[78] that ZANU PF had established a crack unit to co-ordinate and lead a planned violent campaign by ruling party youths and war veterans against the opposition, ahead of the presidential elections in 2002. The person earmarked to lead this unit according to this report was the commander of the air force, Perence Shiri. Dr Hunzvi, and Joseph Chinotimba, another war veteran leader, were also supposed to be key players in the unit.

By-elections and the presidential election

Three by-elections followed the June 2000 elections. The first was in Marondera West. This by-election took place at the end of November 2000. ZANU PF had won in the June election and won again in this constituency.

By the time of the Marondera West by-election, the pattern of intimidation had changed. During the general election there had been widespread physical violence in this area. Against this backdrop the agents of the ruling party were now able to use somewhat less blatant methods of intimidation. The leader of the war veterans, the notorious Dr Hunzvi, travelled extensively around the constituency with a small entourage of war veterans stopping regularly at places like growth points. Given his reputation, his mere physical presence was seriously intimidating. People were also convinced that the war veterans were now being deployed in uniform to keep people under surveillance. Increasing numbers of war veterans seemed to be carrying weapons. At the local level the army, police, and CIO were involved with war veterans in co-ordinating and implementing action. Many people were scared to vote and stayed away from polls to avoid reprisals. There was a reduction in the percentage poll by comparison with the June election.

The second by-election was in Bikita West in January 2001. The Bikita West constituency was one of the few rural constituencies won by the MDC, albeit narrowly. Given its key nature it was inevitable that the ruling party would pull out all the stops to win back this constituency. This time, the ruling party was also determined to ensure that there would be a sizeable turnout of voters. The whole state machinery was mobilised to ensure that the ruling party would win convincingly. Already in December, there were reports of considerable levels of violence in this area.

One newspaper reported that about 100 ZANU PF supporters, mostly war veterans and youths, had been deployed in the area, and base camps had been set up from which to intimidate people. Dr Hunzvi, Joseph Chinotimba, and Francis Zimuto (better known as 'Black Jesus') were

---

[78] The *Financial Gazette*, 21-27 December 2000.

also travelling around the constituency.[79] In late December, the MDC claimed that ZANU PF thugs had already injured one hundred of its supporters.[80] The ZANU PF militias set up camps at various places. By January about 200 militia personnel were located at key points around the constituency. They had access to many motor vehicles.[81] Widespread intimidation took place. People were forced to attend rallies and many MDC supporters were assaulted. Chiefs and headmen were warned that they would lose their privileges unless they organised the people in their areas to vote for ZANU PF.

As he had done in Marondera West ahead of that by-election, the Minister of Youth Development, Gender and Employment Creation, Border Gezi, visited Bikita West a few weeks ahead of the by-election and disbursed Z$3 million for development of youth projects. The Minister of Education, Samuel Mumbengegwi, was reported to have warned villagers at one meeting that their votes would not be secret. He said all chiefs and headmen would be instructed to register all people voting and, from those registers, ZANU PF would be able to tell how people had voted. He went on to say that anyone voting for the MDC would be ruthlessly dealt with, as they wanted to cleanse the area of all anti-ZANU PF elements. He also said that all government social welfare officers would be instructed to give free maize seeds only to ZANU PF supporters. At the same meeting the Minister of Foreign Affairs, Stan Mudenge, reportedly told villagers to inform on all teachers, nurses and other officials who supported the MDC so the government could use its planned civil service staff reduction programme to fix these persons by retrenching them.[82]

On the polling day chiefs and headmen were seen marshalling people to vote. War veterans were allegedly placed in uniforms at numerous roadblocks to discourage MDC voters from travelling to polling stations.[83]

Whereas in Marondera West the MDC had refrained from campaigning because of the violence, in Bikita West the MDC was not prepared to give up so easily. In January, the MDC decided to send in youths to try to protect their supporters and clashes occurred between the two sides. In

---

[79] *The Daily News*, 19 December and *The Daily Mail*, 15 January 2001.
[80] The *Financial Gazette*, 21-27 December 2000. In *The Daily News* on 1 January 2000, it was reported that war veterans and ZANU PF youths had beaten up people indiscriminately, and hundreds had been injured. Many houses had been destroyed and a lot of property damaged.
[81] Hunzvi, and a number of his militiamen using four vehicles chased, at speed, a vehicle containing some foreign journalists while Hunzvi uttered obscenities at them. *The Daily Mail*, 15 January 2001.
[82] The *Financial Gazette*, 11-17 January 2001.
[83] Towards the beginning of January, one newspaper alleged that weapons were being clandestinely taken from the police armoury and given to war veterans. The *Financial Gazette*, 4-5 January 2001.

one of these clashes between MDC and ZANU PF supporters, a supporter of ZANU PF was stabbed to death.[84] Some of these clashes seem to have been instigated by MDC youths. A female MDC supporter, Ropafadzo Manyame, who was badly beaten by war veterans in Bikita West, died several days later.[85] Many MDC youths were arrested and some of these were allegedly tortured.[86] In the aftermath of the election it was reported that war veterans and ZANU PF supporters went around the entire area seeking to root out MDC sympathisers and that teachers had been a particular target of this campaign.[87]

The result in Bikita West was that ZANU PF won the seat with a substantial majority.[88] Voter turnout was about 50 per cent. The third by-election was in Bindura. This election was held on 21 and 22 July 2001. In the lead-up to this election the ZANU PF candidate for this seat, Governor Elliott Manyika, conducted a campaign of violent intimidation in the area. ZANU PF youths operating from seven bases they had set up in the area allegedly raped some women and assaulted suspected MDC supporters. On 22 July 2001, ZANU PF youths attacked a convoy carrying the MDC president, Morgan Tsvangirai, the party's candidate for the Bindura constituency, Elliot Pfebve, and several senior members of the party. The convoy was en route to venues in Bindura. Stones thrown by the youths damaged the vehicles and one car was set on fire, but none of the MDC officials was injured. However, several MDC supporters were injured, some seriously; one was said to be in a critical condition. A few kilometres on, an even bigger mob advanced threateningly towards the vehicles, but was stopped by the intervention of the police. Armed policemen then accompanied the MDC team to two rallies.[89]

The multiple roles of the war veterans

The Dr Hunzvi-led war veterans have become increasingly powerful and ever more dangerous.[90] The ruling party has made use of this coterie of

---

[84] The circumstances of this death still remain unclear.
[85] *The Daily News*, 19 January 2001.
[86] Ibid. 15 January 2001, reports that these youths were beaten with rifle butts and sticks, burned with cigarettes, and subjected to assaults on their testicles.
[87] *The Daily News*, 23 January 2001.
[88] The ZANU PF candidate received 11 993 votes. The MDC candidate received 7 001 votes which was about the same number as MDC had received in the June 2000 election in this constituency.
[89] See *Independent* 6 July 2001, *The Daily News* 9 July 2001 and *The Daily News* 22 July 2001.
[90] The power and influence of the war veterans had been growing since 1998, after they had staged a series of demonstrations that forced Mugabe to grant them large, tax-free, lump-sum payments and lifetime monthly stipends. These pay-outs had not been budgeted for and had a serious negative effect on the economy. They also led to the freezing of balance of payment support from the World Bank.

particularly violent war veterans to achieve various political ends.[91] During this period leading to the presidential elections, any sector of the community perceived to be opposed to the ruling party was in danger of being attacked by war veterans. The range of activities of the war veterans were:

- As storm troopers in the farm invasions.
- As the hit force against MDC supporters.
- In the lead up to the ZANU PF congress in December 2001, they were used to root out ZANU PF provincial executives who were perceived as being likely not to support the continued leadership of President Mugabe.
- To harass members of the private press and sometimes physically assault journalists.[92] They demanded the sacking or transfer of police officers considered sympathetic to the MDC.
- To close district council offices where they believed that the civil servants were sympathetic to the MDC and force the removal or transfer of district administrators considered to be aligned with the MDC.
- In January 2001 when the MDC threatened mass action, Dr Hunzvi announced that the war veterans would invade any factories that did not operate during any stay-away and would take them over just as they had done with the commercial farms. He went on to say that the MDC would never come to power while he was still alive.[93]
- Again in January 2001 when civil servants went on strike, the war veterans attacked them, assaulted teachers who joined in the strike, physically forced some of the strikers to go back to work and told others they discovered to be on strike that they no longer have their jobs.[94]

Conclusion

The rule of law has been under savage attack in Zimbabwe. A power-hungry regime, that is not prepared to brook political opposition, has brought Zimbabwe to the brink of disaster by casting aside legality and constitutionality. Recently President Mugabe and his two vice-presidents

---

[91] A number of war veterans with far more credible war histories than most of the members of this coterie have publicly expressed their disapproval and condemnation of the activities of members of this group.
[92] For instance they assaulted a journalist from an independent daily during a demonstration against the newspaper and in support of slain Democratic Republic of Congo (DRC) leader.
[93] *The Daily News*, 20 January 2001.
[94] The *Financial Gazette*, 25-31 January 2001 and *The Daily News*, 25 January 2001.

have all made statements that seem to indicate that they would not be prepared to allow the MDC to rule the country even if the MDC were to win an election.[95] These statements amount to a total denial of democracy that is premised upon acceptance of the popular will of the people expressed in free and fair elections.

To counteract the serious political threat posed to its continued hold on power, the regime has unleashed forces of violence, intimidation, and disorder throughout the country. It enlisted the war veterans, unemployed youth, and members of the intelligence service and military in this campaign of violent intimidation.

As part of this process, the regime also initiated a violent land grab. It did this despite the fact that it could have brought about substantial redistribution of land in a way that would have avoided the enormous economic harm that has emanated from the frantic and unplanned land grab. This land grab has more to do with power politics than it has with genuine concern for the needs of the landless. It has been used both to punish whites who have had the effrontery to support a political opposition party, and to try to bribe the rural voters into supporting the ruling party.

The law enforcement agencies have either actively collaborated in these lawless activities or were rendered powerless to act. The partisan nature of the police force was further evidenced when, in mid-January 2001, the Commissioner of Police, Augustine Chihuri, publicly proclaimed that he supported ZANU PF because it was the ruling party and he would resign as commissioner if another political party came to power.[96]

Supporters of the ruling party who engaged in these activities were granted an amnesty to confirm that they were above the law and had a licence to continue to engage in violent intimidation against the opposition supporters. The end result of these events has been to plunge Zimbabwe into a state of ever-increasing lawlessness and repression and to doom the country to economic destitution.

The starting point for putting the country back on the rails will be to restore the rule of law and respect for the basic ground rules of democracy. After this is done, however, it will take a long time to repair the enormous damage done by the government's irresponsible economic policies and destructive land resettlement programme.

---

[95] See the comment upon this pronouncement in *The Daily News*, 16 January 2001.
[96] They made these statements in late January 2001 at political rallies, The *Financial Gazette*, 1 February 2001. Msika said that there was bound to be a second war of liberation should Zimbabweans elect the MDC. The *Financial Gazette*, 1 February 2001. *The Herald*, 29 January 2001.

There is no doubt that a major, orderly and sound land reform initiative will remain an urgent imperative, even more so given the heightened demand for land engendered by the ruling party's fast-track resettlement. Clearly, by the time that any rethinking of the process of land reform takes place, large quantities of land will already have been parcelled out to communal farmers and black entrepreneurs, many of whom are likely to be supporters of the ruling party. This will complicate any replanning exercise in relation to land reform. Land resettlement that has already taken place cannot simply be reversed. What will probably have to happen is that proper support will need to be given to some of the resettlement schemes to make them work and other schemes may have to be reorganised and rationalised. The blatantly partisan political basis of land allocation will also need to be corrected.[97]

---

[97] The International Monetary Fund recently suggested that to gain domestic and international support the Zimbabwean government would have to implement an orderly land reform programme and that a speedy return to the rule of law would be important in rebuilding the confidence of domestic, regional, and international investors and international donor support.' The response of the Zimbabwean government was th the provision of financial support for an accelerated resolution of the land issue ' 'facilitate enforcement of the due process of law'.

Zimbabwe: The Past is the Future

Sticks and stones, skeletons and ghosts

A. P. Reeler

One of the more enduring consequences of the organised violence and torture in Rhodesia in the 1970s, and in Zimbabwe in the 1980s, is the number of people who have been handicapped by the experience. The effects have been well researched. Medical or, more properly, forensic evidence, is particularly important because it has increasing significance in criminal tribunals and can provide the only hard evidence when there are no eye-witnesses. Scientific evidence is significant in understanding organised violence and can provide the 'hardest' facts to prove that extra-judicial executions and torture have taken place. Torture is a particularly useful indicator of human rights observance, since both the physical and psychological effects can be detected many years after the original injuries were inflicted.

But evidence of human rights violations is not confined to the so-called hard sciences. It can also be deduced from other areas of social life. For example, an examination of the freedom of the press and other media gives a measure of human rights observance in a country. The number of harassed, attacked, detained, imprisoned, tortured and dead journalists gives a good idea of whether a country respects human rights. In Zimbabwe today there is evidence of continual harassment and violence against journalists and newspapers.

In South Africa, it has been possible to face up to broad problems of accountability. The country did not opt for blanket impunity but for a Truth and Reconciliation Commission that combined accountability with reconciliation and the enactment of a broad range of laws governing human rights observance.

It should be noted that Amani Trust, Harare; Amnesty International, London; The CCJP (CCJP), (Salisbury) and Harare; Human Rights Watch, New York; International Rehabilitation Council for Torture Victims (IRCT), Copenhagen; Research and Rehabilitation Centre for Torture Victims (RCT), Copenhagen; Physicians for Human Rights, Denmark; the Zimbabwe Human Rights (NGO) Forum (ZHRF) Harare, all research and publish their own reports. Thus their details are only provided once in each reference.

By contrast, Zimbabwe has a world record[1] for impunity rather than accountability. In the decades immediately preceding independence and subsequently, Zimbabwe has had epidemics of organised violence and torture. Invariably, these have been followed by planned forgetting and silence, underpinned by laws granting indemnity and impunity. Judges who try to administer the law impartially are under attack. The police are in contempt of the courts and declare partisan adherence to the ruling party, violence is routinely reported and serious allegations are made of human rights violations.[2]

These are now known facts, but they were also common in Zimbabwe's past. The particular configuration of abuse and violation differs over the decades, but the cycle continues almost on prescription: gross human rights violations – during periods of war or insurrection – followed by acts granting formal immunity. This is how we, Zimbabweans, continue to solve our political disputes and there is an uncommon sadness that we learn so little from our history.

Perhaps Zimbabwe is ill, as commentators and traditional leaders have noted. Indeed, for the *vasvikiro* (spirit mediums) of Zimbabwe, the country is plagued by the ghosts of the unburied dead.[3] Many of the walking wounded that I have met hold this opinion, though few Western scientists might do so. Yet research by the Amani Trust supports my

---

[1] See Reeler, A. P. (2000), 'Can you have a reparations policy without justice?' *Legal Forum*, 12, 202-09.

[2] See ZHRF (2000), *Who is responsible? A preliminary analysis of pre-election violence in Zimbabwe*. ZHRF (2000), *Report on political violence in Bulawayo, Harare, Manicaland, Mashonaland West, Masvingo, Matabeleland North, Matabeleland South and Midlands*. ZHRF (2000), *A report on Post-Election Violence*. ZHRF (2000), *Report on Pre-election Political Violence in Mberengwa*. ZHRF (2001), *Report on Election-related Political Violence in Chikomba*. ZHRF (2001), *Human Rights and Zimbabwe's June 2000 election*. ZHRF (2001), *Who was responsible? Alleged perpetrators and their crimes during the 2000 Parliamentary Election Period*. ZHRF (2001), *Politically motivated violence in Zimbabwe 2000–2001. A report on the campaign of political repression conducted by the Zimbabwean Government under the guise of carrying out land reform*. ZHRF (2001), *Complying with the Abuja Agreement*. ZHRF (2001), *Complying With the Abuja Agreement: Two Months Report*. ZHRF (2002), *Human Rights and Zimbabwe's Presidential Election: March 2002*. ZHRF (2002), *Teaching them a lesson. A report on the attack on Zimbabwean teachers*. ZHRF (2002), *Are They Accountable?:Examining alleged violators and their violations pre and post the Presidential Election March 2002*. ZHRF (2003), *Torture by State Agents in Zimbabwe: January 2001 to August 2002*.

[3] See Mupinda, M. (1995) 'Loss and grief among the Shona: the Meaning of Disappearances', *Legal Forum*, 9, 41-49.

view.[4] Zimbabwe requires explanation in both cultural and psychophysical terms and, when the story is told, it becomes easier to understand. But the full record cannot be given here. It would require a truth commission or a criminal tribunal.

My particular aim is to describe the ZANU PF government's use of violence against its citizens. It is a use learnt in the time of Rhodesia to which we have regressed. The two stories cannot be disentangled and indeed many of the protagonists in both eras are the same people. I began by mentioning victims and it is from their perspective that I shall proceed.

---

[4] The following brief case taken from the Mupinda study [see ft. 3 above] illustrates the importance of disappearances.
Cured by a goat's head. Mr Mapurisa is an elderly village head, aged sixty-five. He has six surviving children from a polygamous marriage. Two of his children, a son and daughter, went to join the liberation war in 1976 and 1979 respectively, but did not return after the war. He has standard two education and was employed as a dental therapist assistant before being laid off during the war. He earns his livelihood from subsistence farming. Mr Mapurisa was informed of the death of his two children soon after independence by former guerrillas from his village, who had witnessed the death of his son in an ambush by security forces on the border with Mozambique. Some comrades had also witnessed the death of his daughter at Chimoio, Mozambique, during a raid by security forces. After receiving the news and overcome by grief Mr Mapurisa did not consider that he needed to do anything about it. Apparently at the time that he went to war his son left behind a daughter now aged 13. His daughter left behind a son now aged 12. Due to financial difficulties, Mr Mapurisa could not afford to send the two children to school. It was only recently that they started attending school such that at 13 and 12 they are only in Grade 2 and 1 respectively. Mr Mapurisa had not experienced any unusual problems till about two years ago. His two grandchildren began to suffer from a mysterious illness. They had nightmares and spoke in their sleep. They also reported various symptoms but no disease was diagnosed at the hospital. Mr Mapurisa also reported that they behaved oddly. These occurrences propelled him to consult traditional healers, who informed that these problems were being caused by the spirits of his two children that sought to be brought back home. For Mr Mapurisa it was not possible to find the body of either of his children. His daughter had been buried in a mass grave in Mozambique and his son's body had been ferried away by security forces. Nonetheless burial rituals had to be performed. As already mentioned, all death has very important social and spiritual consequences in Shona family life such that all death requires appeasement and ritual management. In accordance with traditional custom, Mr Mapurisa thus invited all villagers to witness the burial of his children. For each of the children he took a goat's head and wrapped it in a piece of white cloth. Together with items of clothing belonging to the disappeared, the goat's head was buried in a proper grave with the respect accorded to the dead. All procedures that are normally followed at the burial of a deceased person were followed. His family is now preparing for the cleansing ceremony where it is believed that the spirits of the disappeared children will rise with the power of the spirit to take their eternal place in Nyikadzimu (the spirit world). Mr Mapurisa reported that the mysterious illness affecting his grandchildren stopped after the burial rites were performed. The children are also no longer manifesting strange behaviour. As he said this, he was pointing to the two graves that lay side by side on an anthill in a field to the west of the homestead. For Mr Mapurisa, his family can expect to enjoy the eternal protection from his kin who have gone before him. This has a great psychological impact since ancestor spirits play significant roles in influencing and conditioning practically all Shona outlook to life.

The 1970s

The War of Liberation in the 1970s was a time of large-scale human rights violations.[5] African people were forced to spend seven or eight years in 'protected villages', living in near-refugee-camp conditions with inadequate sanitation, poor diet and a high risk of being killed or maimed. By 1977, nearly 750,000 people were confined to such villages, a significant percentage of the then population of about five million.[6] Hundreds of thousands more were in refugee camps in neighbouring countries where they had to endure Rhodesian attacks. Tens of thousands were killed and many survivors remain deeply traumatised. Such experiences alone can lead to life-long psychological disorder and disability. There is ample evidence for all of this from the survivors of Chimoio, Nyadzonia, Tembwe, and Camp Freedom.[7]

Torture was a high risk for everyone, since political loyalty was demanded by all sides. There is no evidence that any white person was ever tortured, though some were summarily executed. This is remarkable in such a bitter war. For black people the story was very different. Accusations of disloyalty or betrayal from either side was a common experience for many rural people. Rhodesian torture could range from the more sophisticated horrors of electrical shock, mock drowning, suspensions, and drugs, to slaps, punches, kicks, and beatings with sticks. It could be inflicted by anyone, especially after the Smith government passed the Indemnity and Compensation Act in 1975. Since the Act gave impunity, it is scarcely surprising that there were few inhibitions in using torture for obtaining information. Active supporters of the liberation army ran the risk of torture on multiple occasions. Some people experienced torture at the hands of the security forces on more than six occasions.

The guerrillas' methods were less sophisticated, but more likely to be lethal. The '*pungwes*' (all night morale-raising sessions) that brought people together in solidarity of purpose and action also acted as the courts of the liberation movements. Rightly or wrongly, people were accused, and often convicted, of being 'sell-outs'. They might receive a 'thorough beating', leaving the victim unconscious, or with broken bones, that caused great pain and could leave a person handicapped for life.

---

[5] See Amani Trust (1998), *Survivors of Torture and Organised Violence from the 1970s War of Liberation*. See also Reeler, A. P. (1995), 'Surviving Torture: A Zimbabwean Experience', in D. Irmler (ed), *Old Ways – New Theories: Traditional and Contemporary Family Therapy Connect in Africa*, Harare: Connect. Also Reeler, A. P. (1998), 'Epidemic violence and the community: A Zimbabwean case study', *Community Development Journal*, 33, 128-39.

[6] See CCJP (1975), *The Man in the Middle*. CCJP (1976), *Civil War in Rhodesia*.

[7] See Reeler, A.P., and Mupinda, M. (1996), 'An Investigation into the psychological sequelae of Torture and Organised Violence in Zimbabwean war veterans'. *Legal Forum*, 8, 12-27.

There were no easily available medical facilities for anyone during the latter years of the war. People were also executed: sometimes by beating, but also by cutting, burning, hanging, and even stoning. These public executions have left many with the most horrible memories of the liberation war.

Torture was such a common event that nearly two decades later, one can see the victims with relative ease in every rural clinic and outpatient department in Zimbabwe. Epidemiological studies have shown that about one in ten adults over 30 years old in a Mashonaland clinic have either been tortured or experienced organised violence.[8] Generally, they have chronic depression or similar disorders. They often have accompanying physical disabilities – bad back pain is a frequent symptom. They are poorer than their neighbours, with a range of other socio-economic handicaps.[9] It does not make much difference who tortured them. Moreover, despite all they have suffered, they might even be proud of their contribution to the freedom struggle and a bit philosophical about their 'un-dead' relatives and friends: all those buried in mass graves in foreign countries and all those that 'disappeared'.

Families remain deeply traumatised by these absent relatives. Many are dealing with the ghosts that haunt them and cause continued problems, particularly of illness. Many survivors are accepting and empowered in themselves, but nonetheless handicapped in some way. The economic liberalisation programme of the Zimbabwe government and the subsequent economic collapse have brought exceptional challenges to their ability to cope. And now, in addition, they are facing a second experience of organised violence and torture. Although there have been many accounts of the liberation war – and largely unsuccessful attempts through the War Victims Compensation Act, to offer redress to the victims – the human rights history still remains virtually unexplored. The violations committed by the Rhodesian forces are known, but not those of the liberation forces. The attempt to compensate its thousands of victims has been derailed by the fraudulent disbursement of the funds. Impunity has left its mark on the social and political processes of Zimbabwe.

It is clear that ZANU PF can take credit for the liberation of Zimbabwe from a brutal regime but, unlike the ANC in South Africa, it has never admitted its own violations, except in passing. There still remain issues to be explained. The Nhari rebellion, the assassination of Herbert Chitepo

---

[8] See Reeler, A. P., Mbape, P., Matshona, J., Mhetura, J., and Hlatwayo, E. (1998), 'The prevalence and nature of disorders due to torture in Mashonaland Central Province, Zimbabwe'. *Torture*, 11, 4-9.

[9] See Reeler, A. P., and Mhetura, J. (2000), 'The psychosocial effects of organised violence and torture: A pilot study comparing survivors and their neighbours in Zimbabwe'. *Journal of Social Development in Africa*, 15, 137-69.

and the dissolution of ZIPA are still shrouded in mystery. And the various impunities render this history even more opaque.

The 1980s

The events of the 1980s have been examined in, for example, the report of the Catholic Commission for Justice and Peace and the Legal Resources Foundation, *Breaking the Silence*.[10] This decade too has skeletons and ghosts,[11] as well as sticks and stones. Violence and torture were experienced in the southern half of Zimbabwe and particularly by the Ndebele-speaking people, who were assumed to be supporting 'dissidents'. Methods used to punish the recalcitrant during the liberation war returned in a new and devastating forms: *'pungwes'*, 'thorough beatings', torture and public executions were all used, predominantly by the Fifth Brigade, a special force reporting to the Prime Minister and ZANU PF. The difference with the liberation war was that this time no one was spared. Whether a person was a member of PF-ZAPU, a former member of ZIPRA or merely an ordinary resident of Matabeleland, he or she could be a victim. This was not a war for the hearts and minds of the people but a terror campaign to destroy the will of a whole community.

Any ordinary person might suffer torture, frequently in public and even in front of relatives and friends. They could be forced to attend a *'pungwe'* and sing ZANU PF songs and listen to speeches denigrating their tribe and leaders. Sometimes they witnessed the execution of friends or relatives. Such horrible occurrences are clearly detailed in *Breaking the Silence*. People were subjected to a curfew and faced near-starvation as food supplies were interfered with. Some were even told they would be deliberately starved. Many lived with the immediate memory of the cruel deaths of friends and relatives whose bodies were thrown into shallow graves without the opportunity of grieving or a proper burial. They were told not to touch the dead on pain of further torture. Loved ones still reside in those graves today. Others disappeared altogether, having been taken away and undoubtedly killed. This has been a particularly bitter legacy of the Gukurahundi, as is attested by recent research.[12] The process of exhumation and reburial will take years and this alone is proof of the violence of the 1980s period in Matabeleland.

---

[10] CCJP and LRF (1997), *Breaking the Silence. Building True Peace: A Report on the Disturbances in Matabeleland and the Midlands, 1980 to 1988*. See also Zimbabwe Human Rights Association (1999), *Choosing the Path to Peace and Development: Coming to Terms with Human Rights Violations of the 1982-1987 Conflict in Matabeleland and Midlands Provinces*. There is a short form of the *Breaking the Silence* report available at http://www.hrforumzim.com.

[11] See Amani Trust (1999) 'A "Report on the Exhumation and Reburial Exercise" Overseen by the Amani Trust in Gwanda District, 25 July to 3 September 1999'. Bulawayo: Amani Trust.

[12] Ibid.

Former soldiers or members of PF-ZAPU often met equally severe fates. Imprisonment and vicious torture by the Central Intelligence Organisation were frequent in one of the notorious detention centres, such as Bhalagwe or Stops Camp. Such victims knew others receiving similar treatment, many of whom did not survive, and were never seen again, their bodies disposed of in nearby mine shafts. The scale and the intensity were truly enormous. Few people in Matabeleland North and South escaped without some exposure to these events and the effects can be seen quite clearly today. Epidemiological studies show us the scale: nearly five adults in ten attending rural clinics or hospitals as outpatients are victims of the organised violence and torture of the past decades and over 90 per cent of these derive their trauma from the 1980s.[13] All the available evidence indicates that this epidemic of organised violence and torture can be blamed on the Fifth Brigade, the CIO and ZANU PF Youth. These were all organisations that reported to ZANU PF or the Prime Minister. This is common cause and there are ample reports of the Prime Minister, the government and the commanders of the Fifth Brigade confirming this chain of command. There has been no credible attempt to provide redress for the victims and no attempt to investigate the allegations of government-sponsored violence and torture. The government's own reports have been suppressed, and it is only due to the efforts of non-government organisations, such as the Legal Resources Foundation, the Catholic Commission for Justice and Peace, ZimRights, and the Amani Trust, that any of this history has been publicised. Even in 2001, the government was reluctant for local newspapers to serialise *Breaking the Silence*. It is clear from the information available that the organised violence and torture of this period differ significantly from what occurred during the liberation war. The methods were similar, but the aim was different. The liberation war was bitter and the loyalty of the 'man in the middle' was crucial to success. The human rights violations of that time cannot be condoned but at least they were understandable. The guerrillas needed the unquestioning support and loyalty of the rural population in order to survive and the security forces could not manage without the information rural people could give.

The situation was quite different during the Gukurahundi. The ZANU PF government faced a weak dissident threat and one that to some extent it had itself created through its partial treatment of ZIPRA and PF-ZAPU. The response was massively inappropriate. The record shows the army, the Support Unit of the police and the police themselves were rarely

---

[13] See Amani Trust (1998), *Survivors of Organised Violence in Matabeleland: Facilitating an Agenda for Development, Report of the Workshop*. Bulawayo: Amani Trust.

implicated in gross human rights violations.[14] But the forces that reported directly to the party and were outside military or police control – were major perpetrators, with the Fifth Brigade the overwhelming culprit. This speaks right to the crux of the problem: ZANU PF remained at heart a liberation movement, and had not made the transformation to a civilian, democratic, party. This becomes a factor in understanding the problems of the new millennium.

The 1990s

The story of the 1990s differs from the previous two decades. There were relatively few victims of politically inspired, organised violence and torture for most of the decade. Moreover, there was an increasing ability on the part of civil society to monitor and document the behaviour of the State, and this was described in a number of reports.[15] The victims during this period were likely to have suffered at the hands of the police as suspects in criminal investigations or they may have run foul of political party supporters during the general election in 1995. There was at least one well-known assassination attempt – on Patrick Kombayi – that followed the well-used pattern. Kombayi's assailants were found guilty of attempted murder and were immediately pardoned by the President, Robert Mugabe.

Yet the numbers of victims in the 1990s were fewer than in the previous decade as can be seen both in the reports of Zimbabwean human rights organisations, such as the Catholic Commission for Justice and Peace or ZimRights, and in the reports of outside bodies such as Amnesty International. People could be forgiven for believing the nation was making the all-important transition from a liberation war ideology to modern democratic principles. But by the end of the decade this belief evaporated.

Students had few illusions about the police and especially the riot police. At every demonstration they experienced unrestrained violence with beatings, tear gas and dogs unleashed on their campuses. Every occasion the riot police met the students, the principle of minimum force was abandoned by the Zimbabwe Republic Police riot squad. The student body increasingly rejected ZANU PF as a result.

The most renowned incidents of organised violence and torture during this period were the treatment of Harare residents during the Food Riots in 1998 and the abduction and torture of *The Standard* journalists, Mark Chavunduka and Ray Choto, in 1999.[16]

---

[14] See again *Breaking the Silence*. (op.cit. ft. 10). For a more detailed exposition see also, J. Alexander, J. McGregor, and T. Ranger (2000), *Violence and Memory: One Hundred Years in the 'Dark Forests of Matabeleland'*. Oxford: James Currey.

[15] See ZHRF (1999), *A Consolidated Report on the Food Riots, 19-23 January 1998*. Report compiled by the Amani Trust on behalf of the ZHRF. See also ZHRF (2000) *Organised Violence and Torture in Zimbabwe in 1999*.

[16] See ZHRF, (1999), *Organised Violence and Torture in Zimbabwe in 1999*.

The journalists' case attracted enormous publicity and exemplified the classical view of torture. Taken by a security agency – it is still not known whether this was the army or the CIO – the two journalists were subjected to beatings, mock drowning, electrical shock, falanga (beating on the soles of the feet), abnormal postures, and a variety of threats and intimidation. In short, this was what we all understand by torture. To date, there have been no arrests and not even a credible investigation of this state-sponsored crime.

The victims of the food riots in the late 1990s were apprehended by the police or the army, or both, on the street. They were tear-gassed, threatened, beaten and sometimes taken into custody as 'suspected looters'. People were tortured in their own homes together with members of their family and in front of their children. If their family members were unable to account adequately for their possessions, they too could be taken into custody as 'suspected looters'. Some people were even shot.

When taken into custody, people might be further tortured in an effort to make them confess to looting. Victims were kept in crowded and insanitary conditions and were acutely aware of their ill-treatment or torture. They were denied bail for several weeks and then simply released for a lack of evidence or properly formulated charges.

In their treatment of the so-called rioters, the security forces – both the police and the army – frequently referred to people as 'enemies of the State', reserving special viciousness for students. By the end of the decade the compact between the State and its citizens was breaking down again, as it did in the time of Rhodesia. There was conflict between the President and the judiciary and the independent press.[17] There were demands for constitutional reform and for a new relationship between the government, workers and employers. With the launch of the opposition Movement for Democratic Change (MDC), the scene seemed set for unprecedented civic confrontation. Yet few could have predicted what was about to happen.

The story today

Since the government lost the constitutional referendum in February 2000, there has once again been an epidemic of organised violence and torture in Zimbabwe. This has been documented as in no other period before.[18] More importantly, the reports emanating from Zimbabwean organisations have been corroborated by the reports of international

---

[17] See ZHRF (2000), *Organised Violence and Torture in Zimbabwe in 2000*.
[18] See ft. 2 above.

organisations.[19] Additionally, there have been reports on the election petitions being heard before the High Court of Zimbabwe.[20] So it is possible to provide a very clear analysis of both the violence and who is responsible for it.

Victims of the most recent organised violence and torture are members, or suspected members, of the MDC, the National Constitutional Assembly and other civic organisations – as well as civil servants and ordinary citizens. The violence is targeted at any person or group suspected of not actively supporting ZANU PF. The notion of a 'sell-out' has a new and broader meaning: no one is safe unless they support the governing party.

Particular attention has been paid to commercial farmers and farm-workers because of the so-called 'land reform policy'. The evidence does not support the view that the violence is due to clashes over land or between ZANU PF and MDC supporters.[21] Overwhelmingly it indicates a systematic campaign of violence, close to the level of low-intensity war, perpetrated by government agencies and supporters against commercial farmers and farm-workers.[22]

Deaths, in the form of extra-judicial killing or summary executions, were not as common as in former periods of organised violence and torture. By August 2001, a total of 112 deaths could be confirmed, but it is also clear that this is an underestimate. There were very few arrests in connection with these murders, even though people often knew who the perpetrators were.

Torture in this present period can mean being attacked and 'thoroughly beaten' at home in front of one's own family by a group, sometimes a mob, of ZANU PF supporters. Other members of the family

---

[19] See Amnesty International (2000), *Zimbabwe: Terror tactics in the run-up to the parliamentary elections, June 2000*. Amnesty International (2002), *Zimbabwe: The Toll of Impunity*. Human Rights Watch (2002), *Fast track land reform in Zimbabwe*. IRCT (2000), 'Organised Violence and Torture in Zimbabwe', 6th June 2000, Copenhagen and Harare: IRCT and Amani Trust. IRCT and RCT (2001), *Organised election violence in Zimbabwe 2000*. IRCT (2001), 'Organised Violence and Torture in Zimbabwe', 24th May 2001, Copenhagen and Harare: IRCT and Amani Trust. Physicians for Human Rights (2002), 'Zimbabwe 2002. The Presidential Election: 44 days to go'. 24 January. Physicians for Human Rights (2002), 'Zimbabwe: Post Presidential Election – March to May 2002. "We'll make them run"', 21 May. Physicians for Human Rights (2002), 'Zimbabwe: Voting ZANU For Food: Rural District Council and Insiza Elections', August to October 2002.

[20] See Amani Trust (2002), *Organised Violence and Torture in the June 2000 General Election in Zimbabwe*. Amani Trust (2002), *Neither Free nor Fair: High Court decisions on the petitions on the June 2000 General Election*. Amani Trust (2002), *Organised Violence and Torture in the By-Elections held in Zimbabwe during 2000 and 2001*. Amani Trust (2002), *Heroism in the Dock: Does testifying help victims of organised violence and torture? A pilot study from Zimbabwe*.

[21] Reeler, A. P. (2003), 'The role of militia groups in maintaining Zanu PF's political power'. <www.zimnews.com>

[22] See Reeler, A. P (2003), 'Who should be sanctioned?', <www.zwnews.com> for a report on the involvement of government officials and others in the organised violence and torture.

may also suffer the same fate. Even if the torture was mild, the intimidation may have been frightening and traumatising. Homes have been vandalised even to the point of near-total destruction. Food stores have been destroyed or stolen. Civil servants – teachers or administrators – have had mobs descending on their places of work, threatening them and demanding their dismissal.[23]

In all of these events people have often decided that discretion was the better part of valour and gone into hiding or left their job. Nearly 9,000 people did this during the pre-election period in 2000. This became an increasing problem again in 2001, 2002 and 2003. This is a form of psychological torture. The UN Compensation Commission considers being forced into hiding by threats a gross human rights violation requiring compensation.

All of this has been condoned, or at least not condemned, by the leaders of ZANU PF. From the President downwards they are continuously on record making hate speeches, racist remarks, encouragements to violence, and threats.[24] The remarks did not cease even after the parliamentary elections. Dr Chenjerai Hunzvi was probably the most egregious of those making hate speech,[25] but there were many others.[26]

---

[23] See ZHRF (2002), *Teaching them a lesson. A report on the attack on Zimbabwean teachers*.

[24] 14 December 2000: President Mugabe tells the ZANU PF congress that the commercial farmers have 'declared war' on the people of Zimbabwe. He says that the white man is 'not indigenous' to Africa and is part of an 'evil alliance'. He tells his audience 'we must continue to strike fear into the heart of the white man, our real enemy'. His audience reply with chants of '*hondo*' (war). The President continued, 'The courts can do whatever they want, but no judicial decision will stand in our way . . . My own position is that we should not even be defending our position in the courts. We cannot . . .brook interference court impediment to the land acquisition programme.' (The *Zimbabwe Independent* 15 December and *Financial Gazette* 14 December 2000.)

[25] Dr Chenjerai Hunzvi (Member of Parliament for Chikomba) made a number of public statements after the Parliamentary elections: 'We are not afraid of the High Court . . . this country belongs to us and we will take it whether they like it or not. The judges must resign. Their days are numbered as I am talking to you . . . I am telling you what the comrades want, not what the law says.' 10 December 2000. On 14 December 2000 Hunzvi said, 'Whosoever is killed, it's tough luck.' On 3 March 2001 he said that all white judges must leave, 'If they want us to use violence we are going to use that.' In late March 2001 he said that ZANU PF will establish 'mobilisation bases' in Zimbabwe's cities as part of 'an aggressive plan'.

[26] Addressing about 1,000 people gathered at the Masvingo Civic Centre hall to receive cheques from Border Gezi, Governor Josaya Hungwe said a war would be declared if ZANU PF lost the mayoral election. Hungwe said, 'If you do not vote for ZANU PF in the coming mayoral election, people are going to be killed. I want to tell you, someone is going to die.' The MDC called for the immediate arrest of Josaya Hungwe, the Masvingo provincial governor, for threatening Masvingo residents with death ahead of the mayoral elections scheduled for next month. (*Daily News* 4 April 2001). Dr Jonathan Moyo was yet another person. Whilst briefing the Co-ordination Committee on press freedom, Moyo warned that Zimbabwe's independent media must expect violence for 'provoking' supporters of President Robert Mugabe's regime. He said it was 'understandable' that journalists who were seen as supporting an anti-ruling party agenda would be threatened with violence. (*The Standard* 13 May 2001).

We even had senior members of the defence forces threatening treason if ZANU PF lost. These statements indicate the mind-set of the governing party and the unreconstructed liberation war ideology that underpins the party. It also indicates there is at least tacit condoning of the violence, even approval and facilitation. It is hard to conclude otherwise when even the President refers to the opposition in Parliament as 'enemies'.

The scale of the current violence is difficult to estimate, but it approaches that of the 1980s. The number of deaths is, however, much fewer. One estimate has put the number of persons that experienced a gross human rights violation in 2000 at about 200,000.[27] Physical and mass psychological torture comprises nearly 90 per cent of this total, with extra-judicial killings and disappearances making up the rest. This is all a matter of record.

The effects of impunity

As indicated earlier, Zimbabwe has an unenviable reputation for the use of impunity in dealing with its human rights violations. This pre-dates Independence, and so ZANU PF has only continued what it learnt from the Rhodesian Front. But at least the Rhodesians were at war whereas ZANU PF uses organised violence and torture, as an ordinary means of government, in a time of peace. This has disastrous effects upon society, for, apart from the terrible consequences of the victims knowing that their assailants will always walk away free, the perpetrators learn that extreme violence is never punished. This is an encouragement to more violence. Indeed, many victims have been bluntly informed by their torturers that this is, indeed, the case. The Clemency Order of October 2000 confirmed this. Some of those pardoned by this order re-appeared as persons implicated in further torture in the by-elections of 2001, and the Presidential Election of 2002.[28] Most notorious of those forgiven in the amnesty was Dr Chenjerai Hitler Hunzvi, the leader of the so-called 'war veterans'. This qualified doctor was implicated in the torture of MDC supporters during the Bikita West by-election in January 2001.

Impunity has had some minor beneficial consequences. After it was granted in 1980 and 1987, the violence ceased. In 1980 the amnesty formed a basis for peace, although the ending of the war was, in itself, probably a strong enough motivation on its own for peace. Undoubtedly there was a need to reassure soldiers on both sides that peace would

---

[27] See Reeler, A.P (2001), 'State Sponsored Violence in Zimbabwe'. Paper presented to 'Crisis in Zimbabwe: Implications for South Africa and Southern Africa', South African Institute of International Affairs, 14 February 2001, Johannesburg, South Africa.

[28] See Reeler, A.P (2003), 'Who should be sanctioned?'. <www.zwnews.com> for a report on the involvement of government officials and others in the organised violence and torture.

exclude personal accountability. With hindsight, however, the decision to declare impunity in 1980 can be regarded as a decision made too hastily. It prevented Zimbabweans from learning the real benefits of accountability. The policy of reconciliation did not prevent the violence of the Gukurahundi, nor has it prevented the re-emergence of hate speech, racism, and violence today. It also would seem to be the case that having impunity as a precedent encourages its further use, and perhaps even encourages the use of violence as a political problem-solving device. It would even seem, in the current violence, that ZANU PF uses impunity as the final part of its 'campaign' strategy.

Conclusion

ZANU PF has a long history of using violence: the President and senior members of the government even boast about this. The legacy of the liberation war seems very hard to shake off. All significant threats to the party's political power are met with force and violence. The major change over the years has been the shift away from the use of violence as a way of defence, to it becoming a weapon of offence, presumably because the party has learnt how effective a weapon it can be.

So in Zimbabwe's history, briefly sketched here, torture and summary executions were used during the war to protect the guerrillas from informers, and to ensure compliance from the rural population. In a war there can be no neutral position, and the 'man in the middle' was an important strategic resource for all sides. Terrible things are done in war and justified by war, even though morality and international humanitarian law condemns them. Immoral things are done in pursuit of a moral aim, the overthrow of a treasonous and racist regime. This indeed may have justified the amnesty in 1980 and allowed peace to come to Zimbabwe.

But in the subsequent peace it is not so easy to justify a return to the methods of the 1970s, seen so graphically in the gross human rights violations committed by the Fifth Brigade, the CIO and ZANU PF Youth. They cannot be explained as the use of immoral means to pursue a moral goal. The mass terrorising of the southern half of Zimbabwe was out of all proportion to the threat, and put the government very much in the same position as the Smith regime, albeit with a constitutional mandate rather than a treasonous one. Old methods of ensuring compliance were revived and given a terrible new purpose: not to ensure the survival of a guerrilla army, but to ensure the political supremacy of ZANU PF. Immoral means were used for an immoral goal. This is not to suggest that there was not a crisis, nor that there was no dissident problem, but all available evidence shows, especially in respect of the latter, that the dissident problem was being contained successfully by conventional military means. It is noteworthy that most casualties inflicted upon the dissidents came from the regular army and the Support Unit of the police. In contradistinction, the other 'political' forces were responsible for the human rights violations. The lessons learned about enforcing compliance in the 1970s were used again in the 1980s.

The same lessons were applied again in an abbreviated fashion during the food riots in 1998, on a massive scale during 2000 and 2001, and still continue into 2003. The new twist in 2000-2003 is the predominant use of torture and the minimising of summary executions. The world frequently failed to understand this, and comments about the small number of deaths during the pre-election period were common. There is a terrible learning that has occurred over the decades, and that is that summary executions are not necessary to maintain compliance: this can be done by torture alone. Here we have the strategic aim behind the violence in 2000-2003.

So we are left with the legacy of several decades of organised violence and torture as we move towards a new democratic dispensation in Zimbabwe. We hope that we will learn our lessons this time around, perhaps assisted by the knowledge that South Africa has done so in a new and revolutionary development in the field of human rights accounting. The skeletons and ghosts will need their truth commission. Only then can we finally settle our differences and deal with the issue of changes in political power without sticks and stones.

14

Opportunities for political renewal in Zimbabwe

Fay Chung

The Zimbabwe African National Union Patriotic Front (ZANU PF) is an alliance of many groups, most notably of the Zimbabwe African National Union (ZANU) and the Zimbabwe African People's Union (ZAPU), an alliance solidified by the Unity Accord of 1987. By amalgamating so many group interests into one political party, it is not surprising that ZANU PF is often pulled in different directions, as the interests of different groups battle for dominance. The interests of the white and black business communities have not always coincided. And the interests of the business community have not always coincided with those of the workers, nor those of workers with those of peasants. The governing party has managed to maintain some form of unity for the first two decades of independence, but the time has now come for it to break up into its constituent parts. The break up of ZANU PF should be fraternal rather than fratricidal.

The history of the liberation struggle

The genesis of ZANU and ZAPU is based on the liberation struggle against Ian Smith's settlerism and colonialism. In this struggle all forces, regardless of class and political orientation, were united. There were major areas of agreement which included the following:

- The re-distribution of land so as to remove the historic grievance of the best land being given by successive colonial governments to a handful of white farmers.
- The opening up of educational opportunities for black people. Only 35 per cent of blacks were in primary school at independence, and only 4 per cent at secondary school. The percentage at university was minuscule, with only a few hundred being able to enrol each year.

- The end of racism. Blacks suffered severe forms of racial discrimination including the inability to purchase land in cities and designated white areas, to hold professional and technical posts, and to hold senior positions in the civil service, army and police.

The different groups that joined together to support the liberation struggle included
- the peasantry who still form 70 per cent of the population,
- the black agricultural and urban workers numbering about one million,
- the black business class who were joined by some progressive business people of other races,
- black intellectuals and professionals who were also supported by people of other races, and
- a large body of high school and university students who were to form a substantial number of the freedom fighters.

Whilst all these groups were totally united behind the liberation struggle, their interests did not always coincide. The differences became more accentuated after the first decade of independence, by which time gains had been made in terms of the resettlement of 62,000 peasant families on two million hectares of former commercial farming land; primary education for all; secondary education for the majority, and tertiary education had opened up to include the offspring of both peasants and workers. Racism had been overcome in terms of blacks being able to purchase land in urban areas and in former white farming areas. A proactive policy of appointing blacks to the civil service and to the armed forces brought a speedy end to racial discrimination in government.

The differences between ZANU and ZAPU were not fundamentally ideological, but were based on different strategies. Whilst ZAPU enjoyed widespread popular support in the 1960s, it was ZANU which managed to spearhead the armed struggle in the 1970s. Because of its military prowess, ZANU was able to gain control of a larger area of influence than ZAPU by the time of independence in 1980. Moreover, these differences were exacerbated by the issue of ethnicity, with ZANU having predominantly Shona support and ZAPU predominantly Ndebele.

Another major difference between ZANU and ZAPU before independence was ZANU's dependence on elections to choose its leadership, whereas ZAPU retained a more traditional system of appointment of leaders by the President of ZAPU, Joshua Nkomo. The superiority of the system of elections was demonstrated in the 1970s when ZANU, beginning with an army of only twelve freedom fighters, was able to dominate in the armed struggle. ZAPU's problem was that even though they had a superior army of over 600 very well-trained freedom fighters, decisions were usually made by non-military leaders located in Lusaka. ZAPU's problems were in evidence in the July 1967 incursion of over 100 Zimbabwe People's Revolutionary Army (ZIPRA) and the African National Congress (ANC) freedom fighters through Wankie (now Hwange). Through poor strategy most of these were either killed or captured. ZANU's military wing, the Zimbabwe African National Liberation Army (ZANLA), was able to win the right to make its own decisions in the field. ZANLA's military superiority was evident when, by 1974, it had become sufficiently powerful to seriously threaten the Smith regime. That same year the whole of colonial Rhodesia was on a war footing, with every eligible white man being called up for military duty.

Despite the differences in the way they chose their leaders, ZAPU and ZANU both inherited traditional ways of selecting their kings or chiefs. Among the Ndebele the eldest male son became the new king. Amongst the Shona the new chief was chosen by spiritual leaders from one of the ruling houses, who rotated this duty in accordance with ancient custom. The spiritual leaders were supposed to represent the interests of the ordinary people, but in fact there was no form of democratic election. Once chosen, the leader was free to choose his lieutenants.

Another characteristic of traditional leadership was patronage, by which a chief provided positions as well as physical possessions to his followers. Patronage was the cement of social stability, with loyalty to the leader being seen as the most valuable characteristic of the follower. Criticism was seen as tantamount to subversion and rebellion. Traditionally any opposition to the leader could lead to violent, even capital, punishment. It is within this context that the conflict within ZANU PF itself, and between ZANU PF and the Movement for Democratic Change (MDC) must be viewed. President Mugabe and the governing party see opposition as equivalent to treason, and feel justified in using force to remove it.

The first decade of independence

In accordance with the Lancaster House Agreement, no attempt was made in the first decade of independence to forcibly take over white farms. Instead the 'willing buyer willing seller' system was instituted. Under this system only three million hectares of the fifteen million hectares of land originally owned by white commercial farmers was transferred for resettlement, with two million going to peasant farmers and one million going to the ruling elite. Resettlement stopped in 1984 for a number of reasons, the main one being the growing predominance of the black middle class in political power as compared to the dominant role played by the peasantry during the liberation struggle. Giving land free of charge to the peasantry was regarded as a retrogressive step by many of the middle class, who feared that the newly acquired farms would soon become like those in the communal areas. They felt that land resettlement should benefit the middle class rather than the peasantry. This land struggle was exacerbated by the British government reneging on its promise to fund the purchase of white farms, whilst the Zimbabwe government itself decided not to utilise its own funds for this purpose. This impasse was to lead to a crisis two decades later.

Meanwhile, the peasantry and the workers were assuaged by their gains in education, and by the opening up of both job and land ownership opportunities denied them during the colonial period. The establishment of a minimum wage regime was initially highly advantageous to workers, although these gains were gradually eroded by inflation.

The Economic Structural Adjustment Programme (ESAP), 1992

The introduction of ESAP in 1992 had a major impact not only on the economy, but also on the political system. ESAP caused a shrinking of the economy for a number of reasons. One was the impact of competition. Zimbabwean industries suddenly found themselves facing lower cost and higher quality products from Asia. It became cheaper to import than to manufacture. Another serious problem was that even when a company was efficient and produced high quality goods, the constant devaluation of the Zimbabwean dollar meant it could face sudden bankruptcy, especially if it had been so unwise as to borrow from overseas banks. The sudden opening up of the banking system meant that some companies could choose to borrow from abroad, and given the weaknesses of the Zimbabwean banking system, many did so. Yet it could also mean that a company's debts literally doubled overnight. With about 200 to 300 companies closing each year, the Zimbabwean economy began to shrink.

However, ESAP was advantageous for a small group of the elite, particularly those who were able to enter the import business. ESAP strengthened the powers of the black middle class, giving them a greater say in the political development of the country. Contrary to ESAP theory, this middle class did not invest in industrialisation in Zimbabwe, but overseas or, if in Zimbabwe, in housing and consumer goods. Nor did the government implement an aggressive industrialisation policy. In other words ESAP did not contribute to an expansion of the economy.

The losers under ESAP were the workers, who not only suffered from constant devaluation, but were also retrenched in large numbers. They blamed government for their woes. The Movement for Democratic Change (MDC), based as it was on the trade union movement, was able to make political use of this discontent.

Raiding of the War Veterans Fund, 1996-97

The collapse of the Zimbabwe dollar occurred in 1997, following the raiding of the War Veterans Compensation Fund in 1996-97. About $1 billion was given mainly to the ruling elite. Some received as much as $850,000. The majority of freedom fighters did not receive any benefit from the fund. This led to the revolt by war veterans, and the subsequent handout of an estimated $4 billion to placate them. As government did not have $4 billion at hand, it gave in to the temptation of printing money, leading soon afterwards to the collapse of the Zimbabwe dollar.

The raiding of the War Veterans Fund was part of growing corruption within government. It also marked a strong resurgence of protest and power by disenchanted war veterans, particularly by ex-ZIPRA fighters who had been excluded from receiving any of the fruits of independence. Branded as 'dissidents' during the internal conflicts of the 1980s, they received an amnesty as a result of the Unity Accord. But their social and economic re-integration was left to a non-governmental organisation, the Zimbabwe Project.

The war in the Democratic Republic of the Congo

Zimbabwe's entry into the war in the Democratic Republic of the Congo in 1998 exacerbated the situation within a country that had already been struck by ESAP, by corruption, and by the war veterans' revolt. Whilst the war gave the opportunity for some businesses and some individuals to become billionaires, it did not benefit the country as a whole.

Political divisions in present day Zimbabwe

Serious political divisions, which had always been there, emerged in 2000 when the government lost the referendum on a new constitution. However, a few issues have acted as a catalyst to the present destabilisation.

Both ZANU PF and the MDC believe that the narrow defeat of the MDC was due to the violence meted out by ZANU PF against MDC supporters. The MDC was also guilty of indulging in fighting back with violence, under the impression that only violence can stem violence. Morgan Tsvangirai, the MDC leader, even threatened to end ZANU PF's reign through a violent uprising. The sorry episode of mutual violence has not yet ended. My own view is that the violence against the ordinary people has done nothing to win support for either party.

The underlying causes of the dissatisfaction with the ZANU PF government are not difficult to see. They include:
- Rising unemployment. This was partially due to Structural Adjustment. It was also partially due to the fact that government

has never seen a role for itself in ensuring the expansion of the productive base, with the result that per capita incomes have fallen. Structural Adjustment exacerbated the trend. As a result we probably have some two million unemployed and therefore dissatisfied youth, a potent force for destabilisation.
- Halting of land resettlement in 1984. The refusal to continue this programme for whatever reasons was a major failure of the ZANU PF government, and led to growing scepticism about the government's commitment to land resettlement. The sudden revival of land resettlement in 2000 and 2001 came about as the government realised that without speedy land resettlement it would lose power. However, the process used has been far from smooth. It can be argued that there was no way that the whites would have given up the land peacefully. Others may point out that the government itself made little move to take over white farms even after legislation was changed ten years ago to make it possible.
- Corruption within government – the worst example of this being the raiding of the War Veterans Compensation Fund in 1996 and the consequent revolt of the war veterans, directly causing the present problems.
- Neglect of war veterans after the first few years of Independence up until 1997. Whilst more than half the war veterans were integrated into the army, the police, the CIO, and the civil service in general, a large proportion were demobilised. They were given about Z$3500 (about US$7000 at that time – 1980) de-mobilisation allowance, and then left to fend for themselves. About ten thousand managed to upgrade their academic qualifications through Ministry of Education scholarships. Some thousands were successfully resettled through NGOs such as ZIMFEP and the Zimbabwe Project. Funding for NGOs came from outside donors and these funds eventually dried up.
- However, the panic that led to the government distributing an estimated $4 billion it did not have to war veterans in 1997 meant that government printed money rather than working out careful programmes for the integration of the former fighters into productive jobs. Instead of receiving land, houses, training or jobs, they were given paper money, leading – as already mentioned – to the drastic devaluation of the Zimbabwe dollar. A quick short term solution has led to a long term problem.

The combination of devaluation and the violent take-over of farms led to the flight of capital. Whereas only three years ago Zimbabwe earned over US$2 billion a year in foreign exchange, the official amount today is drastically lower. In addition, a large black market for foreign exchange has erupted, further destabilising the economy. Zimbabwe will not be able to regain its legitimate foreign exchange earnings until the present violent unrest ends. The totally free market sale and purchase of foreign exchange punctuated by sudden returns to exchange control have added to the volatility of the foreign exchange market. What is needed is a long term vision of foreign exchange, which combines both a degree of control and a healthy respect for market forces. It also requires certainty, predictability and stability, something that Zimbabwe has lacked over the last three or four years. Unpredictability leads to panic, and panic to the flight of foreign exchange.

Is there an alternative?

Yes there is. This lies not in the MDC, but within ZANU PF itself. ZANU PF has many intelligent and capable leaders within its ranks. Despite the present dominant view amongst those surrounding President Mugabe that there is no one capable of leading ZANU PF and Zimbabwe at this stage, the fact remains that ZANU PF includes some of the most brilliant and most capable people in Zimbabwe. Many of them are tried and tested, with wide experience of government as well as of the private sector. However, it is important that the gains of the past two decades are not lost. ZANU PF's next leader must remain loyal to certain ZANU PF precepts. These precepts should include:

- Large scale employment creation both through public works such as dam building and through the expansion of agricultural and industrial production as well as the utilisation of information and communication technologies. The output of agriculture and industry needs to be doubled over the next decade, so that all our young people can be gainfully employed. A policy to boost the number of employed is absolutely essential both for political and economic survival.
- Land to the tiller. Land must be given to good farmers, in particular to black farmers. This is one of the most important principles of the liberation struggle, and was betrayed by ZANU PF itself between 1984 and 2000. However, the chaotic and violent modalities utilized in the past three years must be halted, and land re-distribution must be done in a technically sound way. Unless we do this, Zimbabwe will be threatened with starvation. Land is a precious resource and must be in the hands of good farmers. There are millions of good farmers in Zimbabwe. They are not necessarily chaotic and violent.
- No theft or corruption. The rules followed by freedom fighters during the liberation struggle was not to take anything from the people, and this basic precept has been betrayed by some of those in power.

- Carefully designed programmes for war veterans so that they have farms and houses, and can earn a reasonable living through their work.
- Financial and economic stability through a long term plan for economic expansion, particularly through the establishment of a modern black entrepreneurial class so that the present imbalance where the economy is dominated by the white minority is changed. One of the major weaknesses of ZANU PF over the past two decades has been its inability to expand the economy so that the black entrepreneurial class becomes larger than the white.

Conclusion: fraternal rather than fratricidal politics

Zimbabwe has reached a crossroads. ZANU PF has reached such crossroads many times before. 1963 was one when ZANU was formed. 1968, when ZANU began the armed struggle with the Chinhoyi Battle, was another. The defeat of détente and of Ndabaningi Sithole in 1976 was a further crossroad which led straight to Independence. The successful educational and health programmes in the 1980s marked another crossroad. The crossroad of 2004 is whether Zimbabwe can rise to become a highly industrialised economy which can provide a good living for everyone of its citizens or will remain at its present stage of economic stagnation. This cannot be achieved by clinging to the past, however glorious that past may be. The challenges have changed. Today Zimbabweans are highly educated, whereas 20 years ago less than 4 per cent had secondary school education. This is a major achievement. We are proud of it, but we should move forward rather than sit on our laurels. Today there are millions of unemployed Zimbabweans, and many are suffering from hunger. Tomorrow's Zimbabwe should be able to provide employment and food for all. To do this requires a different type of leadership, a leadership which knows how to double and treble the economy of Zimbabwe. ZANU PF must show its legendary ability to renew itself, or else it will become irrelevant.

The natural division of ZANU PF into its constituent group interests is now long overdue. The unity, which was essential during the liberation struggle, is now no longer relevant. The colonial/settler regime has been removed. Political parties now need to represent the interests of their constituencies, and these are the peasantry, the agricultural workers, the commercial farmers, the urban workers, the business class, the intellectuals, etc., regardless of race. The system of unity based on political patronage has now outlived its day. Corruption is the natural offspring of patronage. ZANU PF as the parent liberation movement must allow its children to hold diverse political views. For example, the peasant view of land resettlement is diametrically opposed to the elite's view of land resettlement. And the political elite's view of land resettlement may be diametrically opposed to that of professional black farmers. The workers' view of progress may be diametrically opposed to that of white farmers, although both groups are now united under the MDC. ESAP's view of progress may be very different from those of the industrial class in Zimbabwe, which has witnessed a decade of de-industrialisation.

ZANU PF as the political parent, or even grandparent, now needs to let go of its children and allow them to form their own political views, their own policies and therefore their own political parties. It is incorrect and unsound to punish one's children for having outgrown parental controls. Our children live in a different world from ourselves: they are better educated than we were and they have had more training in industrial skills than we ever had. We of the parent and grandparent generation came from a peasant and missionary background, and were not allowed to participate in industrialisation during the colonial era. Whilst it is true that 23 years of independence is not a great deal, nevertheless, the first post-independence graduates are now in their forties, and ready to take over from us. We should not continue to treat them as recalcitrant and disobedient children.

The sudden mushrooming of the MDC as an alliance of disparate groups in opposition to Mugabe and to ZANU PF in 2000 is a symptom that change is now imminent. The MDC's economic policy appears to be a repetition of ESAP. In other areas the MDC has used the word 'democracy' to cover an inchoate and a very personalised attack on Mugabe. It appears, according to their statements, that all problems would be resolved if Mugabe is removed. However, this is not how I see it. The problems Zimbabwe faces today would be there with or without Mugabe. ZANU PF's inability to address many of these issues over the past decade is a symptom of conceptual and political bankruptcy. Since the adoption of ESAP most leaders have concentrated on the accumulation of personal wealth (supported by the ESAP ideology), but have failed to increase the national wealth. Unfortunately the MDC appears to share the same bankruptcy. It is time that Mugabe and ZANU PF accept that they are unable to solve the problems and allow those within the party and within the country to do so. We need a much younger generation of leaders. We need opposing and creative political views that can both research and debate the values of different policies in the open, without fear of being attacked and killed for 'treason'. We need a change. In my view MDC rushed in to fill the vacuum, but it does not provide the answers for Zimbabwe's future. Those who can provide these answers will now come forward, most of them from within ZANU PF. It would be good if ZANU PF could have sufficient parental pride to enable this process to be fraternal rather than fratricidal. Whichever way ZANU PF goes, nevertheless political diversity is inevitable.

Zimbabwe: The Past is the Future

One country, 'two nations', no dialogue

David Harold-Barry

To many in the outside world and within Zimbabwe, Ian Smith, the man, or the symbol was (and for some still is) seen to stand for the white community. He represents the racial polarisation and its oversimplification that is contained in so much of the debate about Zimbabwe. Imagine for a moment that the former leader of the Rhodesia Front looks back over his life and gives one final interview. What would he say? Apologies are in fashion: Tony Blair to the Irish for the famine of the 1840s, Japan to China and Korea for the atrocities of World War Two. Would Smith ask pardon for the way Rhodesia looked primarily to the interests of its white settlers and only reluctantly to those of the indigenous population? Would he admit that policies reaching back to the 1890s lie at the root of our present experience? It seems unlikely. More probably he would repeat some such remarks as he made to BBC interviewer David Frost in the 1970s. He would claim all has turned out as he predicted, 'We fought to prevent what is happening now.' Such self-justification would sadly confirm the chasm that has always existed between black and white.

No knees and no ears

The obduracy of Smith was not a new thing in the politics of this country. It has a long and contagious history. Black and white writers had quite different perspectives on the same facts. In the middle of the last century, Philip Mason and Richard Gray wrote penetrating studies on the divide between black and white. Even the titles of their books – *The Birth of a Dilemma* (1958) and *The Two Nations* (1960) – reveal their awareness of the issues. Such writers knew blacks and whites lived in the same country without speaking to one another on any level that really counted. Yet, despite their sympathetic descriptions of the situation, they would have been astonished by the tone, for example, of Lawrence Vambe's *The Ill-Fated People* (1972). Here is Vambe's picture of the arrival of the whites in 1890:

> My father, who was a very young man at the time, said that these people, with their long animal-like hair and beards, wild eyes, uniforms, hats and shoes, as well as horses, ox-wagons and other accoutrements, were like a circus. For several weeks, all the Shona society around Harare would be irresistibly drawn to gape and often split their sides in wonderment and amusement. Most extraordinary and ridiculous were the Pioneers' habits of living, such as military formations, drilling to the barks of their commanders, bugle sounding and hoisting and un-hoisting of their flag. These strange antics, never seen before, were greeted by the Shona as signs of incomprehensible eccentricity and conclusive evidence that the people 'without knees' were mentally deranged.[1]

Vambe goes on to say, 'a more friendly welcome to any occupying power it would be difficult to find ... [and] if the Europeans had any foresight or real appreciation of human values they might have turned this friendly reception to good account and used it as a foundation stone upon which to build the new society that was the object of their endeavour'.[2] But they didn't and by the 1920s, the old people of Chishawasaha, Vambe's home, had despaired of the settlers, 'who failed them on all fundamental questions such as land, justice, truth and human relationships'.[3] In his book, written 50 years later, Vambe can vividly remember the day a white policemen came to his home and arrested his grandfather, Mizha, using a stream of insulting language, for not licensing his dogs. The trooper was alone and 'did not even pretend to hold his revolver at the ready'. Yet the young Vambe felt a fear which made him 'stand still in helplessness ... a passive instinct of self-preservation', which he goes on to say never existed before 1896 but which now extended to the whole black population. 'We were not only a conquered people, but a people that the conqueror did not even respect.'[4]

The tone of the academic studies of Mason and Gray in the mid-twentieth century was rather different. They were critical of the whites but shared none of the optimism of Vambe that things could have been different. 'It was surely inevitable that to begin with there should be very little understanding between peoples so utterly different in their background as the Bantu tribes of Rhodesia and the British and Afrikaners who made the bulk of the first settlers.'[5] Was it so inevitable? Before 1890, explorers, traders, hunters, and missionaries had negotiated

---

[1] Vambe, Lawrence (1972) *An Ill-Fated People*. London: Heinemann. 93.
[2] Ibid.
[3] Ibid. 167.
[4] Ibid. 18.
[5] Mason in his forward to Richard Gray, (1960), *The Two Nations*. London: Institute of Race Relations and Oxford University Press. ix

person to person for the permissions they sought. Why was it so inevitable that the pioneers should adopt an attitude of ownership and authoritarianism from the moment they arrived? But this is what they did, and we are still living out the consequences of their choices.

The interests of the conquerors

They quickly showed their intentions. They made no attempts to negotiate with the paramount chiefs of the Shona. Land was freely allocated to the settlers and a black police force was recruited to instil acceptance of the new order. The settlers who came to this land were probably no better and no worse than any group anywhere else.[6] They were people of their time who felt they had something to give as well as to receive. Their attitude was assertive and self-protecting but they showed a sense of responsibility, even if it was paternalistic, for the people they now governed. They knew they were invaders, but they subscribed to the imperial myth about 'opening up' the vast interior of Africa. Livingstone was not long dead and his message of a continent in thrall to slavery and longing for order, development and Christianity was still fresh. Terence Ranger (1967) has given descriptions of how they acted:

> In January 1894 a police trooper was sent to Makoni's kraal to tell him that Mr Wood "... was occupying that land on the authority of the [British South Africa] Company. If he has anything to complain of he can represent the matter either to the Civil Commissioner or to the authorities in Salisbury ... but if he allows his people to constantly trespass on the land given to Mr Wood by the Company or to kill Wood's goats ... the Company will be obliged to give Mr Wood protection and punish those who molest him."[7]

The description 'white' is a convenient label, but they were never a homogenous group. The earliest settlers were soldier/adventurers; those who came after 1900 were often fugitives from the persecutions and depressions of Europe, especially Eastern Europe. Oppressed people themselves, they were, as so often happens, disinclined to question the practice of those who oppressed others.

Up to the time of the First World War, the new and the old settlers were more worried about the restraining hand of the colonial office in

---

[6] I claim to know this in the sense that my grandfather's brother was one of them. He came from Ireland in 1893 with the same thought as many like him: to do something with his life. There were few prospects in his home country in those days and 'going out foreign' seemed an attractive option. In the event he was killed in the Jameson Raid of 1895.
[7] Ranger, Terence (1967), *Revolt in Southern Rhodesia, 1896-97*. London: Heinemann. 84.

London than of the reactions of the black population. To them the imperial government was irritatingly concerned about the welfare of the indigenous people. The British South Africa Company normally found ways around instructions from London. Uppermost in their thoughts were the issues of land, labour and cattle. How they acquired these showed little appreciation of the outlook of the people they conquered. Cattle, for example, had to be owned by someone. When the Matabele were defeated, the company set about confiscating the king's cattle but not those of the people. But who, among the Matabele, would make such a distinction? With regard to land, the colonial office in London insisted the Matabele were to retain what was '... sufficient and suitable ... [with] fair and equitable portions of springs and permanent water'.[8] This did not happen.

A gulf in understanding

The two sides settled down to an uneasy coexistence. 'To neither did it seem likely ... that the separating gulf could be bridged in any future that need concern them.'[9] No one in the administration of the colony was ready to reflect on the implications of their policies for the future. Southern Rhodesia decided that white interests were paramount. All legislation would be framed around this central axiom. The vanquished grudgingly accepted what they could not prevent. There is a photo of Kaguvi and Nehanda, spirit medium leaders of the Shona rising, taken shortly before their execution. The former looks defiant while Mbuya Nehanda is serene and dignified. It is as though she knew there was nothing to be done – for now. Both Shona and Matabele had fought the invaders and discovered they were no military match for them. They had to accept the new reality and wait for better times.

A French lawyer, visiting the country in 1912, noted there are 'two societies, one superimposed on the other, ... an aristocracy of white landowners and capitalists [and] a proletariat of blacks'. He noticed 'hate, more or less concealed by the native ... hate expressed by the whites with more or less freedom, according to their level of education'.[10]

Progress on white terms

On the surface, the life of the colony progressed. But there were two progressions and, although they depended on one another, they were not integrated. Vambe tells us that after the First World War, the old people just resigned themselves to passive acceptance, but the younger

---
[8] Mason, Philip, (1958) *The Birth of a Dilemma*. London: Oxford University Press. 185.
[9] Ibid. 213.
[10] Henri Rolin, quoted in Mason, op.cit. 244.

generation began to embrace the new opportunities with enthusiasm. The earlier reluctance to go to school, to work in farming, market gardening, and other skills gave way to a new desire to progress. Instead of seeing this as a welcome sign, the whites saw it as a threat and from this time – the 1920s – began a policy of segregation. Those Africans who wanted to 'enter fully into the system brought by the Europeans, found themselves debarred, hindered and frustrated'.[11] The *Land Apportionment Act* of 1931 and the *Industrial Conciliation Act* of 1934 are the two best-known pieces of segregationist legislation. The former divided the country according to race and the latter provided for the creation of trade unions while explicitly excluding Africans from its definition of 'employee'.

The thinking behind both acts was that they were necessary practical measures for the moment; they were not meant to be permanent. But the acts did not say they were temporary and they were immediately perceived as reinforcing a growing system of separate development. The whites who made such laws were not racial fanatics. Many of them were well-intentioned people motivated by considerations of justice as they saw it. They saw the spectre of economic competition and withdrew behind protective legislative barriers. 'It is one of the sober paradoxes of Central African history that just at the moment when Africans were beginning to demand better education and more opportunities of sharing in the white man's world, Europeans were becoming less and less ready to give active and confident help in this transition.'[12] Once again, they missed an opportunity to welcome black people into the economy and they stoked further the embers of bitterness and resentment that lingered on from the crushed uprisings of 1896-97.

Ineffectual control from London

In such a climate, the efforts of London to modify the ardour of the 'responsible government' in Salisbury were bound to be ineffectual. Lord Passfield, the Secretary of State, had issued a memorandum in 1930 reaffirming the paramountcy of African interests in the colonies. There was to be equal opportunity of access to land; Africans should be 'effectively and economically free to work, in accordance with their own wishes' anywhere; African development was to be considered as a 'first charge'. London seemed far away on another planet.

As tension grew in the 1930s, whites began to think closer union with Northern Rhodesia and Nyasaland would strengthen their position in Central Africa. The government in London set up a commission under

---

[11] Gray, op.cit. ft. 5. 167.
[12] Gray, op.cit. ft. 5. 129.

Lord Bledisloe in 1938 to examine this proposal and found that while whites were in favour, blacks were not. The whole question was put on hold as the Second World War broke out.

Growing confrontation

Just as the First World War led to the dismantling of empires in Europe so the Second World War inaugurated a process, a 'wind of change', that would end the colonial empires in the rest of the world. African soldiers fought in that war and helped to liberate Europe. They came home to find that they themselves remained confined in their own homeland. The whites who immigrated after the Second World War were often ex-military or working class people. They had aspirations to live a middle-class life and were not in a mood to compete with blacks for the limited economic space available to achieve it. Black and white were now firmly set on a collision course. The years of passive submission were over.

In April 1948, in Bulawayo, 'all hell seemed let loose' as hundreds of workers armed with knobkerries, sticks, hatchets, lead piping, and bicycle chains enforced a strike.[13] The reaction of whites to the growing assertiveness of blacks was to hasten the day of federation. All sorts of arguments about the benefits to be gained were proposed, but behind them all was an urgent need to strengthen their own position. It was an updated version of the laager. Godfrey Huggins, the first prime minister of the Federation of Rhodesia and Nyasaland, inaugurated in 1953, spoke of a 'partnership' as in a business 'where the junior gradually works his way up'. But he also spoke of a partnership of 'horse and rider' and everyone knew which was which. 'We must make it clear,' said Roy Welensky, Huggins' successor, 'that even when that day comes [when the African shows his ability to contribute more to the general good] in a hundred or two hundred years' time, he can never hope to dominate the partnership.'[14]

Such sentiments further notched up feelings of resentment and frustration among blacks, and when James Chikerema, Edson Sithole, and George Nyandoro started the Youth League in 1955, they found a ready response. The league swept the elections for the advisory board of the Harare township in 1956. In 1957, the African National Congress (ANC) was launched with Joshua Nkomo as its leader. The white government, which existed in one form or another since 1890, was now faced with the clear voice of the African people. Unfortunately, they had never been accustomed to listen and they were not ready to do so now. The Prime Minister, Sir Edgar Whitehead, banned the ANC in 1959 and

---

[13] *The New Rhodesia*, 23 April 1948, quoted in Gray, op.cit. 289.
[14] Quoted in Martin Meredith (1980) *The Past is Another Country*. London: Pan, 24

its successor, the National Democratic Party (NDP), in 1960. Other repressive steps followed, most notably the *Law and Order (Maintenance) Act*, which Sir Robert Tredgold, the Federal Chief Justice, considered 'removed the last vestige of doubt about whether [Southern] Rhodesia is a police state'.[15] Efforts were made to bridge the gap – most notably in the 1961 constitutional proposals – but the underlying drift towards polarisation was unstoppable. In 1962, the newly formed Rhodesia Front (RF) easily won the general election by proclaiming an uncompromising version of white rule. The Zimbabwe African People's Union replaced the NDP and then was itself banned in 1962, its followers splitting into two new parties – the People's Caretaker Council and the Zimbabwe African National Union (ZANU) – and the leaders of both parties were arrested and detained. The RF followed this up with the Unilateral Declaration of Independence in 1965.

'Moral capitulation'

There followed seven years of RF dominance and black nationalist impotence, reminiscent of the aftermath of the Chimurenga of 1896-97. The British government made three attempts to wrest concessions from Ian Smith, the RF leader. Two were made on warships in the Mediterranean by the Labour government under Harold Wilson and a final attempt followed under the Conservatives when Sir Alec Douglas-Home worked out proposals with Ian Smith. Lord Goodman, working with Sir Alec, defended what was proposed. 'The terms of settlement were not a sell-out. The African had been sold out long before ... during the long years of British colonial administration, which, notwithstanding our reserved powers, accepted discriminatory legislation. ... It is against this background of constant moral capitulation ... that the terms we negotiated ... have to be set.'[16] A commission under Lord Pearce sought public reaction to them and found that whites accepted them while blacks did not. They promised majority rule some time in the future – estimates varied between fifteen and 60 years' time – but the African people were not interested in the niceties of maths. They had long since learnt not to trust whites.

As in the early days, whites were not united. There was a sizeable minority who opposed the flint-like thinking of the Rhodesian Front, most notably the Centre Party under Pat Bashford, which attracted a number of well-known people in public life. But they had no effect before the bludgeoning tactics of the ruling party. Ian Smith called anyone 'who was not with us ... pro-Wilson [and] a traitor'. A generation later Robert Mugabe would brand his opponents pro-Blair and 'enemies'.

---

[15] Ibid. 28.
[16] Ibid. 84.

A bitter struggle

The seven years of intransigence were followed by seven years of armed struggle in an increasingly bitter war. The guerrillas gradually wore down the white minority, but the human cost was terrible. Approximately 60,000 people lost their lives in combat, in 'crossfire' or in massacres. Many more suffered in the breakdown of health services and schooling. When peace came at the end of 1979 there was relief, but there was also anxiety. Legal independence in 1980 was a moment of goodwill and hope. But it was born of blood and it could either lead to a real new beginning or else it would be a time of settling old scores.

Reconciliation?

The new government stated its desire to draw a line under the past and offer the hand of reconciliation. Unfortunately, the history of the previous 90 years cast a long shadow on the early 1980s and no one was big enough to free the country from it. There was reconciliation between Zezuru and Karanga, Shona and Ndebele, black and white. But it did not go deep. A short civil war between Shona and Ndebele was followed by a long period of bloody repression – the notorious Gukurahundi – in which thousands were killed.[17] A formal reconciliation between the two parties was negotiated under duress in 1987, but it did not satisfy the Ndebeles, who remain deeply bitter about the Gukurahundi. Archbishop Pius Ncube, however, pointed out, in a public meeting in Bulawayo in 2001, that the Shona also have memories of Ndebele pillage of their lands in the years before the settlers came and this has to be acknowledged. To this day, the government has never seriously sought to address these issues[18], and its actions at the time of the elections of 2000 and 2002 show it has no appetite to do so.

The whites did not expect the peaceful transition of 1980. Many of them had been duped into believing that Abel Muzorewa – whom Ian Smith had groomed as a man he could control – would win the first 'one man, one vote' elections of 1980. Initiatives in land redistribution and real partnership in the economy were introduced and were quite successful. In September 1980, six months after independence, Robert Mugabe said:

---

[17] Catholic Commission for Justice and Peace, (1997) *Breaking the Silence - Building True Peace, A Report on the Disturbances in Matabeleland and the Midlands 1980 to 1988*. Harare: CCJP and the Legal Resources Foundation. 3.

[18] Only one senior minister, the late Moven Mahachi, expressed regret publicly, '... events during that period are regretted and should not be repeated by anybody, any group of people or any institution in this country'; *The Sunday Mail*, 6 September 1992; quoted in *Breaking the Silence*, op.cit. 5.

At a time when our main concern is the resettlement of our peasantry, the rehabilitation of our economy and social services, we have determined that any measures disruptive of the economic infrastructure must at all costs be avoided. Our socialist thrust will thus restrict itself for now to the area of land resettlement and organisation of peasant agriculture. Here we intend to correct with speed the historical imbalance in the distribution of land between the white commercial farmers and the peasantry by reapportioning to the latter a large percentage of the land now in the hands of the former, much of which is under-utilised.[19]

It was the sort of speech with which everyone could be happy. It promised radical and speedy reform, but at the same time a reform that would not disrupt the economy. It was a moment of euphoria and confidence and it seemed to many, black and white, coloured and Indian, that all the bitterness and frustration of the past was now assuaged. We could all move forward together. People were now free to take decisions about their own lives. Here are the words of a parliamentary candidate in Gutu. 'People's power means here in Munyikwa we are responsible for the decisions on how to run our dipping centres. We, the people, make the decisions. You and me, we are the decision makers ... such things cannot run on decisions of a man in Salisbury.'[20]

The candidate was optimistically using ZANU Patriotic Front's own 1980 election manifesto: '... that the common interests of the people are paramount in all efforts to exploit the country's resources, that the productive processes must involve them as full participants, in both the decision-making processes, management and control ...' It was a beautiful ideal.

Enduring divisions

We now know that 1980 was not the end of an era. The papers in this collection make it clear that independence was sadly not a new beginning. There remained unfinished business from the Rhodesian era. Despite grand sentiments, neither the attitudes nor the instruments – the *Law and Order (Maintenance) Act*, for instance – were left behind. In an uncanny way, the new rulers proceeded just as their predecessors had done. I have already referred to the crushing of the Ndebele. The settling of scores with whites took a little longer.

---

[19] Department of Information (1980) 'The Prime Minister opens Economic Symposium', 8 September 1980.
[20] Davis Mugabe, quoted in Terence Ranger (1985) *Peasant Consciousness and Guerrilla War in Zimbabwe*. Harare: Zimbabwe Publishing House. 288.

The new government took initial steps in the 1980s to expand education and health services, but they gave up trying to sustain these in the 1990s. In that latter decade, they saw threats to their position everywhere, just as the Rhodesians had done in the 1920s and 1930s. The last decade of the old century saw a much-expanded free press, a free trade union movement, an end to government monopoly of telecommunications, a credible political opposition and, perhaps most threatening of all, proposals for a new constitution. After 20 years of having everything its own way, the government suddenly found it had a real fight on its hands. And it was not the easily identified whites it was up against, but a broad coalition of people and organisations across the country who came together in a National Constitutional Assembly (NCA) in 1998. As the momentum grew for a new constitution in 1999, the government became nervous about its lack of control of the process and set up its own Constitutional Commission (CC). The NCA found its access to the media blocked while the 'well-funded CC campaign received prominent and positive news coverage and advertising space in the publicly owned media'.[21]

There was consternation in government circles when the referendum on the new constitution was lost in February 2000. While the president conceded defeat on television that night, saying that the will of the people had to be respected, it was evident that he was very angry. Within days, the farm invasions began. It was the old story: a scapegoat had to be found. White farmers, owning vast tracks of the country's best land, were obvious targets. The dissatisfaction of the people in general was brushed aside, and attention was focused on an ancient score that it would now be very convenient to settle. Much of the government's rhetoric was true, as this paper has tried to show. Land was taken in the 1890s with scant consideration for the people dislocated, and subsequent legislation had stacked up grievances that did not evaporate with the raising of a multi-coloured flag on 18 April 1980. But the tragedy is that the new government learnt nothing from the long history of its own opposition to white rule. It listens to the people no more than its white predecessors did. It manifestly does not believe in its own policy about the people participating in decision-making. And it uses all the old oppressive ways of the Rhodesians; harassing, torturing and killing its own people.

---

[21] The first NCA meeting was attended by approximately 1,000 delegates from 40 organisations. See Richard Saunders (1999) *Never the Same Again*. Harare: Edwina Spicer Productions. 99.

Missed opportunities

Those who inherited the leadership of the new Zimbabwe – both black and white – were unable to disentangle themselves from the tired old battles. Since independence, white people have lived in an unreal world, their way of life hardly different from Rhodesian days. They did not seem to realise that, although the government was mishandling the land distribution, at some stage there would be a reckoning. If land, cattle and labour had been the great issues of the 1890s, only the first of these remained to be settled in the 1990s. But the whites seemed to wait on events. What would have happened had they made some form of affirmative approach to black land-hungry peasants we will never know. What would have happened had the government entered into a serious dialogue, backed up by all their authority, with the white landowners in the 1980s we will never know. What we do know is that confrontational politics persisted into the new Zimbabwe. The government, finally finding itself cornered in the opening months of the new century, in a burst of mindless energy, has – like Samson of old – brought the whole fabric of society crashing down around itself and us.

Why are we where we are now – a nation of 'hunter gatherers' as one wit has put it? In 1980, a new black landowner complained that the people of the adjacent communal land were not respecting his property. He asked:

> *Does Zimbabwe mean that you can take someone's property and tell him to keep quiet? People are taking advantage of the independence of Zimbabwe. A lot of evil is happening because they claim they took part in the armed struggle. Who didn't? .... One begins to wonder what kind of life lies ahead in this country.*[22]

Perhaps it was too much to expect that we would rise so quickly above our ancient quarrels. Two thousand years of Christianity has not filtered into our consciousness anywhere in the world sufficiently for us to say that 'there are no more distinctions between Jew and Greek'.[23] So we live divided. The black/white divide is now almost irrelevant, even if it is constantly invoked as a way of concealing the real division. Once again, as in the 1890s, we are a crushed and broken people.

---

[22] *The Herald*, 9 September 1980, quoted in Ranger (1985) op.cit. 326.
[23] St Paul, Epistle to the Galatians, 3:28.

Encouraging signs

Yet this time there is more hope. While people suffer, they know that the present situation cannot go on for long. The Economist Intelligence Unit predicted chillingly in December 2002 that the government's economic policies are 'ultimately unsustainable, but they can probably be continued for several years bringing ongoing economic decline. In addition, it is increasingly likely that even if comprehensive economic reforms were to be introduced, the country's commercial farming, mining and manufacturing sectors have now been irreparably damaged.'[24]

Despite this gloomy forecast there are some good signs. The divisions among people are not based on tribe or race but on political opinion. In the 1980s, there was an attempt to turn the victory of majority rule into a permanent victory of one party rule. The jibe of the whites – 'one man, one vote, once' – nearly became a reality and in fact the present government acts as though it believes it. Contrary opinions are not seen as expressions of 'loyal opposition' but as treachery. Yet the honing of critical dissent continues and there are many brave people – politicians, judges, journalists and civil rights activists – searching for and speaking about alternative ways forward.

As I write, both Ian Smith and Robert Mugabe are about 80 years old. If this were a play, a Shakespearean tragedy, we would now be in Act V, Scene V. The curtain is about to come down on the era of old men and their worn out dreams. When this happens, we will be faced with an awesome programme of rebuilding. It would be an enormous step in that process if at last people began to listen to one another.

---

[24] Quoted in *The Observer* (UK), 15 December 2002.

Chronology

1979

10 September – 21 December – The Lancaster House Conference, which led to the creation of the new state of Zimbabwe, was held in London, under the chairmanship of Lord Carrington, the British foreign secretary. The participants were the Patriotic Front delegation, led by Joshua Nkomo and Robert Mugabe, and the Salisbury delegation, led by the Prime Minister of Zimbabwe-Rhodesia, Bishop Abel Muzorewa, which included Ian Smith and members of the Rhodesian Front. The conference, over fourteen weeks of hard bargaining with concessions made by both sides, agreed to a return of Zimbabwe-Rhodesia to the pre-UDI colonial status of Southern Rhodesia, a cessation of hostilities between the warring parties, and an election under a new constitution, leading to an independent state – Zimbabwe.

12 December – A British governor, Lord Soames, with wide-ranging powers, arrived in Salisbury to head an interim administration that would oversee the transition to internationally recognised independence. The British government lifted all sanctions against the country and the United States followed suit on 16 December.

21 December – The Lancaster House Agreement was signed and the United Nations immediately called on member states to remove sanctions.

1980

27-29 February – Nine political parties contested the first elections under the new Zimbabwe Constitution. At stake were 100 seats in the House of Assembly: 80 elected from a black voters' roll and 20 on a white voters' roll. The election results under the black roll were: ZANU PF 57 seats, PF-ZAPU 20, UANC 3. ZANU PF gained 63 per cent of the black roll votes while PF-ZAPU had 24 per cent. There was a high voter turn out (84 per cent). The Rhodesian Front won all 20 seats under the white roll. Monitors from Commonwealth countries considered that, under the circumstances following many years of armed conflict, the elections were free and fair.

Zimbabwe's new constitution provided for a two-chamber legislature and a non-executive president, elected for a period of six years by the members of the House of Assembly and Senate acting as an electoral college. The principal power lay in the hands of a prime minister, who commanded the support of a majority of members of the House of Assembly. Elections for a new parliament would be held every five years.

The 30-member Senate comprised: fourteen senators elected by members of the House of Assembly, ten by the Council of Chiefs, and six appointed by the president on the advice of the prime minister.

18 April – Britain formally granted independence to Zimbabwe. The constitutional instruments were handed over by Prince Charles at a ceremony attended by thousands of jubilant Zimbabweans at Rufaro Stadium, Harare.

13 May – The Parliament of Zimbabwe convened for the first time. Robert Mugabe, Zimbabwe's first prime minister, headed a widely representative cabinet that, in addition to members of his own party, included ZAPU members (Joshua Nkomo became internal affairs minister), independent white members of the House of Assembly, and senators.

Early education reforms introduced provided free primary education to all Zimbabweans, secondary education for the majority, and tertiary education for those who qualified on the basis of academic achievement. Health care was also extended to provide a much-improved service to the majority.

November: First Entumbane uprising in which ZIPRA and ZANLA ex-combatants in Bulawayo fought each other in a two-day pitched battle.

The ZANU PF government achieved an almost total monopoly of the news media with its purchase of a controlling interest in the company that owned the country's two daily newspapers, two Sunday newspapers and a weekly. The government also controlled the nation's radio and television stations. There remained only one independent national newspaper, the *Financial Gazette*, a business weekly that carried political news neglected by the state media. This situation lasted until 1996.

1981

February – Second Entumbane uprising. Over 300 people killed and many ZIPRA cadres defect from newly integrated Zimbabwe National Army (ZNA). The Zimbabwe Congress of Trades Unions was set up, as an arm of ZANU PF.

1982

February – The Zimbabwe government found caches of arms on farms and properties in Matabeleland. PF-ZAPU was accused of plotting to overthrow the Mugabe government, and Nkomo and some of his supporters were expelled from the cabinet. Other PF-ZAPU leaders were arrested and jailed. There was anger in Matabeleland at the confiscation of ZAPU farms and businesses. Ex ZIPRA fighters defected from the national army and banditry increased.

1983

January – Despite denials by Nkomo that his party had links with dissidents, the Zimbabwe government deployed the Fifth Brigade, an army unit composed entirely of former ZANLA guerrillas and trained by North Korean instructors, into Matabeleland.

Widespread atrocities by this brigade, other state security agencies and ZANU PF Youth Brigade members, occurred during what became known as the Gukurahundi (the washing away of trash). Curfews were imposed and food shortages caused great suffering. Estimates of deaths are in the tens of thousands. During this period, there were also widespread atrocities by 'dissidents' in Matabeleland. Thirty-three people were murdered on commercial farms between November 1982 and December 1983. Missionaries and tourists were among those killed.

1984

January – It is announced in parliament that since January 1983, dissidents have killed 120, mutilated 25, raped 47 and committed 284 robberies.

During the year, and until August 1985, the anti-ZAPU disturbances led by the Youth Brigade spread into urban areas in Bulawayo, Gweru, Beitbridge, Silobela and Harare. Hundreds were left dead and 4,000 became homeless. No arrests were made. The Chahambakwe Commission of Inquiry took evidence about atrocities committed in 1983 but its findings have not been made public.

The land settlement programme was halted by ZANU PF, and not resumed until 2000. Between independence and 1984, two million hectares were purchased with funds from the British government and distributed to 42,000 families. Subsequently, it was learned that a proportion of this land went not the peasants, but to the middle-classes, particularly members of ZANU PF. The argument being that commercial farming needed investment.

1985

26 June – In general elections, ZANU PF increased its majority, gaining 64 of the 80 elected House of Assembly seats voted for on the common roll. PF-ZAPU won fifteen seats and ZANU-Ndonga one seat. The Conservative Alliance (the new name for the Rhodesian Front, led by Ian Smith) won fifteen of the white reserved seats. Independents took the remaining five white seats. The government was incensed by the success, albeit limited, of the opposition. Three days of rioting against PF-ZAPU supporters followed in Harare and a PF-ZAPU candidate was hacked to death and several civilians were killed.

1986

The Presidential Powers (Temporary Measures) Act was passed. This invested the president with unilateral (albeit temporary) law-making powers.

1987

October – At the end of the seven year period stipulated by the Lancaster House agreement the government was free to introduce changes to the constitution. The ceremonial presidency was abolished and a directly elected executive president was introduced. The provision for 20 white members voted for by a white voters' roll and the Senate were also abolished. The membership of elected members to the House of Assembly was increased to 120, all of whom would be voted for by Zimbabweans on a common roll. In addition, 30 non-elected seats were created. Eight were for governors of provinces (appointed by the president), twelve special interest group representatives (appointed by the president), and ten appointed by the House of Chiefs, who themselves are appointed by the president. Ministers and the vice-president were to be appointed by the president.

22 December – ZANU PF and PF-ZAPU merged under the ZANU PF banner in a pact called the Unity Accord. This was widely seen as the price PF-ZAPU had to pay to end the persecution of the Matabele people.

1988

April – Joshua Nkomo was appointed second vice-president and, later in the year, Senior Minister of Local Government, Rural and Urban Development.

18 April – A general amnesty declared for all dissidents.

June – Amnesty extended to cover all members of the security forces who had committed human rights violations during the Gukarahundi.

12 October – *The Chronicle*, a government-owned Bulawayo-based newspaper, revealed a major scandal involving new motor cars. Due to foreign exchange constraints, it was difficult to buy new cars, and a local company, Willowvale Motor Industries, was provided with funds to import kits and assemble vehicles locally. Government ministers and senior members of ZANU PF were alleged to have used their influence to obtain cars for friends, or bought cars at the controlled price and sold them at a higher price. One minister committed suicide after his involvement was revealed. Top government and ZANU PF officials were prosecuted and found guilty but were quickly pardoned by the president. Other prosecutions were stopped. The editor of *The Chronicle*, Geoff Nyarota, was removed from his post and reassigned to non-editorial duties in the Zimpapers group.

In the same month, Edgar Tekere, Secretary-General of ZANU PF was expelled for openly criticising the party and opposing the creation of a one-party state.

1989

April – Zimbabwe Unity Movement (ZUM) formed and led by Edgar Tekere. President Mugabe dismisses it as the 'joke of the year'.

April – Ex-combatants from ZANLA and ZIPRA form Zimbabwe War Veterans' Association (ZWVA) to articulate their interests.

1990

9-10 March – President Mugabe won the first presidential election, though it was marred by political violence. One of Mugabe's key campaign issues was land distribution to the majority and the establishment of a one-party state. He won with 78 per cent of the votes cast while Edgar Tekere of ZUM garnered 22 per cent. In parliamentary elections, ZANU PF won 117 seats of the 120 elected seats in the House of Assembly, ZUM won two seats and one went to ZANU-Ndonga.

July – The state of emergency, which had been introduced in 1965 and maintained after independence, was lifted.

September – ZANU PF Central Committee rejects proposal to create a *de jure* one-party state.

December – Parliament passed a constitutional amendment empowering it to confiscate land, fix the price and deny the right of appeal to courts for fair compensation. By the end of 1990 more than 1,300 farms, amounting to around 3 million hectares, had been acquired by the Zimbabwe government for resettlement of more than 50,000 families.

The World Bank's Economic Structural Adjustment (ESAP) programme was adopted.

1991

Government began implementing ESAP.

1992

The Land Acquisition Act, 1991, was passed, giving considerable powers to government to implement intensive settlement.

Zimbabwe Human Rights Organisation (ZimRights) established.

Severe drought.

June – ZCTU organised an anti-ESAP demonstration. Police ban demonstration and arrest union leaders.

1993

'Bread riots' in high-density suburbs of Harare.

March – The Forum Party of Zimbabwe formed under the leadership of retired Chief Justice Enoch Dumbutshena. Some Zimbabweans saw the new party as a counterweight to ZANU PF but others accused it of being elitist.

April – Seventy-three farms were designated for compulsory purchase, 50 of which were de-listed after negotiation with farmers. The remainder were not acquired due to failure by government to meet its own prescribed deadlines.

1994

A constitutional amendment removed the Lancaster House constitutional provision guaranteeing compensation for land compulsorily acquired.

July – The Forum Party broke apart. Secretary General Themba Dlodlo forms splinter party, Forum Party for Democracy.

ZCTU estimates over 100,000 formal sector workers retrenched since the introduction of ESAP.

1995

February – Most opposition parties resolved to boycott elections, planned for April, unless electoral reforms were implemented.

8-9 April – Parliamentary elections resulted in a landslide victory for ZANU PF, which captured 117 of the 120 elected seats of which 55 constituencies were not contested. However, Margaret Dongo, a former ZANU PF combatant, standing as an independent, won a re-run for the Harare South constituency after a court ruling that there were irregularities in the first round of voting. Forum did not win any seats but Zanu-Ndonga won two seats. There were widespread irregularities reported by the Zimbabwe Human Rights Association, which concluded the elections had not been free or fair. Because of the boycott and general apathy, the voter turnout was only 27 per cent.

The Private Voluntary Organisations' Act (PVO) replaced the Welfare Organisation Act of 1967 to strengthen the minister's power over community-based organisations and other NGOs. The first case under the act involved the Association of Women's Clubs (AWC) who took their case to the Supreme Court and won. The court viewed the PVO as violating freedom of association and so unconstitutional.

1996

16-17 March – Mugabe was re-elected president in an election where other candidates withdrew, complaining of irregularities. Voter turnout was only about 32 per cent.

During the year the War Victims' Compensation Fund, set up to provide financial support for victims of the armed struggle who had been severely injured or disabled, was plundered by the ruling elite. One billion dollars were paid out for non-existent or minor complaints. The government appointed the Chidyausiku Commission of Inquiry to investigate. It recommended that the fund be suspended. The war veterans revolted.

A public servants' strike saw 160,000 walk out for ten days bringing government to a halt. A settlement was negotiated.

10 May – The *Zimbabwe Independent*, an independent business weekly, was launched, bringing additional coverage of government's management of the economy.

1997

This year saw a rapidly deteriorating economic situation with 230 strikes recorded.

February – The Legal Resources Foundation and the Catholic Commission for Justice and Peace completed *Breaking the Silence*, a report on the violent disturbances in Matabeleland and the Midlands from 1980 to 1987. This report was submitted to the Zimbabwe government, which strongly objected to its publication.

13 April – *The Standard*, an independent Sunday newspaper launched, ending the government's monopoly of the weekend printed media.

21 August – After several weeks of demonstrations, often violent, by war veterans who threatened Mugabe's power base, the president awarded hefty unbudgeted gratuities and pensions to them to retain their support. This enormous expenditure was beyond government's means. International financial organisations' confidence in Zimbabwe's economic competence was undermined and a dramatic decline in the Z$:US$ rate followed, leading to increased inflation.

November – Government announces its intention to compulsorily acquire 1,471 farms.

9 December – ZCTU organised a widely observed national strike against high taxation and the rising cost of living. The strike shut down nearly all public and private enterprises and marked a watershed in state-labour relations. An assassination attempt was made on Morgan Tsvangirai, Secretary General of the ZCTU.

1998

January – Food shortages led to riots in Harare and other towns. The government called out the army to quell disaffection, resulting in loss of life. Three thousand people were arrested amid allegations of brutal treatment by the police and soldiers.

31 January – National Constitutional Assembly formally launched. ZCTU elected to chair the body. Its aim was to create a forum for national debate on the constitution. It comprised approximately 90 organisations and 1200 delegates representing a broad variety of NGOs including women's groups, civic and church organisations, and others. The government was invited to participate but preferred to set up its own Constitutional Commission in May 1999.

3-4 March – ZCTU organises another effective nation-wide strike. Mugabe accuses union leaders of plotting to overthrow the government.

The National Economic Consultative Forum was formed but the ZCTU withdrew citing lack of seriousness on the part of the government.

August – President Mugabe deployed Zimbabwe soldiers to the Democratic Republic of Congo claiming that President Lauren Kabila needed SADC support to maintain his hold on power.

Mid-1998 witnessed a series of farm invasions orchestrated by villagers and war veterans.

9-11 September – An international land donors' conference on land reform and resettlement in Zimbabwe was held in Harare under the auspices of the UNDP. Donors endorsed the need for land reform and agreed that this was essential for poverty reduction, economic growth, and stability in Zimbabwe. While agreement was reached on a two-year inception phase to test a new reform system, differences arose between the donors and the Zimbabwe government over modalities and disbursement of funds for the programme.

(During the second decade of independence less than 20,000 families had been settled on 300,000 hectares, although the government had amended the constitution and legislation to enable it to implement an accelerated programme. Policy shifted in the 1990s away from assistance to the landless peasantry to settlement of individual black commercial farmers. This programme had been discredited following accusations of cronyism and corruption in the acquisition of farms.)

16-28 November – Compulsory acquisition of 841 farms announced, in contravention of agreements reached at land donors' conference in September.

1999

January – Zimbabwe's attorney general stated that the government was committed to acquisition of the properties listed in November 1997 and 'would not let the law stand in its way'.

January – The International Monetary Fund withheld balance of payment support until assurance was given on a number of issues, including that of land. International donors began to withdraw support for the Zimbabwe government.

12 January – Mark Chavunduka, the editor of *The Standard*, was illegally detained by the military police, following the paper's report of a coup plan by disaffected army officers. Despite High Court orders, the Ministry of Defence refused to release Mr Chavunduka.

19 January – Ray Choto, the reporter who wrote the attempted coup story, voluntarily acceded to police demands that he answer charges under the Law and Order (Maintenance) Act (LOMA) of writing a 'false story'. The police guaranteed due process of law, but the same day handed Mr Choto over to the army.

20 January – It was learned that Mark Chavunduka had been tortured by army and Central Intelligence personnel, over several days and nights, in an attempt to learn the names of the officers involved in the coup plot. Ray Choto was also tortured, over a ten-hour period.

21 January – Mark Chavunduka and Ray Choto appeared in Harare Magistrate's Court, facing a charge, under Loma, of publishing and writing a 'false story'. The case was suspended while a ruling was sought from the Supreme Court on the constitutionality of the charge, which was considered *ultra vires* and infringed the declaration of rights in the Zimbabwe constitution.

February – The Supreme Court held that the section of LOMA, under which Mark Chavunduka and Ray Choto were charged, was unconstitutional. The police commissioner was also directed to examine the circumstances of the arrest and torture of the two journalists. No action was ever taken against individuals or state organisations. This confrontation between state and press was a defining moment, and a pointer to what was to happen in later years. Although torture of journalists stopped, assaults and arrests became almost commonplace.

April – *The Daily News* launched to become the country's only privately owned daily newspaper.

21 May – President Mugabe set up a 400-member, ZANU PF dominated Constitutional Commission to assess the possibility of and to propose a new constitution for Zimbabwe. The NCA boycotted the Commission and continued its own constitution drafting process.

July 1 – Joshua Nkomo died.

11 September – The Movement for Democratic Change was formed, with Morgan Tsvangirai, president of the Zimbabwe Congress of Trades Unions, as its leader. This had been suggested by the NCA during its reviews of the conduct of national affairs under ZANU PF. Many NCA members were co-opted into the MDC leadership.

2000

12-13 February – Referendum held on a new constitution proposed by ZANU PF. The NCA, MDC and other civic associations combined their efforts to campaign vigorously against the draft constitution. The government's constitution was rejected by 55 per cent of voters – the first electoral defeat suffered by the Government. President Mugabe said he would abide by the result, but within weeks war veterans were evicting white farmers, who, Mugabe believed, were behind the MDC.

28 February – The Minister of Home Affairs instructs occupiers to vacate the land. This statement was immediately reversed by the president, after which the occupations increased in intensity.

March – High Court declared land invasions illegal, and ordered police to remove the invaders.

April – *The Daily News* offices bombed. No arrests were made.

Following intense lobbying by the Commercial Farmers' Union, Acting President Msika ordered all war veterans and their followers to vacate occupied farms. President Mugabe was in Cuba at the time, and when he returned he reversed the order and announced that the occupiers could remain.

20 April – ZANU PF rushed through parliament a clause from the rejected draft constitution to amend the constitution so as to remove the obligation of the government to pay compensation to owners of land acquired for land reform purposes.

24-25 June – ZANU PF was shocked by the results of the parliamentary general election. ZANU PF gained 62 seats, but the fledgling MDC gained 57 in 50 per cent voter turnout. Without the 30 unelected seats ZANU PF would have found it almost impossible to govern. President Mugabe lost the ability to alter the constitution, since he needed a two-thirds majority in parliament. MDC launched court appeals in 37 seats won by ZANU PF.

29 June – The Commercial Farmers' Union reported that 1,525 farms (28 per cent of all farms owned by its members) had been invaded. Britain offered to pay £36 million towards land reform, but only if invasions were halted.

10 September – Meeting held between the Zimbabwe government and Southern Africa Development Community leaders to discuss the Zimbabwe crisis. Afterwards, the SADC chairperson, President Bakili Muluzi of Malawi said that state-sponsored land invasions and violence, rather than land reform itself, were responsible for the overall crisis in Zimbabwe.

11 September – MDC headquarters in Harare bombed.

October – MDC leader Morgan Tsvangirai was threatened with charges of treason, after he called for Mugabe to resign before he was overthrown. There were three days of anti-government protests in Harare. Army and police suppress riots.

6 October – President Mugabe issued an amnesty to pardon politically motivated crimes committed during the election campaign but the amnesty did not cover murder, rape and robbery.

November – Supreme Court declared land invasions illegal, and ordered police to remove the invaders.

14 December – At a ZANU PF congress, President Mugabe described the 'white man' as the 'real enemy'.

During the course of the year, violence against MDC members increased and eight party members were killed by supporters of ZANU PF (six blacks and two whites).

There were reports that senior ZANU PF members were allegedly being given businesses and mining ventures in the DRC as part of the price for Zimbabwe's continuing military support. The army refused to publish casualty figures.

During the year more than 1,600 commercial farms were at one stage forcibly occupied. These farms predominantly, belonged to white commercial farmers, but also included land belonging to black farmers, multinational corporations and even state farms.

2001

1 March – The printing works of the *The Daily News*, Zimbabwe's independent daily newspaper were bombed. No arrests were made.

July-August – The government announced its intention to acquire more farms: up to 5,200 out of a total of about 5,500. White farmers clashed with land invaders on farms, some white farmers arrested. Widespread looting of farms was reported in many areas.

6 September – Abuja Agreement at Commonwealth meeting in Nigeria stated Zimbabwe was 'a threat to the socio-economic stability of the entire sub-region and the continent at large,' and threatened Zimbabwe with sanctions and expulsion.

September – Restructured Supreme Court reverses previous orders against land seizures.

December – US passes Zimbabwe Democracy and Economic Recovery Act, a carrot-and-stick measure promising Zimbabwe aid to rebuild the economy in return for political reforms and establishment of the rule of law.

2002

January – Public Order and Security Act (POSA) and General Laws Amendment Act were passed by parliament. POSA replaced the repressive colonial Law and Order (Maintenance) Act (LOMA), first introduced to provide extraordinary powers to counter the rising African nationalist movement. LOMA was maintained after Independence up to 1990. POSA reintroduced all the extraordinary powers of LOMA and, in some respects, was more draconian. The General Laws Amendment Act effectively disenfranchised an estimated two million Zimbabweans living outside the country. Most crucially, stringent controls on independent and foreign election observers were introduced.

23 January – UN World Food Programme began food deliveries to Zimbabwe, after a drastic fall in local food production.

1 March – Zimbabwe's chief justice, Anthony Gubbay, forced into early retirement by the Zimbabwe government with still some fourteen months of his term to serve. He was succeeded by Judge Godfrey Chidyausiku, a former ZANU PF minister and close colleague of President Mugabe.

March – The Access to Information and Protection of Privacy Act (AIPPA) became law. Its principal purpose was to control the private media, requiring that all newspapers and magazines, and all journalists operating in Zimbabwe be registered with the government-appointed Media and Information Commission. *The Daily News* and its journalists refused to register and instead appealed to the Supreme Court, on the grounds that the act violated freedoms enshrined in the constitution. The chief justice determined the issue was not urgent, and no date for the hearing was set.

7 March – US executive order froze assets of senior members of government and ZANU PF, and prohibited any financial transactions between US citizens and those named.

9-10 March – Presidential election together with mayoral/council elections in Harare. After a pre-election campaign of intimidation and violence against the MDC and its supporters, President Mugabe won a third term, gaining 56 per cent of the vote. Morgan Tsvangirai won 42 per cent. MDC wins in municipal elections. Voter turnout was 54 per cent in presidential election. Many domestic and international observers and organisations declare presidential election neither free nor fair. Some neighbouring countries, notably South Africa, take an opposite view. Commonwealth suspends Zimbabwe: US and European Union impose 'targeted sanctions' on top government and ZANU PF officials.

26 August – President Mugabe sets up 'war cabinet'.

30 September – Morgan Tsvangirai indicted on treason charges. Announcement that troops in DRC to be withdrawn by the end of the year.

2003

18-19 March – Stay-away organised by the MDC; many economic activities grind to a halt. Massive reprisals by police and army followed.

End of March – MDC wins two by-elections in Harare.

23-25 April – ZCTU, with the support of the MDC, calls for mass stay-away to protest tripling of fuel prices.

2-6 June – MDC calls another mass action campaign, dubbed 'final push' to force Mugabe, to step down. Action paralyses some economic activity. Many arrests follow, including that of Tsvangirai, on a second treason charge.

September – Supreme Court rules that *The Daily News* is operating outside the law. Police force closure of paper.

27 October – A commission, set up by President Mugabe to review the government's four-year land reform programme, reports disappointing results. Just over a third of the officially resettled peasant families had actually moved on to the land allocated to them. In the case of black commercial farmers, 50,000 families had received allocations, but only 4,800 had moved on to the land.

7 December – Zimbabwe withdraws from the Commonwealth, after the organisation announced it would extend its 2002 suspension for a further year.

2004

10 January – Iden Wetherell, the *Zimbabwe Independent's* editor was arrested on charges of defaming President Mugabe. News editor, Vincent Kahere, and reporter Dumisani Muleyi were also arrested. The three were released on bail on 12 January, but on 14 January *Zimbabwe Independent's* reporter, Itai Dzamara, and the paper's general manager Raphael Kumalo, were also arrested on the same charges. These arrests followed an article written by Muleya and Dzamara which said that Mugabe had 'commandeered' an Air Zimbabwe airliner for a trip to East Asia, leaving passengers stranded. The paper noted this was the second time Mugabe had diverted an Air Zimbabwe flight.

23 February – Associated Newspapers of Zimbabwe (ANZ), publishers of the independent *Daily News* and *The Daily News on Sunday*, announced its virtual closure after an almost six-month battle with the government and the Media and Information Commission (MIC) to obtain a licence to publish.

Since 11 September 2003 the company has published only one issue of *The Daily News* and has been forced to lay off 250 of its 300 staff. The remaining 50 journalists and support staff are being retained in the event of a licence to operate being granted.

When the Access to Information and Protection of Privacy Act (AIPPA) became law in March 2002, ANZ challenged its constitutionality and announced it would not seek a licence until this basic issue was resolved. It was not until 11 September 2003 that the Supreme Court dismissed the ANZ application and ruled that the paper should register under AIPPA before its petition could be heard. The company found itself in a state of limbo as the MIC refused to grant a licence because the ANZ application was submitted eight-and-a-half months after the closing date of 31 December 2002. Despite High Court and Administrative Court decisions allowing ANZ to publish, the MIC refused to grant registration. Over the next six months, ANZ was the subject of constant harassment, with the police invading the company's offices and its printing factory, assaulting and intimidating journalists, and preventing publication. It was only on one day, 25 October 2003, that an issue of *The Daily News* was published, resulting in yet another invasion of the newspaper's offices and the arrest of eighteen journalists and staff. On two occasions, executives and directors of the company were arrested and charged with publishing without a licence.

The journalists themselves had petitioned the Supreme Court in November 2002, claiming that the forcible registration of journalists and the powers of the

MIC to deny journalists a licence were *ultra vires* the constitution. The journalists were particularly vulnerable, for if the ANZ was refused permission to publish, the journalists employed by the company would be denied registration also. The Chief Justice said that this was not an urgent matter, and did not hand down a ruling until 5 January 2004. He said the regulatory body (the MCI) was constitutional and laws prohibiting journalists from practising without accreditation were legitimate. He did concede, however, that Section 80 (1) (a), (b), and (c) of AIPPA was deemed to criminalise the abuse of journalistic privilege. 'Criminalising the abuse of a privilege is patently oppressive', the judgement said. Parts of this section had already been struck down in an earlier ruling by the same court and were also amended by parliament last year.

March – A survey of opposition MPs and unsuccessful opposition candidates for parliamentary seats, *Playing with Fire*, indicates government's sustained attack on dissent in Zimbabwe over the previous four years. Fifty elected MPs and 28 unsuccessful candidates were asked to detail their experiences since the parliamentary elections in 2000. There were two deaths: an unsuccessful candidate in the 2000 elections and a candidate's brother were beaten to death. Ninety per cent of MPs reported personal violations, including attempted murder, torture, assaults, arrests, or illegal detention. The 78 people interviewed reported 616 violations of human rights against themselves or those close to them. Forty-four per cent also reported vandalism of their homes and six per cent reported total destruction of their homes by arson. Forty-eight per cent reported vandalism of vehicles and attacks of their business premises. Twenty-two per cent of MPs families were attacked. Torture took place in police custody in some cases. MPs reported the police, the CIO or the army as perpetrators of the violence.

Zimbabwe: The Past is the Future